A New Spirit in Christian-Muslim Relations in India

Three Jesuit Pioneers

Jesuits have made significant contributions to the fields of comparative religion and interfaith relations. However, these are not as well-known as they ought to be. This book seeks to address that need in a systematic fashion. It presents a range of views and approaches by three Jesuits who understood the value of learning about other faiths, in their case, about Islam in India, and opened new pathways to interfaith relations. Over the years, these Jesuits inspired many others to walk that same path in the service of peace and justice. The author, himself a Jesuit, and an accomplished scholar and teacher of interfaith dialogue, is among these. In this work, Edwin combines his deep knowledge of Islam and Christian-Muslim relations with his understanding of the history of Jesuit approaches to other religions. The Jesuits studied here realized, each in his own way, that their knowledge about Islam will remain incomplete without building relationships with Muslims. The book includes accounts of these friendships reflecting the values that are central to the practice of faith.

Dr Irfan A. Omar, Associate Professor of Islamic and Interfaith Studies, Marquette University, USA

Edwin's book demonstrates once again two key aspects of Christian-Muslim relations in our time: the Jesuit heritage and the South Asian context, a unique combination that is centuries old and yet timelessly relevant. His cogent analysis of the contributions of three important Jesuit scholars – Victor Courtois, Christian W. Troll and Paul Jackson – demonstrates that peaceful and productive relations between Christian and Muslim peoples depend not only on exemplary scholarship of both traditions, but an openness to the presence of the Divine in the other, and an embrace of the other believer as brother or sister. The groundbreaking scholarship and prophetic partnerships of these three Jesuits with South Asian Muslims underscore the fertile ground that India's multireligious culture presents to the scholar and the practitioner of interreligious dialogue and relations. Fr Edwin shows us that the caliber of their scholarship and the quality of their relationships are both vitally important and foundational for correcting the errors of the past and building a future that reflects the best of our respective traditions.

Prof. Michael D. Calabria, OFM, Director, Center for Arab and Islamic Studies, St Bonaventure University, USA

Christian scholars have found a new approach to the world of Islam. This book offers succinct and helpful insights into the contribution of three Christian scholars who were pioneers in the field. The book will be especially helpful to those who wish to understand the context of Christian-Muslim dialogue in the sub-continent of India and Pakistan.

Prof. Herman Roborgh, Head of the School of Religion and Philosophy, Minhaj University, Lahore, Pakistan

The originality of Edwin's book is a competent gaze and spiritual discernment on the thought of three Jesuit pioneers and their encounters with Islam. Such a book goes beyond the reading of living experiences on Christian-Muslim interfaith relations in India: it will be surely an inspiring source for many toward further developments of interreligious dialogue in the world.

Prof. Ambrogio Bongiovanni, Pontificia Università Gregoriana, Rome, Italy

Edwin's book has provided us with an in-depth and stimulating scientific contribution to inter-religious and interfaith dialogue. Investigating the lives and work of three pioneers in the field of relations between Christianity and Islam in South Asia, the book traces a solid path towards a future of dialogue and reconciliation between communities of different faiths. Love, reason and spirituality are the three key words that identify and capture the commitment of the Jesuit Fathers Courtois, Troll and Jackson. It is precisely from the creative circularity between words and personalities that Edwin draws a series of new, relevant and motivating indications for a renewed commitment to dialogue. Undoubtedly, the book marks a significant contribution to the effort of dialogue in South Asia by Christians and Muslims.

Prof. Gaetano Sabetta, Urbaniana University, Rome, Italy

A New Spirit in Christian-Muslim Relations in India

Three Jesuit Pioneers

Joseph Victor Edwin SJ

Foreword by
Cardinal Michael L. Fitzgerald

HENRY MARTYN INSTITUTE (HMI)
2021

A New Spirit in Christian-Muslim Relations in India: Three Jesuit Pioneers— Jointly published by the Indian Society for Promoting Christian Knowledge (ISPCK), Post Box 1585, Kashmere Gate, Delhi-110006 and Henry Martyn Institute (HMI), Hyderabad-500052.

Online order: http://ispck.org.in/book.php

Also available on amazon.in

ISBN: 978-93-90569-26-7

Laser typeset by

ISPCK, Post Box 1585, 1654, Madarsa Road, Kashmere Gate, Delhi-110006 • *Tel:* 23866323

e-mail: ashish@ispck.org.in • ella@ispck.org.in
website: www.ispck.org.in

To my parents

Contents

Acknowledgements

Whatever contributions the present work makes, if any, will be in large part due to those scholars who have been my mentors during its composition. They are Prof. Akhtarul Wasey, Jamia Millia Islamia, Delhi, Dr Samuel Packiam, Henry Martyn Institute, Hyderabad, Prof. Leo D. Lefebure, Georgetown University, Washington, Dr Ataullah Siddiqui, Markfield Institute of Higher Education, Leicestershire, Prof. Aloysius Pieris SJ, Tulana Research Center for Encounter and Dialogue, Colombo, Dr Yoginder Sikand, Bangalore, Prof. David Baker, University of Delhi and Fr Thomas V. Kunnunkal SJ, Delhi. They have all read the work in different stages of its growth and offered me helpful critique and academic support. I am sincerely indebted to them, for their personal accompaniment. Their assistance has both humbled and inspired me.

I express my deep gratitude to Cardinal Michael L. Fitzgerald for the 'Foreword' that he offered for the book. I cannot imagine a better introduction to my humble work.

I am deeply grateful to my religious superiors who encourage me and guide me in the ministry of dialogue with Muslims. Thanks to Fr George Pattery SJ, Fr Stanislaus D'Souza SJ, Fr Michael T. Raj SJ, rector, and Fr P.R. John SJ, principal, and the faculty of Vidyajyoti College of Theology, Delhi, for their support and encouragement. I deeply appreciate the wonderful academic and spiritual guidance that I continue to receive from Fr Christian W. Troll.

Thanks to Prof. Felix Raj SJ, the director of The Goethals Indian Library and Research Society, and Fr K.T. Chandy SJ, the Librarian of the Vidyajyoti College of Theology, for allowing me to use the resources of these specialized libraries for my research work. I thank Mr. Masroor Ahmad, the retired Library Assistant, for his kindness and help while I spent many hours in the Library while writing this work.

In the course of editing this work for publication, I have benefited from the careful copy editing of Fr Myron J. Pereira SJ. I express my gratitude for his kindness and support. I am sincerely grateful to Dr Samuel Packiam for his generous contribution towards the printing of this book. I thank Ms Laura Ottaviani for designing the cover pages and Fr K.T. Thomas SJ for proofreading and preparing the text for publication.

I would like to thank my brother Edward and his family, my friends: Fr A. Cyril SJ, Guna – Vincent Manoharan, Amy –Michael Yeung, Zen – Peter Kenmore, Jeyashree–Martin Robert, and Lily– Andrew Alexander for their spiritual closeness and blessings. I thank God for you all!

Foreword

In India, with its vast population of some 1.2 billion the majority of whom are Hindus, there exist different religious minorities, including Christians and Muslims. Of course, there is a notable difference in number between these last two groups, since there are about 25 million Christians, whereas the Muslims are six times as many. With their 170 millions, the Muslims in India are as many if not more numerous than in the whole of the Arab world.

It could be imagined that, as fellow minority groups, there would be close relations between Christians and Muslims. In fact Christians, in their desire to build up an Indian church, in their efforts at inculturation, whether in liturgy, theology or spirituality, seem to have paid more attention to the Hindu majority. Relatively little importance has been given to relations with Muslims. It is this situation that has brought Fr Victor Edwin to produce the present volume about three Jesuits who have dedicated their lives to relations with Muslims, two dead, Victor Courtois and Paul Jackson, and one still happily living, Christian W. Troll.

Of course the Jesuits have a long history in India, and they were already present in the 16th century at the time of the Mughals. They were well received at the court of Akbar where they took part in theological disputes, yet their polemical attitude did little to win friends and to advance the cause of Christianity in India. The Jesuits presented in this study have taken a different tack.

Courtois, anticipating the teaching of the Second Vatican Council, insisted on treating Muslims as brothers (and sisters), members of the one human family, and so worthy of respect. He taught that the riches of their tradition are to be discovered and valued. Jackson and Troll have followed in his footsteps, particularly in the fields of spirituality and theology respectively.

Fr Victor's presentation of these three Jesuits, a Belgian, an Australian and a German, does not remain at a biographical level. He makes a thorough study of their thought, based on the *Notes on Islam* produced by Courtois, and the many publications of Troll and Jackson. Key words that jump out of the pages are "curiosity", "love", "presence", "discernment", "freedom", "human dignity", and "coherence". All three Jesuits insist upon the importance of learning the language(s) of the other, and have given an example in this respect. Also significant is the insistence on "listening" and "receiving", before one attempts to give something to others. Such listening opens the way for true conversation (as illustrated in the motto of St John Henry Newman: *cor ad cor loquitur*, "heart speaks to heart"). The cultivation of friendship, through cooperation in learning and teaching, results in personal transformation. As is stated in the document *Dialogue and Proclamation* published in 1991 by the Congregation for the Evangelization of Peoples and the Pontifical Council for Interreligious Dialogue: "Interreligious dialogue does not merely aim at mutual understanding and friendly relations. It reaches a much deeper level, that of the spirit, where exchange and sharing consist in a mutual witness to one's beliefs and a common exploration of one's respective religious convictions. In dialogue, Christians and others are invited to deepen their religious commitment, to respond with increasing sincerity to God's personal call and gracious self-gift" (DP 40).

The individual presentations of these three Jesuits are preceded by two helpful preliminary chapters. One looks at how Christians and Muslims see one another. It examines first the teaching of the Qur'an and Islamic tradition and goes on to consider how the political and social climate influences the attitudes of Muslims towards Christians. Then it shows how Christians, both of the East and the West, have envisaged Islam and Muslims down the ages. The second preliminary chapter concentrates on Christian-Muslim relations in India, considering not only the Jesuits and Catholics, but also the endeavours of other Christian individuals or groups. It also pays attention to the varying attitudes of Muslims towards Western/Christian culture.

This book is concerned with the past and the present, but it is also immensely relevant for the future. Pope Francis has written: "Interreligious dialogue is a necessary condition for peace in the world, and so it is a duty for Christians as well as other religious communities" (Pope Francis, *Evangelii Gaudium*, no. 250). Turning specifically to relations with Muslims he adds: "In order to sustain dialogue with Islam, suitable training is essential for all involved, not only so that they can be solidly and joyfully grounded in their own identity, but so that they can also acknowledge the values of others, appreciate the concerns underlying their demands and shed light on shared beliefs" (EG 253). The example of these three Jesuits provides both material and a stimulus for this essential training, not only in India, but world-wide.

Cardinal Michael L. Fitzgerald

Author's Introduction

This book tells the story of three Jesuit pioneers: Victor Courtois, Christian W. Troll, and Paul Jackson, who triggered a new departure in Christian-Muslim relations in India. This departure came about when they distanced themselves from polemics, began studying Islamic texts with respect and reached out to Muslims with love.

They imagined and worked toward a revolution in the relationship between Muslims and Christians, from one poisoned by fear and rivalry, to one rooted in mutual understanding and fraternal correction. By gaining a deep knowledge of the intellectual and spiritual riches of Indian Muslims, they respected them and their religious convictions.

The lives of these Jesuits are marked with a new spirit of Christian-Muslim relations as they ventured to build bridges between Christians and Muslims, without ever losing their identity as Christians. It is no exaggeration to say that their lives were challenged and shaped by both their own faith and that of Muslims. The significance of their life and work emerges from the high level of integration they attained in living as Christian friends among Muslims. The vistas they opened up for Christian-Muslim relations in India are in coherence with the teachings of the Church. Courtois anticipated the open attitude of Vatican II. Troll and Jackson, in the light of the teachings of Vatican II, deepened their commitment to the relations between Christians and Muslims in the area of theology and spirituality respectively. They have shown the way to build bridges between the followers of these two religions and to live in harmony and peace, and contribute to a harmonious nation.

Pope Francis has rejuvenated the life of the Catholic Church in the world by his servant model of leadership. He has taken several initiatives in building rapport with Muslims around the world. Something beautiful happened on the Maundy Thursday of the year 2013, when Pope Francis celebrated the liturgy in a prison in Rome. One of the poignant moments of the Maundy Thursday liturgy is the 'washing of the feet' ceremony. The main celebrant washes the feet of twelve persons. This is done in remembrance of Jesus washing the feet of his disciples. This observance symbolizes 'abandoning one's will to do the Will of God' and a 'willingness to serve the other without holding on to one's honour'. Pope Francis as the main celebrant, washed the feet of twelve prisoners that included a Muslim and a woman. Usually popes celebrated this liturgy in St John Lateran Cathedral in Rome and washed the feet of twelve Church officials who held important positions in the Vatican.

Pope Francis's act of washing the feet of a Muslim inmate could be one of the most significant moments in the history of Catholic-Muslim relations. It could even be said that it is one of the peak moments in relations between the people of these two religious traditions. The implications are weighty. First, Pope Francis washed the feet of a Muslim during a sacred liturgy that symbolizes the heart of Christian worship. Through this action Pope Francis affirmed that people of other religions, especially Muslims, are integral to his spirituality and mission as the servant leader of the Catholic Church. Secondly, it could also be said that positive attitudes of previous popes, especially of Pope John Paul II towards Muslims have come to fruition in this beautiful act of Pope Francis. In short, the act of Pope Francis essentially calls upon every Christian to establish new contacts with Muslims and deepen existing ones. He expects Christians to cross many borders and meet with others who are 'out of bounds', and thus build cross-border communities. He affirmed unambiguously that "Dialogue is born from a respectful attitude toward the other person, from a conviction that the other person has something good to say. It supposes that we can make room in our heart for their point of view, their opinion and their proposals. Dialogue entails a warm reception and not a preemptive condemnation".[1] To dialogue, one must lower the defenses, to open the doors of one's home and to offer warmth.

Pope Francis's kind and respectful gestures did not go unnoticed in the Muslim World. Omar Abboud, Islamic Center, Buenos Aires who knew the Pope personally, reflecting on his outreach to Muslims said:

> Bergoglio was the one who showed us and taught us about dialogue… How can a Muslim learn from a Catholic priest? I learned the dynamic of Islamic mercy through his words…From Bergoglio it was a whole lesson in the exercise of mercy, in improving your view of the other by putting yourself in their shoes.[2]

Another Muslim cleric, Imam Mohamad Bashar Arafat pointed out that the "Pope Francis is really doing a wonderful job in terms of outreach, in terms of contributing to world peace…This was the message of St Francis and this is the message of Ibn Arabi…and this is the spirit of all the Muslim saints and Sufis around the world".[3]

Pope Francis articulated his outreach in his official teachings too. He called upon the Christian faithful to appreciate the spirituality of Muslims as they live out in their personal lives. He wrote in *Evangelii Gaudium* (no.252): "…it is admirable to see how Muslims both young and old, men and women, make time for daily prayer and faithfully take part in religious services. Many of them also have a deep conviction that their life, in its entirety, is from God and for God. They also acknowledge the need to respond to God with an ethical commitment, and with mercy towards those most in need".

He further emphasized that human dignity and freedom of religion and conscience should be the common ground for Christian-Muslim dialogue. He wrote: "…We Christians should embrace with affection and respect Muslim immigrants to our countries in the same way that we hope and ask to be received and respected in countries of Islamic tradition. I ask and I humbly entreat those countries to grant Christians freedom to worship and to practice their faith, in light of the freedom which followers of Islam enjoy in Western countries. Faced with disconcerting episodes of violent fundamentalism, our respect for true followers of Islam should lead us to avoid hateful generalizations, for authentic Islam and the proper reading of the Qur'ân are opposed to every form of violence" (Evangelii Gaudium no. 253).

Going further down the road, in February 2019, Pope Francis and Shaykh Ahmad al-Tayeb, the Rector of Al-Azhar University, Cairo issued a joint statement 'Human Fraternity'.[4] It is once again an excellent example of what one may call applied dialogue. 'Human Fraternity' reminded us of our relational reality, "we are related and are dependent in more ways than we often realize", comments Dr Irfan Omar, who teaches theology in the Jesuit-run Marquette University, USA. He further said that 'Human Fraternity' powerfully reminds us that we are all brothers and sisters. [5]

On 30 November 2015, Pope Francis said loudly and clearly:

> Christians and Muslims are brothers and sisters. We must therefore consider ourselves and conduct ourselves as such … those who claim to believe in God must also be men and women of peace. Christians, Muslims and members of the traditional religions have lived together in peace for many years. They ought, therefore, to remain united in working for an end to every act which, from whatever side, disfigures the Face of God and whose ultimate aim is to defend particular interests by any and all means, to the detriment of the common good. Together, we must say no to hatred, no to revenge and no to violence, particularly that violence which is perpetrated in the name of a religion or of God himself. God is peace, God *salaam*.[6]

Roll back thirteen years in history, it was on 13 October 2007, that 138 Muslim scholars signed a document entitled "A Common Word between Us and You" (ACW) and addressed it to 28 Christian leaders worldwide.[7] ACW invited Christians to recognize a common ground: the belief in one God as a basis for working for peace in the world along with Muslims. ACW made a case for this common ground with scriptural under pinning, Qur'ânic as well as Biblical. ACW, by avoiding the polemics of the past and treating the biblical verses that it cited with respect and seriousness, signaled new departures in Christian-Muslim relations.[8]

The Pope's 'gestures' and the Muslims' 'letter' are spiritually and intellectually inspiring moments for those who carefully observe the relations between the followers of these two great faiths. The importance of these two events will shine even more brightly when they are placed on the larger canvass of many world events in the recent times that have heightened tensions between Christians and Muslims. The attacks on the Twin Towers in New York on September 11, 2001, the US-led invasions of Afghanistan and Iraq, and several bomb attacks on civilian populations involving European Muslims severely strained existing relations between Christians and Muslims.[9] The Pew Global Attitudes Project in its report released on June 22, 2006 noted: "Many in the West see Muslims as fanatical, violent, and as lacking in tolerance. Meanwhile, Muslims in the Middle East and Asia generally see Westerners as selfish, immoral and greedy – as well as violent and fanatical."[10] Earlier, S. P. Huntington had predicted that the crucial and central aspect of conflict in the future would be between different civilizations. He wrote: "The fault lines between civilizations will be the battle lines of the future."[11] The Muslim signatories and Pope Francis have shown that a deep rootedness in one's religious faith and a respectful openness for the faith of others can and should open up new pathways for peace.

We live in a global village. The emerging new attitudes of the Catholic Church towards Muslims and Muslim efforts to reach out to Christian world have global implications that apply especially to South Asia. Muslims and Christians have been living together as neighbors in this subcontinent for centuries now. The contacts between them differ from one place to another depending upon social and cultural contexts in which they live. It becomes relevant to look for the positive contribution of Christians and Muslims in India for mutual understanding and active building of bridges between these two groups of believers.

Three Jesuits, as noted at the outset, Victor Courtois, Christian W. Troll, and Paul Jackson contributed significantly to Christian-Muslim relations and continue to inspire students and scholars of Christian-Muslim relations in India. This book will present the following three characteristics: their love for Muslims that is expressed in their personal relationship with them, their intellectual curiosity and honesty in engaging with the intellectual and spiritual traditions of South Asian and Indian Islam, and their ability to integrate and bring about coherence in their life as Jesuit missionaries and promoters of Christian-Muslim relations. All this make their contribution relevant, stimulating and important in the present context.

The book will show that these Jesuits ushered in a new spirit in Christian-Muslim relations by reaching out to Muslims as bridge builders: loving them and learning from them. This new spirit was nourished by their deep Christian faith and courageous openness to the faith of their Muslim friends. In other words, they were enabled to reach out because their Christian faith was robust. They unhesitatingly emphasized the fundamental importance of God's revelation to each community and the centrality of the human person in their extensive writings. Their lives manifest the high level of integration they achieved in bringing both the cognitive as well as the 'heart-dimension' in building relations between Muslims and Christians. The creative integration of their life and work, rooted and founded on Christ, make their voices significant in the arena of Christian-Muslim relations. In short, they crossed borders, expanded the scope of interaction by touching upon a number of contexts, and emphasized the important of 'personal experience' in relations between Christians and Muslims.

The first chapter of this book presents in broad strokes how Christians and Muslims saw each other. This is to help both Muslim and Christian readers, especially students of theology and Islamic studies to know the past so that we can learn for the future. The larger picture that emerges in the discussion of this chapter is polemics and debates, which dominated Christian-Muslim relations in the past. The few silver lines in this picture often gets obscured in the high decibel polemics. The second chapter will present briefly the Indian scene before the advent of these three pioneers. These two chapters will provide the general readers, both Christians and Muslims, with a background for understanding and appreciating the pioneering work of these three Jesuits. The students of the history of Christian-Muslim relations, as well as Christians and Muslims who are interested in dialogue between these two great faiths may profit from the endnotes and bibliography which indicate a number of serious studies on this subject.

The next three chapters present the stories of Courtois, Troll and Jackson and the new spirit that emerged in the lives and works of these three Jesuits. They reached out to Muslims in love, exploring the elements that bring them closer to each other, discovering and highlighting the intellectual and spiritual wealth of Indian Islam. The present writer hopes that their lives and work may similarly inspire students of Christian-Muslim relations to reach out to the other, to learn, to share, to build bridges between communities, and thereby establish peace and harmony among all peoples.

Endnotes

[1] Pope Francis, "Talking across the political divide," http://www.catholicmessenger. net/2019/05/talking-across-the-political-divide/[accessed November 11, 2020].

[2] Austen Iverigh, *The Great Reformer: Francis and making of a Radical Pope* [New York: Henry Hold and Company, 2014], 322.

[3] Cindy Wooden, "Muslim leader says pope is model of what religious leader should be," https://www.ncronline.org/news/parish/muslim-leader-says-pope-model-what-religious-leader-should-be [accessed March 25, 2020].

[4] Pope Francis, "Human Fraternity," http://www.vatican.va/content/francesco/en/travels/2019/outside/documents/papa-francesco_20190204_documento-fratellanza-umana.html [accessed November 11, 2020].

[5] I. Omar, Interview by author, Delhi, February 20, 2020.

[6] Address of his holiness Pope Francis at the Central mosque of Koudoukou, Bangui (Central African Republic), http://www.vatican.va/content/francesco/en/speeches/2015/november/documents/papa-francesco_20151130_repubblica-centrafricana-musulmani. html [Monday, 30 November 2015], [accessed March 25, 2020].

[7] A Common Word, https://www.acommonword.com/ [accessed March 25, 2020].

[8] For academic responses to ACW, https://www.acommonword.com/publications/ [accessed March 25, 2020].

[9] The Madrid train bombings (March 11, 2004), the London bombings (July 7, 2005) and some 30 major failed plots in Europe happened in the five years following the Twin Tower attack. See M. Perry and H.E. Negrin, eds., *The Theory and Practice of Islamic Terrorism: An Anthology* [New York: Palgrave Macmillan, 2008], 92.

[10] Pew Research Centre [Pew Global Attitudes Project], The Great Divide: How Westerners and Muslims View Each Other, http://pewglobal.org/2006/06/22/the-great-divide-how-westerners-and-muslims-view-each-other/ [accessed March 25, 2020].

[11] S. P. Huntington, "The Clash of Civilizations?" *Foreign Affairs* 72, no.3 [Summer 1993]: 22. Also see S.P. Huntington, The Clash of Civilizations and the Remaking of World Order [London: Simon & Schuster, 1996], 213-214, 238, 242, 262, and 264.

Chapter 1

How Muslims and Christians see Each Other

Muslim Approaches to Christianity and Christians

Muslim attitudes to Christianity and Christians have taken many forms: cooperation and conflict, dialogue and diatribe, and tolerance and hatred. A dauntingly large amount of material is available on this subject.[1]

The Qur'ânic teachings and the *traditions* of the Prophet Muhammad (*ḥadīth*) on the subject[2] provide a theological framework for Muslim approaches towards Christianity and Christians. Moreover, the actual political and social contexts in which both the groups of believers lived, and continue to live, play a crucial role influencing the Muslim mindset towards Christianity and Christians.

The Qur'ânic Teachings on Christianity and Christians

The Arabic term for Christians 'masīḥiyyūn' never appears in the Qur'ân. The Qur'ân addresses Christians as "People of the Book" or "Scripture People" (*ahl al-kitāb*). This term occurs some 54 times in the Qur'ân. At one time Christians are referred to as "Gospel people" in the Qur'ân (Q 5:47). Both Muslim and non-Muslim scholars have interpreted the Qur'ânic word *al-naṣārā* (sing. *al-naṣrānī*) referring to Christians. This word occurs in the Qur'ân 14 times.

The Prophet Muhammad regarded the Qur'ân as consonant with the Bible. The Qur'ân directed the Meccan detractors of Muhammad to check with the People of the Book if they (Meccan people) had any doubt in the message of Muhammad (cf. Q 10:94). The Qur'ân guided Muslims to check with the People of the Book if they had any doubts about the Message and then to be reassured (cf. Q 16:43). The Book encouraged social intercourse between Christians and Muslims (cf. Q 5:5) and instructed Muslims not to dispute with the People of the Book except in the fairest manner (cf. Q 29:46). There are positive comments as well as sharp criticisms about Christians in the Qur'ân.[3] The Qur'ânic text commends Christians as friends of Muslims because there are monks among them who do not behave arrogantly (cf. Q 5:82). In other passages monks are criticized for consuming people's wealth and turning them aside from God's ways (cf. Q 9:31, 34). Expressing serious reservations on such attitudes of erring monks, the Qur'ân critiques monasticism as an unwarranted innovation (cf. Q 57:27). Further, the Qur'ânic text admonishes Muslims that they should not take Christians as their friends – though Christians might give a friendlier reception to them than most others (cf. Q 5:51).

Further on the critical side, importantly, the Qur'ân accuses Christians of corrupting the Bible. The corruption (*taḥrīf*) of Christian scriptures is an important theme in Christian-Muslim theological debates. Many Muslim scholars found reason to argue that the Jewish and Christian scriptures were corrupted.[4] While some argued that the texts were deliberately corrupted, others explained corruption as the misinterpretation of the Bible.

Muslim authors have used the following four words in describing how the Jewish and Christian scriptures were corrupted: *taḥrīf* – to corrupt a book; *tabdīl* – to substitute one text for another, *layy* – to turn one's thought in one's mouth (mispronounce the revealed text in order to give it another meaning), *kitmān* – to hide, to hide a book or part of a book. *Taḥrīf* was understood as either the distortion of the biblical text (*taḥrīf al-nass*) or the distortion of meaning (*taḥrīf al-ma'ni*). The charge of concealment of truth (*ikhfā'*) is also levelled against Jews and Christians (Q 2:159; 2:174). They concealed the truth of the coming of Muhammad and make no reference to it in their scriptures. Jews were reprimanded for "dismembering the *tawrāt*, making it into separate sheets 'for show' which conceal much of its contents" (Q 6:91). Christians were told that they have forgotten a good part of the message that was sent to them.[5] The Qur'ân is, in a word, ambivalent about Christians and Christianity.[6]

Some scholars like al-Tabarī (d. 855 CE), al-Qāsim ibn Ibrahim (d. 860 CE), ibn Qutayba (d. 889 CE), and al-Bīrūnī (d. 1048 CE) tended to accept the text but questioned the interpretation. One of the most important theologians who argued this position is al-Ghazālī (d. 1111 CE). He, whom many Muslims consider as the 'proof of Islam' and a great renewer of their religion, follows this second approach. He considers that Christian scriptures are misinterpreted and they need a Muslim interpretation. His views appear in a book entitled *al-Radd al-jamīl li-Ilāhiyyāt 'Isābi-ṣarīh al-Injīl* (An Excellent Refutation of the Divinity of Jesus from the text of the Gospel).

Al- Ghazālī recognizes, on the one hand, that Islam alone holds the truth for humanity, but at the same time he, holds that the Christian scriptures are authentic. The actual words of Jesus alone, he contends, convey the truth of his message.

It will be helpful to consider how al- Ghazālī looks at biblical texts. The author differentiates between three types of texts in the Bible. First, he focuses on the texts that deal with the divinity of Christ. He wants those texts to be taken allegorically. As an example he presents the statement: "The Father and I are one" (John 10: 30), and insists that this has to be explained metaphorically. Secondly, he picks out texts that imply the humanity of Christ; texts like the cursing of the fig tree (Mark 11:12-14) and ignorance of the hour (Mark 13:32): these have to be taken literally. This may give an insight into al-Ghazālī's mind. One can well infer that he views Christ as merely a human messenger. Thirdly, he chooses texts like "the son will submit himself" (1 Corinthians

15:28), "the God of our Lord Jesus Christ" (Ephesians 1:16-17), "God is one, one is the mediator: the man Jesus" (1 Timothy 2:5) and "a man who told you the truth" (John 8:39-40) and explains that Jesus uttered them with special permission from God.

The Qur'ân honors Jesus as one of the prophets and criticizes Christians for deifying Jesus. One of the experts in Christian-Muslim relations, M. Borrmans writes:

> The Qur'ân sees Jesus simply a prophet among others . . . it makes him a perfect 'prophet of Islam.' His name, too, '*Isa*' is different from that in the Gospels, *Yasu*' (God saves). Certainly 'the Messiah, Jesus, Son of Mary,' is a prophet and a messenger, a perfect 'servant of God,' 'very pure,' 'blessed by God,' and 'gentle toward his mother, not violent nor wicked,' but rather 'set among the number of the saints' and 'of those who are close to God,' for He has bestowed on him 'of His bounty.' Created directly by God, like Adam, he is announced by John, son of Zachary, who is Mary's guardian. 'Word came from God,' and 'placed in Mary,' he depends on an intervention of 'the Spirit' which God 'breathes into Mary,' and he is many times 'strengthened by the Spirit of holiness.' 'Jesus the Messiah, son of Mary, was (no more than) a messenger of Allah, and His Word, which He bestowed on Mary, and a spirit proceeding from Him' (4:171). Despite all these unique qualities, the Qur'ânic Jesus, is a good 'Muslim prophet. Moreover, he did not die on the cross and awaits his return as 'sign of the (Last) Hour': it is then that he will be made manifest as a Muslim prophet and disciple of Muhammad.[7]

Further, the Qur'ân rejects: first, the conventional Christian doctrine of the Trinity (cf. Q 4:171; 5:77), the Qur'ân makes several observations about different aspects of the Christian faith. Some of these observations, Muslim exegetes claim, deny the Christian teaching on the Trinity. The Qur'ân seems to challenge Christians on three important aspects of their faith with regard to the triune nature of God. 1. Is Jesus God? 2. Is God, the third of three? 3. Does God have a son? A closer look at different passages elucidates this.

The following passage is said to address the first question:

> They indeed have disbelieved who say: Lo! Allah is the Messiah, son of Mary. (Q 5:17)

The following Qur'ânic verse is said to concern the second question:

> They surely disbelieve who say: Lo! Allah is the third of three; when there is no God save the One God. If they do not desist from so saying a painful doom will fall on those of them who disbelieve. (Q 5:73)

The following Qur'ânic verse is understood to concern the third question:

> O People of the Scripture! Do not exaggerate in your religion nor utter aught concerning Allah save the truth. The Messiah, Jesus son of Mary, was only a messenger of Allah, and His word which He conveyed unto Mary, and a sprit from Him. So believe in Allah and His messenger, and say not "Three" – Cease. (it is) better for you! - Allah is only One God. Far is it removed from His transcendent majesty that he should have a son. (Q 4:171)

Secondly, the Qur'ân rejects both the doctrine of the Incarnation (cf. Q 4:171; 5:17, 72, 73, 116, 117), and the Christian view of the Crucifixion (cf. Q 4:157).[8] In the Qur'ânic perspective, Christians who propound these doctrines go to an excess and say more than what the true religion teaches. This is because their leaders follow the whims of people who had gone into error (cf. Q 5:77).

The Qur'ân portrays Christians as fallen away from the faith of Abraham.[9] Though Christians received revelations through Jesus, they have lost the purity of that revelation. The Qur'ân and Muhammad simply invite Christians to be faithful to the revelations given to Jesus. Christians who are faithful to Jesus will recognize Muhammad as the last prophet and find Islam the true and original religion. Christians who respond favorably to Muhammad's message are assured of Paradise and the recalcitrant Christians are assured of hell.

A number of both classical and modern Muslim scholars work out a possibility of salvation outside Islam. Tom Michel writes: "In working out how this can be possible, Mohamed Talbi refers to earlier theological attempts, such as that of Abu Hamid al-Ghazali (d. 1111) in medieval times and of twentieth-century thinkers such as Muhammad Abduh, Ahmed Amin, and Yusuf Ali. In arguing the possibility of salvation for non-Muslims, Talbi relies on Qur'ânic verses such as 2:62; 5:62, 69; and 4:150".[10]

D. Marshall writes:

At the heart of the Qur'ân there is a vision of religious history which includes an ideal form of Christianity. This consists of a Jesus and a Mary who are precursors of Muhammad; a Scripture which is a precursor of the Qur'ân; and Christians who are precursors of the followers of Muhammad. Initially, this ideal understanding of Christianity is not greatly challenged, but gradually the ideal collides with the actual. The ideal of a Christianity which must find its proper goal in Muhammad and the Qur'ân runs up against the actual forms of Christianity adhered to by the Christians encountered by Muhammad. Their failure to acknowledge Muhammad and the Qur'ân reveals that such Christians are distortions of what followers of Jesus should be; that they hold a distorted understanding of Jesus ...; and that they have distorted the scripture brought by Jesus.[11]

The Teachings of the *Ḥadīth* on Christianity and Christians

There are numerous references to Christians in the *hadīth*.[12] The word for Christians in the *hadīth* is *naṣāra* (sing. *naṣrānī*). The *hadīth* literature is concerned with social relationships between Christians and Muslims. It does not give much attention to Christian doctrine as such.[13] The *hadīth* literature comes from an era when Muslims had already established political control over many parts of West Asia and North Africa. So its concern is mainly with the question of how to relate with Christians and not their doctrine. In these narrations Muslims are profiled as a distinct religious group. The *hadīth* literature also reflects an attitude of mistrust both towards Christians and Jews. It is important to note that there are positive traditions about them too. It insists on the need of Muslims to be wary of Christians.

In the words of M. Speight:

The *hadīth* show that, as the Islamic Community marked its distinctive nature, it evoked scriptural and theological issues vis-á-vis the other religion, even if at a rudimentary level, and examined its social relationships with Christians. The reports testify as to how the dominant Muslim population found a place for Christians in the scheme of things by assigning them to the *dhimmī* status. The social and religious inferiority with which the Muslims regarded their *dhimmī* population is clearly delineated. And yet the accounts are not without certain touches of human warmth. Religiously, the ruling element isolated the Christians while at the same time acknowledging some ties with them. In general, ḥadīth served to strengthen the foundations of an exclusive theology which afterwards would set Muslims firmly apart from the People of the Scripture.[14]

Political and Social Influences on Muslim Approaches Towards Christians and Christianity

In the early Islamic centuries, when Muslims ruled over a vast number of Christians, they were to assert their Islamic identity in a Christian milieu and make efforts to preserve the distinctiveness of their Islamic way of life. During these times, Muslim theologians developed a systematic critique of Christians and Christianity. Polemics played an important role in their theological language.[15] At heart of the Muslim approach to Christianity there were two themes.[16] "The first is essentially a historical one – (as indicated in the last section) that during the course of Christian history, the original message of Jesus had become corrupted. The second is at heart a philosophical one – the argument that Christianity is fundamentally irrational".[17] H. Goddard provides an example of each trend. 'Abd al Jabbar's (d. 1025) thinking represents the first trend.

> The gist of 'Abd al Jabbar's argument is that Christians since the time of Jesus have developed beliefs and practices that are contrary to the teachings of Jesus. 'Abd al Jabbar isolates seven areas in which Christians have blatantly gone against the specific teachings of Jesus: he observed ritual purity in prayer, he recited prayer texts from the Bible, he turned towards Jerusalem in order to pray, he was circumcised, he fasted on Jewish fast-days, he observed the Jewish Sabbath, and he abstained from pork, so that in all these things he obeyed the precepts of the Law. But the Christians abolished the Law: they ceased to observe ritual purity in prayer, they used poems composed by their own scholars as prayers, they turned to the east to pray, they gave up the practice of circumcision, they introduced fasting in Lent, they replaced Sabbath with Sunday, and they authorised the eating of pork.[18]

The second trend is effectively represented by the work *al-Radd al-jamīl li-Ilāhiyyāt 'Isābi-Ṣarīh al-Injīl*. This is a work associated with the great Muslim theologian al-Ghazali (d. 1111).[19] The Christian idea of Incarnation is the chief item of discussion in this work. The author, commenting upon different texts, argues that the doctrine of the incarnation is completely incongruous. The Divine and the human are mutually exclusive, and so they cannot be predicated of one and the same substance. The conclusion the author draws is that Christianity is an irrational religion.[20]

The implications are: Christianity is considered a religion that has deviated from the original path and needs to be corrected by the message of the Prophet Muhammad and Christians need to heed the Qur'ânic injunctions,[21] Islam is the final religion, the Qur'ân is the final revelation of God and the Prophet Muhammad is the final prophet.

A relatively amicable situation prevailed between Muhammad and Christians while he was alive, but some overt antipathy was shown towards Christians after his death. Later Muslim approaches towards Christians became less hostile and more accommodating when Muslims began to rule over a large number of Christians in the conquered territories. For example, the 'Abbasid caliph al-Ma'mun (C.E. 813-33) encouraged intellectual exchanges. There were debates that took place between representatives of these two faiths in his court under his patronage. Christians played an important role in the translation of cultural and scientific texts from Greek and Syriac to Arabic.[22] But things turned for the worse later during the reign of al-Mutawakkil (C.E. 847-61).[23]

H. Goddard writes:

There are a number of possible reasons for this change in attitude: on the one hand there are practical factors such as the greater feeling of security engendered by the Empire's having existed for over two centuries and its no longer being vulnerable to outside attack, and on the other there are more theological factors such as the emergence of a more sophisticated Islamic system of thought, not least as a result of the controversies of the time concerning the status of the Qur'ân, but whatever the reason, there can be no denying a change of attitude towards Christians.[24]

Though theology gave a framework for Muslim approaches towards Christians and Christianity, socio-political factors either amplified or reduced conflicts between the two communities. One could say, for example, that the context was like a microphone. It conditioned the voice, the theology. It should be said that theology and its context together played a major role in shaping Muslim approaches to Christians and Christianity.

In recent history, another important dimension is added that complicates the situation further. The association of Christianity with the West has increasingly become crucial in shaping Muslim approaches towards Christians and Christianity. The link between Western imperialism and Protestant missionaries is one of the main reasons for the apparent closeness of Christianity with the West.

A large number of Muslims think about Christianity as inherently a western phenomenon. As one author puts it, "the Christianity of today is inseparable from the culture of the West".[25] This association is often implicitly treated as an accident of history. But some Muslim writers take it for granted that there is a divergence between the West/ Christianity and the East/Islam. K. Zebri points out that the American Jewish convert, M. Jameelah, and Isma'il al-Faruqi both assert that Christianity is inherently Western and essentially inimical to Islam.[26]

The assertion of Christianity as a Western phenomenon by these authors needs to be critically assessed in the present context of Christianity's rootedness in Asia. The inculturation of Christian Faith among Asian countries, birth and growth of indigenous Christian theologies in the context of religions and cultures appear to challenge their assertion.

M. Jameelah argues that from the time St. Paul presented Christianity to gentile Christians in Graeco-Roman terms, Christianity took root in Western civilization and remains inseparable from the West.[27] She continues that when West Asian and African Christians quickly embraced Islam, Western Christianity remained always hostile to Islam. She also claims that Christianity cannot attract Asians' or Africans' hearts since Christianity as a religion is a religion of colonizers. Al-Faruqi, in a similar vein, says that Christianity appeals only to crude minds.[28]

Since these authors perceive that Christianity is a Western phenomenon, they have no difficulty in twinning Christianity with Western imperialism and seeing Christian missionaries as the representatives of imperialists. Lebanese scholars like 'Umar Farrūkh and Muṣṭfā Khālidī argue that Christian missionaries not only took advantage of Western imperialism and political dominance to spread Christianity but also deliberately paved the way for it.[29] A number of Muslims consider Christianity is all out to subjugate Muslims and Islamic countries. In the light of Western dominance, it is said that the Muslim view of Christians and Christianity has become highly politicized.[30]

The following points emerge from the foregoing discussion. There is consistency in the realm of Islamic theology: Islam offered Christians a place within its theological vision. Accordingly Christians, the disciples of Jesus, as indicated earlier, should find fulfilment in the Prophethood of Muhammad. They should understand the finality of the Qur'ân. But Christians refused to see this truth and continue to follow corrupted teachings.

It should be said that the theological image of Christianity and Christians is certainly based in the Qur'ân and the *hadīth*. Muslims have become accustomed to look at Christians and Christianity through Qur'ânic lenses. No doubt in these Islamic sources there is a definite, clear portrait of Christians and Christianity.

Islam in the Eyes of Christians

Eastern Christian View

One of the first observations on Islam and Muslims was made by the Armenian bishop Sebos (died after 661). He considered Muslims as descendants of Ishmael, and, consequently Islam as a self-conscious movement of the Abraham-Hagar-Ishmael connection.[31] It was his considered opinion that God has realized his promise that he made to Abraham in Islam. Meanwhile, the so-called Nestorian, as well as the so called Monophysite Christians,[32] who were routinely persecuted by Chalcedonian Christians, rejoiced at the rise of Islam and considered the new religion as God's pronouncement of punishment for their oppressors.[33] One of the early Christian theologians, John of Damascus (d. 753),[34] dismissed Islam as a heresy.[35] He believed that the Qur'ân was an ignorant imitation of the Bible.[36]

It should be observed: these first responses were guarded and cautious. There is a positive affirmation when Islam was judged as God's promise fulfilled. The second response has more to do with what was happening between different Christian groups, coupled with a judgment that Islam was God's punishment on Christians who followed the Chalcedonian formulation of faith. It is more of a judgment against the Chalcedonian Christians than on Muslims. The third opinion was made considering common elements and differences: Islam should be considered as a heresy. One can notice that in these views there are no harsh words for the Prophet Muhammad or for the Qur'ân. One reason could be that these opinion-makers lived under Muslim rule. Any condemnation either of the Qur'ân or of the personality of the Prophet Muhammad was not to be taken lightly. Another reason could be these theologians lived among Muslims, read Arabic and thus had a certain familiarity with Islam and Muslims.[37]

The tone of the Christian critique of Islam changes when one moves into Byzantine-ruled territories. Writings on Islam by Christians who lived in the Byzantine territories were sharply polemical since they did not need to fear the Muslim rulers. They were also largely ignorant of Islam. Ignorance and political enmity are lethal; they are a source of biting polemics. It will suffice to give the examples of Theophane the Confessor (d. ca. 813), and Nicetas of Byzantium (d. ca 912) both belonging to the 9th – 10th century.

Theophane the Confessor opened up many vistas for confrontation with Islam. He called Muhammad a false prophet. About the Qur'ân, he claimed that it was a set of teachings that Muhammad received from Christians.[38] Carrying forward this polemical legacy into the mid-9th century, Nicetas of Byzantium condemned Islam not just as a heresy but also as idolatry. He claimed that the Qur'ân was not just a garbled collection from Christians but that it was of demonic origin and that Muhammad was both a charlatan and a false prophet.

There were flashes of positive streaks of light in this otherwise dark, negative horizon. For example, Emperor Leo III (d. 741) agreed that Christians and Muslims worship One God. This was a very bold statement in an era where Islam was reviled as idolatry. In a similar vein, Emperor Manuel (d.1180) advised his officers not to force the Christians who were converts from Islam to anathematize the God of Muhammad lest it be seen as if Christians and Muslims worship different gods. In other words, both these Emperors affirmed that Christians and Muslims worshiped one God. It is an important assertion. However, it is not clear how they would explain the differences of this worship. It can only be speculated that while the Emperors recognized that Muhammad led the Arabs from idolatry to faith in one God, still they implicitly held that he was not given the gift of faith in Jesus Christ. On the other hand, they may have followed John of Damascus and thought that Islam was a Christian heresy. In the first sense, Christianity would be believed to be the fulfillment of Islam or Islam would be on the way towards its fulfillment. In the second sense, Islam would be construed as a heresy that should be corrected and brought back to Christian faith. Whatever may be the case, with Meyendorff one can affirm that in Byzantium there were two views on Islam: one was closed and the other somewhat open.[39]

It must be noted that prejudices, biases, and stereotypes flourish where there is no real contact between different groups. Muslims and Christians may live among one another, but if there is no real interaction between them, invariably the imagination takes over and makes the other an enemy. In this drama of perceptions, politics play a vital role.

This brief discussion on the Eastern Christian views on Islam shows the two faces of this relationship as indicated in the last passage: one view is closed and the other is somewhat open. The next section will pay attention to the Western Christian perception of Islam.

Western Christian View

Goddard argues that the events that unfolded in Spain in the 9th century gave birth to a distinctively Western response to Islam. In Spain, Christians, though not persecuted openly for their faith, were disadvantaged and lived under severe restrictions. Two Cordovan Christians, a priest by the name of Eulogius and a lay person named Paul Alvarus, responded to this situation in a dramatic way. It came to be called in history the Spanish Martyrs' Movement (850-860).[40] Both Eulogius and Paul Alvarus considered Islam as the precursor of the coming of the anti-Christ. They developed this view when they looked at the Bible for guidance, especially the book of Daniel.[41] They abused Muhammad and called for conversion of Muslims to Christianity. Both these actions made one liable to suffer capital punishment in a Muslim-ruled state. Despite warnings, Eulogius and Paul Alvarus continued to provoke Muslims to abandon Islam and adopt Christianity. They were put to death. Their killing inspired more Christians to take their path. In those ten years, between, 850 to 860 around 50 people were executed by Muslim authorities. It is said that their killings were etched in the memory of the Western European peoples and continues to influence negatively their opinion of Islam.[42]

The next major episode that damaged Christian-Muslim relations was the Crusades. The Crusades were launched by the Pope Urban II (d. 1099) in 1095-96 at the request of the Byzantine Emperor Alexius I Comnenus (d. 1118) and left an indelible mark on the psyche of Muslims at large, which lasts even today. Without any doubt the Crusades have become a very big road-block in the relationship between Christians and Muslims.

Some positive approaches towards Islam began to surface in the 12th century. Petrus Alphonsi (c. 1106-1110) alerted Christians that one should be careful to separate the factual from fictional. William of Malmesbury (c. 1090-1143) said that Islam is not idolatry nor a pagan religion but a monotheistic religion and Muhammad is a prophet of God. Otto of Freising (c. 1143-1158) confirmed that Muslims worship one God. These approaches indicate the movement towards a new direction that challenged ignorance and blind prejudice. This new direction was a fruit of openness towards true learning.

This approach gained momentum in the work of Peter the Venerable (d. 1156). He suggested that Islam should be studied from its sources. James Kritzeck calls this as a momentous event in the intellectual history of humankind.[43] It is a unique approach since it encouraged Christians to meet Muslims not with weapons but with reason and love. In July 1143, Robert Ketton completed the translation of the holy Qur'ân into Latin. Roger Bacon (d. 1292) encouraged the learning of Muslim languages. Saint Francis of Assisi (d. 1226), an apostle of love, was convinced that the Crusades would not promote among Muslims a proper knowledge of Christ. In the spirit of friendship, he called Muslims to a fellowship in Christ. These Christian leaders taught that the mission among Muslims should be engaged in with serious study and deep love for Muslims.

In the 12th and the 13th century, there was a movement for learning from the sources of Islam. St Francis of Assisi brought another important dimension into Christian-Muslim relations, that is, love for Muslims. This is a gentle movement that introduces a new starting point in Christian-Muslim relations: learn from the sources of Islam and add love in relationship with Muslims. However, these movements were feeble and failed to catch the imagination of Western Christians. This is especially true with regard to the approach of St Francis of Assisi.

Renaissance and Humanist Thinking

The papacy under the French domination (1309-76), the forty-year Great Schism (1378-1417), and the Black Death (1347-50) shook people's confidence in the certainty of the teachings of the Church and undermined the prominence of the pope and clerics. The hegemony of the clerics was challenged and unsettling questions were raised against their 'inviolable' doctrinal knowledge. Simply put, the control the Church exercised on the common man was challenged.[44]

A new understanding of the human person and his/her existence emerged in the writings of the humanist authors of what is called the 'Renaissance'. 'Renaissance' thinkers and artists began to focus on the human person, not simply as the creation of God, but as the highest form of life in the universe. Earlier, life in the world was regarded as a sentence of exile in a valley of tears. This was a punishment for human transgressions. Among the humanists, human dignity was considered the foundation for all values. Ultimately, this humanism gave rise to a declaration of human rights during the French Revolution (1789). Human rights and human dignity came to be regarded as central to philosophical thinking in Europe. Responding to the cultural shift that was taking place around her, the Church began to look for ways to reconcile faith and obedience to God with humanism. Islamic thinking meanwhile continued to be a thinking that was rooted on God's Law. Thus, the Christian view of human life became incompatible with the Muslim view of human person and God.[45] J.M. Gaudeul explains: that "Christians and Muslims seemed to be standing on two floating islands or icebergs, always drifting farther from each other".[46]

How do Christians respond to Muslims in such a situation? George of Trebizond (d. 1484) looked for a truly Christian response to Islam. He believed that God wanted unity among all people. He affirmed that God has given the Sultan political power over the whole world to unite all people in a common faith. However, for George of Trebizond the common faith was nothing but the basic truth of Christianity.

He advised Christians to renounce any form of violence against Muslims. He stressed that his fellow believers should avoid rash judgment against Muslims. He further insisted that Christian believers should rectify their prejudices against Muslims. He called on them to give up their hatred towards followers of Islam. He went on to suggest that Christians and Muslims should frequently meet one another and discuss different elements of their faith. He advocated that Christian-Muslim peace conferences be organized and doctrines of both religions be studied during those meetings. Moreover, he encouraged the Christians to study the Qur'ân. J.M. Gaudeul writes: "He seemed to accept the Qur'ân as a revealed scripture, but interpreted it in accordance with Christian doctrine, adding that what could not be interpreted in this way had been falsified".[47] This approach is similar to that of Paul of Antioch and of Basetti-Sani.[48]

George of Trebizond breaks the old barriers of prejudices and looks for ways to discuss issues of faith with Muslims. No doubt the attitude of the 'Renaissance' is present in his approach when he explores ways for unity among Christians and Muslims. However, as J.M. Gaudeul rightly points out, he minimizes the differences between the two religions. Minimizing differences is a dangerous trend that denies the specific richness of a religious tradition.

While George of Trebizond recognized the Qur'ân as a revealed scripture, John of Segovia (d. 1458) did not believe that the Qur'ân was a revealed book and argued for a rigorously exact translation of the Qur'ân so that what he believed were its contradictions and errors could be exposed. He believed that the natural mode of expansion of Islam is by war where as Christianity spreads only through peace.[49] However, like George of Trebizond, he also recommended conferences between Christians and Muslims. He desired that those conferences study the different themes of Qur'ânic criticism.[50]

A curious, similar attitude like that of George of Trebizond can be noted in the writings of Cardinal Nicolaus from Cusa (d.1468). In his work *De pace fidei*, he maintained that the three Abrahamic religions coincide in their fundamental truths but differ in manifold customs and rites.[51] However, later Nicolaus changed his views. Gaudeul writes: "Nicholas' first attitude was based on a false optimism [...] which saw the opposition between Islam and Christianity as superficial and slight. He then began to study the question methodically as a true scholar, attempting to prove that the real meaning of the Qur'ân was Christian".[52]

While the aforementioned authors showed certain openness in dealing with Muslims, there were many others who did not share the optimism and goodwill of these men. For example, Jean Germain (d. 1461) and Pope Pius II (d. 1464) advocated a tough stand against Muslims. Jean Germain insisted that Islam was the enemy of Christians and religious discussion with them would only weaken the Christian position.[53]

An important affirmation was made in the beginning saying that Christians and Muslims worship one God. As observed earlier, this is a very important and positive affirmation in the history of Christian-Muslim relations. Following this, a gentle approach insisting on knowledge of Islam and love for Muslims gained momentum with Peter the Venerable. This positive approach suffered a small setback when Christian meaning was sought to be read into the Qur'ân. In and around the fifteenth century, there were a number of Christians who showed a certain openness towards Muslims. Their eirenic approach was based on a false understanding that the differences between these two religions could be minimized. As Christians, they wanted the Muslims to recognize the truth of the Christian faith. There were many

Christians who remained antagonistic towards Muslims. It is also that individual Christians made efforts while the official Church did not appear to positively respond either to Muslims or to Islam.

Endnotes

[1] The Brill is publishing a series of volumes of the History of Christian Muslim relations titled *Christian-Muslim Relations, a Biographical History*. Till date 43 volumes have been published by them https://brill.com/view/serial/HCMR?rskey=rHRmga&result=1 [accessed May 30, 2020].

[2] *ḥadīth* – "(narrative, talk) with the definite article *al-ḥadīth* is used for Tradition, being an account of what the Prophet said or did, or of his tacit approval of something said or done in his presence". See *The Encyclopedia of Islam*, New Edition, s.v. "Ḥadīth".

[3] H. Goddard, *Muslim Perceptions of Christianity* [London: Grey Seal, 1996], 1-16.

[4] G.S. Reynolds, "On the Qur'ânic Accusation of Scriptural Falsification (taḥrīf) and Christian Anti-Jewish Polemic," *The Journal of the American Oriental Society* 130, no. 2 [April-June 2010]: 189-202.

[5] A. Saeed, "The Charge of Distortion of Jewish and Christian Scriptures," *The Muslim World* 92, no. 3-4 [September 2002]: 419-436.

[6] H. Goddard, *Muslim Perceptions of Christianity*, 1. Also see D. Marshall, "Christianity in the Qur'ân," in *Islamic Interpretations of Christianity*, ed. L. Ridgeon [Surrey: Curzon, 2001], 24-25.

[7] See M. Borrmans, "Islam as it understands itself," in *Catholic Engagement with World Religions: A Comprehensive Study*, ed. K.J. Becker and I. Morali [Maryknoll, New York: Orbis Books, 2010], 502. G. Parrinder gives an excellent portrait of Jesus in the eyes of Muslims in his book. See G. Parrinder, *Jesus in the Qur'ân* [London: Faber and Faber, 1965].

[8] A number of scholars have reflected on the Qur'ânic rejection of crucifixion of Jesus. See M. Borrmans, "Muslims and the Mystery of the Cross: Rejection or Incomprehension?" *Encounter* 2, no.25 [1976]: 3-13; E.E. Elder, "The Crucifixion in the Qur'ân," *The Muslim World* 13, no.3 [July 1923]: 242-258; M. Ayoub, "Towards an Islamic Christology II: the death of Jesus, reality or delusion?" *The Muslim World* 70, no. 2 [1980]: 91–121; G. S. Reynolds, "The Muslim Jesus Dead or Alive?" *Bulletin of the School of Oriental and African Studies* 72, no.2 [June 2009]: 237-258.

[9] Encyclopedia of the Qur'ân, New Edition, s.v. "Christians and Christianity".

[10] See I.A. Omar, ed., *A Christian View of Islam: Essays on Dialogue* [Maryknoll, New York: Orbis Books, 2010], 38.

[11] D. Marshall, "Christianity in the Qur'ân," in *Islamic Interpretations of Christianity*, 24-25.

[12] M. Speight, "Christian in Ḥadīth Literature" in *Islamic Interpretations of Christianity*, 30-48.

[13] Ibid., 32.

[14] Ibid., 48-49.

[15] D. Thomas, *Anti-Christian Polemic in Early Islam* [Cambridge, 1992].

[16] H. Goddard, *Muslim Perceptions of Christianity*, 1.

[17] Ibid.

[18] Ibid. Also see G.S. Reynolds, *A Muslim theologian in the sectarian milieu: 'Abd al-Jabbar and the critique of Chrisitan origins* [Leiden, 2004].

[19] There is disagreement over the authorship of this work and it cannot be assumed that al-Ghazālī wrote it. See H. Goddard, *Muslim Perceptions of Christianity*, 30.

Al-Ghazali's views appear in a book entitled *al-Radd al-jamīl li-Ilāhīyyāt 'Isā bi-sarīh al-Injīl.* There is disagreement over the identity of the author of this work. Scholars like Massignon and Chidiac held that the content of this book was the teaching of al-Ghazali; a student of his who attended his lectures compiled it as a book (See H. Lazarus-Yafeh, *Intertwined Worlds: Medieval Islam and Bible Criticism* [New Jersey: Princeton University Press, 1992], 124. This view is rejected by H. Lazarus-Yafeh, who held that a Coptic Christian convert to Islam was the author (See H. Lazarus-Yafeh, *Intertwined Worlds*, 124).

[20] H. Goddard, *Muslim Perceptions of Christianity*, 29.

[21] N. Daniel, *Islam and the West, The Making of an Image* [Edinburgh, 1993], 47.

[22] F. Robinson, *Islam and Muslim History in South Asia* [New Delhi: Oxford University Press, 2000], 28-42.

[23] It should be remembered that during al-Mutawakkil's time the conflict was not just between Christians and Muslims; the intra-Muslim conflict was also sharp.

[24] H. Goddard, *Muslim Perceptions of Christianity*, 32.

[25] M. 'Ata ur-Rahim, *Jesus, Prophet of Islam* [Elmhurst, New York: Tahrike Tarsil Qur'ân, 1991], 205.

[26] The chapter "Towards an Asian Theology of Dialogue" in *Towards a Theology of Dialogue* makes a relevant reading here. See E. Chia, *Towards a Theology of Dialogue* [Bangkok, Thailand: publisher not mentioned, 2003], 230-256.

[27] M. Jameelah, *Islam Versus Ahl al-Kitab: Past and Present* [Delhi: Taj Company, 1989], 351-352.

[28] Isma'il al-Faruqi, *On Arabism: 'Urubah and Religion* [Amsterdam: Djambatan, 1962].

[29] See M. Ayoub, "Roots of Muslim-Christian Conflict," *Muslim World* 79, no.1 [1989]: 25-45, for an exposition of the ideas of these authors.

[30] K. Zebri, "Muslim Perceptions of Christianity and the West," in *Islamic Interpretations of Christianity*, 188-190.

[31] J. Moorhead, "The Earliest Christian Theological Response to Islam," *Religion* 11, no. 3 [July 1981]: 265-274.

[32] Many Eastern Christians rejected the Council of Ephesus (431) that taught Mary is the mother of God. They argued that this means that Jesus would be absorbed wholly into the divine nature. They stressed that both the human nature and the divine nature in the person of Jesus should remain distinguished. They call themselves "Eastern Orthodox Christians". They are erroneously called Nestorians.

Monophysites rejected the Council of Chalcedon (451). This council taught the doctrine of two natures in one person; Jesus fully human and fully divine. Monophysites recognized only the divine nature of Christ.

The terms "Nestorians" and "Monophysites" are not accepted by the church to which they are applied, and these churches have asked the Catholic Church not to use those words. The first is the Assyrian Church of the East the latter collectively are the Oriental Orthodox churches. Note that the Catholic Church has signed ecumenical agreements with the Assyrian Church of the East and the Oriental Orthodox churches (the Copts, the Armenian Orthodox, and the Syrian Orthodox) resolving the several disputes.

[33] H. Goddard, *A History of Christian-Muslim Relations* [Edinburgh: Edinburgh University Press, 2000], 37. Viewing Arabs as the scourge of God implies that the conquests were believed to be limited in time. See H. Suermann, "Early Islam in the Light of Christian and Jewish Sources," in *Texts and on the Qur'ān, Qur'ān in Context: Historical and Literary Investigations into the Qur'ānic Milieu*, ed. A. Neuwirth, N. Sinai, M. Marx, vol.6 of *Texts and Studies on the Qur'ān*, ed. G. Böwering and J.D McAuliffe [Leiden and Boston: Brill, 2010], 135-148.

Some also saw this as punishment upon themselves. "Preaching on the Christmas day 634, in the midst of the invasions, the patriarch of Jerusalem explained to his trembling flock that God has sent 'the godless Saracens' as punishment for 'countless sins and very serious faults'. 'Let us correct ourselves', he exhorted. 'If we constrain ourselves . . . we would see their final destruction.'" See W. E. Kaegi, "Initial Byzantine Reactions to the Arab Conquest," *Church History* 38, no. 2 [June 1969]: 139-149; D. Nirenberg, "Christendom and Islam" in *Christianity in Western Europe c. 1100 – c. 1500*, vol. 4 of *The Cambridge History of Christianity*, ed. M. Rubin and W. Simons [Cambridge: Cambridge University Press, 2009], 149-169.

[34] John of Damascus was an important official in the administration of the Umayyad Caliphs, who retired from his position due to the diminishing influence of non-Muslims in the administration. See G. Hawting, *The First Dynasty of Islam* [London & New York: Routledge, 2000], 61-65.

[35] H. Goddard, *Islam: Towards A Christian Assessment* [Oxford: Latimer House, 1992], 13; J.W. Voorhis, "John of Damascus on the Moslem Heresy," *The Muslim World* 24 [1934]: 391-398.

[36] D.H. Sahas, *John of Damascus on Islam, the "Heresy of the Ishmaelites"* [Leiden: Brill, 1972], 132-133.

[37] R. G. Hoyland, *Seeing Islam as Others Saw It: A Survey and Evaluation of Christian, Jewish, and Zoroastrian Writings on Early Islam* [Princeton, New Jersey: The Darwin Press, 1997].

[38] Many Christian and Jewish scholars tried to claim that Islam is systemically related to their religion. While scholars like W.Rudolph, R. Bell, T. Andrae, and J.S. Trimingham argued for what they believed was a dominant Christian influence on the Qur'ân, others like R. Dozy, A. Geiger, D. Sidersky, C.C. Torrey, A. Katsh, A. Zaoui and J. Bouman alleged the Jewish influence on it.

C. Adang in her book (C. Adang, *Muslim Writers on Judaism & the Hebrew Bible: From Ibn Rabban to Ibn Hazm* [Leiden: E.J.Brill, 1996]) helpfully lists some of the most important of these scholars and their principal works:

W. Rudolph, *Die Abhangigkeit des Qorans von Judentum und Christentum* [Stuttgart: W. Kohlhammer, 1922].

R. Bell, *The Origin of Islam in Its Christian Environment* [London: Macmillan & Co. Limited, 1926].

T. Andrae, *Der Ursprung des Islams und das Christentum* [Uppsala: Stockholm, 1926].

J.S. Trimingham, *Christianity Among the Arabs in Pre-Islamic Times* [London, New York: Longman, 1979].

R. Dozy, *De Israelieten te Mekka. Van Davids tijd tot in de vifde eeuw onzer tijdrekening* [Haarlem: A.C. Kruseman, 1864].

A. Geiger, *Judaism and Islam* [New York: KTAV, 1898].

D. Sidersky, *Les orgines des legendes musulmanes dans le Coran et dans les vies des prophetes* [Paris: Geuthner, 1933].

C.C. Torrey, *The Jewish Foundations of Islam* [New York: KTAV, 1967].

A. Katsh, *Judaism in Islam: Biblical and Talmudic Backgrounds of the Koran and its Commentaries* [New York: Sepher-Hermon Press, 3rd ed., 1980].

A. Zaoui, *Jewish Sources of the Koran* [Jerusalem, 1983].

J. Bouman, *Der Koran und die Juden: Die Geschichte einer Tragodie* [Darmstadt: Wissenschaftliche Buchgesellschaft, 1990].

However many scholars like W.M. Watt, (See W.M. Watt, *Muhammad at Mecca* [Oxford, 1953], 1-29), M. Gaudefroy-Demomlyness (See M. Gaudefroy-Demomlyness, *Muhammad* [Paris: Albin Michel, 1969], i-xxii.) and H.A.R. Gibb (See H.A.R. Gibb, "Pre-Islamic Monotheism in Arabia," *Harvard Theological Review* 55, no. 4 [1962]: 269-280) do not agree with any such view and have claimed that

Islam grew out of an Arabic background without any influence from Judaism and Christianity.

In the 1970s, scholars such as J. Wansbrough, (See J. Wansbrough, *Qur'ânic studies: Sources and methods of scriptural interpretation* [Oxford: Oxford University Press, 1977]; J. Wansbrough, *The sectarian milieu: Content and composition of Islamic salvation history* [Oxford: Oxford University Press, 1978]) claimed that the Qur'ân was part of literary activity that reflects salvation history and has been created "by choosing texts from a much larger pool of originally independent traditions". See H. Motzki, "Alternative accounts of the Qur'ân's formation," in *The Cambridge Companion to The Qur'ân*, ed. Jane D. McAuliffe [Cambridge: Cambridge University Press], 59-75.

Muslims on their part reject any such theory that questions the direct divine authorship of the Qur'ân. They maintain that the Qur'ân does not borrow from any source. They consider that the Qur'ân was sent down by God and in it God speaks directly. It is the literal word of God. Muhammad simply receives the Book that is sent down to him.

[39] J.Meyendorff, "Byzantine Views of Islam," *Dumbarton Oaks Papers*, 18 [1964], 113-132. See also C.L. Hanson, "Manuel I Comnenus and the 'God of Muhammad': a Study in Byzantine Ecclesiastical Politics," in *Medieval Perception of Islam*, ed. J.V. Tolan [New York and London: Garlan, 1996], 55-82.

[40] K. Ihnat, "The Martyrs of Córdoba: Debates around a curious case of medieval martyrdom," https://onlinelibrary.wiley.com/doi/pdf/10.1111/hic3.12603 [accessed on 10 January 2018] See also H. Goddard, *A History of Christian-Muslim Relations*, 81.

[41] It is interesting to note both the Eastern as well as Western Christians looked for guidance in order to evaluate Islam. The Eastern Christians approached the Jewish scriptures and came to conclude that in the Muslims God fulfilled his promises. Western Christians especially who lived in Cordoba approached the Book of Daniel and came to conclude that Islam is the precursor to the anti-Christ. Both these groups of Christians followed proof-text style of interpretation. They arrived at what they wanted to prove using the biblical texts!

[42] R.W. Southern, *Western Views of Islam in the Middle Ages* [Harvard: Harvard University Press, 1962], 16-25; A. Cutler, "The Ninth-Century Spanish Martyr's Movement and the Origins of Western Christian Mission to the Muslims," *Muslim World* 55 [1965]: 321-39; J. Waltz, "The Significance of the Voluntary Martyrs' of Ninth-Century Cordoba," *Muslim World* 60 [1970]: 143-159 and 226-236; H. Goddard, *A History of Christian-Muslim Relations*, 84.

[43] J. Kritzeck, *Peter the Venerable and Islam* (Princeton: Princeton University Press, 1964).

[44] *The Oxford Companion to Christian Thought* [Oxford: Oxford University Press, 2000], s.v. "Renaissance".

[45] J.M. Gaudeul, *Encounters & Clashes: Islam and Christianity in History I A Survey* [Rome: Pontificio Istituto di Studi Arabi e d'Islamistica (P.I.S.A.I), 1984], 189.

[46] J.M. Gaudeul, *Encounters & Clashes: Islam and Christianity in History II A Survey* [Rome: Pontificio Istituto di Studi Arabi e d'Islamistica (P.I.S.A.I), 1984], 191.

[47] J.M. Gaudeul, *Encounters & Clashes: Islam and Christianity in History II A Survey*, 192.

[48] Paul of Antioch in his "Letter to Muslim Friends" tried to drive home the claim that Islam teaches that Christianity was the true religion. He used Qur'ânic verses to achieve this end. See D. Thomas, "Paul of Antioch's Letter to a Muslim Friend and The Letter from Cyprus," in *Syrian Christians under Islam: the First Thousand Years*, ed. D. Thomas (Leiden, 2001), 203–221.

Basetti-Sani accepted the Qur'ân as an inspired scripture and claimed that the Qur'ân truly lead one to the light of Christ. See G. Basetti-Sani, *The Koran in the Light of Christ* [Chicago: Franciscan Herald, 1977].

[49] That Islam spread by sword has been one of the prejudices against Islam. J.L. Esposito states that this statement is historically incorrect. He writes: "The assertion that Muhammad commanded the spread of Islam by the sword was strenuously rejected by Muslim and non-Muslim scholars as inaccurate". See J.L. Esposito, *The Future of Islam* [Oxford: Oxford University Press, 2010], 187-188.

[50] J.M. Gaudeul, *Encounters & Clashes: Islam and Christianity in History II A Survey*, 194.

[51] See M. Bauschke, "Islam: Jesus and Muhammad as Brothers," in *Christian Approaches to Other Faiths*, ed. A. Race and P.M. Hedges [London: SCM Press, 2008], 196.

[52] See J. M. Gaudeul, *Encounters & Clashes: Islam and Christianity in History I A Survey*, 195-197.

[53] See J.M. Gaudeul, *Encounters & Clashes: Islam and Christianity in History II A Survey*, 198.

Chapter 2

Christian-Muslim Relations in India

Christian-Muslim relations in India are not monolithic, but have several dimensions that include political, cultural, economic and religious understanding. We pay attention to the religious dimension, since mutual understanding and real respect for others as persons is founded on understanding and respecting the religious convictions of the other. From early times Muslims had contacts with people of other faiths in the Malabar region. We restrict our focus to the Gangetic plains, since the three pioneers we present in the book worked in these regions.[1] The following general overview will help the reader to understand the context in which the pioneers open new vistas.

The Jesuit Mission at Emperor Akbar's Court

The first scene of Christian religious interaction unfolded in the Mughal Court. The Jesuit mission to the Mughal court has been a topic of much interest among scholars.[2] The Jesuits themselves have left a number of documents, including letters explaining their work. The present writer is fascinated by the way in which the Emperor Akbar befriended the Jesuits. On their arrival Jesuits were received cordially in the Court of the Emperor. They were given large sums of money and accorded quarters in the palace. The Jesuits politely refused the large sums and accepted only what was needed for their sustenance. They also preferred to live in modest quarters rather than in the palace. These gestures expressed the interior life of the Jesuits. Akbar was impressed by the simplicity of the Jesuit priests. The Jesuits received their meals from the royal table, which was no ordinary gesture of the Emperor.

On several occasions Akbar demonstrated his love and friendliness towards the Jesuits openly. When Antony Monserrate was ill, Akbar visited him and wished him well in Portuguese. Many times, the Emperor asked the Jesuits to sit next to him even as a gesture of familiarity and love. He walked with his hands around the neck of Rudolf Acquaviva. He used to take them to his inner chamber for private discussion. He shook hands with Jesuits in a most familiar way. Such gestures were simply Akbar's expression of his love for Jesuits. No other person in his court would even dream of such familiarity with the Emperor.

Akbar showed great respect while entering the Jesuit chapel. He appointed his minister to teach the Jesuits Persian and asked the Jesuits to teach him Portuguese and good morals. He charged Abu'-l-fazl to translate the gospels into Persian. He gave full freedom to the Jesuits to preach and make converts. He appreciated the love Jesuits had for one another. When Monserrate rushed to meet Acquaviva on learning he was sick, Akbar openly praised their concern saying: 'See, how they love each other'. Akbar's relation with Jesuits was warm and friendly.

However, it is surprising and sad to find that the Jesuits at Akbar's court, instead of making a new beginning, started off with polemics.[3] The Jesuits' main concern was to prove Christianity was the superior religion to Akbar. To achieve this end, they sought to demonstrate the articles of Christian faith through reason. They expounded their reasons for their belief in the authenticity of the Jewish and Christian scriptures. Then they fired up their motivational cylinders into full-scale attacks on the Qur'ân, on Muhammad and on Islam. They first attacked what they thought were the fallacies and errors of the Qur'ân. Second, they contrasted the holiness of the life of Jesus with what they regarded as the 'irregularities' in the life of Muhammad, and the holiness of the law of Christ and the pure life of those who spread it with the supposed impurity of the law of Muhammad and its alleged spread by the sword.

Such attacks raised the anger of Muslim courtiers at the Court. However, Akbar allowed the Jesuits to complete their arguments. Later, his only suggestion to the Jesuits was to be moderate in their arguments. Akbar was practicing a high level of religious tolerance around the same time as when Giordano Bruno was burnt at stake for heresy at the Campo dei Fiori in Rome.

The Jesuit expectation was to convince Emperor Akbar of the claim of the truth of Christianity. By convincing him of this claim, the Jesuits hoped that he would request baptism. Once the emperor was baptized, it would pave way for Christianizing India. A tall expectation indeed! Their dreams were never translated into reality.

Reflecting on the pastoral and theological aspects of this mission, Paul Jackson observes:

> The Jesuits were perfectly familiar with the European scene of sixteenth-century religious discord and had a lively appreciation of the important, often crucial, role played by the king: *cuius regio, eius religio* was, very often, only too true. Conditions in India however were quite different from those in Europe where many sincere people could understandably pledge allegiance to what was present as a "reformed" Church where Christ's position was absolutely central. It would be quite another matter for an ordinary Muslim, however, to reject the Qur'ân as the "Word of God" and Muhammad as "the Apostle of God" in order to embrace Jesus Christ as "the Son of God" That would be a far too radical change to expect of them, even if their king took the step.[4]

Jackson makes eminent sense when he critiqued the approach of the Jesuits at the Mughal court. Their letters and communications highlight the certain urgency that they showed in their mission; however, they did not seem to understand the Muslims. They appear to have dismissed Islam lightly, and they tried to convince their listeners of their claim of the true value of Christianity. They missed connecting with the broader concerns of Akbar and his politics. The Jesuits, without any doubt, were unaware of the diversity of the Indian society and the political and religious concerns of the Emperor. That was the reason that though Akbar showed such familiarity with the Jesuits, he did not respond to the proselytizing concerns of these Catholic priests. It should be said that the Jesuits did not do enough home work in reflecting on the nature of the mission that they had to undertake once they were aware of the ground realities. They simply stuck on to their earlier motivation, which was to convert Akbar and then convert India, without critically reflecting upon this agenda.

Mughal rule began to disintegrate after the death of Emperor Aurangzeb (d. 1707). The rulers who came after Aurangzeb were incapable of stemming the uprisings of the Sikhs, the Jats and the Marathas. The resurgence of non-Islamic forces unsettled Muslims, especially the *'ulamâ*. The great Delhi theologian Shah Walli Allah (d. 1762) addressed the dilemma of declining Muslim influence in the face of growing non-Islamic powers in his writings.[5]

Protestant Evangelism

How did the Muslims perceive the growing strength of the East India Company? In the year 1803, the Mughal heartlands fell into the hands of the British East Indian Company. Initially, the Company did not allow missionaries to carry out any proselytizing activities.[6] The reason was because the Company was interested in setting up their business and not in proselytization. Consequently, the Company officials did not want to meddle with the religious traditions of its newly-acquired subjects. Moreover, some Company officials had an admiration for Hindu culture and did not share the common missionary prejudice about the 'depravity' of Indians.[7] It took some ten years for the British Parliament to give permission for Protestant missionary activities to begin in 1813.[8]

These Protestant missionaries were evangelical Christians. One among them was Henry Martyn. [9] He is considered to be the first missionary among Muslims in India.[10] Evangelicalism started in Europe as a reaction to the intellectualism[11] and rationalism[12] that undermined the Christian faith in Europe.[13] Evangelicals felt that the Gospel had to be experienced personally and communicated passionately. God's word was central to their life and faith. They affirmed that the Bible was the necessary connection between God and Christian life. Evangelicals asserted strongly the place of God's grace in one's life. Claiming intuitive knowledge of God, they emphasized the importance of one's religious experience, one's new life in Christ, and the whole process of sanctification.[14]

In the words of British historian David Bebbington, the life and mission of an evangelical was marked by: "Commitment to the necessity of personal conversion, recognition of the importance of Jesus Christ's atonement, acknowledgement of Biblical authority and devotion to the active propagation of the Christian gospel".[15]

Evangelicals not only proclaimed salvation through faith in Christ but also forcefully affirmed their claim of the sinfulness and vanity of all other religious paths. They told Muslims that they lived in a state of sin and that, therefore, they were in need of redemption offered in Jesus Christ. Islam, they claimed, could not redeem them from their present status, and Muhammad, who, they said, was not sinless, could not be a mediator. Such preaching was at the heart of the evangelical approach towards Muslims at that time. The Christians' emphasis was on the person of Christ. They did not try to convince the listeners with rational arguments. Rather, they appealed to the heart and emotions of their listeners and called them to conversion. Their religion was a religion of the heart. Though they preferred to appeal to emotions and not reason, not all evangelicals completely abandoned rationalist tendencies.[16] Martyn, for example, would be one who in his ministry among Muslims integrated heart and mind.

In the first decades of the 19th century, the intellectual isolation of the *'ulamâ* from European learning, and the absence of any restrictions from the British side for pursuing their traditional occupation and scholarly interests made the *'ulamâ* remain unmindful of their new rulers. However, Muslims did not fail to realize that their land was losing its identity as *dar al – Islam* (land of Islam). Some of the *fatawa*[17] (plural form of *fatwa*) pronounced the northern part of India as *dar al-harb* (land of war).[18] Abd al-Aziz, one of the Delhi's *'ulamâ*, decreed that Muslims could cooperate with the British. But they should not compromise with the Islamic values and the Muslim way of life while associating with the foreigners. Could a Muslim work under the British? Al-Aziz instructed his fellow Muslims in the following way:

> If someone accepts a post under them [infidel Government] to kill a Muslim or to destroy a [Muslim] state or to promote infidel practices or to find faults with Islam just for the sake of criticism, then all these services are grave in sin and near to *kufr*.[19]

Like Abd al-'Aziz, the *Shî'î mujtahid* in Lucknow too took a similar view. They cautioned Muslims to avoid situations likely to compromise the Islamic way of life.

Though Sunni and Shia theologians differed considerably on a number of theologically weighty points among themselves, they responded similarly to an external threat to their faith, as described as above. Though they were open to social contacts with the British, they insisted that this openness should be exercised with caution. They both advocated a pragmatic approach. Their approach avoided open conflicts between Muslims and East India Company officials who were Christians. Hence, it becomes clear that the *'ulamâ* kept the British at arm's length.

The loss of political power hit the Muslims hard. A Muslim state, right from the time of the Prophet Muhammad, is considered to be a politico-religious state. Many Muslims still hold that the politics and religion are not two isolated entities but two sides of the same coin. The Prophet Muhammad himself was a political genius and statesman as well as a religious leader. Muslims hold that the Prophet provided them a perfect state during his life time in Medina. That was the model state to be copied. The political power Muslims wielded remained an important aspect of Islam.[20]

In India, since the 12th century a Muslim state came to be established by Muslim rulers. Later on, the Mughal emperors expanded the state territorially. Now that Muslim state was breaking up. The Muslim rulers lost their power to the British. Besides, there were missionaries preaching Christianity in many parts of Bengal and other provinces among Muslims. Therefore, Muslim intellectuals felt that both their politics and religion were under attack. In short, the Islamic way of life was in danger.

How did they deal with this new reality? As already shown, the Muslims kept up the social intercourse with Company officials without compromising their faith. What was their attitude towards the missionaries?

It is important to note that the missionaries themselves did not focus their attention on Muslims in the beginning. Scholars point out various reasons for this attitude. First of all, Christian preachers felt that the Hindus lived in depravity and deeply sinful conditions and they merited immediate attention. Indian Muslims, on the other hand, in the missionary outlook, did not exhibit debased behavior and so did not merit their immediate attention. Secondly, missionaries felt that converting Hindus would be comparatively easier than converting Muslims. Thirdly, missionaries considered Muslims as intruders into India and as not meriting special attention.[21] Evangelical preachers did not meddle in Muslim affairs initially; Muslims, too, were not suspicious of the missionary presence. One has to recognize that this situation was to change rapidly in a few decades.

It was within this context of indifference towards Muslims that **Henry Martyn** approached Muslims. Thus, he was appropriately called the first Christian Evangelical missionary to Muslims in India. He felt a call to go to India as a missionary. He quickly picked up Hindustani (Urdu) while at Cambridge. Initially, he wanted to work among Hindus. However, he turned his attention towards Muslims since he felt that God had assigned him to work with Muslims.[22] He wanted to be a full-time missionary among Muslims in India, but due to financial constraints he could not realize this dream of his. He eventually accepted to go to India as a chaplain to Company officials and families.

Once in India, however, as a Company chaplain he did not have the freedom that he wanted to preach to Muslims. He was aware of his limited knowledge of Islam. As a starting point, he read the Sale's translation of the Qur'ân. He also studied carefully Maracci's *Refutatio*. Afterwards, he read about Islam from whatever material he could lay his hands on. However, he learnt a great deal about Islam and Muslims from his Muslim staff, *munshi*s whom he employed to assist him in his vernacular Bible translation. One among them was Nathaniel Sabat. He was an Arab Christian who had been a Muslim with a lineage connecting with the Prophet Muhammad. The missionaries thought that the conversion of Sabat was a turning point. As a Christian from *ashraf* Muslim background, he would, they thought, be able to attract many Muslims to the Christian fold. However, Sabat turned out to be temperamental in character. He ended up as a disappointment for great missionary plans. Sabat changed his religion as if he were changing his coat. He had been Muslim twice ... and a Christian twice! While he was a Christian, he argued for Christianity, and then he argued against Christianity when he returned to the fold of Islam. His arguments against Christianity were incorporated into the first responses from Muslims against Christianity.

Martyn's translation of the Bible into Arabic, Urdu and Persian also helped to open up a new channel of communication with the Muslim debaters.[23] Martyn thought that once the educated Muslims read the New Testament, they would turn to the Christian faith. The polemical Persian tracts on Islam that Martyn wrote were the result of his discussions with the 'ulamâ in Shiraz, Persia. They were collected and translated into English and later missionaries used them for polemics.[24] This contributed negatively to a developing tradition of Protestant anti-Islamic polemics. The movement from indifference to disputation is palpable. Both the missionaries and the 'ulamâ took keen interest in attacking each other's religion. The contemporary context and the way they understood their religion contributed to this phenomenon.

It is worthwhile here to make a few comments on the work of the missionaries. The Protestant preachers were keen on converting the *ashraf* Muslims. They wanted to convert elite Muslims in the hope that it would create a momentum for further conversions. The Protestants followed a religion of the heart and wanted to appeal to the emotions of their listeners. In their mission they simply imposed their evangelical passion on Muslims in India. In the West, they preached to Christians who did not take their religion seriously. However, in India Protestants failed to consider that they would be preaching to a group of believers, the Muslims, who took their religion seriously. This was a serious lack of judgment on the part of the missionaries. Moreover, as it was mentioned, the missionaries preached a religion of the heart. The Sufi spirituality is also a religion of the heart. The missionaries seemed not to have considered this aspect of Islam (Sufism) in their missionary approach. These factors could be considered as serious lacunae in the missionary rationale towards Muslims in that era. We can only speculate that if the preachers had given some consideration to Sufism, probably the seeds of fruitful dialogue would have been sown, instead of debates and disputations. We had to wait for long for the arrival of Victor Courtois, Christian W. Troll and Paul Jackson for a new approach!

An Era of *Munazara* (polemics): A New Christian-Muslim Interface
There are very few references to exchanges between Muslims and missionaries in the first three decades of the 19th century. There were intensive debates between Shia and Sunni scholars but no such intense prolonged theological discussions between Christians and Muslims. One of the first tracts that appeared with an anti-Christian stance was *Taqwiatul-Iman*. It was composed by Shah Muhammad Isma'il (d. 1831), one of the leaders of the reform movement (*tariqa-i-Muhammadi*). Without any reference to contemporary Christians, he censured Christianity as one of the mistaken religions. His condemnation of Christianity was based on the Qur'ânic teachings. A priori assessment of Christianity as a falsified religion has been one of the characteristics of Islamic critique of Christianity.

'**Abd al-Masih** (d. 1826) was a Muslim convert who seemed to have taken part in some conversations with Muslims. Powell points out that though Abd al-Masih's journal refers to such contacts, there were no corroborations from contemporary Muslim writings. There were some Muslim converts to Christianity, though eventually these returned to the house of Islam. These converts created the early interface with Islam. Muslims who listened to Abd al-Masih's preaching responded in different ways: sometime their response was "witty and nonchalant" and other times "bitter and abusive". Abd al-Masih was able to make some impact in Lucknow. He was invited into Muslim homes and asked to explain his conversion. Nevertheless, Muslims practically ignored him in Delhi, his place of birth.[25]

The first *munazara* took place at the court of the Nawab in Lucknow. Both Muslims and Christians kept an account of these debates. It was something new, since the previous debates did not keep an account from both parties. The Nawabs at Lucknow provided a congenial atmosphere for *munazara*. Once again, the head of the shia *'ulamâ* encouraged and participated in these *munazara* encounters.

One of the important figures in munazara with *shia 'ulamâ* was **Joseph Wolff.** His approach was to find an immediate point of contact with the shia theologians of the city. The shia belief with regard to the immanent reappearance of the hidden imam caused them to attach significance to the teaching of Wolff with regard to the second coming of Jesus. Prophecy and fulfilment of prophecy were another topic of disputation between them.

In short, in the earlier stage, both the *'ulamâ* and the missionaries generally ignored each other: missionaries ignored Muslims as they fixed their gaze on Hindus in their design for a future Christian Indies; Muslims, on the other hand, ignored missionaries for they were small in number and did not interact with Muslims. Thus, the first Christian-Muslim contact was marked by mutual disinterest in one another. The second stage was striking for the display of ignorance of each other's beliefs and an insistence to view the other from one's own point of view.

Both Muslims and missionaries were talking **at** each other, not talking **to** each other. There was no real communication between them, but only misunderstanding. Common grounds were not explored, but only battle grounds were readied for the next stage of conflict.

Moreover, a number of British officials sympathetic to the missionary cause attended the *munazaras* where the missionaries and the *'ulamâ* disputed with one another according to court etiquette. These disputations would later erupt into a full-blown conflict when "the British presence became more positively intrusive, and when missionary activity was extended to the heartlands of India.[26]

The Agra Debates (1854 CE)

C. Shirrmacher affirms that the 1854 Agra-debate is a historical milestone. The German missionary **Carl Gottlieb Pfander** (d. 1865) was "the greatest of missionaries to the Mohammedans [sic]", sent by the Church Missionary Society.[27] He was a product of the pietistic movement in Württemberg (Swabia) and was trained in devotional Christian theology.[28] He did not have training in the critical approach to the Bible. This fact had an important consequence in his debates with Muslims. One notices the contrast with Henry Martyn, who, though being an evangelical and a preacher of religion of the heart, was, due to his training at Cambridge University, more academically-oriented than Pfander. Pfander was a preacher with much affectivity. Henry Martyn, as noted earlier, was temperamentally not suited to dealing with ordinary Muslims, whereas Pfander had a congenial attitude that was suitable to making many contacts.

Before coming to India, Pfander had worked in the Russian Caucasus and Persia. He realized that verbal discussion was not enough to convince Muslims. He prepared a general exposition of the evangelical Christian belief which was adapted to the Muslim mind. The spiritual needs of the individual soul and a firm denial of the role of human reason in the search for religious truth marked his writings. He composed *Mizan al-haqq* ('Balance of the Truth') in German.[29]

What is the central focus of his writing? True revelation must fulfill and satisfy the greatest need of people for eternal and never-ending well-being. It should be in accordance with the dictates of the human conscience that God has established. Pfander emphasized that people *need to know the truth* concerning God and concerning themselves. They *need forgiveness* for their sins. They *need to be pure and holy* if they expect eventually to rest in God. He stressed that if these needs are not attended to in a particular religion or its scripture, then that religion and scripture are not from God. It was his contention that these needs are met only in the Christian faith. However, he had to respond to one of the main accusations of Muslims against Christian scriptures – it was the issue of corruption of the Bible.[30]

Pfander categorically denied any corruption of the Bible. He emphatically tried to convince his Muslim readers that the divinity of Christ and the doctrine of the Trinity were mysteries of God's nature and so beyond the reach of human reason and that they should be believed as they are mentioned in the Bible.[31] He selectively quoted from the Qur'ân and demonstrated that the Qur'ân gave a high place to the Bible. Similarly, by quoting from the writings of the Muslim scholars he argued that they showed a certain amount of openness towards the Bible and Christianity.[32] H. Dorman observes that this type of approach tries to argue that the Qur'ân honors Christianity and venerates its beliefs.[33] It should be mentioned here that Dorman's opinion is very debatable.

When Pfander wrote for a Muslim readership, he claimed that Christianity alone could satisfy the inner needs of the soul and that here Islam fell short of Christianity. In other words, in Pfander's view Christianity dealt more with interior needs of the human heart. He did not accuse Islam either of being a false religion or a heresy.[34] The medieval polemics and Jesuit polemics against Islam considered that Islam was a false religion. While speaking about Muhammad, Pfander focused on what he claimed were the Prophet's deficiencies and contradictions and as a result of which, he argued, the Prophet would not be able to mediate for the sins of others. Pfander did not accuse him of being a false prophet. The Bible appealed to the heart, whereas, he argued, the Qur'ân occupied the mind with its cold speculation and left the heart unaffected. Islam did not preserve the whole divine truth, he claimed. It rejected Christ, he contended. Thus, Pfander wanted to establish his claim of the superiority of Christianity over Islam. However, Powell shows that when Pfander wrote for a European readership he reviled Islam with hard words. Hence, there is a contradiction in his scholarly opinion of both Islam and Muhammad.[35]

On his arrival in India (1839), Pfander got a misleading impression that Indian Muslims were on the verge of turning to Christianity.[36] With a sense of optimism he translated his book *Mizan al-haqq* ('Balance of the Truth') into Urdu. This book became the focus for a Muslim counter-attack on Christianity. Just as Henry Martyn thought that once the educated Muslims had the Bible in their hands they would turn to Christianity, Pfander possibly thought that once Muslims got to read *Mizan al-haqq*, they would come flocking into Christianity.

Having introduced Pfander, let his fellow debater from the Muslim side **Rahamatullah ibn Halîl al-'Utmânî al-Kairânawî** (d. 1891), be briefly introduced here. C. Shirrmacher calls al-Kairânawî a shia theologian. Rahamatullah ibn Halîl al-'Utmânî al-Kairânawî was not a shia theologian, but a Sunni 'alim, of the Hanafite-Maturidite school of jurisprudence and theology. He wrote a number of tracts to answer the questions that missionaries raised against Islam.[37] In his tracts, he argued that the doctrine of the Trinity was absurd, irrational, and impossible.[38]

Finally, the big day arrived. On the 10th and 11th of April 1854, several hundred Muslims and Europeans gathered in the school room of Agra's Church Missionary Society to listen to a series of public debates.[39] C. Shirrmacher explains the importance of the place where the debate took place:

> In the 19th century Agra, the former symbol of Mughal power, developed into one of the centers of Muslim learning and culture in India. The British government transformed it into their administration center for the North-West Provinces. In addition, the British government allowed

foreign mission agencies to enter the country. Especially in Agra, mostly British missionaries were stationed and they opened a huge orphanage after a disastrous famine in the year 1837. Several children were baptized as Christians, so that the growing influence of the Christian mission was universally recognized. In Agra itself several polemical Christian books against the Muslim creed had been published. All of these facts made the Muslim population extremely aware of the presence of Westerners and missionaries as an instrument of British colonialism.

The debate was slated to focus on the Trinity, the Qur'ân as the word of God and the Prophethood of Muhammad. However, the discussion focussed on the corruption of the Bible.[40] Kairânawî succeeded to set an agenda in the following order: *naskh* (abrogation), *taḥrîf* (corruption), *taslis* (Trinity), *risalat-i-Muhammad* (Prophethood of Muhammad), and finally the Qur'ân. Powell comments: Kairânawî's "persistence and astuteness in establishing a procedure which was favorable to his objectives was to prove vital to the outcome".[41]

Kairânawî attacked the textual integrity of the Christian Scriptures, using for the first time, in addition to evidence drawn from the Bible, arguments and evidence culled from liberal Biblical Criticism recently published in Europe and America.[42] While the evangelical debaters were determined to defend the Bible and their belief in its purity from the attacks of the Muslim debaters, Kairânawî stole the show by using this unexpected weapon: western Biblical criticism. His "impressive citation from European theological and historical literature was unprecedented among scholars anywhere in the Muslim world".[43] Though this question of corruption has been an old issue which Muslims consistently debated, the debate at Agra gave a new twist to this old tale in which the Muslim debaters used Western sources of Biblical criticism. By showing the Bible is corrupted Kairânawî wanted to demonstrate once for all the inferiority of Christianity in order to make his fellow believers strong and not be shaken by the onslaught of Christian mission activities. Pfander fumbled under such a formidable attack from his opponent. In this drama Kairânawî achieved a momentum that irreversibly damaged the strategy of Pfander.

Kairânawî composed a book 'Demonstration of the Truth' (*Izhâr al-Haqq*), as a response to Pfander's *Mîzân al-Haqq*.[44] It became so popular that the noted Egyptian theologian Rashîd Ridâ (1865-1935) made extensive use of it when dealing with Christianity. Similarly Muhammad Abû Zahra, in his famous 'Lectures on Christianity' (*muhâdarâtfî n-nasrânîya*) made use of al-Kairânawî's commentaries on the Christian creed.

Earlier, certain dogmas were refuted and Christianity was believed to contain some truth. In his far-reaching polemic, Christianity itself seemed undermined by Kairânawî. His effort was to show that Christianity is a flawed religion.

The preceding discussion presents a window into the Muslims' view of Christianity and Christians in the pre-1857 era. This was in the context of growing British power in the Indian sub-continent and the evangelical fervor of the missionaries who worked assiduously for gaining converts among Muslims to the Christian faith, which intensified the conflict between these two groups of believers. There was pressure from two fronts; political as well as religious. Muslims had dealt with religious controversies with Christians before. Both Christian and Muslim theologians in the 9th and 10th centuries had produced a number of polemical treatises. But Christian political domination, that, too, taking over from Muslim political power, was a new phenomenon. Political and religious pressures intensified the polemics.

The Muslim scholars studied here assessed Christianity as a corrupted religion, a mistaken religion, or even an irrational religion and finally a false religion. Their emphasis on Christianity as a corrupted religion was based on the Qur'ânic teachings about Christianity. This indictment has been repeated over the centuries. There is corruption at the heart of the Christian religion and this can be cleansed if Christians attune their hearts to the voice of the Qur'ân. The Qur'ânic teaching, to use the contemporary computer software language, has an antivirus program. It identifies the corruption. The antidote to corruption is the clear message of the Qur'ân. If Christians are receptive to the message of the Qur'ân, they will recognize the truth. Then one will find the oneness of the message between the books: the Torah, the Gospels, and the Qur'ân. The Qur'ân, no doubt, gives the final and uncorrupted version of the word of God.

Muslim interlocutors laid stress on the purity of the Qur'ân vis-à-vis the Bible. Though both these scriptures are from the Mother Book, only the Qur'ân remains clear of any trace of corruption. The Bible does not share in this privilege. This has been one of the most important talking-points for Christian-Muslim debates over the centuries. By critically establishing the corruption of the Bible, the Muslim scholars wanted to show the unreliability of the Biblical texts that are in the hands of Christians. Thus, they believed that they would be able to establish the superiority of Islam over Christianity. To attain this end Kairânawî used a new weapon, the treatises on Biblical criticism that appeared from the Western universities. Biblical criticism by Christian scholars encouraged those Muslim counterparts to affirm that the Muslim point of view of corruption of the Bible had been vindicated in these new researches done in the portals of many western universities.

The evangelicals simply stressed belief in the redemption offered in Christ for humanity, and of Christ the sinless, being the mediator between God and humanity. Consequently, they argued, Islam could not offer redemption since the Muslim Prophet Muhammad, who, they claimed, was not sinless, could not be a mediator. Evangelicals contrasted Jesus and his life with the Prophet Muhammad and his life.

As a quick observation it should be said that it was a pity that in their theological evaluation of the 'other', both the groups of scholars failed to understand as well as respect what the other party held to be true. It is also important to notice the Muslim approaches were provoked by the British politics as well as the work of evangelical missioners.

One notices that Muslims interpreted the variant readings in the Bible as the corruption of the Bible. Moreover, the Qur'ân, too, teaches them that the Bible is corrupt. It is a Muslim reading of the Bible from their point of view. Christians will reiterate these discrepancies, or put in other words, the variant readings found in the Bible do not obfuscate their theological vision. The different accounts, they say, are different expressions of different communities that experienced the power of the Crucified and Risen Christ.

Christians, for their part, insisted on the issue of redemption that made no sense to Muslims. Muslims consider that each person works out his/her own salvation by living in obedience to the will of God as revealed in the Qur'ân and also by following the model of Prophet Muhammad. Moreover, the notion of one man suffering for the sins of the others does not belong to the theological thinking of Islam.

The discussions between Muslims and Christians proceeded in two different directions without a common ground. They discussed issues and categories that did not make sense to the other party. In contrast to medieval polemical debates, the present debates did not produce any nuanced theological arguments. The only fruit of such heated polemical debate is that Christianity is not just a corrupted religion but an unreliable and false religion.

While the pre-1857 is marked with such hostility, what was in store for the post-1857 era? This is discussed in the following section.

The Post-1857 Era

The first war of Indian independence in 1857 led to a major political rearrangement in the governance of India. The East India Company was relieved of its responsibility to oversee the administration of India and that task was taken over by the British Crown. The British thought that Muslims were primarily responsible for the Uprising. Consequently, they were repressed by the British.[45] This period was particularly traumatizing for the Indian Muslims. An elaboration of 'what and how' of the events does not fall within the focus of the present study: however, how Muslims responded to the British and the missionaries is relevant.

W.C. Smith, in one of his seminal works, *Modern Islam in India: A Social Analysis*, correlating the changes that occurred in the Indian economy as well the aforementioned political rearrangements under the British governance, highlights three distinct Muslim responses to the British religio-cultural outlook: *the movement in favor of contemporary British culture, the movement in favor of the Muslim culture of the past, and the movement in favor of a new culture of the future.*[46]

A Movement in Favor of Contemporary British/Christian Culture

In the second quarter of the nineteenth century, a group of scholars began translating treatises on science and western learning into Urdu. Such a process reminds one of the translation bureaux in Baghdad, where both Christian and Muslim scholars translated Greek texts on Optics, Physics, Medicine, Geography, Astronomy, Mathematics and Philosophy into Arabic. It could be said that the liberal spirit of Baghdad in scholarship could be identified in India at this particular period of time. But this sort of liberalism came to an abrupt end with the Uprising.

After the 1857 Uprising, once again there was an effort along these lines mainly by Sir Sayyid Ahmed Khan (d. 1898), [hereafter Sir Sayyid]. Sir Sayyid affirmed that Islam is compatible with science, business methods and the humanitarianism of the West. He realized that Muslims had to engage with the British in order to affirm their place in India, which was effectively controlled by the British.[47] The movement stressed the similarity of the fundamentals of Christianity and Islam.[48]

A Movement in Favor of Islamic Culture of the Past

This movement was based on the understanding that Islam is not only compatible with but is the very source of Western liberalism, and that Christianity is a rival and inferior religion. The movement was "accompanied by [a] burst of enthusiasm for the glory of Islamic culture in the past and particularly the brilliant 'Abbāsī age, from which modern science and civilization were now derived".[49] Amir Ali is the best-known face of this movement.

How do these two movements differ from one another? It could be said that when *the movement in favour of British culture* argued that Islam was not inimical to progress, *the movement in favour of Islamic culture of the past* seem to present Islam as that very progress.[50]

W.C. Smith writes: "Sir Sayyid's objective was to prove to that audience [Western audience] that Islam is a respectable religion and should not be disdained [or] attacked. Amir Ali is more ambitious, more confident: he hopes to attract Western seekers to Islam. He goes further, [by stating] that Islam is already making headway in the West, in the form of Unitarianism and Theism, which are Islam without its discipline".[51]

This movement described by Amir Ali argued that Islam is not just compatible with modern ideas on subjects like war, intolerance, women, slavery, the scientific spirit, rationalism and democracy but that Islam's teaching and its spirit are precisely made of those ideas.[52]

A Movement in Favor of a New Culture

This movement claimed that there is dynamism at the heart of Islam. This dynamism of Islam supersedes liberalism, and points to a new future. Enthusiasm and creative enterprises are the marks of this movement. "This movement repudiates not only the West, as did the preceding one, but also Westernism itself, instead of claiming liberalism as its own, as Islamic, it supersedes liberalism with a new creative vision. Its pride is no longer in the 'Abbāsī culture of the Muslims, for that was too 'imperialistic'; rather it stresses the very early period of Islam, the *Khilāfat al Rāshidah*, and dubs all subsequent Islamic history an aberration".[53]

Islam gave dignity and serenity to humankind which faced adversity. It helped people to be charitable towards their fellow men and women. If it should function in a similar way in this modern world it has to be revived in its original and true spirit. Such refashioning was rendered by Sir Muhammad Iqbal, an outstanding poet and philosopher.[54] He decried the ascetic dualism of Christianity, especially its separation of the sacred and the secular.[55]

The Indian scene that began with the Mughal courts, unfolded through centuries, the discourses between Muslims and Christians were largely dominated by supremacist attitudes from both sides and did not create an ambience either for mutual enrichment or of mutual understanding. In the next chapters we will find the pioneers will unfold a new era of understanding and fruitful interaction.

Endnotes

[1] C. W. Troll, "Christian-Muslim Relations in India," *Islamochristiana* no. 5 [1979]: 119-145; C.W. Troll, "New Light on the Christian-Muslim Controversy of the Nineteenth and Twentieth Century," *Die Welt des Islam* 34, no. 1 [1994]: 85-88.

[2] Jesuits sent three missions to the courts of the Great Mughal emperors Akbar and Jahangir. The first mission consisted of Fr. Rudolf Acquaviva, Fr. Antony Monserrate and Brother Francis Henriques. Fr. Acquaviva and his companions reached Fatehpur Sikri in 1580. Fr. Edward Leitao, Fr. Christopher de Vega and Brother Stephen Ribero were members of the second mission, that reached Lahore in 1591. In the third mission, Fr. Jerome Xavier was accompanied by Fr. Manuel Pinheiro and Brother Bento de Goes. They arrived in Lahore in 1595. See E. Maclagan, *The Jesuits and the Great Mogul* [London: Burns Oates & Washbourne Ltd., 1932]; P. Du Jarric, *Akbar and the Jesuits* [London: George Routledge & Sons Ltd., 1926]. A. Camps, *Jerome Xavier, S.J. and the Muslims of the Mughal Empire: controversial and missionary activity* [Schoneck: Nouvelle revue de Science missionnaire Suisse, 1957]; M.A. Chaghatai, *Mirat ul-Quds: An Illustrated Manuscript of Akbar's Period about Christ's Life* [Lahore: Lahore Museum, 1994]; J.A. Correia, *Letters from the Mughal Court: the first Jesuit mission to Akbar, 1580-1583* [Anand: Gujarati Sahitya Prakash, 1980]; J. Flores, *The Mughal Padshah: A Jesuit Treatise on Emperor Jahangir's Court and Household* [Leiden/Boston: Brill, 2015].

[3] It must not be forgotten that when the Jesuits expounded Christian tenets a Portuguese artist who accompanied them to the Mughal court in 1597 CE was pressed into the service to produce scores of small oil paintings of Christ and making copies of the Madonna, including copies of the emperor's extensive collection of European Renaissance religious pictures and prints. The Jesuits often used the emperor's paintings to illustrate their arguments. "It is an episode from one of the most remarkable cultural exchanges in the history of East-West relations: the three Jesuit missions to the Great Mughal Emperors Akbar (1542-1605; reigned 1556-1605) and Jahangir (1569-1627; reigned 1605-27)", writes G. A. Bailey. See G. A. Bailey,

The Jesuits and the Grand Mogul: Renaissance art at the Imperial Court of India, 1580-1630, Occasional Papers 1998/ Vol. 2 [Washington DC: Freer Gallery of Art Arthur M. Sackler Gallery, Smithsonian Institution, 1998]. See also G. A. Bailey, "The Catholic Shrines of Agra," *Arts of Asia* 23, no. 4 (July-August 1993): 131-37; G. A. Bailey, "Counter Reformation Symbolism and Allegory in Mughal Painting" (Ph.D. diss., Harvard University, 1996); G. A. Bailey, "The Lahore Mirat al-Quds the Impact of Jesuit Theater on Mughal Painting," *South Asian Studies* 13, (1997): 95-108; G. A. Bailey, "The Indian Conquest of Catholic Art: The Mughals, the Jesuits, and Imperial Mural Painting," in *Art Journal* 57, no. 2 (spring 1998): 24-30.

[4] P. Jackson, "Jesuits at the Mughal Court," *Vidyajyoti: Journal of Theological Reflection* 44, no. 3 [1980]: 108-109.

[5] S.A.A. Rizvi, *Shah Wali Allah and his Times* [Canberra, 1980]. Muslim scholars of this era panicked and took refuge in the Qur'ân and *ḥadīth*. They emphasized the need to abide by the Qur'ân and Sunnah, return to origins, revival of *ijtihad*, and *ḥadīth* studies, rejection of innovation and imitation (*taqlid*) in matters of law, and rejection of Sufism. Shah Wali Allah too wanted reformation. As a religious genius he adopted a conciliatory approach..

[6] A.A. Powell, *Muslims & Missionaries in Pre-Mutiny India* [London: Curzon Press, 1993], 76. Also see P. Spear, *Twilight of the Mughals* [Cambridge, 1951, reprinted Delhi, 1969].

[7] A.A. Powell, *Muslims & Missionaries in Pre-Mutiny India*, 76-79.

[8] C. Shirrmacher, "Muslim Apologetics and the Agra Debates of 1854: A Nineteenth Century Turning Point," *The Bulletin of The Henry Martyn Institute of Islamic Studies* 13, nos. 1 and 2 [January-June 1994]: 74-84. The first Anglican Bishop was secretly consecrated on 8 May 1814 in Lambeth Palace, Calcutta. See H. H. Dodwell (ed.), *The Cambridge History of India*, [New Delhi, 1932], 6:124.

[9] H. Martyn, *Journal and Letters*, ed. S. Wilberforce [London: R.B. Seeley and W. Burnside, 1837]; A.C. Benson, *Men of Might: Studies of Great Characters* [London: Edward Arnold, 1921], 188-212; E. Foster, *Heroes of the Indian Empire; or, Stories of Valour and Victory* [London: Cassell & Co., 1886],169-184; J. Hall, *The Life of Rev. Henry Martyn* [Philadelphia: American Sunday-School Union, 1831]; H. Martyn, *Journal and Letters* ed. S. Wilberforce [London: R.B. Seeley and W. Burnside, 1837]; C. Padwick, E. *Henry Martyn: Confessor of the Faith* [New York: George H. Doran Co., 1923]; J.S. Rhea, *Life of Henry Martyn: Missionary to India and Persia, 1781-1812* [Chicago: Women's Presbyterian Board of Foreign Missions of the Northwest, 1888]; J. Sargent, *Memoir of the Revd Henry Martyn* [1st American ed. Boston: Published by Samuel T. Armstrong, and Crocker & Brewster, 1820]; G. Smith, *Henry Martyn* [London: The Religious Tract Society, 1892]; V. Stacey, *Life of Henry Martyn* [Hyderabad: Henry Martyn Institute of Islamic Studies, 1980].

[10] A.A. Powell, *Muslims & Missionaries in Pre-Mutiny India*, 89-90.

[11] The term 'intellectualism' generally designates a philosophical or theological system in which intellect or conceptualization is accorded primacy, as opposed to will or affectivity.

[12] A theory that exaggerates reason's independence from the senses in philosophy or from supernatural revelation in religion is rationalism.

[13] A.A. Powell, *Muslims & Missionaries in Pre-Mutiny India*, 78.

[14] *The Oxford Companion to Christian Thought* [Oxford: Oxford University Press, 2000], s.v. "evangelicalism".

[15] *Encyclopedia of mission and missionaries* [New York and London: Routledge, 2007], s.v. "evangelicalism".

[16] I. Bradley, *The Call to Seriousness* [London, 1976], 19. Henry Martyn is one of the good examples. He grew up listening to the preaching of evangelicals like Cornwall and others. He learnt to appeal to the feelings of listeners. However, his Cambridge education put him on a solid platform of logical thinking. He preached human sinfulness with such a force, a fellow traveler commented, that he never ceased to send his listeners to hell every Sunday. Martyn, while getting translated the Bible to Urdu and Persian, could not resist his temptation to argue in favor of the authenticity of the Bible.

[17] *Fatawa* (sing. *fatwa*): a ruling by a *mufti* a Muslim juris consultant who is qualified to interpret the Islamic law.

[18] This is in reference to a *fatwa* issued by Abd al-Aziz. Though this *fatwa* noted northern India as a land of war, it did not advocate *jihad* (a struggle waged by Muslims to achieve the upholding of Islam) or *hijrat* (migration to a Muslim land). See S.A.A. Rizvi, *Shah' Abd' Aziz: Puritarianism, Sectarian Polemics and Jihad* [Canberra, 1982], 577-579.

[19] A.A. Powell, *Muslims & Missionaries in Pre-Mutiny India*, 72

[20] Shah Wali Allah argued for a strong Muslim State that lived according to *shari'a*. Later, Maulana Abul ala Maudūdī, in his concern for the future of Islam, called for an Islamic state. See R. Jackson, *Fifty Key Figures in Islam* [London & New York: Routledge, 2006], 154-159 and 190-196.

[21] D. Kopf, *British Orientalism and the Bengal Renaissance: The Dynamics of Indian Modernization, 1773-1835* [Calcutta, 1969], 103.

[22] S. Wilberforce, ed., *Journals and Letters of Henry Martyn*, 471.

[23] C. Bennett, "The Legacy of Henry Martyn," *International Bulletin of Missionary Research* 16, no.1 [1992]: 10-15.

[24] Martyn debated with Mohammad Reza in Shiraz. These debates were collected, edited and published by Samuel Lee (d. 1852) under the name *Controversial Tracts*.

[25] A.A. Powell, *Muslims & Missionaries in Pre-Mutiny India*, 110-116.

[26] Ibid., 75.

[27] E. Headland, *Revd. Karl Gottlieb Pfander, D.D.: Sketches of CMS Workers* [London: CMS, 1897]; S. M. Zwemer, "Karl Gottlieb Pfander," *Moslem World* 31 [July 1941]: 217-26; See Church Missionary Society, ed. *One Hundred Years: Being the Short History of the Church Missionary Society* [London, 1898], 78.

[28] C. Shirrmacher, "Muslim Apologetics and the Agra Debates of 1854: A Nineteenth Century Turning Point," *The Bulletin of the Henry Martyn Institute of Islamic Studies* 13 [January-June 1994]: 76.

[29] C. Shirrmacher writes: "His controversial book 'Balance of Truth' (*mîzân al-haqq*) is still a current topic of debate in the Muslim world today. This apologetical work, written in 1829, originally in German (The original handwritten text is still to be found in the archives of the Basle Mission Society headquarter (Basle Mission), Switzerland) in refutation of Islam, intends to convince its readers of the supreme values of Christianity, mostly by defending the integrity of the Old and New Testament and refuting the Muslim charge of the deviation of the Christian scriptures (*taḥrîf*). After its first publication in 1831 in Armenian it was quickly translated into at least half a dozen Muslim languages, including e. g. Urdu (1840), Persian (1835), Turkish (1862) and Arabic (1865) and has had an enormous influence. This book 'Balance of Truth' (*mîzân al-haqq*) still is both quoted by and refuted by Muslim apologists today. ...'Balance of Truth' (*mîzân al-haqq*), the "standard work of encounter between Christianity and Islam", was used by generations of Christian missionaries as an apologetical tool to refute Islam, and for this reason was reprinted many times up until the present. Despite the fact that we also hear severe critiques concerning the work, especially in the 20th century, we can date the last Arabic and English reprints back to the year 1986". See C. Shirrmacher *The influence of German Biblical criticism on Muslim apologetics in the 19th century*, http://www.contra-mundum.org/schirrmacher/rationalism.html [accessed 10 March 2012].

[30] See C. Bennett, *Understanding Christian-Muslim Relations* [London: Continuum, 2008] chapters 1 and 2 for a good summary of such polemics.

[31] Christians and Muslims understand revelation in two different ways. The revelation of the Qur'ân as the Word of God is understood by Muslims as "the final, unique and fully authentic manifestation of the Word of God, addressed to humankind through the ministry of Muhammad." (See M. Borrmans, *Guidelines for Dialogue between Christians and Muslims* [New York: Paulist Press, 1990], 104-105; also see Y. Michot, "Revelation," in *Classical Islamic Theology*, ed. T. Winter [Cambridge: Cambridge University Press, 2009], 180-196). For Christians the story of revelation comes to its fulfilment in Jesus of Nazareth, who is the Word made flesh (John 1:14), and public revelation ends with the death of the last Apostle. See K. Rahner, "Revelation," in *Sacramentum Mundi: An Encyclopedia of Theology*, ed. K. Rahner, C. Ernest, K. Smyth, vol. 5 [London: Burn & Oates], 358.

[32] C. Shirrmacher, "Muslim Apologetics and the Agra Debates of 1854: A Nineteenth Century Turning Point," *The Bulletin of the Henry Martyn Institute of Islamic Studies*, 77.

[33] H.G. Dorman, *Toward Understanding Islam* [Edinburgh, 1948], 31.

[34] One of the early Christian theologians, John of Damascus (d. 753), dismissed Islam as a heresy. He believed that the Qur'ân was an ignorant imitation of the Bible. See G. Hawting, *The First Dynasty of Islam* [London & New York: Routledge, 2000], 61-65; H. Goddard, *Islam: Towards A Christian Assessment* [Oxford: Latimer House, 1992], 13; J.W. Voorhis, "John of Damascus on the Moslem Heresy," *The Moslem World* 24 [1934]: 391-398; D.H. Sahas, *John of Damascus on Islam, the "Heresy of the Ishmaelites"* [Leiden: Brill, 1972], 132-133).

[35] A.A. Powell, *Muslims & Missionaries in Pre-Mutiny India*, 145-46.

[36] Ibid., 132.

[37] Kairânawî wrote three polemical works defending Islam. They are as follows: *Azalat al-auham, Azalat al-shukuk, and Asahh al-ahadis fi ibtal al-taslis.*

[38] A number of medieval Muslim theologians wrote with some originality their objections against the doctrine of the Trinity. See D. Thomas, *Anti-Christian polemic in early Islam: Abū 'Isā al-Warrāq's "Against the Trinity"* [Cambridge: Cambridge University Press, 1992]; D. Thomas, "Two Muslim-Christian debates from the early Shi'ite traditions," *Journal of Semitic Studies* 33 [1988]: 53-80. D. Thomas, *Christian Doctrines in Islamic Theology* [Leiden: Brill, 2008]; S. Rissanen, *Theological Encounter of Oriental Christians with Islam during the Abbasid Rule* [Åbo: Åbo Adademis Förlag-ÅboAdademi University Press, 1993].

[39] C. Shirrmacher, *The influence of German Biblical criticism on Muslim apologetics in the 19th century*, http://www.contra-mundum.org/schirrmacher/rationalism.html [accessed 10 March 2009].

[40] Ibid.

[41] A.A. Powell, *Muslims & Missionaries in Pre-Mutiny India*, 246

[42] Ibid.

[43] Ibid., 231. He consulted the following editions of Christian commentaries. T.H. Horne, *Introduction to the Critical Study and Knowledge of the Holy Scriptures*, 3rd ed., 4 vols. [London, 1822]; *A Commentary upon the Holy Bible extracted from Henry and Scott*, 6 vols. [London, 1834]; N. Lardner, *Works*, 10 vols. [London, 1827]; G.D'Oyly and R. Mant, *Notes, Explanatory and Practical, to the Holy Bible* [London, 1848]; S. Horsley, *Biblical Criticism on the first fourteen Historical Books of the Old Testament*, 4 vols. [London and Edinburgh, 1820]; R. Watson, *A Collection of Theological Tracts*, 6 vols. [Cambridge, 1785].

[44] It was written in Arabic in 1867 by request of the Ottoman sultan Abdül Aziz I. (1861-1876). The book has seen several translations into Turkish (1876/1877),

French (1880), English (ca. 1900), Urdu (1968). Like 'Balance of Truth', the book 'Demonstration of the Truth' (*izhâr al-haqq*) has been reprinted up until the present. In 1964 a new edition came out, supervised by the 'Department for Islamic Affairs of the Kingdom of Morocco', and a foreword was added by the adab-professor 'Umar ad-Dasûqî. The last Arabic editions date from the year 1978; one of the two was authorized by the late Shaikh 'Abd al-Halîm Mahmûd of al-Azhar-University, Cairo. In 1989 a short version in English came into being, published by Ta-Ha Publishers in London.

[45] P. Hardy, *The Muslims of British India* [Cambridge: Cambridge University Press, 1972], 63-91.

[46] W.C. Smith, *Modern Islam in India: A Social Analysis* [London: V. Gollancz, 1946].

[47] Sir Sayyid felt that the British Raj was too powerful to be resisted, and too useful to be ignored; the Muslim who wanted to 'get ahead' should align himself with the British. See W.C. Smith, *Modern Islam in India* [Lahore: Anarkali, 1943], 5.

[48] It is not clear what it means to have similarities in fundamentals between Christianity and Islam. Both Muslims and Christians worship one God. From the Catholic Christian side, the Vatican Council II has affirmed this truth in a number of her documents (for example): *Nostra Aetate* ["They worship God, who is one, living and subsistent, merciful and almighty, the creator of heaven and earth, who has also spoken to men".] and *Lumen Gentium* ["But the plan of God also includes those who acknowledge the Creator, in the first place among whom are the Muslims: these profess to hold the faith of Abraham, and together with us they adore the one, merciful God, mankind's judge on the last day"]. Muslims question the Trinitarian expression of one God. A recent document on Christian-Muslim Relations; *A Common Word between Us and You*, without explicitly questioning, but implicitly indicating the problem extended the hand of friendship towards Christians and called them for working with them (Muslims) for world peace.

[49] W.C. Smith, *Modern Islam in India*, 3.

[50] Ibid.,49.

[51] Ibid.

[52] Ibid.,50.

[53] Ibid.,3.

[54] Ibid.,109.

[55] M. Iqbal, *The Reconstruction of Religious Thought in Islam* [New Delhi: Kitab Bhavan, 1981], 9-10.

Chapter 3

Victor Courtois:
A New Christian Attitude
Towards Muslims in India

The study of Islam should lead to greater love and better appreciation of Muslims. Insistence should always be made not on what separates Christians and Muslims, but on what may bring them together closer to one another and to the heart of Christ. We study them not as enemies but as brothers [and sisters]. To study, we shall add much prayer.[1]

Introduction

Victor Courtois's approach to Muslims was born of his familiarity with the Qur'ân and his love for his Muslim friends and neighbours. In other words, a deep love for Muslims and deep respect for their sacred scripture the Holy Qur'ân, marked his approach to Muslims. Courtois's story will show the type of theology he exemplified and highlight his significant contribution to Christian-Muslim relations. We will find his vision for Christian-Muslim relations expressed in three relational actions that are underlined by three relational principles.[2]

This chapter has two sections. The first section will present a brief biography of Courtois and his theological vision for Christian-Muslim relations. This section will give particular attention to the intellectual, cultural and theological background of Courtois. The second section narrates the *relational principles* that were operative in the life and mission of Courtois that crystallized in three **relational actions** in which his theological vision was enfleshed. It will be shown that three *relational principles* underpin these *relational actions* that give coherence and authenticity to his Christian vocation among Muslims. It will be argued that his theological vision is at the heart of his relations with Muslims. The theological vision inspired him and gave clarity and authenticity to his work among Muslims. Any serious endeavour in Christian-Muslim relations needs a strong foundation in theology and an ambience of respectful relationship.

The Theological Vision of Courtois

Courtois envisions Christians and Muslims as brothers and sisters belonging to the one large family where God is father of both groups of believers. Courtois emphasises his vision many times in *Notes on Islam*, a review that he published till he died. This is a theological vision that grows out of Courtois's own new paradigm which *interrelates* both text and context, in a living theology.

Courtois emphasised that Christians and Muslims are brothers and sisters to each other. He wrote elsewhere: "It would be grand if the Muslims could realise that they have in the Christians of today not merely the descendants of the Crusaders with whom their knights crossed swords, but brothers, real brothers, big brothers who are eager to tell them the way to the only true renovation, to guide them on to the One who is the source of life ... it is the aim of *Notes on Islam* indirectly to hasten the day when Muslims and Christians will make one big family under the benevolent leadership of Jesus, the Son of Mary." [3] We find several references that express the foundation for his theological vision for his mission among Muslims.[4]

He affirmed that the purpose of his journal *Notes on Islam* is to help Christians to recognize the rich quality of religious life of Muslims. He wrote: "*Notes on Islam* would like to discover a little the unknown riches of those hearts so that in them we may recognize the features of our Heavenly Father and love them as Brothers [and sisters]. Were they better known, they would surely [be] better loved, and where there is love, there is God."[5]

This stunningly vibrant and fresh vision charts a new course in Christian-Muslim relations in India.[6] In this vision one can trace the summary of his approach. An analysis of his vision points towards a universal family where Christians and Muslims live together as brothers and sisters. In stark contrast to the polemics that characterized the strained relationship between Christians and Muslims, this vision ushers in a new era, in which Christians and Muslims belong to a single family.[7]

The following three *relational principles* underpin Courtois's life and work. These principles are as follows: one, mutual understanding and appreciation; two, look for what unites and not what divides; and three, work not just for coexistence but for a binding family love.

With these *relational principles*, Courtois puts his vision into action through the following self-evident *relational actions*: He first 'demonstrates deep and sympathetic knowledge of Islam: revelation in Islam, Muhammad, the Qur'ân and Islamic renaissance';[8] secondly, he 'defends Muslim faith in the face of unsavory comments from his fellow Christian missionaries'; and thirdly, he 'presents Christianity to Muslims in a beautiful way,[9] This vision will be discussed in depth later. However, brief comments on his vision are in order here.

Courtois's theological vision urges Christians and Muslims to recognize and explore the unknown riches of the Muslims' faith-life and then to recognize in their lives the features of our Heavenly Father and love them as brothers and sisters.[10]

This vision implies a spiritual relationship between both sets of believers. One can sense here a widening and deepening of Louis Massignon's vision that emphasized the Abrahamic connection between Christians and Muslims.[11] This vision reverses any negative approaches and appealed for a positive approach.

Courtois's theological vision was influenced by his exposure to Muslims both in West Asia and in India. It could be said that his mature theological vision of Islam is the fruit of the interaction between his inner conviction and the outer influences. He wanted Christian witness among Muslims in the present to be unencumbered by the baggage of negative attitudes of the past in meeting Muslims. In other words he did not want the conflicts of the past to overshadow their present relations.

The implication of the vision is that as members of one family Christians and Muslims are encouraged to be in constant *conversation* with one another. Polemical debate should end, and *family conversation* should begin. Each should witness to one's faith conviction in an atmosphere of mutual love.[12] In one stroke this vision does away with polemics which had been the mode of interaction between Christians and Muslims as shown in the first chapter.

The newness is that the interaction between Christians is conversation within the family of God where both continue to give *witness* to one another's faith. Witnessing to one's faith is at the heart of Christian-Muslim relations. How does a Christian do this? Courtois teaches that a Christian should help his Muslim brother or sister to come to love Jesus, as the Gospel presents.

'Maulvi Saheb' Courtois: A Biographical Note:[13]

Courtois was born in Louvain on the 18 September 1907.[14] His father was an artillery officer and his mother a home maker. Courtois's mother was a devout person and she was the one who shaped the life of her son on the foundations of the Catholic faith. Courtois did his schooling at the Jesuit high school of St Servais, Liege. Courtois was a good sportsman, especially a good swimmer. He enjoyed skating, too. He had learnt at home to be practical and self-reliant. He was a cook, a photographer, a motor-mechanic, a book-binder and a good nurse.[15]

He joined the Society of Jesus at Tronchiennes in Belgium on 23 September 1926. From his school days Courtois had taken a keen interest in the Jesuit missions in the Congo,[16] and after joining the

Jesuits he volunteered to be sent there.[17] He was fascinated by St. Paul the missionary, and imagined himself as a missionary also.[18] Something unexpected happened at this juncture that changed the course of his life. In the Jesuit community where he lived, he noticed that one of his companions was in great difficulties: Jesuit superiors wanted him to go to India, but his parents refused to give their consent; they would, however, allow him to go to the Congo; for parents in Belgium this difference was significant. Courtois went to the Rector and offered to go to India instead of his friend. His offer was approved by the higher authorities. Courtois started learning English and prepared himself to go to India.

In the summer before he left for India, he was assigned to participate in a history seminar. While preparing for the seminar, Courtois chanced upon the books on the Mughal period and found them fascinating. It was an important landmark in his life. This chance encounter with the history of the Mughals in India must have awakened in him his personal vocation to work with Muslims in India.[19]

Preparing Himself Intellectually

Science and Positivism

A short helpful note on the philosophical and theological trends that shaped Courtois's thinking and his preparation for his work among Muslims is necessary here to appreciate his overall concern for Islam and love for Muslims.

Since Newton's *Philosophiæ Naturalis Principia Mathematica* (1687), science and its methodology impacted the life and thinking of the European peoples. A great emphasis was laid on science as the only valid knowledge and on facts as objects of knowledge. Scientists and philosophers who drew inspiration from science and its methodology, searched for principles that were common to all the sciences, and used those principles for human conduct and as basis for social organizations. Works of the English empiricists like

Francis Bacon and the cultural climate of the Industrial Revolution underpin 'positivism'. Positivism extended scientific methods into the realm of philosophy. This philosophical movement exercised a great influence on the intellectual climate of the second half of the nineteenth century and the first decades of the twentieth century. The proponents of this trend emphasized that science has demolished the theological and metaphysical foundations of medieval society. They stressed that with the ascendance of science, humanity had entered into a new era in which positive philosophy would underlie the new society.

In this new society, according to the philosophers who pushed this trend, scientists and industrialists would hold spiritual and temporal power respectively.[20] Negation of God was one of the main characteristics of this trend. This positivist humanist philosophy, while on the one hand it denied a place to God in the human conscience, on the other hand it gave absolute value to human life and drifted to atheistic humanism. This atheistic humanism impacted social, political and individual philosophies of life.[21] At the same time, there was also an increased awareness and emphasis on "a practical concern for human life in its concrete details."[22]

Personalism and Existentialism

While the methods of science influenced the thinking of people, Personalism placed great stress on personality as of supreme value and a key constituent giving meaning to all of reality. The personalist philosophers stressed the value of man/woman as persons and moral selves with freedom, and endowed with dignity, and responsibility. Humanists recognized the dignity of the human person and took human nature, its limits or its interests, as its theme.

The Existentialists asked: how does one exist as a true human being? The existence in question here is not that of abstract man, or of man in general. Human existence, human living, as the existentialist views it, is always achieved by a man in the 'here and now', in a concrete situation with a host of particular and accidental circumstances surrounding it. The concern of the existentialist is not with the general and the universal, but with the singular and the individual. As S. Toulmin noted, concrete details received a great emphasis.

Existentialists explored human subjectivity in the concrete situations and crises of everyday. It was an invitation to authenticity. Authenticity lies not in abstract analysis and reflection but in concrete details. In this exploration, atheistic existentialists like Nietzsche and Camus rejected God and placed great emphasis on human autonomy. Another group of Existentialists like Heidegger and Jaspers were neither atheistic nor theistic. A third group demonstrated their theistic credentials as they worked with Existentialism.

Søren Kierkegaard (d. 1855) the leading light of the third group expressed some extraordinary insights into a loving care for the plural world.[23] First, he was convinced that it is of no use appealing to the authority of the Church to deal with the present world. Christianity "needs to recognize reality"[24] and face the modern world to make herself meaningful. The starting point is not what the Church thinks but where the others stand. If the modern world celebrates the freedom of the individual subject, Christians should begin to make sense for themselves and for others. Kierkegaard suggests that Christians should start with human freedom that is valued in modernity, and then should move on to arrive at a deeper understanding of freedom, "to the point at which it [the modern world] learns its needs of God."[25] For him every authentic existence is a Christian existence. He called the Church for a reality-check. One could say that 'here and now' is the key word for Kierkegaard. The 'other' is the essential point of reference for any meaningful faith reflection.

Gabriel Marcel (d. 1973) used these insights for his reflections. He emphasized that one should do philosophy as a participant and not as an observer. He brought the notion of participation in *doing* philosophical reflection.[26] One can recognize how different his philosophical idea is from that of Descartes who emphasized thinking in abstraction. Marcel highlighted the relational aspect of life. For him, the other is not a problem to be solved but a mystery to participate in. Moreover, for him the human vocation is revealed in human communion. He believed that only in love, hope and fidelity is the other experienced. For him the 'I-Thou' relation is a pivotal form of participation.[27] He underscored that any authentic relation is based on love, hope and fidelity.

Courtois appears to draw a number of insights from personalist and existentialist philosophers. He seemed to put these insights into practice when he articulated his theological vision. One could see that in the way Courtois dealt with Muslims. He did not meet Islam with the prejudices of his times but met Muslims as brothers and sisters. Moreover, he met them not as adversaries but as friends. Meeting them as brothers and sisters was the starting point for a meaningful interaction. He was not a mere observer, but a participant in their lives. His authentic relationship with them was based on love, hope and fidelity.[28] One could recognize that relationality was the key to Courtois's work among Muslims. Thus his theological vision had sound philosophical foundations. One should not overlook here the striking closeness his ideas have with some points of *Nostra Aetate*, a document which was issued during the Vatican Council II.

The philosophical principle that governed Courtois's conviction seems something like this: Muslims and Christians should experience a fulfilled life as members of God's one family. In this context giving witness to one's faith is essential.

Courtois in India

In January 1931, Courtois arrived in India. He was sent to Sacred Heart College, Shembaganur (South India), for his studies in Philosophy.[29] After a period of three years of studies in Philosophy, he taught at St Xavier's School, Calcutta for a year. In 1935 he left for West Asia to learn Arabic to prepare himself for a fulltime work in Christian-Muslim relations. He studied classical Arabic (that is Qur'ânic Arabic) at Beirut, Damascus and Cairo and gained a good working knowledge of that language. On his return in 1936 he did another year of teaching at St Xavier's and in 1937 he went to St Mary's College, Kurseong (Darjeeling), to study theology as an immediate preparation for his ordination to priesthood.

While studying theology, at Kurseong, Courtois deepened his knowledge of Islamic thought and started writing on Islamic subjects for the Indian Academy.[30] In 1938 he wrote an excellent report on the Muslim World for Fr. Ledochowsky, the Superior General of the Society of Jesus. This report was very much appreciated at the Jesuit headquarters (Rome) for its clarity and preciseness.[31] He was ordained a priest in 1939 and made his final commitment in the Society of Jesus on 15 August 1942 at Hazaribagh.[32] Courtois spent one year in Kidderpore (Calcutta) and Lucknow for Urdu studies. Thus, Courtois acquired command over both Arabic and Urdu. Fully equipped with the linguistic capability to deal with Muslims he dedicated himself to work among Muslims. Courtois was "energized by an inner passion both to know and to understand [Muslims] and was guided by an extraordinary self-discipline and sensitivity to the spiritual dimension of things."[33]

On 11 July 1944 Courtois and Celeste Van Exem[34] joined the Islamic Section of the newly-founded Oriental Institute in Calcutta.[35] In 1950, another Jesuit, Albertus Magarmaans too joined them.[36] From 1944 till 1960, first in collaboration with Van Exem and Magarmaans and later alone, Courtois devoted most of his time and energy to this work.[37] He methodically gathered a considerable library and a large amount of information about the Muslims in India,[38] besides lecturing in a number of Christian centers on Islam and Christian-Muslim relations. He was a frequent and much appreciated visitor in Kurseong, Ranchi, Poona, Allahabad, Barisal and other centers where students were trained to become priests. His courses were invaluable: clear, practical, learned and well-informed, and pleasant.[39] Besides his lectures, he edited his **Notes on Islam** for 14 years.[40]

He had many Muslim friends, both poor and rich. In the most influential and cultured circles Courtois was loved and esteemed. He was an active member of the Iran Society and he did much for this association, even becoming its Secretary and Vice- President. The Iran Government recognized his work and presented him with a Silver Medal, in 1959 in appreciation of his services in promoting Indo-Iranian cultural relations. He also obtained the collaboration of the best Muslim scholars to publish two important and learned works for the Iran Society.[41]

Poor Muslims enjoyed his special love and care. He made himself so wonderfully one of them, that his friends teasingly but lovingly called him '*Maulvi Saheb*' or '*Father Maulvi*'. His reddish beard, his knowledge of Muslim manners and etiquette, and much more, his constant devotion to all Muslims in a spirit of delicate Christian zeal and charity fully justified this familiar nickname.[42] Some Muslim converts to the Christian faith were the object of his fatherly care and priestly zeal; he followed them with affection and devotion long after he had baptized them; they formed a little family very close to his heart.[43] He helped many poor Muslims to obtain work; and placed many of them in Government service.[44] His charity was constructive and wise.[45] He was always surrounded by poor people, whom he helped in various ways. He loved them unsparingly.[46] They felt at home with him; his room was theirs, his time ungrudgingly theirs.[47] Unexpectedly, Courtois died on 21 December 1960.[48] He was a devoted priest and a wonderful spiritual guide whose retreats and sermons were both solid and practical.[49] Many nuns and priests owe him much, and so do countless lay people.[50] As a confessor he was paternal, encouraging, pacifying, a precious and devoted adviser.[51]

Courtois's Christian *Vocation* among Muslims

Courtois realized his call to be a Christian witness among Muslims. He was not a pure academic concerned only about the Islamic texts. As much as he worked with the texts in the library during morning hours he spent the afternoons among his Muslim friends. As mentioned, he was not just an observer, but a participant in their life. He, like Gabriel Marcel, believed that only in relationships founded on love, hope and fidelity can the other be experienced, celebrated and treasured. As a brother of Muslims, he wanted to give witness to his faith among them.

The polemicists and debaters, as shown in the introductory chapters, were also passionate about giving witness to their faith. However, in their misguided enthusiasm they attacked Islam and its prophet and thus invited the wrath and disgust of Muslims rather than their admiration and love. They did not display humility and charity which is a must for interacting with a person of another religious tradition. They were not concerned about what Muslims believe. Their focus was to prove the Muslim faith untenable.

In contrast to their attitude, Courtois enters into their life as a brother. He writes: "Those whose calling it is to be 'Other Christs' cannot see such a vast multitude without taking pity on them, for they are like sheep that have no shepherd. They are waiting for their hearts to be healed by the virtue which issues forth from the Christ – those hearts capable of so much generosity, afire with so much zeal for the name of the only God, treasuring unawares immense reserves of love."[52] His words may seem to reflect a patronizing or condescending attitude towards Muslims and one may hesitate to use such language today, but one cannot deny that Courtois was affectionate and warm towards Muslims. He wanted to be a Christian among Muslims.

Courtois's approach could be said to be modeled after the work of Raymond Llull (d. 1315) to a certain extent.[53]

Courtois writes:

Llull knew well that men's hearts and minds are not conquered by sword; love and mutual understanding are far more powerful weapons: they subdue without hurting. Ramon, therefore, studied Islam trying always to **discover not what divides, but what unites** [*emphasis the present writer's*]. It is this spirit which must be revived today, a spirit of intellectual fairness and charity. Prejudices, indeed, against one another are still many both among Christians and Muslims; untrue or grossly distorted statements disparaging the other's religious belief or practice are still found in books of recent dates or heard in conversations in Christendom as well in the world of Islam.[54]

It appears that he has also drawn inspiration from other Christians who have made new approaches towards Muslims in the Near East, though he does not mention any of these. One can mention here Cardinal Lavigerie (d. 1892), Charles Foucauld (d. 1916) and Louis Massignon (d. 1962).

Lavigerie for instance insisted so much on this theme [becoming one among Muslims] that he forbade his missionaries to preach Christianity to Muslims as long as they were not so completely integrated into the Muslim society and its culture as to be totally accepted by the group as men of God and Brothers.[55] Courtois painstakingly studied the liturgical language of Muslims, acquired the ability to read and understand the Qur'ân, the holy book of Muslims, and learnt the etiquettes of Muslims. As mentioned in the previous section he participated in the daily struggle of poor Muslims and fully involved himself in the intellectual life of the highly educated Muslims. Lavigerie instructed his fellow workers that they should give priority to live a life of disinterested love among Muslims thus giving witness to the love of Christ.[56] It will be of no exaggeration to say that what Lavigerie intended for his men in the previous century, Courtois put in practice.

Charles de Foucauld lived the mystery of Jesus's life at Nazareth by living a life of poverty among Muslims.[57] His goals were to live a life of poverty, to be a silent presence among Muslims, express love in daily occupations, and to adopt the way of life of Muslims as Christ adopted human nature, and to esteem and foster their friendship.[58] The labor of love that Courtois spent in the library and the hours of walking around Muslim colonies meeting Muslims could be compared to the hidden life Foucauld lived among the Bedouins. The reviews and articles Courtois wrote for *Notes on Islam*, amidst his work in the school, library, and in the centers for formation of Christian priests could very well be considered 'hidden life'. In such a work, it should be said that he shared in the mystery of Jesus's life at Nazareth.

Massignon (d. 1962) was a scholar of Arabic and Islamic mysticism.[59] He wanted to become one with Muslims by becoming their brother and loving them. He lived a life of an agnostic before converting to the Catholic faith. He regained his Christian hope when he was cared for and cured by a Muslim family in Baghdad when he fell ill. He later became the professor of Arabic and Sufi thought at the College de France. Massignon experienced harmony in the face of differences that exist in the world. He recognized that this harmony is brought about by secret keys or links that connected persons and events. The symphony of beauty where voices blend together could give a glimpse of the differences in oneness and oneness in differences. Similarly he observed that religious figures and Prophets from different religions complement and complete one another to produce harmony in the world.

Massignon affirmed the Abrahamic connection of Islam. R. Caspar explains this in the following words:

> Islam, according to Massignon, is the heir of Hagar and Ishmael, the 'excluded', driven into the desert but enjoying a special blessing (Gen. 16: 11-20; 21: 17-20; 25: 12-18). Muhammad receives this blessing of Ishmael at the providential and symbolic hour: exiled from his homeland, Mecca, like Abraham from Ur and Ishmael driven into desert, he claims the inheritance of Abraham against Israel (the Jewish people) unfaithful to their Covenant, and against the Christians unfaithful to Jesus.[60]

Massignon recognized that God can make use of Islam to draw men and women to himself in marvelous ways. Fitzgerald writes: "Islam's role is thus, as it were, to goad Jews and Christians to return to the correct understanding of their own religions."[61] Massignon affirmed that this was not due to 'Christian influence' but due to the presence of the Spirit of Christ that people are brought closer to God in and through Islam. In his opinion Islam should be judged by the fruits of the Spirit that are found within Islam and not by the defect-filled lives of some Muslims.

He guided many to enter into Muslim homes and Muslim lives and to learn from them the values of Islam. In other words a Christian should enter into the lives of Muslims in order to understand Muslims. He was convinced that when Christians experience hospitality, they in turn will be able to provide hospitality for Muslims. In short, relationship is at the heart of positive Christian-Muslim relations. In mutual relationship and hospitality, a Christian will 'become all things to all men' (1 Cor 9, 19-22). Massignon carries these reflections to a further level. While contemplating the mystery of Christ offering himself on the Cross for humanity ... he experienced himself among an 'invisible community' that offers their life to the Father for Muslims, for their salvation in union with Christ crucified for all men and women.

What does this vision encourage one to do? It finds that a Christian who is *sent* to build bridges of understanding between Christians and Muslims must be in solidarity and in communion with Muslims so that his/her struggles become meaningful in the mission. In Courtois's writings, his reviews for *Notes on Islam*, teaching Islam in many Catholic colleges where clergy were trained, his interaction with scholarly Muslims in the universities, his contacts with many Catholic theologians who are involved in Christian-Muslim relations, and his service to poor Muslims, he stood in solidarity with Muslims. His connected life with all who care for Muslims reflects in more than one way the 'invisible community' that offers their life to the Father for Muslims.

The Underpinning Relational Principles of Courtois's Theological Vision

Courtois, emphasizing sympathy and regard for one another, writes: "The little bulletin (*Notes on Islam*) likes to re-dedicate itself to the great task that it has chosen as its own: mutual understanding and brotherly love between the estranged children of the same Heavenly Father, the Muslims, especially and the Christians. Enlightened knowledge must take away the sharp sting of prejudice and open the way to more sympathy and regard."[62]

In his mind, Christians and Muslims are estranged children of the same heavenly Father. These alienated, separated and divided brothers and sisters should return to live as one family. It should be pointed out here that Courtois is not making a theological judgment on Islam saying its followers strayed from the family of God. He laid emphasis on the fact that prejudice and ignorance divided Christians and Muslims.

Narrow-mindedness and intolerance had set brothers upon each other. They must remove the 'sharp sting of prejudice' and grow together in mutual 'sympathy and regard'. How do these brothers and sisters of this one family grow in love for one another?

Principle 1: Develop Mutual Understanding and Appreciation

Courtois considers mutual understanding and appreciation to be the first step towards 'brotherly love' (children of heavenly father). *Notes on Islam* will toil towards this goal in a small way,[63] because "both Christian and Muslim apologists have said crazy things about each other in the past is no reason to perpetuate that wrong approach to mutual understanding. Let Christian[s] and Muslims try to appraise each other better and they will soon discover that they have a common Father to serve and to love."[64] It should be emphasized that his attitude is in complete contrast to that of the Protestant missionaries at Agra, discussed in the second chapter. Mutual understanding and appreciation were absent in their approach. In the context of such polemics his principle of mutual understanding and appreciation is like 'snow drops' at the end of a hard winter!

Principle 2: Highlight the Goodness of Muslims and their Culture

Courtois laid down the agenda for his relations with Muslims. At the outset he announced that in relating with Muslims, he "would ... abstain from polemics."[65] It is a huge and significant step, and an original approach in an era when polemics dominated Christian-Muslim relations in India. In the first and second chapters it was shown that such polemics generated a lot of heat but hardly any light! Polemics created animosity and hostility but not understanding. Courtois showed a great awareness that his Christian vocation called for understanding and friendship. It is a courageous step that announced a spring time in Christian-Muslim relations in India.

He explains his reason for his new approach elsewhere in the following words:

> Do not insult Muslims. We do not live in the Crusader's era. In that era insulting one's adversary was part of military tactics. Banish all disparaging words against Islam and Muhammad, the prophet of Islam. To call them 'dirty Muslims', 'impious Muslims' is not the way to befriend them; to speak only of their immorality, often grossly exaggerated, is unjust to them; to add the adjective 'false prophet' when speaking of their founder is to court martyrdom uselessly. We must be able to see what is good in the Muslims and their culture. Alas, some dare not acknowledge any good in Islam.[66]

Courtois understood that it was not enough to abstain from polemics. He underlined the need that Christians should change their heart and mind so that they could see what is good in Muslims and their culture. Thus, Courtois invites Christians to learn from the devout life of Muslims. Acknowledging goodness in Islam and Muslims is a pioneering step. While commenting on a meeting in which Jews, Christians and Muslims met in a friendly atmosphere to discuss the spiritual values they have in common, Courtois writes:

> Aloofness is out of mode in religious things as well as in politics and economics. World peace and mutual understanding between nations cannot be achieved merely by pacts and treaties however solemn they may be, nor [sic] by financial organizations however altruistic their aims may appear. Brotherly love between men cannot be manufactured and imported ready-made, like a commercial commodity; it has to be implanted in the heart of man, and there take root, and grow, and blossom under the light of his intelligence and the warmth of his will.

> The condition for mutual love between men is mutual knowledge, a knowledge which penetrates beyond the outward appearance of man to reach his very self ... to understand my neighbor, therefore, it is the believer whom I must seek; I must discover the higher principles that guide him in his daily routine; I must listen to the secret longings of his heart, the petitions he places before God, the tale of misery he repeats, the pardon which he begs from his Lord for his failures in his life. All this will explain my brother's attitude towards his fellowmen and towards the world.[67]

Focus on What Unites, not What Divides

This is the principle that governed Llull's work among Muslims. Courtois assimilates this attitude. While commenting upon the friendly interactions between Muslims and Christians in an international convention on Christian-Muslim relations, Courtois wrote: "they were seeking not what divides, but what unites the hearts of men, the consciousness that they belong to the same human family and that all have a common Father in heaven."[68]

It should be noted that this is one of the qualities of pioneers. When petty minds focus on divisions, pioneers focus on what brings different groups together. This does not mean the differences are whitewashed. Courtois recognized that differences can be a source of enrichment, and they can mutually challenge and replenish everyone; they are not necessarily causing division. Courtois was aware that differences would continue. However, what he wanted to drive home was that division born of prejudices will not. What unites Christians and Muslims is divine, and what divides them is not.

Courtois firmly believed that focusing on commonalities, Christians and Muslims may be able to synergize each other to fight the forces that dehumanize humanity. As believers in one God, Christians and Muslims can face the challenges of the world and transform it from within. He writes:

> Now although they [Christians and Muslims] have been living side by side for many centuries, they yet practically ignore one another: the Christian knows hardly anything about the religion of Islam, and the Muslim knows still less about Christianity. If genuine concord is to be obtained if Muslims and Christians are to appreciate one another, they have to meet on religious grounds, they have, in other words, to meet at the feet of God to realize that they are brothers, children of the same Heavenly Father. Only then will they be able to shed mutual prejudices, [and] find fields where collaboration will be possible against materialistic atheism, the common enemy of Islam and Christianity and all believers in God, only then will they be able to work together for the betterment of the world. [69]

Courtois further attaches importance to proactive coexistence. He writes:

> The *Notes on Islam* aims at much more than 'co-existence' between
> Muslims and non-Muslims – co-existence is only synonym for toleration,
> a negative concept! The *Notes* endeavors to bring about mutual esteem,
> nay brotherly love between Muslims and non-Muslims, be they Hindus,
> Christians or Jews. It is brotherly love, indeed, that the common Father
> of all men, God almighty, desires to see burning in the hearts of all the
> members of the big human family.[70]

In his writings one can notice a number of elements that are new and
path-breaking. First, Courtois recognizes a brother and a sister in a
Muslim. It is a strikingly fresh approach. The old attitude of adversaries
is discarded for good. A new approach of gaining their love is adopted.
In a deeper sense, brothers and sisters are loved and accepted. This
acceptance, without fail, must include respect for their way of life and
convictions including their religious convictions. Calling them brothers
and sisters, Courtois unambiguously expresses his love and respect for
them as individuals and people belonging to a community of another
faith.

Secondly, he has demonstrated in the first two volumes of *Notes on
Islam* the new approach he had adopted; that is keeping himself away
from polemics and any form of insult to Muslims. He had highlighted
what is good in the Muslims and their culture by presenting realities
as objectively as possible.

Thirdly, in his carefully worded editorial he wrote: "It is the aim of
Notes on Islam indirectly to hasten the day when Muslims and Christians
will make one big family under the benevolent leadership of Jesus, the
Son of Mary."[71] A brief and clear commentary is needed to understand
this sentence. His call for one family under the benevolent leadership
of Jesus, the Son of Mary should not be understood as a call for the
conversion of Muslims. This call to form one family should be seen in
the light of his affirmation of Muslims as his brothers and sisters and
the brotherly respect for their religious convictions, and thus it is not a
call for abandoning Islam and joining the Christian fold. The *one family*

that Courtois indicates is the family of those who worship one God; that is Muslims and Christians, albeit in different ways.

Courtois refers to Jesus, the son of Mary, as the benevolent leader of both Christians and Muslims. Courtois by referring to Jesus as son of Mary is drawing from the sources of Islam. Muslims know Jesus as the son of Mary. Since *Notes on Islam* is for both Muslims and Christians, he implicitly invites Christians to present to Muslims the Jesus they have discovered in the Gospels by their words, deeds and life. It is an invitation to live as '*alter christus*' among Muslims.

In other words, Courtois simply reminds Christians of their baptismal grace which is for mission: the mission of presenting Christ. In their baptismal grace, each baptized person is given the gift of relationship with Jesus. Christians will explain that gift of relation with Christ as dying and rising with Christ, a sort of new and communitarian life. This gift is not only for the personal sanctification of a Christian, but for mission. This mission is to present Christ to others.

This presentation has nothing to do with aggressive proselytization. It is simply sharing the gift with others who are willing to be enriched and willing to mutually share the treasures of their faith with Christians. In the process both are mutually enriched. Note the words of Courtois, when he writes: "Muslims and Christians will make one big family", he did not say Muslims becoming Christians to make one family! As members of one family they will be enriched mutually, under the 'benevolent leadership of Jesus', the son of Mary. Jesus, son of Mary, is theologically sensitive to Muslims and Christians. It is a sort of common ground, where the believers of these two great faiths can meet and share in depth their specific understanding of Jesus.[72]

There is an interesting element one can read into the invitation of Courtois. Often Muslims have blamed Christians for exaggerating their faith. Courtois's invitation is that the Christian faith is authentic and not exaggerated, though it is different from the Muslim's faith; and similarly, for a Christian it is important to respect the faith of Muslims even if it differs from the Christian understanding of Jesus. As a Christian it is a joy for Courtois to invite his Muslim neighbours to come to his home without losing their identity of being Muslims.

Courtois affirms the faith of Muslims, and presents the Gospel by word and deeds among Muslims: a new paradigm for India. This had been done earlier by Massignon and Foucauld in another part of the world. Courtois introduces this approach in India, taking into account the specificities of the Indian political and religious situation. Courtois wanted Christians to recognize the features of our heavenly father and love them as brothers. The Father draws Muslims to himself in ways known to him. Christians recognize that this act of God is an act in the Spirit. Christian responsibility is to love them as brothers and sisters. Having seen the vision and the principle, the next section presents the action program: how this vision is put into action with these underpinning principles.

Enfleshed Vision

Courtois Demonstrates Sympathetic and Critical Knowledge of Islam

Courtois, the Christian member of the family of God, demonstrates sympathetic and critical knowledge of Islam. His writings are witness to this fact. Four major areas of concern are touched upon by Courtois in his writing. They are revelation in Islam, Muhammad (prophet of Muslims), the Qur'ân and Islamic renaissance in the sub-continent.

Revelation in Islam

In the essay *The Notion of Revelation in Islam* (written in the beginning of his theological studies in 1937)[73] Courtois proposes that one should carefully consider the following elements in order to understand the concept of revelation in Islam: the religious situation of Arabia before Muhammad's call, the idea of revelation according to the Qur'ân, the idea of revelation developed by *ḥadīth*, and the way philosophers and Sufis understood revelation.

First Element: Arabia Before Muhammad's Call

Courtois writes that according to the Qur'ân "in sixth century Arabia, there were groups of men who pretended to have received from the Divinity, a *kitab*, where the Law of God was expressed."[74] The Qur'ân identifies them as Jews, Christians, and Sabeans. There was another group who claimed to have some connection with the world of spirits and were poetic in their utterance. They were considered to be *Kahins*, or *sha'irs* (poets). There were also individuals, who did not belong to any of the aforementioned groups, but who too worshipped one God and these were identified as *Hanifs*.

The Second Element: Revelation According to the Qur'ân

Courtois emphasizes that one should carefully distinguish between the Meccan period and Medinan period of Muhammad's life in order to understand revelation as presented in the Qur'ân. Courtois recognizes that the *Higira* "has been a turning point in the Prophet's career."[75] He notes that *Higira* may fittingly serve as a limit between Muhammad's idea of revelation 'in fieri' (while being evolved) and in 'facto esse' (after being produced).

Courtois explains Muhammad's concept of revelation 'in fieri'. He invites the readers to a *hadîth* recorded by Al Bukhari. The *hadîth* says as follows:

> The first manifestation of the Revelation which the Messenger of Allah gave was true vision in sleep; the vision always came to him like the dawn of the morning. Then solitude became dear to him, and he used to go alone to the cave of Hira and practice *tahannuth* (bewailing of sins) there, for several nights before he returned to his family. After some time, the Angel came to him and said: 'Recite'. He said: 'I am not going to recite'. So, he seized him and squeezed him until he was in distress. He repeated this three times and finally said: 'Recite in the name of thy Lord, who created man ...'[76]

This *hadîth*, according to Courtois, marks three elements in Muhammad's vocation. The elements are: "the dream, the need of solitude, and vision of the angel".[77] Following authors like Lammens and Margoliouth,

Courtois affirms that the Qur'ân is the only reliable source and ḥadīth material could be spurious if not confirmed by the Qur'ân.

With regard to the vision of the Angel, Courtois writes: "If then we open the Qur'ân we find that there is no evident mention of Gabriel before the Medinan sura of the Cow (Q. 2: 97), i.e., at least ten years after the supposed call. The idea therefore of the inspiring Angel Gabriel cannot have been first in Muhammad's concept of Revelation. In the beginning he [Muhammad] thought of no Angel".[78] Courtois concludes that the vision of Angel is an invention. What about solitude? Courtois writes that solitude is not "in keeping with the character of Muhammad"[79], and concludes: "The spiritual retreat of Muhammad previous to his mission seems to have been invented to liken him to the real prophets of God: John the Baptist, Jesus, etc".[80]

Coming to dreams, Courtois argues that Muhammad was disgusted with the ills of the society in which he lived. Muhammad had a deep desire to regenerate his people, and thoughts of reform filled his heart and mind. He meanwhile heard Christian monks praying and chanting from their sacred scriptures. He could not but ask himself: How could he pray if he had no Scripture? Had God left out the Arabs? Courtois seems to affirm that a desire for regeneration of his people and a yearning for scripture for his fellow men and women were in Muhammad's unconscious mind that eventually surfaced in the form of dreams. Following Tor Andrea, Courtois thinks that Muhammad's prophetic revelations are formed in advance in his thoughts as he seriously thought about the ills of the society.[81] These conscious thoughts assumed the form of dream. Courtois states that Mahammad considered the contents of his dreams as revelations.

The Qur'ân uses the word *wahy* for revelation.[82] The author of *wahy* is not necessarily God. Hence the general meaning of *wahy* can be 'a suggestion', 'a prompting', or 'an inspiration'. The hearers of Muhammad, too, did not think of any supernatural character for the revelation of Muhammad. It could also be interpreted that the truth was manifested or at least suggested by God in a dream.

Courtois considers that this scene changed as Muhammad moved to Medina. He was nonplussed by the refusal of Jews and Christians to see in him a messenger of God. Both Jews and Christians mocked and sneered at him. According to Courtois, Muhammad, instead of discerning the basis of its veracity became more rooted in his conviction that he was a prophet. Muhammad also came to the conclusion that Jews and Christians could not recognize him since they had corrupted their scriptures. After this Muhammad began to deal with Divine Inspiration lightly. His conviction that he was a prophet, instead of getting clarified, deepened and strengthened according to Courtois.

In Medina, Muhammad came to believe that every utterance of his, whether after a dream or in reflection to solve a problem, or to justify a decision, was to be considered as revealed by God or by his angel. Was this a hostile comment? Should it be seen as yet another negative approach of western writers on Islamic revelation? When Courtois wrote this essay, he was just 30, and at the beginning of his life as a young theologian. He moves gently for a deeper understanding once he developed a theological vision, which is at the heart of his bridge-building efforts.

Third Element: The Idea of Revelation Developed by Ḥadīth

As the years rolled by, the ḥadīth added another layer of meaning to revelation saying that revelation is the pure word of God without any admixture. This idea was noticeable already during the life time of Muhammad but gained force in the ḥadīth.

Fourth Element: Philosophers' and Sufis' Understanding of Revelation

Philosophers and mystics added another dimension to the understanding of revelation. Their views were based on the distinction between God's essence and existence. Under the impact of Greek philosophy, Christian dogmas and Gnostic theories, Muslim philosophers discussed the nature of God and his attributes. The rationalists/Mutazilites recognized eternity to be of the essence of God but denied eternity to God's attributes.

They thought that if the attributes have to share eternity, being distinct from God, there will be more than one God. They suggested that what the Qur'ân predicates as an attribute of God should be understood allegorically. For them God is a pure essence. If God is reduced to pure essence, God cannot be said to possess the Word of God. In other words, God is stripped of his ability to possess speech. Revelation, in that case could only be understood symbolically. They reduced revelation to subjective intuition. There would not be any special intervention or extraordinary communication. The prophet through intuition can access the will of God. 'Revelation' of God is merely an allegorical way of speaking.

The orthodox Muslim theologians disagreed with the rationalists. They affirmed the real and eternal attributes in God. They understood that these attributes exist in God in an analogical way. To illustrate: a human person is able to speak. In other words, speech exists in man. Speech exists in God but all the qualities of speech that are incompatible with the immutability of God's essence are absent in the speech of God. In other words, attributes are neither God nor are they distinct from God. The divine speech is *verbum mentis* (a mental word). Sounds and signs are accidental to *verbum mentis* and do not exist as such in God.

According to Courtois, this understanding is close to what Catholic theologians called *lex aeterna*. This is the Divine wisdom eternally conceived in the mind of God. However, Christian theologians consider that man and woman can access this wisdom of God through the study of Natural Law. Natural Law provides a moral and ethical way of living what is enshrined and inbuilt in the rational thinking of every human being. Natural Law is understood as an inbuilt commitment in human persons that seeks to do good and avoid evil. It could be said that divine law enlightens the human intellect to seek good and avoid evil. This commitment reflects the way God has made humanity. Thus, Natural Law participates in divine law (eternal law). Courtois comes from within this tradition.

Muslim theologians think differently. They consider that *Verbum mentis* contains the positive and negative precepts that a human person has to subscribe to. Orthodox Muslims like the great theologian al-Ghazali taught that natural reason is incapable of accessing or knowing these prescriptions. The moral principles that a human person can recognize through his rational faculty may not have value since God can change it as God wills. God is above every law, including metaphysical laws. If God does not reveal these to human beings, then they cannot know the moral principles that they should live by. God alone can reveal them. God reveals them in a way that a human person is capable of knowing. God uses material signs, voices and sounds. This is *wahy*, according to al-Ghazali. Al-Ghazali in this way rescued this concept from exaggerated rationalism. There is a great stress laid on the divine origin of Islamic revelation.

Courtois could not agree with these explanations. Courtois argues that the human person is rational and he should put rationality to good use. He should delve deep to recognize the moral virtues and live accordingly. In the opinion of Courtois, the prompted word falls short of responding to the exigencies of human reason. This is the reason why revelation as understood by Muslims does not give credit to human capability. He drew the conclusion that the traditional Islamic doctrine of Revelation neglects the human side of the same and lays exaggerated stress on divine intervention.

Muslims understand the concept of revelation on the basis of two different roots: *wahy* and *nuzūl*. *Wahy* is commonly understood as revelation.[83] *nuzūl* denotes the ideas of 'coming down', 'descending', or 'sending down'. This root has a strong place-related connotation. In the Qur'ân the words like *'nazala'*, *'nuzul'*, *'nazzala'*, and *'anzala'* which come from the root *nuzūl* are more used than the words that come from the root *wahy*. It should be noted that the word *'tanzil'* refers to the manner of revelation. It is the considered opinion of scholars that taken together these two root words and their derivatives that occur in the Qur'ânic revelation show an awe-inspiring communication from above, not just an inspiration. Islam stresses its transcendent communication from above. This transcendent communication takes place in history through the medium of prophets and messengers. In order to proclaim the unique lordship of God one has to subscribe to God's moral will as God reveals it. Courtois's reflection is limited to reflection on *wahy* and words derived from this root. Courtois seems not to give attention to root *nuzūl*. As a result the discussion Courtois initiated did not give overall attention to the convictions of Muslims with regard to revelation. This is a shortcoming in Courtois's presentation.

Both Courtois as a Catholic theologian and Muslim theologians would agree that the human person is a moral agent. However, where they disagree is about the capability of humans. Courtois will argue that God created humans in such a way that they are by creation fundamentally open to God. This openness cannot be ignored. In such a fundamental openness, man and woman recognize their moral responsibilities. In other words, in their conscience they recognize that something is good and some other things are not. Orthodox Muslim theologians will insist that revelation from above is necessary without which moral life is impossible.

This discussion points towards the different ways in which revelation is understood in both these religious traditions. The Qur'ânic understanding of revelation expressed in the word *wahy* is related to speech and inspiration and implies the idea of worship and obedience. God is the absolute sovereign and all are called to be servants and worshippers. For according to Islamic revelation, the purpose of creation of the human being is to worship God (Q 51:56). The purpose of revelation is a call to humanity to worship and obey the commandments of God.[84]

Courtois held that God revealed himself as a forgiving, healing and redeeming God. God's love is genuine, self-giving, unconditional and extended to sinners and even to enemies. Moreover, Courtois firmly held that God revealed himself ultimately in Christ, and the purpose of this revelation is to invite humanity to enter into a new kind of personal and communitarian life clothed with Christ, to use the Pauline terminology. In other words; The word of God became human in order to transform the humans to become sharers of the divine. Through the incarnate word we [human beings] become sharers of the divine nature. This is called *theosis* or divinization.[85]

It must be admitted that these two views differ from one another. Differences cannot be resolved by brushing them aside. They must be recognized and an effort has to be made to reach a deeper understanding of them within their respective wider contexts. The recognition and affirmation of differences teach an important lesson for the students of religion. It is necessary to understand the differences with sympathy. Sympathetic understanding is an effort to understand how one believes or presents his/her case.

Moreover, Courtois would affirm God's revelation in Christ as the third and final stage of the progress in revelation. Natural revelation (God is known through conscience as well as from contemplating the natural order) and God's special revelation to Israel are considered to be the first and second stages of revelation.[86] This is typical of the eighteenth century understanding of Islam. During the age of enlightenment, Islam became a typical form of deism and Muhammad became the font of natural and rational religion. Islam does not believe in the progress of revelation. It believes in the constancy of revelation. For Muslims, Islam is a call back to what was revealed to Adam and every prophet who came after him. All prophets received essentially the same revelation and preached the same message that God is one.[87]

What status does Courtois give to the Islamic revelation? From the analysis of his essay, one could draw a conclusion that Courtois along with other Christian theologians place the Qur'ân within the natural order of revelation with an added complexity that any God-knowledge beyond the natural order that is present in the Qur'ân is gathered from the Hebrew and Christian Scriptures. However, the matter does not end here. Christian theologians like Augustine and reformers like Luther and Calvin, all claiming Pauline authority, would argue that the human person is marked with sin, that natural knowledge is tinged with sinfulness, and that it becomes the source of sin and not salvation. Consequently, one cannot fully rely on the first stage of revelation. They would emphasize that human persons as inveterate sinners cannot save themselves by their own effort. God has to save them. God saves them by humbling himself and sharing with humanity in the person of Jesus. Jesus, the sinless by his death and resurrection renews humanity and opens up a new way for humans to be with God. This is completely unacceptable to Muslims.

How would Courtois respond to this complexity? He neither indicates this intricacy in his essay nor develops the theme later. Pushing him on this matter, he would most probably say Muslims through their attitude of faith (fides qua) adhere to belief in One God and share a commonality with Christians (and Jews) despite fundamental differences. Since Islam considers faith as a gift of God and an invitation to enter into His mystery, such faith disposes Muslims to accept God and lead a life according to His will to walk in the path towards salvation.

It should be kept in mind that this essay, written in the first year of theological studies shows Courtois's effort to make a serious reflection on Revelation in Islam. It was a bold venture when his fellow Jesuits largely ignored Muslims and their faith. While other Jesuits who wrote for the Indian Academy were recycling the polemical views, he inaugurated an approach of serious study of Islamic concepts among Jesuits in India.[88] His essay demonstrates his creative ability to bring both Catholic and Islamic theologies into dialogue. Without hesitation it should be said that Courtois has sown the seeds for greater appreciation of the faith of Muslims. A scientific approach is at the heart of Courtois's approach. This deeper critical reflection leads the reader to a mutual understanding and appreciation. It is not polemics: at the heart of polemics there is a dismissal of the other as undeserving. In critical appreciation, there is conversation within the family which recognizes differences and learns to dialogue.

Understanding Muhammad Sympathetically

Medieval writers were unfair and unjust in viewing the portrait of Muhammad. John of Damascus described him as a "false prophet."[89] Muhammad's prophecy was dismissed as the effect of epilepsy.[90] Muhammad was considered to be 'a man of impure life and worldly stratagem' by many writers in the West.[91] They find in Islam and in Muhammad a sinister conspiracy against Christianity.[92] They thought that Muhammad was the anti-Christ because they saw that Muhammad's life was a parody of the life of Christ. The crusaders made the founder of Islam negatively popular in the West. Muhammad's story was woven with fictitious imagination.[93] The negative image of Islam has deep roots.

Courtois focused on bringing about harmonious relations between Christians and Muslims. He wanted to articulate his views about Muhammad in a reasonable way. Courtois writes: "It does not pay to speak disparagingly of Islam, its prophet and its institutions ..."[94] Further he wrote: "Christians should not say that Muhammad is a false prophet."[95] He instructed his Christian readers not to call Muhammad a false prophet; this does not mean that he encouraged Christians to see Muhammad as a prophet. In other words, both what you say about Muhammad and how you say it will be keenly watched by Muslims. Sensitivity to the Muslim mind, honesty in appraisal, at the same time saying this without compromising one's own faith should underpin Christian comments on Muhammad. Courtois demonstrates this beautifully.

The Portrait of Muhammad

Courtois intends to explore the reliable data on the life of Muhammad. He was careful in choosing the threads to weave the portrait. He was neither willing to agree uncritically to the negative material that was churned out by scholars on Muhammad nor prepared to absorb the hagiographical material for his purpose. His essay on Muhammad that appeared in the pages of *Notes on Islam* is the important text to know the mind of Courtois on Muhammad.

Muhammad, the Trustworthy

Courtois presents Muhammad to his readers as a trustworthy person. He writes: "As a boy and as a youth, Muhammad was esteemed for his loyalty and straightforwardness. His contemporaries would have given him the surname *al-amin*, the trustworthy. He was religiously inclined and to all appearances pious, a rare quality among the materialistic Meccans".[96] Courtois highlights the spiritual dimension of Muhammad in contrast with other writers.

Muhammad's Steadfastness in Spiritual Crisis

Courtois informs his readers that Muhammad passed through a moral crisis in his youth. He did not attribute this crisis to any physical ailments as did by many western scholars.[97] Courtois interprets it as a reaction to the worldly and ungodly life of his fellow Meccans. Moreover, Courtois points out during the moment of spiritual darkness, when Muhammad suspected his vocation, Khadija the wife of Muhammad remained as his strength and support.[98]

Thus, Courtois highlights the spiritual sensitivity of Muhammad. Muhammad's "sensitive soul" was offended by his fellow Meccans' "lust for blood, greed, [and] practical materialism."[99] He was longing for honesty in business, justice in society, and justice for the poor, the orphan and the widows. These aspirations according to Courtois denote Muhammad's noble and generous nature. These characteristics impacted the Qur'ân "where equity and social justice are often insisted upon."[100]

Courtois was aware of the over powering strength of materialism in his own times and recognized it as a serious challenge to faith. Courtois finds that Muhammad handles this crisis with deep faith. One can draw a conclusion that Courtois finds in the followers of Muhammad allies to deal with the materialism that alienated men and women of his times from their faith.

Muhammad, the Leader of Men

Courtois writes: "Muhammad was born to be a leader of men. He was trusted and relied upon by his fellow Meccans. He was shy. This natural shyness, Courtois writes, "pointed to real depth of character."[101] Courtois writes further, "He was in fact aflame with a great ideal which he wanted to realize; no rebuke, no scorn, no persecution could make him waver. Muhammad's indomitable will and steadfastness of purpose would make him overcome all opposition and finally triumph. He was a leader of men."[102] It is interesting to note that Courtois interpreted 'shyness' as a pointer towards 'real depth of character'. Many Christian saints have this gentle whiff of shyness. This shyness could be an indication that the person is focused on God. It could be said from this comment of Courtois, that Muhammad was a great leader focused on doing God's will.

Muhammad, a Social Reformer

Muhammad was very daring and deeply conscious of his mission. He certainly tried to remedy social evils. Courtois writes:

> [O]ne of Muhammad's first tasks will be to rise against the oppression of the poor. 'Ye honor not the orphan nor urge ye one another to feed the poor, and ye devour heritages, devouring greedily, and ye love riches with exceeding love' (Q 89: 18-21). He sent to Hell the rich man who did not care for the needy.: 'Lay ye hold on him and chain him, then at the Hell-fire burn him, then into a chain whose length is seventy cubits thrust him; for he believed not in God , the Great, and was not careful to feed the poor' (Q 69: 34). He imposed alms-giving, *zakat*, on every Muslim; alms-giving indeed is the mark of true piety and the way to happiness: 'As to him who gives alms and feareth God ... to him will make easy the way to happiness. But as to him who is covetous and bent on riches, and calleth God a liar, to him we make easy the path to misery' (Q 92: 5-10).[103]

His solidarity with the poor created many enemies among the rich and leaders, and Muhammad and his little flock of followers were persecuted. "But in spite of insults and the inconvenience following the ban imposed on him and his followers; he went on warning his brethren of the Judgment to come and of the necessity of being converted to Allah in order to escape His wrath".[104]

Courtois finds a certain influence of Jewish prophets on him in his thirst for justice. He writes: "Consequent to the lust for fat gains was the practice of usury, *riba*, with all the excesses to which it leads. Muhammad, perhaps influenced partly by Judaism, cursed in Allah's name the usurers and their satellites – their abode is Hell fire (Q 2:276)."[105]

Courtois continues: "... Muhammad tried to improve matters. It was a delicate task in which – when things are looked at from the Gospel level – he seems not to have been completely successful. Yet, he lay down certain regulations in order to raise the standard of morality of the Arabs."[106]

Muhammad, a Spiritual Person

Many scholars have derided Muhammad saying his piety was a mask to capture power.[107] Courtois disagrees with such claim and remarks: "Political and military upstarts do not found religions."[108] He writes further:

> Islam is a religion which has made a very wide appeal to the people of the East, and it has appealed not only to soldiers and adventurers but to more recollected souls as well in search of spiritual guidance. The Qur'ân has been at the origin of their life of prayer. This would hardly be possible unless one found in that book at least the elements of spirituality, of Muslim spirituality no doubt. That spirituality was put in there by Muhammad. Now it is admitted by all that the Qur'ân reflects well the soul of Muhammad. We must then conclude that there was genuine piety in Muhammad's heart and that he really loved prayer.[109]

'Muhammad really loved prayer' is an important comment. It expresses the depth of theological insight of Courtois. Through this comment he affirms two elements: one, the affirmation of Muhammad's earnestness in prayer; two, the spirit that prays in the heart of Muhammad. They are important affirmations that bring about a new way in which Courtois thinks about Muhammad. One should contrast here with what he himself wrote earlier somewhat truculently as a student of theology that Muhammad took 'divine inspiration lightly'. As Courtois continued to deepen his relationship with Muslims, he was able to appreciate more and more the spirit of prayer and genuineness of Muhammad. An interesting methodology that Courtois appears to allude to is the method of learning the faith of the people primarily from people. This approach will be enriched further when the texts are consulted and carefully read and analyzed. In Courtois's life and mission 'reading people' constantly enriched 'reading texts' and vice-versa. It should be noted that he thus developed an important element for Christian-Muslim relations.

Muhammad's Spirit of Detachment

Courtois commends highly Muhammad's esteem for prayer and his complete dependence on God. He writes: "the Prophet of the Arabs cared little for the goods of this world."[110]Muhammad voluntarily embraced poverty restrained himself from seeking comforts in life. He impoverished himself by giving without ceasing and thus lived out the spirituality of the Qur'ânic teaching. "You will never attain righteousness (justification) unless you impoverish yourselves by giving of what you like; and whatever you give, for sure God knows it." (Q 3: 92)

Courtois writes:

Muhammad's poverty and little comfort-seeking were perhaps not exclusively the fruit of abnegation. Lavish hospitality and generosity were one of the conditions for leadership and greatness in old Arabia. Yet, one cannot help admiring Muhammad's detachment from riches. For a man of his position, it would indeed have been easy to amass wealth, and live in great comfort. He preferred the simple way of life of the modest Arab, eating their food when he got it toiling with them. He helped with his own hands in building the mosque of Medina, and in digging the trench round the city when it was to be attacked by the Quraish.[111]

Having enumerated the positive qualities of Muhammad, Courtois also pointed out to his readers of NI what he found unacceptable in the life of Muhammad. This he does with care and sensitivity.

Muhammad and His Enemies

Courtois finds Muhammad lacked forbearance with his enemies at times. He notes that at times Muhammad cursed others. Muhammad prayed for pardon and for success, and for friends and for himself. "He did not pray for his enemies; nay, he sent several to Hell - the nastier ones, and threatened them all with God's eternal punishment ... We regret not to find in Muhammad that spirit of humility, that heroic patience, which makes a saint so very much like Christ."[112] One could notice a tinge of sadness in Courtois expressing that Muhammad failed to imitate Christ.

Courtois finds that Muhammad's hostility towards the Jewish tribe Banu Qurayzah unacceptable in the light of his faith. In Medina, Muhammad found them as a potential group of traitors, and he beheaded around 700 men and made their children and women slaves.[113] Courtois suggests that this should be read in the context of the 7th century when the fate of a conquered nation was hard. However, one cannot equate this situation with a biblical text like Deuteronomy 20: 13-14.[114] Courtois writes: "in A.D. 626 the old law was long obsolete."[115] He meant to say that Christ has abrogated the old law with a new law of love and self-sacrifice.[116] According to Courtois, Muhammad did not see God's purifying hands in those trials. However, behind the angry face and in the angry tone, people recognized a heart that remained kind and generous.[117] The other instance is the assassination of poets who satirized Muhammad.[118] Courtois does not make any reference to this incident.

It should be noted that Jesus showed a new path, a path of love, forgiveness and love even for enemies; 'love your enemies', he said. Muhammad despite all his great qualities of leadership and spirituality, as recognized by Courtois, did fall short of the greater heights that Jesus wanted his disciples to reach. Courtois records this 'weakness' in the character of Muhammad, not in the spirit of polemics, but in the spirit of building up a genuine and honest relationship with Muslims.

Is Muhammad a Prophet for Courtois?[119]

Having discussed what he (Courtois) found commendable and not so exemplary in the life of Muhammad, Courtois deals with the question: Is Muhammad a prophet for Christians? It is an important question that Muslims ask Christians. Many Muslims wonder why Christians hesitate to consider Muhammad a prophet in the same way as Muslims accept Jesus as their prophet. This is a theologically a complex question. If Courtois accepts that he is a prophet, then one may ask why he [Courtois] did not follow him [Muhammad].

Courtois responds to this with clarity. He writes: "Muhammad set himself to organize his followers into a strong community. Muhammad was a master organizer, and had to the highest degree that great quality of the Arab leader, *hilm*, 'political and diplomatical sense.'"[120]

Thus, in the writings of Courtois, Muhammad emerges as a genuine religious genius,[121] great diplomat, sincere worshipper of God who showed a great sense of detachment from worldly goods and greater sense of attachment to do God's will in his life. Courtois tries to show is that it is possible to appreciate Muhammad without necessarily recognizing him as a prophet. Though he did not explicitly state it, it can be recognized from his comments on Muhammad; Courtois is implicitly telling his readers that recognizing Muhammad as a prophet would compromise his Christian faith.

How would recognizing 'Muhammad as a prophet' compromise his faith? Did not the Hebrew prophets commit sin? When Christians continue to honor those Hebrew prophets who were not sinless, why not honor Muhammad as a prophet, too? A quick consideration on how Courtois as a Catholic theologian understood prophecy and Muslims understand prophecy is important here.

The Greek word from which the word 'prophet' derives suggests that a prophet is one who speaks for God. The Hebrew word for 'prophet' in its passive principal form suggests one who is called by God. Thus a prophet brings God's word to humankind; a prophet is an inspired speaker. The primary sense of prophecy in the Bible is to be inspired by God and to speak in God's name. It is revelation and admonition. The prophet received the communicated word of God shared with his people. Muhammad reflects a number of such qualities of prophets.

The serious theological issue is that the biblical understanding of prophecy finds the coming of Christ as the definitive fulfillment of prophecy. The Gospel of Jesus (according to Mathew) develops this concept of fulfillment thoroughly. In short the Christian scripture considers that the whole Jewish scriptures spoke of Jesus.

With such clarity in Christian theology with regard to Prophethood and its fulfillment in Jesus, Christians struggled with Muhammad's claims to Prophethood.[122] First, for Christians the divinely guaranteed expression of the ultimate or eschatological public revelation of God ended with the Apostolic Church and its witnesses. Such a theology did not allow Muhammad to be considered a prophet without compromising their own Christian faith.[123]

Secondly, for Christians, Jesus Christ is the fulfilment of Hebrew prophecy; but more than that, he is the Word of God incarnate. Hebrew prophecy prepared people for the central event of the incarnation. This claim by Christians needs a brief explanation. In Jewish and Christian belief, Hebrew prophets called the people to worship the one God who liberated them from captivity and established a covenant relationship with them. The Hebrew people maintained the integrity of their covenant with God by sacrifices offered by priests in the temple. The sacrifices in the temple were at the heart of their covenant relationship with God.

They faced a religious crisis when they were exiled after the destruction of the temple (587 BCE). The exiled Hebrews nourished a hope for a new temple and thus the revival of sacrifices. However, a new religious thought emerged in the Book of Ezekiel (4:4-6). It asserted that a prophet's bodily suffering would maintain the integrity of the covenant in the place of temple sacrifices. The songs of the suffering servant of God in the Book of Isaiah further clarified this emerging religious thinking. The suffering servant as understood by Isaiah would reconcile humanity with God. Christians understand Jesus to be the suffering servant of God (Isaiah 42:1-7; 49:1-7; 50:4-9; 52:13-53:12). They also recognized Jesus not just as the servant of God but as the Word made flesh and sent among humanity to accomplish the work of salvation which his Father had given him to do.[124] Muslims find this Christian understanding of Jesus quite unacceptable. The essential difference is that, for Christians, Jesus is the embodiment of the Word and the fulfillment of prophecy. For Muslims, Muhammad is the recipient of the last and universal Book, the perfect exemplar of the message, the guide to paradise for the whole of humanity, and the seal of prophecy.[125]

Muslims understand a prophet in the following way: prophets, while speaking in the name of God speaks with divine authority and hence have to be obeyed. Understanding this particular way, a Christian cannot call Muhammad a prophet.[126] If they do so, they would be compromising with some of the key beliefs of their faith. Accordingly for Courtois, Muhammad was not a prophet. Thus, Courtois is well within Christian theology and records his appreciation for Muhammad. He has shown the critical appreciation with much sensitivity.

The way Courtois reflects could be compared to the way in which the Catholicos Timothy I (d. 823) responded to the Caliph al-Mahdī.[127] The Caliph al-Mahdī inquired from Timothy I concerning his opinion on Muhammad. Gaudeul writes: "Any derogatory remark would be considered as an insult. A refusal to acknowledge his Prophethood might be seen as implying that he is a liar. Timothy avoids answering negatively. He does not fall into the trap of recognizing Muhammad's prophethood. Instead, he simply acknowledges Muhammad for having 'walked in the way of prophets.'"[128]

Like Timothy, Courtois showed appreciation for some of the great qualities of Muhammad. But he did not call Muhammad a prophet. Courtois demonstrated that Christians and Muslims can live as a family, by respecting the faith and traditions of others, without necessarily accepting what others consider crucial to their religious faiths. Christians should respect the faith convictions of Muslims. They could recognize that in a number of moments the spirit of God at work in the life of Muhammad. One could discern here the openness of Courtois to learn from Muslims and their understanding of Muhammad. Courtois knew the deep love Muslims have for Muhammad. As he loved his Muslim brothers and sisters, he could develop a sympathetic understanding of Muhammad. It will not be difficult to say that the good qualities that Muhammad enumerates should not challenge Christians for an authentic life according to their faith.[129] Having dealt with two major issues; revelation and Muhammad, Courtois has to deal with the Qur'ân.

Qur'ân: 'The Living Voice' for Muslims

Muslims consider that the Qur'ân is an earthly edition of the heavenly book and it is the revealed word of God word by word. J.D. McAuliffe, the general editor of the *Encyclopedia of the Qur'ân*, explains the place of the Qur'ân in the life of Muslims in the following words:

> For more than a billion Muslims around the globe, the Qur'ân reproduces God's very own words. To hear its verses chanted, to see its words written on mosque walls, to touch the pages of its inscribed text creates a sense of sacred presence in Muslim minds and hearts. For countless generations, Muslim families have greeted a newborn baby by whispering words from the Qur'ân in the infant's ear. For centuries, small children have begun their formal education with the Qur'ân. Seated around the teacher, they have learned to form the letters of the Arabic alphabet and to repeat the words and phrases from which their own recitation of the Qur'ân will develop. In a religious culture that extols learning, those individuals who acquire an advanced knowledge of the Qur'ân are accorded profound respect. People who commit all of the text to memory are treated with reverence. In fact, reverence marks most Muslim interaction with the Qur'ân, whether in silent prayer, public demonstration or serious study.[130]

Most Christians read the Qur'ân with polemical concerns in mind. It was part of 'know the enemy' strategy. This approach was a dominant one during the time of military conquests. The focus of the religious polemic, as discussed in the first chapter, was to discredit its status as divine revelation and to demonstrate its internal inconsistencies. In the later medieval times, there emerged a new approach that showed keen interest in a scholarly translation of the Qur'ânic text.[131] Scholars paid closer attention to the text and produced refutations of the Qur'ân. Philology became a dominant method for the study of the Qur'ân.[132]

Since Courtois was keen on bringing about brotherly and sisterly relations between Christians and Muslims, he kept himself away from any polemics. He simply developed a method along with some "modern, enlightened Muslims" who "while not denying their faith in the Qur'ân do acknowledge a human element in the composition of their holy Book".[133] However, Courtois emphasizes that "credit" should indeed be "given to Muhammad for his acute power of synthesis and his clear vision of the things that were to the welfare of the Arabs of his days."[134]

Courtois regards that the local customs were the first source for the Qur'ân. He is convinced that it was not necessary to bring in 'revelation' to explain the following items present in the Qur'ân.[135] Muhammad had sanctioned a number of old Arab customs and incorporated into the Law of Islam, for example: hospitality, polygamy, and divorce.

While Muslims are "convinced that the Qur'ân is the fruit of a special act of God and a standing miracle",[136] and Muslim theologians "refuse to consider the problem of foreign influence in the Qur'ân,[137] Courtois comments: "unfortunately the circumstances and the content of the 'revelations' are such that they seem satisfactorily explained by [the] normal play of ordinary influences."[138]

Courtois also considers that the dependence of the Qur'ân "on Judaism and Christianity is manifest."[139] Courtois writes:

> Muhammad came to know to some extent the teaching of the Bible from hearsay only, from daily contacts with Jews and Christians, the petty merchants, the small artisans, the slaves of Mekka and of Medina, the former refugees to Abyssinia, and Mary the Copt. This indirectness coupled with the unreliableness of little instructed informants easily explain the discrepancies that exist between the biblical and the Qur'ânic accounts of the same stories, the unfortunate misinterpretations given by the Qur'ân of fundamental religious truths like the Christian Trinity, the Incarnation, the Passion and Death of Christ on the Cross, etc., and its complete ignorance of other no less fundamental dogmas such as original sin, Redemption and Grace.[140]

Two factors need to be highlighted here. In a certain sense Courtois follows Jesuit scholar H. Lammens (d. 1937). Lammens regarded the

Qur'ân as "a heterogeneous aggregate of borrowings from the apocrypha of the Old and New Testaments, mixed with [the] pre-Islamic Arab tradition."[141] This is undeniably a hurtful and hostile approach. What is something new in Courtois despite following Lammens? It is the credit that he gives to Muhammad that he had the "acute power of synthesis and his clear vision of the things."[142] This is an indication of sympathy within the tradition of scholarly understanding. Courtois is both scholarly and sympathetic.

Courtois considered Muhammad as an inspired person who searched for the will of God in his life through the dictates of his conscience.[143] By highlighting the faithfulness of Muhammad to his conscience, Courtois recognizes and appreciates salvific value within the faith experience of Muhammad. This is certainly a new approach.

What is clear is that he did not condemn Qur'ân as 'manipulation' of Muhammad. In the past scholars either condemned it or ignored it. Those approaches were unhelpful.[144] Courtois's approach could be interpreted within his overall approach to Muslims, that Christians should recognize the spiritual significance of the Qur'ân in the lives of Muslims as the Book shapes the lives and spiritualities of over 1.6 billion Muslims today. His approach seems to insist that in order to enter the world of Muslims; Christians need to understand the status and agency of the Qur'ân and the way in which it is respected by Muslims. Courtois seems to be asking, is not the Qur'ân living voice for Muslims?

It should be said that Courtois does not make clear the explicitly negative elements and areas of ambiguity in the Qur'ân for a Christian believer. In the first category the Qur'ân is emphatic that God would be denying himself if he unites himself with humanity in incarnation. Courtois did not develop his response to this critical observation of the Qur'ân on one of the key elements of the Christian faith.[145] Secondly, the Qur'ân is ambiguous in its teaching with regard to relations with Christians. Some verses appeal for positive relations with 'the people of the Book' (read Christians and Jews) [Q 2:62, 5:82] and many other verses advocate hostility and thus are negative [Q 9:29]. Qur'ân provides incompatible moral options [Q 5:45] for those who innocently suffered injustice. The Qur'ân advocates retribution and suggest that to forgo the right to retribution would bring atonement for one's sins.[146] These are some of the key areas that were not given attention in Courtois's work.

Islamic Renaissance in the Indian Subcontinent and Christian Responsibility[147]

Looking at the appalling stagnation in Muslim lands, many politicians and Orientalists had prophesized an early disintegration of Islam. Courtois affirmed that such prophesies would prove wrong. Courtois believes that the energy tonic 'independence' rejuvenated the Muslim world. Muslims are conscious that they have to play an important role in reorganization of the world.[148]

However, Courtois notes that in the Muslim world, there is "still too much loose thinking, too many improvised solutions, too much enthusiasm and not enough reflection."[149] Courtois writes:

> The Renaissance is still at a primary stage; but the life that sprang from newly won independence, the belated discovery of the advantage of modern civilization, the urgent need of adaptation to present conditions if one wants to have a say in the shaping of the future are churning the Muslim masses into a compact block conscious of its strength and convinced of a divine mission for the betterment of the world.[150]

Courtois thinks that Islam will find it difficult to respond to the changing situations, since the interests of Islamic scholars are focused on pressing needs of politics and economics. He writes:

> The present Muslim world is so engrossed in economic pursuits, in political and social reforms, in the fight for existence that it has had no time for quiet thinking. Where, indeed, are the Ibn Sina, the Ibn Rushd, the Ghazzali, the al-Biruni and scores of theologians, philosophers and scientists of the heyday of Islam? Unless the modern generation returns to the feet of these great masters and accepts to be taught once more how to think, love God and His creation Man, modern achievements will fizzle through the darkness of the night like a rocket on Diwali Day.[151]

Where is the problem? Courtois is of the opinion that Islamic religious leaders, at least in India and now in Pakistan, lack the sound philosophical and theological training which alone can open minds to a dispassionate study of truth and enable them to recognize other people's point of view. Courtois agrees with writers like Fareed S. Jafri that the Muslim has to liberate himself from the medieval fancies of theologians.[152]

In a letter to a Jesuit scholar on Islamic Studies he writes:

> I think, indeed, that the time has come for a more intimate and a more 'massive' approach of Islam. I do not mean a Crusade which is bellicose, but a friendly approach. The Muslim world is manifestly passing through a crisis and is in the throes (spasm of feeling, mental agony and anguish) of a renaissance trying to adapt itself to recently won independence. Under foreign rule, Muslims had no real education, while social and political problems were solved by the rulers. But now they have to give an Islamic solution to the many problems which the administration of a free country brings forth. And they are at a loss with the danger of falling as a prey either to misguided fanaticism or to a fatal laxism. Their scholars are busy with politics, and economics which are always opportunist disciplines.[153]

In these letters to his fellow Jesuit scholars and leaders he emphasized the responsibility of Christians towards helping their Muslim brothers and sisters.[154] We should work with Muslims so that they do not go "away from the principles of truth which to a certain extent they share with us."[155]

Courtois urges that it was necessary and urgent that friendly contacts be established with Muslims wherever they are in an effort at gradually influencing the Muslim masses. This can be done by means of properly conceived books on problems to be solved: social questions, philosophy, education and culture. Such books spread among the educated Muslims and adapted to their mindset can have a deep influence.[156]

Our philosophical studies are often purely academic or of interest only to some research scholar or distorted against some western philosopher. Would it not be possible to write such books taking into account the Muslim mentality and studying its philosophers and theologians.[157] Courtois recognizes the importance of Christian-Muslim relations in this particular context. He writes:

> It would be grand if the Muslims could realize that they have in the Christians of to-day not merely the descendants of the Crusaders with whom their knights crossed swords, but brothers, real brothers, big brothers who are eager to tell them the way to the only true renovation, to guide them on to the One who is the source of life ... it is the aim of *Notes on Islam* indirectly to hasten the day when Muslims and Christians will make one big family under the benevolent leadership of Jesus, the Son of Mary.[158]

Courtois essentially makes three important remarks in the context of the Islamic renaissance. He emphasizes making **contacts** with Muslims. He wants the contacts to grow substantial so they could **work together** against all ideologies that alienate the human person from God and from one another. On the deeper level these contacts and working together lead Christians and Muslims to theological and philosophical **conversation**. Once again this is not a debate to prove a point but to share a message, challenge and enrich one another. In working together and speaking to one another Christians and Muslims should make out the bond of love between them and recognize its source in God.

Courtois Defends the Muslim Faith

There is an important event in the life of Courtois that establishes his respect for Muslims and reverence for their beliefs. He energetically defended Muslim faith from the attack of a fellow missionary, the Italian Passoni who belonged to the religious order of PIME [Pontifical Institute of Missions in the East]. It should be said that Courtois *walked* the *talk*.

Passoni prepared a manuscript for a book titled, *Al-Lah vs God* and sent the text to Courtois for his approval. Passoni, like some of the polemical medieval writers condemned Islam as false religion. His dreadful language greatly offended the polite ears of Courtois. Courtois writes to him: "Many of your texts are certainly offensive to Muslims– not to say to Christian – feelings ... I beg you never to publish a thing like that. Such ... can only harm deeply the apostolate among the Muslims."[159]

Refusing to approve his work, Courtois writes to Passoni:

I am afraid it will be difficult for me to approve of your work. I have not
been able to read the whole of it as yet; but what I have read so far has
failed to make an appeal to me. I would even beg of you, for the sake of
apostolate among the Muslims and so as not to endanger the relations
between Christians and Muslims, not to publish your book in any language.
Even if it comes in Italian, it will somehow reach the Muslim public and
they will have a new argument against missionaries who misrepresent
Islam and the rest. I think this is a matter of great importance. Even if
you are thoroughly convinced of the value of the arguments you bring
forth, it is not opportune to bring them out in printed form and risk a
storm against Christian missionaries and missions.[160]

Courtois explains to Passoni why he could not approve his work. He
writes:

I am reading your manuscript; but the impression which the first chapters
of *Al-Lah* leave is that you are playing on words. I do not care what
the original meaning of a word may have been, but what matters is its
content at a definite period. The Hindu concept of God is certainly not
the Christian one, yet we do use the Hindu name of God – Bhagwan –
when referring to our own God. We have only to enrich or even partially
modify its content. This what we have done even with the term Yahweh,
or Jehova which means much more in a Christian mouth than in a Jewish
one. So with Allah. Whatever may be the origin of the word, and its
original connotation its content was certainly enriched by Muhammad
to mean very much what the Christians understand by the term. It would
be interesting to find out whether the term Allah was not used in Arabic
Christian literature before the spread of Islam.[161]

What he finds unpleasant and unfair in Passoni's manuscript is that
he (Passoni) does not find it necessary to consult Islamic sources to
find out the Islamic concept of God. He tried to determine 'ab extra'
what the word al-Lah must mean for a Muslim. Courtois finds that
Passoni gravely misunderstands the etymology of the word Allah.
Courtois writes that Passoni "with malign pleasure ... [you] falsify the
Islamic teaching about Allah and Islamic ritual and social practices to

suit your thesis. This, to say the least, is intellectually unfair." He did not mince words when he wanted to say that Passoni's accusation of Islamic understanding of God 'is sheer nonsense.' Thus, Courtois finds the manuscript unfit for publication.[162]

Recognizing the weight of the matter Courtois consulted a number of Islamologists in Rome. He writes to Passoni again:

> You may be interested to know that when I was in Rome last September, Msgr. Mulla, whose authority in Islamic things cannot be doubted, spoke to me about your book; he naturally was very much dismayed. As a Muslim convert and a good Catholic theologian, he was unable to recognize himself and his earlier beliefs in your presentation of Islam and especially of the God of Islam. None of the scholars whom I met could have subscribed to your thesis: I mean Rev. Fr Abdel Jalil, a convert and a man of great erudition, Professor at the 'Institut Catholique of Paris, Mr Louis Gardet, Rev. Fr Anawati O.P. and many others. In fact I do not know of any serious Islamic scholar that would back you up. It is now commonly accepted, for very good reasons, that Allah, the God worshipped by the Muslims, is the God of Abraham and of the Prophets of the Old Testament, the God whom the Christians and the Jews of Arabia worshipped in the days of Muhammad, in other words the true God.[163]

He further writes: "with regard to the discovery you boast of, namely that Allah, the God of Muslims, has nothing to do with the true God ... is an unwarranted affirmation of yours."[164]

Courtois's conclusion is worth quoting. He writes:

> That the teaching of the Qur'ân and of the Muslims about God is defective in parts, and far from the Christian revelation, most non-Muslims will agree. But the efforts of the Muslims, from Muhammad downwards are to come to know God, the true one, and serve Him as He should, are certainly the most inspiring among all the non-Christian religions, pre-Christian Judaism excepted. Your long study fails to appeal to me, because it is based on a misconception of Islam and leads you to distort its teaching.

> Without judging your intentions ... your presentation of Islam often offends objective truth, and certainly charity and justice. Muslims,

as well as Christians, have the right to be respected, in their beliefs as well as in their persons.

Your study if published – either in India or abroad – will certainly do very great harm to the cause of the Church in Muslim lands and in India.

You should know that any attack on the Prophet Muhammad will be very strongly resented by Muslims, the world over, please do not place us, and the Church in India as well as in Muslim lands, in a false and dangerous position. Do not laugh at these words. I know full well what I am speaking about.[165]

Subscribing to the thesis of Passoni, Courtois writes: "that would be against my conscience." He reiterates his position once again in the following words.

I must, therefore, reiterate my request and beg of you not to publish your book, neither in India nor in Italy. Try to realize the tremendous responsibility you have. In your book you seem to have many illusions as to the way Muslims would welcome your book, and how it would make them turn to the church en masse. The method you have used far from generating friendship, can only offend deeply the religious feelings of the Muslims.

I am sorry I cannot be more encouraging, but in the circumstances, it is not possible. I hope you will not take it in the wrong way. You have several times asked me for my opinion; I am giving it here without gilding it.[166]

Not satisfied with his letter to Passoni, he wrote to the archbishop to stop Passoni from publishing his thesis. He writes:

Permit me to send you herewith for your information a duplicate copy of a letter I sent to Rev. Fr. M. Passoni of Trimulghery.

Fr Passoni has written a voluminous book trying to prove that Muslims are not worshippers of one God.

Already a year ago I had read part of the book in types and had written to the Father that I was unable to agree with his thesis. I begged him never to publish the book either in India or in Italy as it would most certainly be a cause of great embarrassment for missionaries in Muslim Lands and for the Catholic Church in India. Muslims, indeed, are extremely sensitive of the honor of their prophet and of Islam ... Passoni's book is

a direct and most unfair attack on Muhammad who is described as the
... and the practice of Islam. If the book is published ... it is likely to ...
do much harm to the cause of the Church in India.

I have not been able to find out whether the Father has made arrangements
for the printing and publishing of his book. I, thought, however, that I
should inform you of the above and of the intentions of the Father – even
if he has not as yet come to realize them – so as to forestall the publication
of the said book anywhere, anyhow, in any language. Perhaps the matter
could be discretely referred to the CBCI for proper preventive action. It
is easier to prevent the harm than to repair it.[167]

The communication between Courtois and Passoni reveals a number of
things. He firmly rules out polemics in the scheme of things between
Christians and Muslims. In a family conversation differences are
understood, respected and regarded. In a family, when children grow
profoundly different from others in their varied gifts and their responses
to them while rooted in the oneness of family, no one considers such
as deviance and a cause for worry. Though Muslim conception of
God is greatly different from Christian revelation, Courtois affirms,
Muslims from Muhammad onwards worship the one true God. The
deep desire to know God and to do God's will is at the heart of Islam,
is an important lesson that Courtois tries to communicate with Passoni
and the likes who still creep around in the dark shades of polemics.
For Courtois the time has come for Christians and Muslims **to** speak
to each other, not speak **at** each other. It is also time Courtois tells
his readers that both groups of believers should work together for the
dignity of human person.

Muslims have the Right to Know Christ of Christian Faith

It is said that outstanding presentations of Christ for Muslims came
from the ninth and twentieth century.[168] In the early 9th century
Theodore Abū Qurra, Habīb ibn Khidma Abū Rā'ita, and 'Ammār al-
Basrī wrote on Christology for Muslims.[169] It is said that they wrote
for both Muslims and Christians. These scholars wanted to convince
Muslims of the rationality of the Christian faith. They also wanted to

encourage Christians that their faith is rational and "it was acceptable for Christians to hold such views even in a society ruled by Muslims."[170]

Similarly, some other presentations of Christ for Muslims in the last century came from K. Cragg, H. Küng, and J. Hick. These scholars treated Muslims as equal dialogue partners and tried to relate Christian thinking about Christ to Islamic presuppositions.[171] They believed tackling differences is essential. They did a contextualized Christology amidst Muslims. Interestingly the absence of any mention of Courtois in Beaumont's *Christology in Dialogue with Muslims* is an indication of the need for better knowledge of Courtois's contribution.

Presenting to Muslims the Christian Way of Understanding Christ
Courtois emphasized that it was un-pedagogical to start with Christian dogmas. One should begin with the common ground that exists between the Christian faith and Muslim faiths. Courtois wanted that Christians should express Christianity in its simplicity and in its beauty to Muslims. He considered it as the best method. He wanted to excite the interest of Muslims about Christ without offending them. He felt that a Christian should take into account Muslim objections to the Christian faith.[172] Christian sharers of their faith should not use the life of Jesus written for the devout Christians or books on the life of Jesus written for apologetic purposes. Such books are of no use. Perhaps Gospels could be presented to Muslims. However, one should be careful because it can be easily misunderstood. We should have a book on the life of Jesus written for Muslims. In short, Courtois wanted to present Christian doctrine in a way that it could meet the Muslim mind. He wanted to present the Muslim readers in general with a concise and objective exposition of Christian beliefs.[173]

Muslims and Christians Penetrate Each Other's Hearts and Minds
For this Christians and Muslims should know each other well. Courtois felt that Muslims and Christians do not penetrate each other's hearts and minds. It they do so, they may certainly discover the same intimate

longing for inner purification, the same urge to serve God, and the immense treasure of unused love. For Courtois Christians' relationship with Muslims is a way of unlocking the treasure of love that remains locked up in their hearts. Courtois was certain that both Christians and Muslims would make spiritual progress if they penetrated each other's heart and come to know and love each other. The implication is that Christians and Muslims should recognize in each other promptings of the Spirit of God towards a more authentic form of life. If Christians and Muslims learn more about each other, they may respect and appreciate one another better and perhaps end by loving and serving their common Father in the same way like children of one large family.

Courtois believed that Christians should know the hidden treasures of Islam. He wrote that Christians look only at the edifice of Islam. They see the facade, aged and in part defaced. They cannot see the real treasure hidden inside. Islam is like the Levant (countries bordering the eastern part of the Mediterranean) surrounded by a high wall. The casual passerby is unaware of the refreshing fountains of cool water and of bouquets of scented flowers which embalm the atmosphere within the brick or mud enclosure. The wall must be pulled down, the limits transcended, 'so that the Levant may be the mount of Galilee'.

Obstacles

First and foremost, Courtois analyses the problems in presenting Christ to Muslims in India. Courtois observes two difficulties: one, psychological and the other, intellectual.[174] The psychological one is to do with the *prejudices* that a Muslim gathers concerning Christian doctrines about God. Islam teaches that Trinitarian expression of faith is a corruption of monotheistic faith but for a Christian it is not in spite of the Trinity that Christianity is a monotheistic faith, but **because** of it. Muslims consider the Trinitarian faith is a compromise on the unity of God.

God addresses God's word to the world, and the community of faith recognizes it not just as (in the Muslim case) poetry, tales of the ancients, soothsaying, or something the prophet invented, or that he learned from someone else. Rather they recognize it as God's very word, which is inseparable from God's very self. In the Christian case, when God's word is spoken in the flesh, the community of faith recognizes it not just as a prophet, or as a rabbi, or as a politico-religious reformer, but as God's very word, inseparable from God's very self. In the Christian case, further, there is the experience of Pentecost and of the power of God at work within and among those who believe in Christ. Again, this is believed not to be just a power from God or an enthusiasm aroused by God, but God's very self present and at work. These three experiences--of God beyond us, God with us in Christ, and God within and among us as Spirit—Christians take to be experiences not just of three different methods or periods of God's action, but rather God's continued presence with them and with the world.[175]

Courtois writes: "as a protection against deceit and corruption the Muslim is enjoined to avoid the company and friendship of polytheists, including Jews and Christians."[176] A Muslim grows up with such convictions and he/she finds it difficult to accept any of the central Christian doctrines.[177] Courtois articulates the intellectual difficulty in the following way: Islam in general shuns abstract reasoning and speculation. That is why, "Islam likes to treat of spiritual things as it does of material ones, in a concrete way" writes Courtois.[178] Moreover, according to him many Muslim theologians, lack competence in metaphysical analogy and scholastic philosophy (Aristotelian philosophy). He gives an example: "when treating of the infinite Essence of God, they [Muslims] find it difficult to steer clear from agnosticism on the one side and anthropomorphism on the other. In order to avoid the dangerous pitfalls of anthropomorphism they prefer to retire into respectful agnosticism. They do accept and strongly affirm God's existence and the predicate of Him a hundred names ... but they are afraid to say how those predicates are found in God."[179] He further writes: "take the Muslim attitude to the divine Sonship of Christ. For a Muslim, filiation in God is *a priori* impossible and repugnant because true sonship necessarily bespeaks carnal relations. As to spiritual sonship, like the one existing between a *murid* (disciple) and his *pir* (master, guide), it is only a metaphor."[180] He concludes that the turn of Muslim minds to concrete realities is a great obstacle to the understanding of Christian understanding of truth that are expressed in human words.

Muslims do not grasp the teachings of Christians with regard to the Spirit. For the Muslim, spirit is a subtle matter. Thus, spirit is understood as physical or semi-physical. Man, as a semi-physical being has spirit. God has none. This suppresses any similitude and analogy between God and Man. Man has to acknowledge God and obey his commandments as revealed in the Qur'ân. Man cannot aspire or become a child of God. Both are totally two different categories and cannot be united. Thus, the Christian message is unintelligible to Muslims.

Islam and Conversion[181]

Courtois wrote: "We have come to convert India to Christ. The Church would never be secure and safe if it does not rest upon key-pillars – one among them is undoubtedly the Muslim bloc."[182] These words, if stripped of their Courtois-context, are bound to bring up more misunderstanding and lead us back to the age of polemics. So, it is important to situate them within the overall concern of Courtois. Is he talking about a plan to convert Muslims so that they become Catholic Christians? It is important to clarify that these words of Courtois do not mean proselytization among Muslims. It is also not a subtle manipulation to win souls for God. His theological vision and his mission undergirded by the relational principles make it clear that in his scheme of things there is nothing that would support such a claim. He is clearly motivated to build bonds of love between Christians and Muslims.

As a Christian, he cannot but give witness to Christ. Courtois's life is marked by Christ as a baptised person. Every word and action that is done in love configures his life into the life of Christ. So his every word and action is imbued with love for and of Christ. He gave witness to his faith. He also respects Muslims and their right to give witness to their faith within the family of God. He welcomes that Muslims give witness to their faith. He writes: "[T]his should not necessarily lead to a new clash between Muslims and Christians if politics is kept out of the game. We should not fear truly religious people, for in the manifestations of a sincere faith we might recognise features of a lost brotherhood."[183] Once again, the bonds of the family are strengthened. Would he welcome Muslims if they meet Christ in their lives and wanted to follow Christ within the fold of the Catholic Church? He definitely would welcome them and even prayed for such grace.[184] His whole approach is eirenic and transparent.

Summarizing Remarks

This chapter set out to analyze the work of Courtois and to find out his significant contribution to Christian-Muslim relations in India and to highlight the type of theology he lived out in relationship with Muslims.

In conclusion it should be said that Courtois displayed a two-fold awareness in his mission. He recognized first, that the Indian Church was failing in her responsibility by neglecting the vast number of Muslims of India. He strongly felt that Christians should reach out to 'Muslims *not* as adversaries but as brothers [and sisters]'. Secondly, the Church in her relationship with Islam can share the riches of her faith and receive from the rich wisdom and spirituality of Islam in order to grow together. Thus, he realized his mission within the fold of the Church and responded within the emerging Indian Church in the wake of Independence. The concern for the Indian Church and its future in terms of her relations with Muslims engaged him all the time. It was a pity that he was left to plough a lonely furrow.

Courtois, like a well-cut diamond, distinguished himself as a fine Islamicist and devoted his life to present the true faith of Islam to the Catholic Church in India (and elsewhere) and the love of Christ for Muslims. Thus, the overarching concern of Courtois was to introduce a positive methodology in Church's relations with Muslims.

In order to achieve this, first, Courtois upturned the sense of superiority that marked the Christian approach towards Muslims and introduced a sense of equality that prevails among the children of a family with God as their Father. Thus the 'family motif' is at the heart of his work. This motif expressed his respect for the religious conviction of the other. Members of one family do not reject one another for divergent views. He envisioned a joint family in which Muslims and Christians would live as brothers and sisters with God as their Father. He highlighted the common features of their faith and emphasized that these common features bring them closer together and to the heart of Jesus. Thus Courtois's work signifies a major watershed in the attitude of the Catholic Church in India towards the adherents of Islam.

Courtois emphasized that deep knowledge of Islam and sincere love for Muslims should be the two indispensable qualities for Christians to witness to their faith among Muslims. One can articulate this metaphorically in the following way: a bird needs two wings to rise high into the horizon, similarly a Christian should have both knowledge of Islam and love for Muslims to enter into the world of Muslims in order to understand them. Knowledge and love will fructify into wisdom. Such wisdom could be found in the life and work of Courtois.

A full appreciation of Courtois's way could be achieved when it is contrasted with the situation he encountered in his times. It will not be an overstatement to say that mostly ignorance and generally polemics underlined Christian-Muslim relations in India. By underlining a deep knowledge of Islam and a sincere love for Muslims, Courtois brought about a paradigm shift in Christian approach to Islam and Muslims in India. Thus it would not be an exaggeration to call him a visionary par excellence.

Courtois was a mystic. He lived the mysticism of love for Muslims. His theological vision, that Christians and Muslims, as brothers and sisters belonging to the one large family where God is father of both groups of believers, demonstrates his mysticism powerfully. Courtois's relational principles that underpin his actions bring about coherence to this mystical thinking. His principles and work draw nourishment from his theological vision. There is an internal logic and coherence in his vision and the vision inspired principles. Thus, for Courtois, Christians and Muslims coming together and living together is an unfolding of God's plan. The most significant dimension of his work is to raise the awareness among both Christians and Muslims that in family/faith conversation they can truly give witness to one another's faith. In such faith conversations they can recognize in one another the features of their heavenly father, in other words, they recognize in each other the image of God, *imago Dei.*

Courtois's encounter with Muslims and his deep studies of the sources of Islam shaped his perception of Islam and Muslims in India. His methodology was to study both the sources: text and context. His studies of the texts led him to Muslims, and his concerns for them returned him to the texts. One cannot deny a pioneering start of a new theological method in the work of Courtois. This methodology would be used fruitfully later by Paul Jackson, the third author to be discussed in the fifth chapter of this book.

Courtois's work did achieve a fair degree of coherence as it dealt creatively with a number of key issues in Christian-Muslim relations. He did not write comprehensively on each issue. He left many issues without discussing them as has been shown in this chapter. However, the coherence is the result of his ability to hold together simultaneously the theological differences between Islam and Christianity and the Christian responsibility to build bridges through friendly conversations between the adherents of the two faiths. It can be gleaned from his approach that, Courtois approached Muslims "in the Holy Spirit, [with] genuine love [and] truthful speech". (2 Cor 6: 6-7).

In his approach to Muslims, Courtois anticipated the attitudes of Second Vatican Council in a number of ways. There is sufficient textual evidence for such positive approaches. The statement in *Lumen Gentium*

(n. 16) affirmed that Muslims together with Christians worship one God.[185] Courtois held this view without any ambiguity, as brought out in his communication with Passoni. *Ad Gentes* (n. 11) called for respect for Muslims and their faith. This is something part and parcel of Courtois's writings. For solid theological reasons Vatican II documents remain silent on Muhammad.[186] It has been shown that Courtois expresses his admiration for Muhammad without admitting his role as a prophet. As a mystic like Massignon, he gave a qualified role for Muhammad. The Vatican II document (*Nostra Aetate*) cannot afford to do.

Finally, it must be said that Courtois was a pioneer in Christian-Muslim relations precisely because of his theological vision which recognized Christians and Muslims within the family of God, and led them to conversations drawing from their rich theological and spiritual traditions. In this way they could discover in one another a brother and sister and give witness to one another's faith. In other words, Courtois emphasizes through his vision that compromising with one's own faith would not strengthen this family bond. In an atmosphere of 'us against them' Courtois promoted communion, built bridges, and opened doors for mutual understanding and cooperation.

It is obvious from the earlier discussions that Courtois was not a systematic theologian. He did not pay precise attention to a number of theological issues in relations between Christians and Muslims. It is important to point out that he did not give sufficient critical attention to the political dimension of the faith of Muslims. He also did not give attention to experiences shaped by genuinely difficult situations, especially, where Christians live as minorities. This in no way diminishes his stellar contribution. While Courtois provided a mystical frame work and a paradigm shift, Christian W. Troll and Paul Jackson, the next two Jesuits that are studied, will carry forward in the area of theology and spirituality, respectively.

Endnotes

[1] V. Courtois, review of *Christianity Explained to Muslims*, by L. Bevan Jones and *Islam and Christianity*, by L. Levonian, *Notes on Islam* 3, no. 33-34 [May-June 1949]: 60.

[2] Relational actions are three concrete ways in which Courtois registers his appreciation for the faith of Muslims. Three relational principles underpin and connect the concrete plans.

[3] V. Courtois, "Editorial," *Notes on Islam* 2, no. 23-24 [25 July-August 1948]: 77.

[4] "The little Bulletin likes to re-dedicate itself to the great task of that it has chosen as its own: mutual understanding and brotherly love between the estranged children of the same Heavenly Father, the Muslims especially and the Christians." *Notes on Islam* 5, no.1 [January 1952]: 1.

"We pray so that the present movement of reform may bring about not a greater cleavage between the Muslims and other peoples, but mutual understanding and appreciation which are the first step towards brotherly love." *Notes on Islam* 6, no.1 [March 1953]: 3.

"The fact that both Christian and Muslim apologists have said crazy things about each other in the past is no reason to perpetuate that wrong approach to mutual understanding. Let the Christian and the Muslims try to appraise each other better and they will soon discover that they have a common Father to serve and to love." *Notes on Islam* 6, no. 2 [June 1953]: 48.

"[T]hey [Christians and Muslims] were seeking not what divides, but what unites the hearts of men [and women], the consciousness that they belong to the same human family and that all have a common Father in heaven." *Notes on Islam* 7, no. 2 [June 1954]: 45.

"With new hopes and a new zest our little bulletin begins its eighth volume, eager always to foster a better understanding between Christians and Muslims. Ever since the Crusades, Christians and Muslims have always been at daggers drawn or wellnigh so, they have been thinking and at times speaking of each other as enemies, as infidels or kafirs, when they are in truth the children of the same Heavenly Father whom both mean to love and to serve." *Notes on Islam* 8, no. 1 [March 1955]: 1.

"[T]here is in Central Africa a race between Christianity and Islam as to who will win the souls of the people. But this should not necessarily lead to a new clash between Muslims and Christians if politics is kept out of the game. We should not fear truly religious people, for in the manifestations of a sincere faith we might recognise features of a lost brotherhood." *Notes on Islam* 10, no. 1 [March 1957]: 12.

"Now although they [Christians and Muslims] have been living side by side for many centuries, they yet practically ignore one another: the Christian knows hardly anything about the religion of Islam, and the Muslim knows still less about Christianity. If genuine concord is to be obtained, if Muslims and Christians are to appreciate one another, they have to meet on religious grounds, they have, in other words, to meet at the feet of God to realize that they are brothers, children of the same Heavenly Father." *Notes on Islam* 10, no. 2 [June 1957]: 51.

"The *Notes* aim at much more than 'co-existence' between Muslims and non-Muslims – co-existence is only a synonym for toleration, a negative concept; the *Notes* endeavor to bring about mutual esteem, nay brotherly love between Muslims and non-Muslims, be they Hindus, Christians or Jews. It is brotherly love, indeed, that the common Father of all men, God almighty, desires to see burning in the hearts of all the members of the big human family." *Notes on Islam* 10, no. 4 [December 1957]: 130.

[5] V. Courtois, "Editorial," *Notes on Islam* 1, no.1 [25 September 1946]: 1.

[6] The symbol of 'Father's house' was earlier used by A. Keller. She wrote: "Christendom accustomed itself ever since the time of the Crusades to look upon Islam as its most bitter foe and not as a prodigal son to be won back to the Father's house." See A. Keller, "Geisteskampf des Christentums gegen Islam bis zur zeit der Keruzzüge" [Leipsic, 1886]. In Keller's mind, Muslims are the ones' who have gone astray from truth and live in 'sinfulness'. Courtois considers both; Christians and Muslims belong to the house-hold of the heavenly Father. We could even say that in the spirit of Louis Massignon, Courtois might agree that Islam bears the responsibility of bringing Christians closer to God in Jesus Christ. Chiara Lubich (d. 2004) provided her followers a similar vision. She wrote: "We must always fix our gaze on the one Father of many children. Then look at all persons as children of our one Father. With our thoughts and the affections of our heart we must always go beyond every limit imposed by a merely human life and tend constantly, and because of an acquired habit, to universal brotherhood in one Father: God." C. Lubich, *L 'arte di amare* [Roma: Città Nuova, 2005], 29.

[7] As contestants, in the game of polemics, both Christians and Muslims lacked true charity and humility. As brothers and sisters, Courtois wanted them [Christians and Muslims] to approach the other in love and humility.

[8] "One needs to be prudent in what one says to Muslims about Islam. One should avoid negative comments about Muslims. One should avoid attacking Islam either directly or indirectly. Christians should not say that Muhammad is a false prophet. A Tamil book entitled: 'A *short History of Catholic Church*', authored by M. J. Michael (1934), greatly offended Muslims and provoked protests, reactions in Calcutta and Karachi. Missionaries should respect Islam. As missionaries we should speak sympathetically about Islam". This comes from Victor Courtois's Report to the General of Jesuits in the year of 1937. The original text is in French. A copy of the text was available with Jesuit Father A. Huart

SJ. The present writer gratefully acknowledges the services of A. Huart SJ for his help in rendering the French text into English.

⁹ A Christian missionary should express Christianity in its simplicity and in its beauty. It is the better method. Excite the interest of Muslims without offending them. One should take into account the Muslim objections to Christian faith. One should not use the life of Jesus written for the devout Christians or books on the life of Jesus written for apologetic purposes. Such books are of no use. Perhaps the Gospels could be presented to Muslims. However, one should be careful because it can be easily misunderstood. We should have a book on the life of Jesus written for Muslims." The Report of Victor Courtois to the General of Jesuits in the year of 1937.

¹⁰ V. Courtois, "Editorial," *Notes on Islam* 1, no. 1 [September 1946]: 1.

¹¹ L. Massignon acknowledged the Muslim connection with Abraham through Ismael. He considered Muslims as heirs of Abraham's blessings. See G.C. Anawati, "Excursus on Islam," in *Commentary Declaration on the relationship of the Church to non-Christian religions, Dogmatic Constitution on Divine Revelation, Decree on the Apostolate of the Laity,* ed. H. Vorgrimler, vol. 3 of the Commentary on the Documents of Vatican II [New York, London: Burns & Oates/Herder and Herder, 1969], 152. See L. Massignon, *Testimonies and Reflections: Essays of Louis Massignon,* ed. H. Mason [Notre Dame, Indiana: University of Notre Dame Press, 1989], 3-20; C.W. Troll, "Islam and Christianity interacting in the life of an outstanding Christian scholar of Islam: The Case of Louis Massignon (1883-1962)," *Islam and the Modern Age* 15, no. 3 [August 1984]: 157-166.

¹² "We should not fear truly religious people, for in the manifestations of a sincere faith we might recognise features of a lost brotherhood." Victor Courtois Papers, Calcutta Jesuit Province Archives, Calcutta.

¹³ A number of biographical details have been gleaned from a note written by E. Nicaise and P. Fallon. A. Huart, e-mail message to the author, December 29, 2011.

¹⁴ Vidyajyoti Library's collection of 'Catalogus Provinciae Belgicae' begins with the year 1930. On page 172 the name of Victor Courtois is found with the following two dates: Ortus (date of birth) – 18 September 1907 and Ingress (entrance into the Society of Jesus) 23 September 1926.

¹⁵ Interview with A. Huart, November 15, 2011.

¹⁶ Belgian Jesuits served in the Congo as missionaries.

¹⁷ Members of the Society of Jesus are known as Jesuits.

¹⁸ J.S. Das, "Remembering the 'Moulvi Saheb' Contributions of Victor Courtois to Islam – Christian Dialogue," Victor Courtois Papers, Calcutta Jesuit Province Archives, Calcutta.

¹⁹ 'Personal vocation' is precisely a Christian concept that expresses a particular way of life as a response to the call of Christ in one's life. One's "personal vocation"

is not just discovering what one really wants to do, but discovering the very essence of one's being, what is unique and unrepeatable about oneself. Doing flows from being, so this is the spirit that animates everything one does; this is the secret of unity and integration at the heart of life. See H. Alphonso SJ, *The Personal Vocation: Transformation in Depth Through the Spiritual Exercises* [Rome: Gregorian University Press, 2002].

[20] *The Encyclopedia of Philosophy*, Reprint ed., s.v. "Positivism."

[21] H. De Lubac, *The Drama of Atheistic Humanism*, trans. E.M. Riley [London: Sheed&Ward, 1949].

[22] S. Toulmin, *Cosmopolis* [Chicago: Chicago University Press,1990], xi.

[23] *New Catholic Encyclopedia*, 2nd ed., s.v. "Kierkegaard, Søren."

[24] G. Pattison, "Passionate Thinker," The Tablet, May 4, 2013, 6-7.

[25] Ibid.

[26] *New Catholic Encyclopedia*, 2nd ed., s.v. "Marcel, Gabriel."

[27] M. Buber is a famous exponent of dialogue who explored the interaction between I and You. See his *I and Thou*, trans. W. Kaufmann [Edinburgh: T&T Clark, 1970].

[28] "*Notes on Islam* would like to discover a little the unknown riches of those hearts so that in them we may recognize the features of our Heavenly Father and love them as Brothers [and sisters]. Were they better known, they would surely better loved, and where there is love, there is God." *Notes on Islam* 1, no.1 [25 September 1946]: 1.

[29] First time his name appears in the 'Catalogus Missionis Majoris Calcuttensis-Ranchensis, Provinciae Belgicae' in the year 1931.

[30] Courtois wrote four essays when he was a theology student at St Mary's. They are as follows: V. Courtois, "The Notion of Revelation in Islam" [1937], Indian Academy Record Collection, Vidyajyoti, Delhi; V. Courtois, "A Missionary Movement in Indian Islam: the Ahmadiyya Anjuman" [1938], Indian Academy Record Collection, Vidyajyoti, Delhi; V. Courtois, "Arabia in the Gahiliyya or the Cradle of Islam" [1939], Indian Academy Record Collection, Vidyajyoti, Delhi; V. Courtois, "A Conspectus of Islamic Theology" [1940], Indian Academy Record Collection, Vidyajyoti, Delhi.

[31] Interview with A. Huart, November 15, 2011.

[32] Jesuit Provincial's Office, The Calcutta News Letter [1942], no.3.

[33] This is how H. Mason introduces Louis Massignon to the readers. Massignon was a pioneer in Christian Muslim relations. What Mason tells about Massignon could very well be said about Courtois. The present writer is fascinated by the beauty and the depth of this sentence that captures the spirit of Courtois. See L. Massignon, *Testimonies and Reflections: Essays of Louis Massignon*, ed. H. Mason [Notre Dame, Indiana: University of Notre Dame Press, 1989], xv.

[34] The following Jesuits were prepared for the ministry. Courtois writes: "In 1935, Scholastic Victor Courtois was appointed to study Arabic in West Asia. He learnt to read the *Qur'ân* and the commentary and able to acquire knowledge about Muslim thinking. He was sent to theology in 1937. Besides Victor Courtois, Scholastics Jose' de Wolf and Albert Magarmaans are greatly interested in Islam and Muslims and would like to dedicate themselves for the conversion of Muslims. Jose' de Wolf could not come to India but helps the mission with prayers and alms. Magarmaans is doing philosophy. Fr Van Exem is prepared for scripture teaching in Kurseong. But he knows Arabic which he studied in Syria and Egypt. It is hoped that he will be able to render a greater service to Islamic apostolate. Another Jesuit by name Fr Pigeon went to Syria to learn Arabic and Islamic affairs, however he has not been allowed to go in that line." The Report of Victor Courtois to the General of Jesuits in the year of 1937.

The Calcutta News Letter (N.L/18) February 1944 mentions that Van Exem also studied Urdu in North India.

[35] Institutum Orientale (The Oriental Institute) was housed at 146, Bow Bazar Street, Calcutta. "On 11 July, Frs. Courtois and Van Exem moved to Baitikhana, where they were generously welcomed by Fr Rodrigues. They may now launch themselves into the work they had been preparing, and which was planned in Rome during the last general congregation". Calcutta News Letter (N.L/22), 9 August 1944.

Courtois, in the 1954 jubilee number of the Calcutta Jesuits' magazine *Our Field*, writes about the origin of the Islamic section of the Oriental Institute as follows: "It started in 1930. A chance remark of Fr P. De Letter, then a conscript of the Belgian army set the ball rolling: 'Someone should take up the apostolate among the Muslims in India.' Plans were approved by Fr Joseph Fallon, the then Superior regular of the Bengal Mission. In 1934, I was sent to the Near East to study Arabic, then in Northern India, in Lucknow, and at the Jamia Millia Islamia in Delhi to study Urdu. Meanwhile Fr C. Van Exem who was later to join the work, had taken a licentiate in Oriental languages at the University of Louvain, and was also sent to the Near East to study Arabic from the Bedouins in the desert. Then Fr Moyersoen put us up in Baitakhana where we stayed six years till after the departure of Fr Lawrence Rodriguez ..." See Y. De Steenhault, *History of the Jesuits in West Bengal, Part II: 1948-1985* [Ranchi: Catholic Press, 2002], 209.

[36] Magarmaans studied Arabic from February 1947 till the end of the year. Interview with A. Huart, November 15, 2011.

[37] Note: Van Exem who joined the Oriental Institute in 1950 was attracted towards the pastoral apostolate especially helping Mother Teresa to establish her religious congregation. Eventually he left the Oriental Institute to assist Mother Teresa. Magarmaans later left the SJ. Interview with A. Huart, November 15, 2011.

"Some of us, scholastics were dismayed at the way in which Van Exem left the 'Muslim Apostolate'. I asked Van Exem: 'how that is you the most qualified of this apostolate gave up this ministry?' Van Exem told me that he found that the direct service to the poor as the work of redemption. He further said that to help Mother Teresa was his vocation within vocation due to his spiritual experience. To my mind, Father Provincial L. Schillebeeckx should have told him that the Society of Jesus has entrusted the 'Muslim Apostolate' into his hands and should not give up." Courtois felt sad when Van Exem left this apostolate. Though he was downhearted, he was always charitable about Van Exem. Courtois never said a hurting word about Van Exem. Courtois told me: 'It is not eagles that do the ploughing, but oxen.'" Interview with C. Mignon, November 18, 2011.

The Islamic section of "the Oriental Institute of Calcutta was supposed to ... be a Christian bridgehead in the world of Islam. But for reasons I have never understood, it failed." Courtois to Rev. Fr J.B. Janssens, Praepositus Generalis Soc. Jesu, September 18, 1954, Courtois Papers, Calcutta Jesuit Province Archives, Calcutta.

Courtois writes: "... ever since the inception of the O.I. in 1944, I have worked absolutely alone; the former companions in the section, indeed, never actually helped in the work." Courtois, April 1957, Courtois Papers, Calcutta Jesuit Province Archives, Calcutta.

[38] Interview with A. Huart, November 15, 2011.

[39] V. Courtois, "A Conspectus of Islamic Theology" [1940], Indian Academy Record Collection, Vidyajyoti, Delhi.

Subject-matter for the Lectures ...

A general introduction to Islam

The *Qur'ân*

The ḥadīth

Christ in Islam and the Presentation of Christianity to the Muslims

Sūfism

Courtois, Letter to Rectors of seminaries, Victor Courtois Papers, Calcutta Jesuit Province Archives, Calcutta

[40] These '*Notes*' have received much favourable attention in India, Pakistan and Burma as well as in the Near East. They represent an admirable and painstaking labour, and their apostolic utility is great. Interview with A. Huart, November 15, 2011.

Reverend Father General J.B. Janssens writes: "I sincerely recommend your excellent review to Ours in India and elsewhere ... Its aim is truly apostolic and inspirited by Christian charity; you have expressed it yourself, dear Father, in an editorial as being the promotion of mutual understanding and brotherly love between the estranged children of the same Heavenly Father (Vol. 5, Nº 1, p.1). The Review gathers and diffuses reliable information about Islam and the Muslims thereby facilitating a just appraisal of Islamic culture, thus to break down prejudice and open the way to sympathy and regard (Vol. 5 N° 6, p.125). It does this of course in no spirit of indifferentism, but knowing that without knowledge and understanding the ardent charity which is the basis of the apostolate and the condition of its success is impossible ... unfortunately the number of subscribers is small, even smaller certainly than the quality of the magazine ... I am glad to hear you report that the number of Muslim readers is increasing ... *Notes on Islam* is but a small voice, but it has the supernatural power of God's grace behind it." Father General of the SJ to V. Courtois, September 23, 1953, Courtois Papers, Calcutta Jesuit Province Archives, Calcutta.

Archbishop of Calcutta F. Perier SJ writes: "your bulletin is much praised and appreciated not only in India, but also in several countries I passed through recently, like Iraq, Egypt, France, Italy, Belgium, etc. Allow me to congratulate you wholeheartedly on the success that has crowned your endeavors. I feel sincerely grateful to you for your initiative and the masterly way in which you have fulfilled your object, i.e. to get us all informed about the Faith, the aspirations of so many millions of Muslims, with whom we come daily into contact". See V. Courtois, *Notes on Islam* 1, no. 11 [August 1947]: 57.

[41] V. Courtois, ed., *Al-Biruni Commemoration Volume (AH 362 – AH 1362)* [Calcutta: Iran Society, 1951]; V. Courtois, ed., *Avicenna Commemoration Volume (AH 370 – AH 1370)* [Calcutta: Iran Society, 1959]. Courtois wrote the introduction and prepared an exhaustive and complete index for both volumes.

[42] Interview with A. Huart, November 15, 2011.

[43] Interview with C. Mignon, November 18, 2011.

[44] Interview with A. Huart, November 15, 2011.

[45] Interview with C. Mignon, November 18, 2011. It is a telling comment. He did not simply dole out money to his acquaintances. He helped them to stand on their feet. He respected their dignity.

[46] Interview with A. Huart, November 15, 2011.

[47] Interview with C. Mignon, November 18, 2011.

[48] "Nothing had prepared us for his sudden death. He was taken away still working, still smiling, still devoting himself till the very end. His work will have to be continued, though no one is able to take his place. God's ways are mysterious: He will not do the work without us; yet he is in need of no one. His will be done." A. Huart, e-mail message to author, January 22, 2012.

At the funeral ceremony and at the Sealdah cemetery a large number of his friends from all ranks of life; many poor people, many priests and nuns, school children, working-class men and women, a representative deputation of Muslim divines and scholars gathered to bid farewell to Courtois. Interview with A. Huart, November 15, 2011.

[49] Interview with A. Huart, November 15, 2011.

[50] Ibid.

[51] Ibid.

[52] V. Courtois, "Presentation," *Notes on Islam* 1, no.1 [September 1946]: 1.

[53] In the face of frustration Llull showed signs of aggressiveness, whereas Courtois did not allow circumstances to get better of him.

[54] Courtois, *Notes on Islam* 8, no, 2 [June 1955]: 49.

A caveat should be placed here. Llull is considered to be one of the most original thinkers of his time. In the 13th century when Majorca was recaptured by Christians, Christians, Muslims and Jews lived together. There were intellectual disputes and violent struggles between them in establishing their form of truth. At this context Llull decided to live for Christ. He reflected carefully on his desire to live for Christ. He came to a conclusion that to live for Christ is to: one, work for the conversion of Muslims; two, to write the best book as possible in defense of Christianity, and three, to found centers for training missionaries.

Llull wanted to pull down the walls of mutual suspicion that divided Islam and Christianity. He wanted to convince Muslims of the reasonableness of those mysteries that Muslims reject such as Incarnation, Redemption and the Trinity. Through mutual love and respect he wanted to bring about a rapprochement between Islam and Christianity.

Failures and frustration at times got better of him. He wanted to preach in the mosques. He contemplated a new crusade, a military one for opening the lands of Muslims for the preaching of the Gospel. However, he never had any plan for force conversion of Muslims to his faith. Whereas Llull has shown the forceful signs of frustration, Courtois has shown a great sense of maturity in his integral approach.

[55] J-M. Gaudeul, *Encounters & Clashes: Islam and Christianity in History I (A Survey)* [Rome: P.I.S.A.I, 2000], 315.

[56] Ibid., 315.

[57] C. de Foucauld, *Letters from the Desert*, trans. B. Lucas [London: Burns&Oates, 1977]; C. de Foucauld, *Spiritual Autobiography of Charles de Foucauld*, ed. J-F Six, trans. J.H. Smith [New York: P.J. Kennedy & Sons, 1964] and C. de Foucauld, *Meditations of a Hermit: The Spiritual Writings of Charles de Foucauld*, trans. C. Balfour [London: Burns Oates & Washbourne, 1930].

[58] J-M. Gaudeul, *Encounters & Clashes: Islam and Christianity in History I*, 310-313.

[59] G. Basetti-Sani, *Louis Massignon, Christian ecumenist* [Chicago, Franciscan Herald Press, 1974].

[60] R. Caspar, *A Historical Introduction to Islamic Theology* [Rome: Pontificio Istituto di Studi Arabi e d'Islamistica, 1998], 97.

[61] M.L. Fitzgerald, "From Heresy to Religion: Vatican II and Islam," in *Europe and Islam: Evaluations and Perspectives at the Dawn of the Third Millennium, Proceedings of an International Conference, Pontifical Gregorian University – Rome, 6-8 May 2000,* ed. M.S. Elsheikh [Florence: Florence University Press], 52-71.

[62] V. Courtois, "Editorial," *Notes on Islam* 5, no. 1 [January 1952]:1.

[63] V. Courtois, "Editorial," *Notes on Islam* 6, no.1 [January 1953]:3.

[64] V. Courtois, "Editorial," *Notes on Islam* 6, no. 2 [June 1953]: 48.

[65] V. Courtois, "Editorial," *Notes on Islam* 1, no. 1 [September 1946]: 1.

[66] V. Courtois, "Islam and Conversion," *The Clergy Monthly* 10 [July 1946]: 1.

[67] V. Courtois, *Notes on Islam* 10, no. 2 [June 1957]: 49.

[68] V. Courtois, "Editorial," *Notes on Islam* 7, no. 2 [June 1954]: 45.

[69] V. Courtois, "Christian Muslim Conversations," *Notes on Islam* 10, no. 2 [June 1957]: 51.

[70] V. Courtois, "Editorial," *Notes on Islam* 10, no. 4 [December 1957]: 130.

[71] V. Courtois, "Editorial," *Notes on Islam* 2, no. 23-24 [July-August 1948]: 77.

[72] Another Jesuit scholar R.A. Bütler SJ, a contemporary of Courtois writes with a similar understanding. "The figure of Christ stirs love in many a Muslim heart, and herein lies a hope for future developments." See R.A. Bütler, *Trying to Respond,* ed. M.I. Chaghatai [Lahore: Pakistan Jesuit Society, 1994], 407.

[73] V. Courtois, "The Notion of Revelation in Islam," MS [1937], Indian Academy Record Collection, Vidyajyoti Library, Delhi.

[74] Ibid.

[75] Ibid.

[76] Ibid.

[77] Ibid.

[78] Ibid.

[79] Ibid.

[80] Ibid.

[81] Ibid.

[82] Ibid.

[83] "It is a kind of communication that appears impenetrable and perhaps exotic to a third person observing it, yet remains full of meaning for the one receiving it. Given the range of its use, it seems possible, perhaps even preferable; to translate wahy simply as 'communication,' understanding it normally refers to divine communication."

[84] For a comprehensive study of the Islamic concept of revelation, See F. Rahman, *Major Themes of the Qur'ān* [Minneapolis: Bibliotheca Islamica, 1980], 80-105; S. Abul Hasan Ali Nadwi, *Islamic Concept of Prophethood* [Lucknow: Academy of Islamic Research and Publications, 1976]; Jalal al-Haqq, "Epistemology of Prophethood in Islam," *Al-Tawhid* 6, No.2 [1986-1987]:53-71; M. Arkoun, "The Notion of Revelation from Ahl al-Kitab to the Societies of the Book," *Die Welt Des Islams* 28 [1988]: 62-89; and S. Akhtar, "An Islamic Model of Revelation," *Islam & Christian-Muslim Relations* 2 [1991]: 95-105.

In Islam revelation is seen as dictation from God to a prophet of the same timeless message: *God exists, adore Him and Him alone, correct your conduct in view of the resurrection and the final judgement.* Christians understand the intervention of God in history in the following way. In Revelation God makes himself known to the extent of becoming incarnate and dying on a cross to 'show mercy to all mankind' (Rom 11, 32), instead of exacting justice for all.

[85] In Christian theology 'theosis' refers to the transformation of believers in to the likeness of God. In the words of Dionysius, the Areopagite: 'Deification is attaining of likeness to God and union with him so far as is possible. Several biblical passages (See: Matt 5:48, John 14:12, Eph 5:1, 2 Peter 1:4, Ps 82:6, John 10:34, John 14:17, Rom 8:16, Phil 3:21, Rom 8:29, 2 Cor 3:18 and 1 John 3:2) stimulates the Christian deification discourse. See N. Russell, *The Doctrine of Deification in the Greek Patristic Tradition* [Oxford: Oxford University Press, 2004].

[86] J. Dupuis, *Towards a Christian Theology of religious Pluralism* [Maryknoll: Orbis, 1977], 53-157.

[87] F. Rahman, *Major Themes of the Qur'ān* [Chicago: University of Chicago Press, 2009], 83.

[88] J. V. Edwin, "Jesuit Writings on Islam Found in the Documents of the Indian Academy," *Journal of Henry Martin Institute* 39, no. 1 [January-June 2020]: 1-23.

[89] D.J. Sahas, *John of Damascus on Islam: The "Heresy of the Ishmaelites"* [Leiden: Brill, 1972], 132-133; H. Goddard, *A History of Christian-Muslim Relations* [Edinburgh: Edinburgh University Press, 2000], 38-41.

[90] Norman Daniel, *Islam and the West: The Making of an Image* [Edinburgh: University Press, 1960], 83.

[91] R.W. Southern, *Western Views of Islam in the Middle Ages* [Cambridge, Massachusetts, and London England: Harvard University Press, 1962], 6.

[92] Ibid.

[93] Muhammad was accused of being "a Roman cardinal or cleric, frustrated in his ambition, who perverted his own converts to spite the Roman Church." See Norman Daniel, *Islam and the West: The Making of an Image*, 83.

[94] V. Courtois "Christ and Muslims," *Indian Missionary Bulletin* 1, no.2 [June 1952]: 66-75.

[95] "Christians should not say that Muhammad is a false prophet." V. Courtois, Courtois Papers, Calcutta Jesuit Province Archives, Calcutta.

[96] V. Courtois, "An Introduction to the Study of Islam: The Founder of Islam," *Notes on Islam* 2, no. 13 [September 1947]: 2.

[97] N. Daniel, *Islam and the West: The Making of an Image*, 83.

[98] V. Courtois, "An Introduction to the Study of Islam: The Founder of Islam," *Notes on Islam* 2, no. 14-15 [October-November 1947]: 10.

[99] V. Courtois, "An Introduction to the Study of Islam: The Founder of Islam," *Notes on Islam* 3 no. 27 [November 1948]: 19.

[100] Ibid.

[101] Ibid.

[102] Ibid.

[103] V. Courtois, "An Introduction to the Study of Islam: The Founder of Islam," *Notes on Islam* 1 no. 3 [November 1946]: 35.

[104] V. Courtois, "An Introduction to the Study of Islam: The Founder of Islam," *Notes on Islam* 2 no. 16 - 17 [December 1947 – January 1948]: 26.

[105] V. Courtois, "An Introduction to the Study of Islam: The Cradle of Islam," *Notes on Islam* 1 no. 3 [November 1946]: 35.

[106] Ibid., 34.

[107] V. Courtois, "An Introduction to the Study of Islam: The Founder of Islam," *Notes on Islam* 3 no. 27 [November 1948]: 20.

[108] Ibid.

[109] Ibid.

[110] V. Courtois, "An Introduction to the Study of Islam: The Founder of Islam," *Notes on Islam* 3 no. 28 [December 1948]: 27.

[111] Ibid., 28.

[112] Ibid.,29.

[113] The authenticity of this story is challenged by scholars. See W. N. Arafat, "New Light on the Story of Banu Qurayza and the Jews of Medina," *The Journal of the Royal Asiatic Society of Great Britain and Ireland* 2 [1976]: 100-107.

[114] V. Courtois, "An Introduction to the Study of Islam: The Founder of Islam," *Notes on Islam* 2 no. 22 [June 1948]: 70.

[115] Ibid.

[116] Ibid.

[117] V. Courtois, "An Introduction to the Study of Islam: The Founder of Islam," *Notes on Islam* 3 no. 28 [December 1948]: 29.

[118] J.A.C. Brown, *Muhammad: A Very Short Introduction* [Oxford: OUP, 2011], 41.

[119] For a helpful survey of some leading 20th century Christian writers on Muhammad, See D. Kerr, "'He walked in the Path of the Prophets': Toward Christian Theological Recognition of the Prophethood of Muhammad" in Y.Y. Haddad and W.Z. Haddad (eds.), *Christian-Muslim Encounters* [Gainesville: University Press of Florida, 1995], 426-446.

[120] V. Courtois, "Muhammad: In Medina – organizing the Community," *Notes on Islam* 2, no. 19-20 [March-April 1948]: 53.

[121] T. Carlyle saw Muhammad as a prophet and a literary genius. Cf. C.W. Troll, "Christian/Muslim dialog(e)", in Theology Digest 33, no. 1 [Spring, 1986]: 129-133, especially 131; T. Carlyle presented Islam as the work of a genius. See T. Carlyle, *The Hero As Prophet* [Lahore: Islamia Press, 1893].

[122] N. Daniel, *Islam and the West: The Making of an Image*, 88-98. See also T. Andrae, *Muhammad: Man and his Times*, London: George Allen & Unwin, 1956. T. Andrae argues that the religious consciousness and moral character of Muhammad should be taken seriously for any theological reflection on Muhammad and his claim to prophethood.

[123] K. Rahner, "Revelation," in *Sacramentum Mundi: An Encyclopedia of Theology*, ed. K. Rahner, C. Ernest, Kevin Smyth, vol. 5 [London: Burn & Oates, 1970], 358.

[124] P.L. Heck, *Common Ground: Islam, Christianity, and Religious Pluralism* [Washington DC: Georgetown University Press, 2009], 7-42.

[125] S.H. Nasr, *Islam: Religion, History, and Civilization* [New York: HarperOne, 2003], 3.

[126] C.W. Troll, *Catholicism and Islam* [Nairobi: Pauline Publication - Africa, 2012], 38.

[127] W.G. Young, *Patriarch, Shah and Caliph: A study of the relationships of the Church of the East with the Sassanid Empire and the early Caliphates up to 820 AD with special reference to available translated Syriac sources* [Rawalpindi, Pakistan: Christian Study Centre, 1974].

[128] "Timothy's reasons for this affirmation are that Muhammad taught his followers the doctrine of the unity of God, detaching them from idolatry and polytheism; he drove people away from bad works and brought them to good works; he also taught about God, His Word and His Spirit." See M.L. Fitzgerald, "From Heresy to Religion: Vatican II and Islam," in *Europe and Islam: Evaluations and Perspectives at the Dawn of the Third Millennium, Proceedings of an International Conference, Pontifical Gregorian University – Rome, 6-8 May 2000*, ed. M.S. Elsheikh [Florence: Florence University Press], 57.

"It is hard to interpret Timothy's words confidently. He was speaking to the ruler 'in whose hands rested his own fate and that of his community'. Was he therefore perhaps bowing to pressure and saying more than he really believed? But even if Timothy would have said exactly the same in private discussion with fellow Christians, we note carefully chosen words: not 'Muhammad was a prophet (for then Timothy could have been said to have made the Muslim confession of faith), but rather he 'walked in the path of the prophets ...' it is an interesting but elusive episode." David Marshall, email to the author, April 23, 2012.

[129] "In a lecture entitled 'Jesus and Muhammad: the Sufficiency of Prophecy', given at a 2004 seminar of Christian and Muslim scholars convened by Archbishop Rowan Williams, D. Madigan suggested that rather than approaching Muhammad asking only into what theological category they can place him, Christian might instead ask themselves what he has to say to them." David Marshall, email to the author, April 23, 2012.

[130] J.D. McAuliffe, preface, *encyclopaedia of the Qur'ân*, i.

[131] For a brief discussion on the pre-modern Christian approaches to the Qur'ân, See H. Bobzin, "'A Treasury of Heresies': Christian Polemics against the Koran" in Stefan Wild (ed.) *The Qur'ân as Text* [Leiden: Brill, 1996], 157-175.

[132] Scholars like Robert of Ketton (Circa 1150) and Juan de Segovia (d. 1458), though hostile to Islam showed great interest in having the accurate understanding of the Qur'ân. T.E. Burman in his work, *Reading the Qur'ân in Latin Christendom, 1140-1560* [Philadelphia: University of Pennsylvania Press, 1960], suggests that these Christian writers momentarily shown a certain appreciation for the text. His point is that the approach of Latin Christendom towards the Qur'ân is much more complex than a simply polemic agenda. Robert of Ketton worked with one Muhammad "who wanted to ensure ... that the translation would be done '*with the fullest fidelity, without anything left out by deceit*'". See J.M Gaudeul, *Encounters & Clashes: Islam and Christianity in History I (A Survey)*, 144.

[133] V. Courtois, "The Sacred Book of Islam," *Notes on Islam* 3, no. 26 [October, 1948]: 10.

[134] V. Courtois, "The Sacred Book of Islam," *Notes on Islam* 3, no.26 [October, 1948]: 11. T. Carlyle has commented in a similar way. According to him Muhammad in a unique and effective way has translated the spirit of the universe and its holy, unbreakable laws in to the words of the Qur'ân. See C.W. Troll, "Christian/Muslim dialog(e)", in *Theology Digest* 33, no.1 [Spring 1986], 129-133.

It is important to keep in mind that Muslims get offended when the theological dimension their understanding of the term 'prophet' or the mission of Muhammad is devalued in any fashion. The Muslim participants felt offended when a certain Prof. Gregoria Ruiz interpreted the term 'prophet' in a Marxian way. See E.G. Aguilar, "The Second International Muslim Christian Congress of Cordoba (21 – 27 March, 1977)," *Islamochristiana*, 3 [1977]: 207-228.

[135] V. Courtois, "The Sacred Book of Islam," *Notes on Islam* 3, no.26 [October, 1948], 11.

[136] Ibid.

[137] It would be profitable to note here how Christian Monk Bahira (legendary or historical) has different functions within Islamic and Christian traditions. Muslims consider that Christian Monk Bahira confirmed the prophethood of Muhammad. The function of Bahira, accordingly in the Islamic tradition, is to represent those Jewish Christian scriptures to prepare the arrival of Muhammad. The same Bahira in Christian literature was used to accuse the Qur'ân as fraud. Christian polemics against Islam considered Bahira as one who taught heretic Christianity to Muhammad. See S. H. Griffith, "Muhammad and the Monk Bahīra: Reflection on a Syriac and Arabic Text from Early Abbasid Times," *Oriens Christianus* 79 [1995]: 148. See B. Roggema, *The Legend of Monk Bahira: Eastern Christian Apologetics and Apocalyptic in Response to Islam* [Leiden: Brill 2009].

[138] V. Courtois, "The Sacred Book of Islam," *Notes on Islam* 3, no. 26 [October, 1948]: 11.

[139] Ibid.

[140] Ibid., 11-12.

[141] A. O'Mahony, "The Influence of the Life and Thought of Louis Massignon on the Catholic Church's relations with Islam," *The Downside Review* 126 no. 444 [July 2008]: 169-192.

[142] V. Courtois, "The Sacred Book of Islam," *Notes on Islam* 3, no. 26 [October, 1948]: 11.

[143] Muhammad had a deep desire to regenerate his people. Courtois seems to affirm that a desire for regeneration of his people and a yearning for scripture for his fellow men and women were in Muhammad's unconscious mind that eventually surfaced in the form of dreams. Following Tor Andrea, Courtois thinks that Muhammad's prophetic revelations are formed in advance in his thoughts as he seriously thought about the ills of society. These conscious thoughts assumed the form of dream. Courtois states that Muhammad considered the contents of his dreams as revelations.

[144] Some others interpreted the Qur'ân in such a way as if it supports the Christian truth. Paul of Antioch was an important example for this approach from the Christian side. In his "Letter to Muslim Friends" he tried to drive home the point that Islam teaches that Christianity was the true religion. He used Qur'ânic verses to achieve this end. See M.H. Siddiqui, "Muslims and Byzantine Christian Relations: Letter of Paul of Antioch and Ibn Taymiyah," *Greek Orthodox Theological Review* 31 [1986]: 33-45.

[145] Yahaya ibn 'Adi, an Arab Christian theologian responding to such objection argues from God's generosity that unites creation and incarnation. See C.W. Troll, "Who is Jesus Christ in a world of many faiths?" *Report of the Swanwick Christology Conference, September 1999*, 16-35.

[146] E. Farahian and C. van Nispen, "Approaches biblico-theologiques de l' Islam," in P-H. Kolvenbach et al. (eds), *Understanding and Discussion: Approaches to Muslim-*

Christian Dialogue [Rome: Pontificia Universita Gregoriana, 1998], 31-57. Also see C.W. Troll, Catholicism *and Islam* [Nairobi: Pauline Publication - Africa, 2012], 41-42.

[147] Though Courtois uses the word renaissance, he must be using that in the sense of revival/renewal that is expressed in two major set of movements: salafiah and reform movements. A short note is in order here.

iḥyā' (revival) and *tajdīd* (renewal) are two important Arabic words in the context of resurgence of Islam that is reflected in the modern Islamic movements. Both *iḥyā'* and *tajdīd* indicate that a designated purifier would renew the faith and practice of Muslims. Muslim thinkers in the 18th and 19th centuries detected stagnation among Islamic societies. They reflected on ways to bring Muslim communities on par with Europe and its progress. They felt that Islam is not the cause of the problem, but the way Muslims approach Islam has brought about the downfall of Muslim societies. Muslims, they felt, should approach religion in a new way. Two major movements came about to meet the challenge. One is *salafiyah* movement and the other is reformist movement.

The Salafists were concerned about the very survival of Islam. They felt the danger was lurking in *bid'ah* (innovations that are religiously impermissible). They aimed at cleansing religious practices that were alien to the Islamic way of life. They emphasised the unity of God. Consequently they opposed the sufi religious practices which they thought compromise faith in one God. They recommended 'return to the simplicity of early Islam'.

The reformers wanted to rejuvenate Islamic thought and practice among Muslims. They aimed at the role of reason in people's lives. They clearly recognised that the imitation of thoughts and practices of early Muslims would not help this rejuvenation, thus they rejected *taqlid*. They emphasised the importance of *ijtihād*.

[148] V. Courtois, "Editorial," *Notes on Islam* 6, no. 1 [March, 1953]: 2.

[149] Ibid.

[150] V. Courtois, "Editorial," *Notes on Islam* 4, no. 2 [March, 1951]:17.

[151] V. Courtois, "Editorial," *Notes on Islam* 5, no. 5 [September, 1952]: 101. Such comments did not give sufficient attention to the impact of colonialism on Muslim life. Troll writes: "Such comments, presumably, did not hurt as they came from a source sympathetic to Muslims, beyond any doubt. May we add that here and in general the editor may not have given sufficient thought to the humiliation and suffering inflicted upon the Muslim world by colonial rule and to the destruction under it of much of the means and institutions that had formed the basis of the living intellectual tradition of the Islamic world." See C.W. Troll "A Pioneer in Christian-Muslim Relations: Victor Courtois, S.J. (1907-1960)," *Vidyajyoti Journal of Theological Reflection* 44, no. 12 [December, 1980]: 525.

[152] V. Courtois, "Editorial," *Notes on Islam* 5, no. 5 [September, 1952]: 104.

[153] Letter to Thomas O' Shaughnessy, [dated, 24 – 10 -1954], Victor Courtois Papers, Calcutta Jesuit Province Archives, Calcutta.

In his letter to Fr R. J. McCarthy on 24 November 1954 he writes: "I think, indeed, that the time has come for a more intimate and a more 'massive' approach of Islam. I do not mean a Crusade which is bellicose, but a friendly approach. The Muslim world is manifestly passing through a crisis and is in the throes (spasm of feeling, mental agony and anguish) of a renaissance trying to adapt itself to recently won independence. Under foreign rule, Muslims had no real education, social, political problem; those were solved by the rulers. But now they have to give an Islamic solution to all the many problems which the administration of a free country brings forth. And they are at a loss with the danger of falling a prey either to misguided fanaticism or to a fatal laxism. Their scholars are busy with politics, and economics which are always opportunist disciplines." Victor Courtois Papers, Calcutta Jesuit Province Archives, Calcutta.

In his letter to Fr Devenny on 31 December 1954 he writes: "In India and Pakistan, Muslims are being busy mainly with politics, economics, literature and a little history: deep thinking there is very little. Philosophy, theology and mathematics are hardly studied. Here we have a fine opportunity for action and useful contacts." Victor Courtois Papers, Calcutta Jesuit Province Archives, Calcutta.

In a letter to the General of the Society of Jesus Father J.B. Janssens SJ on 18-09-54,

Courtois writes: "Now if ever is our chance of bringing about a rapprochement [establishment or resumption of harmonious relations between two groups] between Islam and Christianity by joining forces against the invading materialism of communism and by helping the Muslim intelligentsia who work at the 'renaissance' of Islam and to keep clear from dangerous rationalism and modernism. At this juncture tact and sympathy may do very much to bring the Muslim thinking world closer to the eternal principles of Truth and closer also to the Christian world which is no longer considered as an enemy.

For centuries almost all the Muslim nations of the world were under foreign domination of some sort: political, economic, social, educational problems were left to the care of the foreign rulers. But now almost all the Muslim groups of the world are either independent or crave so to be; now they themselves have to solve their own problems concerning education, social relations, economics, politics, research ... Engrossed that they are in ensuring economic stability, they have no time to think and are becoming a prey to chap literature, sentimental system of 'thought'. In a recent congress of philosophers held at Lahore, West Pakistan, the few philosophers that gathered there complained of the dismal state of philosophical thought and philosophical pursuit in the Muslim world, especially in Pakistan.

Islam has now no philosophy, its theology has remained static for centuries, its study of the Qur'ân and the ḥadīth is unscientific, it has no real social doctrine, no political doctrine to fit the modern world, not even a system of education adapted to the modern demands ... The few scholars that are, are busy mainly with literary research and criticism, with history of a sort ... There is little real deep thinking. To quote Dr Khalifa Abdul Hakim, President of the Philosophical Conference of Lahore: 'There is no denying the fact that partition brought in its wake many human problems, one of them being a material struggle for existence'. This at times became so intense that all the ultimate and intrinsic values were apt to be neglected.

With awakening that has come about throughout the Muslim world, the philosophers have new role to play in infusing a new life into now stagnant intellectual and spiritual heritage left by philosophers, poets and mystics. Philosophy is a dynamic discipline relentless in destroying error and falsehood.

Is this then not a golden opportunity for us to step in and through friendly contact, by the word or by the pen, gradually influence the revival in the right direction? Unhealthy books on materialism and ultra-rationalism influence the readers because such books are easily available and they are read. I am convinced that if our books were equally easily available, they too would make an appeal to the better type of people; but where is that literature that Muslim can understand? Victor Courtois Papers, Calcutta Jesuit Province Archives, Calcutta.

A report on the needs of the Islamic Section of the Oriental Institute 25 November 1954

There is a wrong opinion among many that Islam is slowly dying out; it is not: it is undergoing a renaissance with the next 50 years the Muslim countries of the world will have formed, continuous block dividing the rest of the world in two; they will be strongly settled on the very birth place of Christianity.

When Muslims were living under foreign rule, they had few living-problems to solve; those were the responsibility for the rulers. But now that the Muslim countries of the world have won their independence or will win it sooner or later, they are faced with those problems which every free nation of the world has to face: educational, economic, political, social problems which have to be solved according to one's leading principles, in our case, according to Islamic principles. But the urgency of problems of organization and mere administration are so engrossing that Muslim leaders have no time to seek for a proper solution to the about mentioned problems; thinkers are busy devising means of living; they are at the stage of 'primum vivere, deinde philosophari', with the result that they are at the mercy of any modernistic, or materialistic movement of thought which is presented to them. In the process of renaissance, the world of Islam is getting open to outside influences. Victor Courtois Papers, Calcutta Jesuit Province Archives, Calcutta.

[154] In an essay titled "The Need for Islamic Studies" the Dutch Jesuit J. J. Houben, a former Professor of Islamology at Nijmegen (Holland) and Beirut (Lebanon) makes similar statement: "Not only the missionaries working in Muslim countries but every Catholic throughout the world must realize that the fate of hundreds of millions of Muslims hangs in the balance and that in order to help them to solve the difficulties along religious lines, a deeper knowledge of their mentality and of Islam in general as a religion and as a polity is certainly one of the most pressing needs for the Catholics of our times."

[155] A report on the needs of the Islamic Section of the Oriental Institute 25 November 1954. Victor Courtois Papers, Calcutta Province Archives, Calcutta.

[156] Ibid.

[157] A letter to the General of the Society of Jesus Father J.B. Janssens SJ on 18-09-54. Victor Courtois Papers, Calcutta Province Archives, Calcutta.

[158] V. Courtois, "Editorial," *Notes on Islam* 11, no. 23-24 [July-August 1948]:77.

[159] An undated letter of Courtois to Passoni, Victor Courtois Papers, Calcutta Jesuit Province Archives, Calcutta.

[160] Ibid.

[161] "There was nothing before Islam that might qualify as Christian Arabic literature. It only begins only after the Arab conquests of the areas where Christians live and Christians eventually start writing in Arabic. Before that the main Christian language there is Syriac, where the word for God is *Alaha*. Arthur Jeffery, *The Foreign Vocabulary of the Koran* observes that it is used long before Islam -- found a lot in North Arabic inscriptions. And, of course, Muhammad's father is `Abdullah (or so they say) so it is certainly pre-Islamic." D. Madigan, e-mail message to the author, May 19, 2013.

Certain early Muslim authorities held that the word was of Syriac or Hebrew origin. However, majority of scholars claimed that it was pure Arabic. Western scholars are unanimous to confirm that the source of this word should be found in one of the old religions. The word came into use in Arabian heathenism long before Muhammad's time. See A. Jerrery, *The Foreign vocabulary of the Koran*, [Lahore: Al-Biruni, 1977], 66.

[162] ... I cannot hide serious apprehensions as to the result it would achieve should it come in print. Before proceeding with the publication of the book, please weigh carefully the damage that it may cause to our missions. Any unfriendly attack on Islam – and your presentation is certainly not friendly is sure to provoke drastic reactions and unpleasant ones ... do not let off an atomic bomb ... it may do more harm than good ... forgive me to write thus and so frankly, but I feel I must."

[163] V. Courtois's letter to Passoni [dated: 17.04.1957]. Victor Courtois Papers, Calcutta Jesuit Province Archives, Calcutta.

[164] Letter to Passoni. An undated letter of Courtois to Passoni. Victor Courtois Papers, Calcutta Jesuit Province Archives, Calcutta.

[165] Ibid.

[166] Ibid.

[167] V. Courtois's letter to archbishop. Victor Courtois Papers, Calcutta Jesuit Province Archives, Calcutta.

[168] I.M. Beaumont, *Christology in Dialogue with Muslims*, Regnum Studies in Mission [Oxford: Regnum Books International, 2011], xxii.

[169] S. Rissanen, *Theological Encounter of Oriental Christians with Islam during Early Abbasid Rule* [Åbo: Åbo Akademi University Press, 1993].

[170] I.M. Beaumont, *Christology in Dialogue with Muslims*, xxii.

[171] Over the past fifty years a number of books have been written on Jesus as depicted in the Quran. See D. Wismer, *The Islamic Jesus: An Anotated Bibliography of Sources in English and French* [New York: Garland Publication, 2011], G. Parrinder, *Jesus in the* Qur'ân [London: Faber and Faber, 1965], E. Hahn, *Jesus in Islam* [Nagercoil, T.N.: IELC Board for Literature, 1975].

[172] M.M. Ayoub, "Towards an Islamic Christology: (I) An image of Jesus in early Shia'I Mulsim literature," *Muslim World* 66 [1976]: 163-188) and "II: The death of Jesus, reality or delusion: A Study of the death of Jesus in Tafsir literature," *Muslim World* 70 [1980]: 91-121. On the spiritual Jesus as perceieved in Islam, see J. Nurbaksh, *Jesus in the Eyes of the Sufis* [London: Khaniqahi Nimatullah Publications, 1983].

[173] V. Courtois, *The Christian Doctrine: An Exposition*, [Calcutta: Oriental Institute, 1954]. V. Courtois, *The Christian Doctrine: An Exposition – Abridged Edition* [Calcutta: Oriental Institute, 1954].

[174] S.H. Nasr identifies another contextual reason for the re-emergence of polemics over Christ on the Muslim side in the following way: "Centuries of confrontation with the Christian West followed by a period of intense missionary activity, which still continues in certain regions of the Islamic world in new form, have created among some contemporary Muslims an aversion not only to Christianity but, in the case of some of the modernised classes, even to the Islamic conception of Christ and Mary." S.H. Nasr, "Jesus Through the Eyes of Islam," in *Islamic Life and Thought* [London: Allen&Unwin, 1981], 209-211.

[175] "By the logic of the Qur'ân, the names and attributes of God are not human constructs for praising him or describing him; they are God's own revelation of himself using humanly understandable categories – the human mode of God's self-disclosure … Because he is 'the One with … integrity" (Q 59:22) then these must be a *true* disclosure of his *true* self. Having so many names or attributes

does no violence to the unity of God for they are not revelations of different parts of Him but of aspects of his being and his ways with human beings. Christians would want to affirm something similar about the names we give to God; Father, Son and Spirit – God *for* us, *with* us and *within* us. There is no part of God which is Father and another part which is Son or Logos and a third part which is Spirit. No; there is One God who has revealed to us that He is *for* us, with us and *within* us". See D. Madigan, "Are there some ways of relating Christian Trinitarian faith to the Quran's presentation of God?" *Salaam* 6, no. 2 [1985].

[176] V. Courtois "Christ and Muslims," *Indian Missionary Bulletin* 1, no.2 [June 1952]: 66-75.

[177] There is an ambiguity in the Muslim understanding of Christ. Oddbjørn Leirvik identifies two problems. He writes: "On the Muslim side there was from the beginning an ambiguity in the approaches to Christ. One tendency was to enrich the rather scanty references to Christ in the Qur'ân by drawing on the Christian legend and Gospel material, culminating in the centrality of Jesus in mature Ṣūfism. The other tendency was to refute the specific Christian teachings about Christ, and argue against the reliability of the Christian sources, culminating in the medieval polemic of Ibn Hazm. Both tendencies may be said to have their origin in the Qur'ân, whose non-polemical reference of the Meccan period to a more polemical confrontation in the Medinan context. See O. Leirvik, *Images of Jesus Christ in Islam* [Uppsala: Swedish Institute of Missionary Research, 1999], 8.

[178] V. Courtois "Christ and Muslims," *Indian Missionary Bulletin* 1, no.2 [June 1952]: 67.

[179] Ibid., 67-68.

[180] Ibid., 68.

[181] V. Courtois "Islam and Conversion," *The Clergy Monthly* 10, no.1 [July 1946]: 1-14.

[182] Ibid., 1.

[183] V. Courtois, "Editorial," *Notes on Islam* 10, no.1 [March, 1957]: 12.

[184] He cared for individual converts from Islam to the Catholic faith. He taught catechism only after they received the gift of faith. It is the opinion of the present writer that Courtois' care for the converts to Catholic faith has a broader consequence. He respected the freedom of individuals in choosing a religion of their choice according to their conscience. It should be said Courtois anticipated the UN human rights convention (article 18) in his approach.

[185] Fitzgerald alerts that many Christians and Muslims may have difficulty with this statement. Some Christians may find it difficult to accept this affirmation since the notion of Trinity is rejected by Muslims. Some Muslims would also find it difficult to affirm this because the Qur'ân contains a reference to the Trinity as God, Jesus

and Mary (Q 5. 116). See M.L. Fitzgerald, "From Heresy to Religion: Vatican II and Islam," in *Europe and Islam: Evaluations and Perspectives at the Dawn of the Third Millennium, Proceedings of an International Conference, Pontifical Gregorian University – Rome, 6-8 May 2000*, ed. M.S. Elsheikh [Florence: Florence University Press], 62-63.

[186] A. Siddiqui, *Christian-Muslim Dialogue in the Twentieth Century* [London: Macmillan, 1997], 35.

Chapter 4

Christian W. Troll:
Informed by the Past, Free for the Present

The only future for the pluralistic, globally networked societies of the world is a shared future. If we wish to avoid the 'clash of civilizations' there is no alternative, whether in the Western world or elsewhere, to a dialogue between religions and cultures that is honest, critical, and open. If the goal is coexistence in diversity, then all religious communities need to ask themselves how their inherited faith, moral principles, and religious laws should be understood and applied in the context of culturally and religiously pluralistic societies.[1]

Introduction

Christian W. Troll's profound understanding of Muslims and Islam as a religion and polity and his insightful knowledge of the history of Christian-Muslim contacts have shaped his theological thinking on relations between these two sets of believers.

This chapter will show that the two building blocks: 'discernment', and 'witness to faith', characterize his commitment to 'bridge-building' between Christians and Muslims. These two building-blocks, then, could be called components for establishing and nurturing deep relationships with Muslims.

These are not two different or separate components. They are two inter-dependent dimensions of his lifelong work in the field of Christian-

Muslim dialogue. Metaphorically, it could be said these two 'dimensions' have become the 'spiritual and intellectual glue' that binds his work. Ultimately, his faith, nourished by the Gospel and the teachings of the Catholic Church, underpin his commitment to dialogical engagement between Christians and Muslims *glocally* (both globally and locally).

The first component; **discernment** marks his method of approach towards Muslims.[2] This component needs a brief explanation here. Discernment is a spiritual discipline. It demands total openness to God and complete inner freedom to do the will of God in one's life. Such openness assists the seeker to recognize movements within his/her heart towards God or away from God. The Spirit of God strengthens and directs the one who seeks to respond to God totally. The heart and soul of a person remain in desolation when the person moves away from God. As he applies this method, *mutatis mutandis*, to his contacts with Muslims and his studies on Islam and its culture, Troll recognizes the marks of the Spirit of God in Islam through the spiritual lives of many credible Muslims whom he meets and relates with. Without doubt the life of Muslims is shaped by the Qur'ân. This method helps him as a Christian both to appreciate the presence of God in different elements of Muslim faith and culture, and to be critical of the absence of the Spirit of God in several other features of Muslim religious thinking, especially in its political dimension that disregards religious freedom, plurality and diversity. This method also alerts him to the absence of the Spirit of God in the prejudices that Christians continue to nurture against Muslims. Thus, this method creates the space for an open and honest dialogue with Muslims.

The second element, '**witness to faith**', highlights Troll's faith commitment as a Catholic theologian in dialogue with Muslims. He thus seeks knowledge of Islam not as a secular researcher, but as one *missioned* or *sent by the Church* for establishing deep friendship with Muslims by affirming the common spaces and differences between Christian and Muslim faiths.

In dialogue, he seeks to give witness to his Christian faith. At the same time, in 'being sent among Muslims' he displays openness to remain in a respectful disposition to the witness of a Muslim to his/her faith. This bipolar openness mutually challenges and enriches both Muslims and Christians and offers hope for deep mutual understanding.

For Troll, dialogue means fundamentally thinking and talking together; discovering, recognizing, and listening to the Spirit of God in one another's point of view. He neither rejects nor underestimates others' approach to truth. It is something like, 'I want to talk with you who think differently from me, so I can learn from you.'[3] Learning is mutual here. Both parties learn something from each other and change accordingly. Such learning calls for personal transformation.[4] This process leads both groups of believers to respect diversity in the pluralistic world and to build up communities of peace. In other words, the credible lives of Muslims and their faith challenge and transform Troll's perceptions.

This chapter will further argue that at the heart of Troll's theology lies his firm belief that Christians and Muslims can live together in peace and contribute to justice inspired harmony *only if* they both remain faithful to their moral obligation to give reasonable account of their faith to others. In other words, Christians and Muslims should remain faithful to 'mission' and *'da'wa'* respectively. It would be helpful to remember that Courtois too had a similar attitude when he wrote that both Christians and Muslims should not fear the mission dimension of one another's life "... for in the manifestations of a sincere faith we might recognize features of a lost brotherhood."[5]

In dialogue, one neither compromises nor disguises his/her faith. In witnessing to one's faith one neither degrades the faith of the other nor lures the other to one's faith. Using a metaphor, one could say like a compass (a hinged V-shaped instrument that one uses for drawing circles) one foot is established in one's faith ... the other foot reaches out to the people of other religions. In short, the *freedom of conscience* of others is respected in genuine dialogue. Partners in dialogue are called to respect the *freedom of conscience* that underpins the *religious freedom* of every individual. This *religious freedom* is founded on their *dignity as human persons*. Since both Christianity and Islam are missionary religions, Troll affirms that any effort for mutual relationship between Muslims and Christians that does not give sufficient attention to the 'witness-dimension' of their faiths is bound to be either superficial or ephemeral. It will be like a castle built on sand and its durability is short-lived. Also any effort to force one's religious conviction on the other is an insult and affront to the dignity of the other. In short, it is abuse of freedom.

Troll's approach is significant precisely because he locates his case for fruitful relations with Muslims unambiguously within the context of one growing in awareness of human rights as ratified in the Universal Declaration of Human Rights by the United Nations (1948)[6], and respect for the dignity of persons embodied in the teachings of the Catholic Church in the Vatican Council II documents, especially in *Dignitatis Humanae* (7 December 1965)[7]. This approach takes very seriously both the development in the human history and the 'updating' within the Catholic Church. The significance lies specifically on the ability to bring a religious principle (mission) and a secular principle (human rights) in cohesion with one another.

Following the teachings of Paul VI, as expressed in his encyclical *Ecclesiam Suam*, Troll inculcated reciprocal communication, mutual friendship, and respect, as well as a joint effort for the sake of shared goals, all in the service of a common search for the fuller realization of the truth as important qualities for a relationship with Muslims. This unambiguous clarity brings coherence to his efforts to dialogue with Muslims.

Consequently, this chapter focuses on the motivating forces that have contributed to shape Troll's approach towards Muslims. The chapter has two sections. The first section presents Troll's *commitment to pursue a deeper understanding of Muslims and Islam*. The second section explores his engagement with Muslims and Islamic movements especially in South Asia and his theological engagement with Muslims everywhere.

In this chapter the word **mission** is used. One finds that business, industry, and large organizations develop a mission statement that focuses on the key result they want to achieve. In India many people often misunderstand 'mission' as proselytization.[8] It should be clearly understood at the outset that 'mission' is used to indicate that the person lives a mission or purpose-driven life to 'give witness' to the love of Christ and His mission to build a new world on earth, which He called kingdom of God and to share responsibility with others in order to live peacefully in the 'shared ' future.

Mission at the Heart of Troll's Early Upbringing

Troll heard and felt a *calling* to serve God in a special way even before he became a teenager.[9] He *discerned* that this experience was an invitation to become a missionary priest. He read books on mission and missionaries with keen interest. The geographical maps that were preserved at his family library carried his imagination to far-off continents and sustained his *mission* motivation. When he turned thirteen, he revealed his desire to become a missionary priest to his parents.[10]

Troll was sent first to a school administrated by the Missionaries of the Divine Word and then to one by the Redemptorists. In both schools, he had countless opportunities to learn about far-off countries from missionaries who were returning to Europe for holidays. With much interest he listened to them about missions in Asia and Africa. Their slides and other visual aids grabbed his attention. He was fascinated about the people and country the missionaries had adopted. His interest in missions persisted throughout school years. In both schools the regular practice of liturgical and personal prayer as well as meditation on Holy Scripture played a central role in shaping the personality of this future missionary. After completing his *Abitur* (Secondary School Leaving Certificate) he asked to be admitted as a seminarian in the Archdiocese of Cologne.[11]

Motivated for Mission in the University

As a seminarian in the university, he took the initiative of founding a study group consisting of students from overseas who were studying in various faculties of the university. Many of them were Muslims, Hindus, or Buddhists. The group met every week during the semester in a private home. One of them gave a talk about a topic of interest usually related to her or his home country, culture or religion. These meetings made a lasting impression on him and kept alive his mission desires.[12]

Entering into the World of Muslims and Islam

Troll's commitment to pursue deeper understanding of Muslims and Islam and of their culture and religion developed gradually during the years 1957 to 1961. In 1959 he worked under the guidance of the Church historian Hubert Jedin while writing a seminar paper, "The China Missions in the Middle Ages".[13] One day, by chance, Troll came across the essay "The Need for Islamic Studies" by a Dutch Jesuit J. J. Houben, then Professor of Islamology at Nijmegen and Beirut. The following statement, made in the context of discussing the importance of a renewal of religious thought in contemporary Islam, impressed him:

> Not only the missionaries working in Muslim countries but every Catholic throughout the world must realize that the fate of hundreds of millions of Muslims hangs in the balance, and that in order to help them to solve the difficulties along religious lines, a deeper knowledge of their mentality and of Islam in general, as a religion and as a polity, is certainly one of the most pressing needs for the Catholics of our times.[14]

Houben stressed that the problem of Islam is not simply political but deeply religious. The crisis has its roots in the way Islam is linked to its political expressions. In other words, the critical question that should be asked: is the concept of an Islamic State part and parcel of Islam? Houben proposes that Catholic intellectuals should offer to help Muslims to break the hold that the traditional, orthodox theological schools had on Islam. His approach touched upon the importance of the intellectual dimension of the Christian approach to Islam and

Muslims. This approach appears to have made a lasting impression on the mind of Troll.

Soon after reading Houben's essay, Troll managed to meet Houben in person. Houben stressed the need for proper study of Arabic and of Islam for Troll. Houben also entrusted Troll with a letter addressed to archbishop Josef Cardinal Frings of Cologne, in which he proposed that Troll should be allowed special studies in Arabic and Islam. Troll delivered that letter to the cardinal during his first official meeting with him in June 1961 on the occasion of the completion of his university studies in preparation for the priesthood. The cardinal immediately expressed his agreement with Houben's proposal, and sent him to the Centre Religieux d'Études Arabes (CREA), the language school attached to the Université Saint Joseph, Beirut for Arabic studies.[15]

Missioned to Study Arabic and Islamic Culture

With regard to Troll's quest to understand Muslims and Islam, these two years of intensive study of Arabic in CREA (1961–63) were the most formative period in his life. This intensive and demanding effort to enter into the Arabic world together with the first encounter with central foundational texts of Islam in the Arabic original left a lasting impression on him and shaped his later encounter with Muslims, their culture and their faith. In the summer of 1962, Troll felt a desire to join the Society of Jesus. He approached the Jesuit provincial of the Near East Province of the Society of Jesus who advised Troll to finish the course in Arabic for which the Archbishop of Cologne had sent him to Lebanon. Troll followed his advice and completed the Arabic studies with the *Diplôme de Langue Arabe* of the Université St Joseph, Beirut.[16]

Discernment, the Key to His Method for Approaching Muslims

Troll returned from Lebanon to Germany and entered the Jesuit novitiate in Westphalia. Like every Jesuit novice he made a *thirty days' spiritual retreat*. This retreat acquainted him with the method of discernment in spiritual matters. This was an important stage in his life as a trainee Jesuit and his future scholarly studies on Islam. As mentioned in the introduction to this chapter, discernment is a particular way of reflecting on what is happening to one and drawing conclusions for future action. The primary question that is asked in a process of discernment is: "What does God want of me in this concrete situation? And, what should one do in circumstances that are not clear and where reflection and conclusions do not result in a clear answer?"[17] Troll learnt that the method of such discernment included total openness ('indifference') in the face of God and of all reality. This openness gradually led him to a real encounter with the Jesus of the Gospels, which enabled him to recognize in his heart different movements both positive and negative. After the two years of spiritual training, he had two years of study for the Licentiate in Philosophy in Bavaria. In addition, the study of philosophy made him convinced of the need to understand religious traditions.

Encountering South Asian Islam

During the first half of 1966, Troll travelled to Pakistan in order to engage in the study of Muslim culture. Then he proceeded to the School of Oriental and African Studies (SOAS) in London and began with a BA (honors) course in Urdu Language and Literature. The honors course included the study of classical Persian and of medieval and modern Indian history.[18]

The decade in London from 1966–76 was a period of intensive study and encounter with Muslims, most of them from South Asia. The first two years were dedicated almost entirely to acquiring basic language skills in Urdu and Persian. The Urdu course was designed to enable the student, practically from the beginning, to converse with Urdu speakers. He spent many weekends in Urdu-speaking homes practising the language, talking about the South Asian Muslim tradition, reading Urdu poetry or listening to its recitation, and watching Urdu videos and films. In this way he entered into the world of Indian and Pakistani Muslims. As far as Persian is concerned Troll remained on the level of reading texts of classical works of historiography and literature and of Sufism in the original. During those years he also had the opportunity of spending several extended summer holidays reading selected classical Sufi texts in Arabic and Persian under the personal guidance of the outstanding scholar of classical Sufism, Richard Gramlich, S.J.[19]

The British academic system allowed him to spend a whole year of his course travelling through Iran, Afghanistan and South Asia, visiting Muslim scholars and institutions, and finally taking tutorials with Urdu scholars in Lahore. During his years of doctoral research under the guidance of the historian of South Asia, Dr Peter Hardy, he again traveled to Pakistan and India, meeting scholars knowledgeable in the field of his research and frequenting the relevant libraries in Aligarh, Rampur, and Patna. Troll's travel, and his meeting people and seeking knowledge distinguished him as a serious Christian scholar in the field of Islam and Christian-Muslim relations.[20]

The Catholic Inspiration for Mission among Muslims: Vatican II and the Post-Conciliar Documents

Spiritually and theologically the process of the Second Vatican Council (1962–65) and its final documents turned out to be crucial for the whole of Troll's later engagement with Muslims and Islam. At the time of the announcement of the Council by Pope John XXIII, on January 25, 1959, Troll was still pursuing his theological studies at Bonn University. Hubert Jedin, the well-known historian of the Council of Trent and later a key advisor to Pope John XXIII in organizing Vatican II, was his main tutor at that time. Immediately after the announcement of the council, he "prophetically" impressed upon his students the extraordinary impact this council would make on the future life of the Church. Two other *periti* (experts) of the council, Joseph Ratzinger (later pope Benedict XVI) at Bonn and Hans Küng at Tübingen, brought *aggiornamento* (*the spirit of updating*) of the Council close to Troll's attention. This made him ask analogous questions regarding the development of contemporary Islam. These parallel and corresponding questions paved the way for him to develop clarity and deeper understanding of Islam and Muslims. This is one of the ways in which Troll specifically applied discernment in the context of the Catholic Church's *aggiornamento, mutatis mutandis* development of religious thinking in Islam.[21] Jesuit Father Houben's idea that Islam is in crisis and Catholic intellectuals have the responsibility to help Muslims to get out of their religio-political mess firmly underpins his approach to Islam and Muslims.

The Vatican Council II documents and post-Conciliar texts further guided him to focus on his work. It is important to highlight the teachings of the documents that inspired him to persevere in his vocation as a Catholic theologian among Muslims.

The Vatican Council II brought a new way of relating with other religions, especially Islam.[22] The paragraph no. 16 of the Dogmatic Constitution on the Church (*Lumen Gentium*) reads:

> But the plan of salvation also embraces those who acknowledge the Creator, and among these the Muslims are first; they profess to hold the faith of Abraham and along with us they worship the one merciful God who will judge humanity on the last day.[23]

Troll wrote that this document, besides placing Islam first among the non-Biblical religions, boldly affirmed that Muslims adore the same God.[24] This inspired him to confidently enter into the mission of dialogue between Christians and Muslims.[25]

The second document the Declaration on the Relationship of the Church to Non-Christian Religions (*Nostra Aetate*), especially its paragraph three inspired him further. It is important to quote the text here.

> The Church also looks upon Muslims with respect. They worship the one God living and subsistent, merciful and almighty, creator of heaven and earth, who has spoken to humanity and to whose decrees, even the hidden ones, they seek to submit themselves whole-heartedly, just as Abraham, to whom the Islamic faith readily related itself, submitted to God. They venerate Jesus as a prophet, even though they do not acknowledge him as God, and they honor his virgin mother Mary and even sometimes devoutly call upon her. Furthermore they await the day of judgment when God will requite all people brought back to life. Hence

they have regard for the moral life, and worship God especially in prayer, almsgiving and fasting.

Although considerable dissensions and enmities between Christians and Muslims may have arisen in the course of the centuries, this synod urges all parties that, forgetting past things, they train themselves towards sincere mutual understanding and together maintain and promote social justice and moral values as well as peace and freedom for all people.[26]

Troll notes that first, this document emphasizes the importance of affirming both similarities and differences between Christianity and Islam.[27]

Secondly, this document opens up the possible collaboration between these two sets of believers.[28] Troll writes: The opening sentence of the 3rd paragraph of *Nostra Aetate* ... in fact constitutes a unique statement and an absolutely new beginning insofar as it is an official declaration about Islam issued by the highest teaching authority of the Church. The faith in God as One and his adoration are the centre and heart of Islam. This is also the first article of the Christian faith: 'Credo in unum Deum' - even if, for Christians, the divine Oneness opens itself to the trinity of the persons.[29] Troll recognizes this affirmation as an important base for theological dialogue between Christians and Muslims.

The third document, the Declaration on Religious Freedom (*Dignitatis Humanae*), became for him a key point of reference and a constant source of motivation. This point will be discussed at length in the third section of this chapter. Further Troll wrote: "personally, however, I was especially impressed by Pope Paul VI's encyclical letter *Ecclesiam Suam* of August 6, 1964. The key elements emerging for me from Paul VI's and the council's teaching on interreligious dialogue were these: reciprocal communication, mutual friendship, and respect, as well as a joint effort for the sake of shared goals, all in the service of a common search for the fuller realization of the truth."[30]

Moreover, Troll indicates that the dominant theme in all post Vatican II papal teaching is the submission to the same unique, personal God.[31] This continues to inspire him in his contacts with Muslims.[32] This submission to one God provides the link of fraternity among Muslims and Christians and gives them a common vision and mission to serve humanity for the greater glory of God.[33]

Priestly Ordination as a *Servant of Reconciliation* (2 Cor. 5:18f)

Troll was ordained priest in July 1971. The grace of ordination not only intensified his desire to spend all his energy in the study of Islam but also gave him the knowledge of doing this work in the name of the local and universal Church. He felt that the Church, by assigning him as an ordained priest to this work, had committed herself to the task of intensive Christian–Muslim dialogue. He says:

> Studying a Muslim text possibly for weeks or spending whole weekends discussing with educated Muslims trends in contemporary Islamic thought, I considered being an expression of my priestly apostolate. These activities—including, for example, the learning of a language like Turkish relatively late in life—constituted for me one and the same process of being drawn ever more deeply into a presence, an encounter to which I had been empowered and sent officially by my religious order and thus by the Church. I have never lost this sense over the years. Meeting Muslims and thus Islam at a deep level, I consider being my way of participating as a priest in the larger and centuries-old encounter between Church and Mosque.[34]

Missioned to India: Into the Cradle of Cultures and Religions as '*Servant of Reconciliation*'

Early in 1976, the Jesuit Superior General missioned Troll to teach Islam and Christian–Muslim relations at the Vidyajyoti Institute of Religious Studies, the Jesuit Faculty of Theology in Delhi. "In this way I was to be of help to the Indian Church in the effort of entering into dialogical relations not only with the Hindus but also with the Muslims of India and their Islam."[35]

In Delhi his main assignment was to introduce the Catholic students of theology to Islam, Indian Muslim culture and to make efforts to create an ambience for dialogue between Muslims and Christians. Already at his priestly ordination in 1971, he had chosen the motto from the

Second Letter to the Corinthians: "Servant of Reconciliation" (2 Cor. 5:18f). Now in India he saw himself being called in some small way to help the Church in her task of promoting reconciliation between the worlds of Hinduism and of Islam. In India, at Vidyajyoti Institute, as well as at various other faculties and seminaries throughout the country, he taught students of Christian theology, introducing them to Islamic faith and practice, South Asian Islam and Christian–Muslim relations past and present. He was the founder of VIDIS [Vidyajyoti Institute of Islamic Studies] for broader academic interaction.[36]

Soon after arriving in India in 1976, Troll met Paul Jackson, S.J., in Patna, Bihar. Jackson, inspired by the late Courtois, was engaged already in the study of Islam, especially of South Asian Sufism and the dialogue with Muslims. They began to meet regularly and eventually formed JAMI [*Jesuits among Muslims in India*] which in 1983 became ISA [*Islamic Studies Association*]. The founding of the Islamic Studies Association was due to the vision of the Second Vatican Council. It aims to help the Catholic Church in India to reach out through the various well-known forms of dialogue to the Muslims just as the Church reaches out to Hindus, Jains, Sikhs and others. ISA wants to encourage the Christians to get to know and to relate to Muslims better on all levels and in the various components of national life: neighborhoods, villages, towns and cities, states and national institutions. It hopes that in this way Muslims, too, will gradually acquire a more adequate and better informed knowledge of Catholics and their Church so that mutual relations may become more and more characterized by respect, mutual knowledge and the determination to join hands wherever possible for promoting common national goals in the spirit of the service of God and neighbour.[37]

During the same year (1983) the quarterly publication *Sulaam* was initiated. The small group of Indian Catholics organized in ISA, made it possible to maintain the vision, and to pursue the work, of initiating dialogue at various levels—contacts as neighbors in everyday life, teaching and publishing, discussing questions of common social, cultural and religious interest and so on—within an environment that was and remains largely uninterested, if not at times hostile to it, because reaching out deliberately to the Muslims was seen then as weakening the inculturation of Christian life in Hindu culture and religion.[38]

Rootedness among Muslims: Troll's Muslim Contacts in Delhi

Troll established academic as well as personal relationship with many Muslims in Delhi. Here it will be pertinent to hear him speak:

> The lasting friendships with a number of Muslims who represent to me some of the finest qualities of Indo-Muslim culture and religion. I can mention here only a few of them: Sayyid Vahiduddin (1909–98) who over the years conveyed to me a unique synthesis of Hindu and Muslim philosophy, modern Western thought, Sufi wisdom and contemporary Christian theology. Sayyid Vahiduddin made me understand and appreciate essential aspects of the Qur'ânic idea of God and of the meanings of Islamic prayer. Then Khwaja Ahmad Faruqi, the accomplished scholar of English and Urdu literature, Muhammad Ishaq Khan, the outstanding historian of Sufism, past and present, in the Kashmiri environment, Maulana Wahiduddin Khan, the remarkable leader of the Al-Risala movement, these and many others—among whom especially those who collaborated with me for the book series *Islam in India: Studies and Commentaries*—became dear and esteemed colleagues, and some even admired friends.

> From the day I arrived in India to be member of the staff of Vidyajyoti, I experienced through the 12 years there a great openness and eagerness, not least among Muslims, to meet, to get to know one another and to exchange on matters of shared cultural and religious concern. This hospitality was offered to me mostly by Muslim individuals whom I met as a scholar of religion and of Islam, as a Christian theologian and as a Catholic priest. It constitutes one of the most precious gifts I have received during my life. In Delhi I used to visit regularly a small number of respected Muslim scholars. Between us developed bonds of trust and friendship that facilitated an open conversation on basic questions of religion, the history of Islamic thought and spirituality, and not least on issues common to Christians and Muslims. After his retirement from Delhi University, Professor Sayyid Vahiduddin had moved to Hamdard Nagar in Tughluqabad, where, with Sayyid Ausaf Ali and others, he worked on the translation of Avicenna's monumental works on medicine

and philosophy, esp. *al-shifā'* and *al-qānūn*. I used to visit Professor Vahiduddin at least once a month; we exchanged new publications and became trusted friends. I owe him, above all, an understanding of Islam as unconditional surrender to the God of creation and the Qur'ân, the Transcendent and yet Near One who remains the Hidden (*al-ghaib*), inspiring us with reverential fear and attracting us by His mercy and love (*jalāl-o-jamāl*). Sayyid Vahiduddin's name brings to mind the name and personality of another, quite different but equally respected scholar, Maulana Wahiduddin Khan, the founder of the *al-Risālah* Movement. Only a few days after my arrival at Vidyajyoti Institute in Old Delhi in the summer of 1976, he knocked at my door. From that afternoon onward we have been continuously in friendly contact. The conversations with, and study of, the development and thought of this remarkable *'alim* has not ceased to fascinate me.

From 1976 onwards I also met Dr Sayyid Abid Husain (1896-1987), one of the three intellectual pillars of The Jamia Millia Islamia. With his initiative had started in 1970 the 'Islam and the Modern Age Society' for which he edited the periodical 'Islam and the Modern Age', now edited by Prof Akhtarul Wasey, the director of the Zakir Husain Institute. Dr Abid Husain introduced me to the basic ideas underlying his Institute and its publications. Thus I also met Professor Mushirul Haq (d. 1990) and Prof. Ziyaul Hasan Faruqi. Both had studied in that renowned Indian institutions of Muslim learning and, later, under Wilfred Cantwell Smith at McGill University in Montreal, Canada. Here again very friendly relations developed. I was introduced into a deeper understanding of the South Asian Muslim tradition, past and present and regularly was invited by the scholars named and by others for instance to Aligarh, Patna's Khuda Bakhsh Library, Osmania University in Hyderabad and to Asghar Ali Engineer's Institute in Bombay/Mumbai in order to participate in seminars and meetings discussing various aspects of past and present Indian Muslim culture. At Delhi University the renowned scholar of Urdu literature, Prof. Khwaja Ahmad Faruqui (1917-1986) invited me regularly to his home. Over breakfast we exchanged and thus he helped me to keep alive and deepen my love for Urdu prose and poetry. The Ghalib Academy sponsored by Hakeem Abdul Hameed (1908-1999) of the Hamdard group and inaugurated by President Dr Zakir Hussain in 1969 and the Dargah of Hazrat Nizamuddin Auliya offered regularly opportunities to attend *mushāira*s as well as *qawwāli* sessions. Those Thursday evenings spent at Nizamuddin remain unforgotten. Being a professor at the Vidyajyoti, Institute of Religious Studies, and editor of the series *Studies of Islam in India*, and between different Muslim institutions, helped me greatly to develop cordial and fruitful collegial relations with a good number of Muslim colleagues belonging to various academic institutions all over India, from Srinagar to Hyderabad (Deccan), from Ajmer to Calcutta.[39]

This account appears to be just a narration of Troll's contacts with Muslims in India. However, it is not so, if viewed from the point of view of the long history of Jesuit contacts with Muslims in India. In the second chapter, it has been shown that till the time of Courtois, polemics was the preferred genre of contacts between Jesuits and Muslims. In the third chapter it was shown how Courtois reversed such negative trends by launching positive contacts. Here one can affirm that Troll deepened and widened such a positive approach.

While Calcutta was the centre of Courtois's activities, it is fruitful to note that Delhi was the centre of gravity of Troll's contact during his ministry in India. The contacts that Troll developed in Delhi and around the north western part of India have specific theological significance. In the first half of the nineteenth century, missionaries who worked with people of other religions in these areas were either inspired by the Evangelical Revival that happened in Great Britain during the mid-eighteenth century, the Great Evangelical Awakening of the United States of America in the early nineteenth century, or German pietism. All these methods insisted upon outdoor preaching and the distribution of tracts and scriptures to reach people with the Gospel message. They called upon individual conversion and inner piety that leads to a deep relationship with God through Christ.

Troll, a missionary himself, followed a different route which is both faithful to the Gospel and to the teachings of the Vatican II. First, he begins with a positive affirmation of what the finest qualities of Indo-Muslim culture could offer for a sincere dialogue between Christians and Muslims. Secondly, many Muslims he met became his esteemed colleagues and they together worked on projects of common interest. Some of these colleagues turned to be his admired and trusted friends.

Thirdly, bonds of friendship and trust led to open conversations for mutual listening, learning and understanding. Fourthly, it is important to notice here how academic dialogue was nourished by the dialogue of life and vice-versa. Troll's approach in Delhi was indeed something new and refreshing in contrast to the perspective of mission that was exercised around Delhi by other missionaries earlier. In this sense Troll was a trailblazer in Delhi in terms of dialogue with Muslims.[40]

Return to Europe

In 1988 the Centre for the Study of Islam and Christian-Muslim Relations at the Selly Oak Colleges, Birmingham, officially invited Troll to join its staff. In the study centre at the Selly Oak Colleges, Muslims and Christians together engaged in studying, teaching, and researching in the field of Islam and Christian–Muslim relations. Its academic courses and exams formed part of the program of the Faculty of Theology of Birmingham University and included undergraduate and postgraduate courses, up to the level of PhD.[41]

At Selly Oak he entered naturally into regular conversation with religiously well-educated young Muslim women and men hailing from different parts of the world, where Christians and Muslims together were trying to enter into meaningful dialogical relations with one another. Staff and students at Selly Oak were united in the effort to deepen their own and one another's understanding of Islam and of Christian–Muslim relations, in a common academic framework. He taught "The development of Islamic religious thought from the Qur'ân to our time" in close collaboration with the Pakistani scholar Dr Khalid Alawi (d. 2008). "This turned out to be a refreshing and satisfying experience for me in both human and academic terms", he said.[42] "Also, initiating together with my Muslim and Christian colleagues on the staff at Selly Oak, a new international bi-annual (later to become quarterly), *Islam and Christian-Muslim Relations*, brought me into regular contact and intellectual exchange with Muslim and Christian scholars of Islam and Christian–Muslim relations the world over."[43]

Crossing Another Border: Into the World of Turkish Muslims

In 1993 Troll was assigned to take up a professorship at the Pontifical Oriental Institute in Rome, an academic institution mainly dedicated to teaching and research about the Oriental Churches. The main reason for asking him to move to Rome was to enable him to go regularly—in the name of the Pontifical Gregorian University Consortium—as exchange guest professor to the University of Ankara's Ilahiyat Fakültesi. A Turkish professor from the Ankara Faculty taught on aspects of Islamic culture and faith at the Pontifical Gregorian University in Rome, and in return Troll gave lectures and seminars on Christian and Christian–Muslim themes at the Ankara faculty, and from there, as it turned out, sporadically in a number of other Muslim theological faculties. He taught at the Ankara faculty over a period of nine years, on each occasion for one to two months. After having been engaged in India and in England in explaining aspects of Islam and Christian–Muslim relations to Christians, especially students of Christian theology, he was asked now to do the opposite, namely to explain aspects of Christian faith and practice, such as the biblical scriptures and the history of the Christian Churches and of their relationship with Islam, to Muslims. Frequently he was also asked to discuss more recent Christian developments such as the Protestant Reformation and the Catholic Counter-Reformation, the Christian responses to the Enlightenment, and to modern, critical scholarship, the ecumenical movement and the First as well as the Second Vatican Councils.[44]

He took advantage of the opportunity to learn Turkish at the well-known 'Tömer Institute for Turkish Language' at the University of Ankara. There he found himself learning Turkish from the scratch, in the company of students—most of them some thirty-five or even forty years younger than himself—hailing mainly from Central Asia and from the Caucasus region. In these and countless other fascinating ways he was able to approach great geographical and cultural regions of the Islamic world, different from, and yet also in many ways related to, the world of Arab and of South Asian Islam.[45]

Back to Germany: Continuing Teaching Mission

In 1999 he returned to Germany, first to the Catholic Academy of Berlin, where he established the Forum for Christian–Muslim Dialogue. There he became acquainted with a city that had turned into a major centre of Turkish and Muslim immigration and permanent presence. However, after two-and-a-half years, in 2001, he left Berlin to become once more part of an academic setting, the Jesuit Faculty of Philosophy and Theology of Sankt Georgen, in Frankfurt. There he started a certificate course called 'Introduction to Islam and Christian-Muslim Relations' for students and professionals.[46]

To Sum Up

This brief biographical sketch pays attention to the central aspect of the life and work of Troll: the **mission** and its specific Islamic dimension. Houben enkindled a fire at the heart of Troll for mission among Muslims imbibing a deep desire for an intellectual approach towards Muslims and Islam from him. Troll pursued his desire for mission as he began to acquire deep knowledge of Islam. Then as a Jesuit he carefully discerned his desire for mission and its specific dimension, Islamic Studies.

Quite another aspect of Troll's work that emerges in this brief life sketch is the importance he has given to interaction with Muslims. He comes across as someone who is really interested in Islamic religious thinking in this part of the world. His interactions with Arab Muslims, South Asian, Turkish and European Muslims during different stages of his life and work attest to this important dimension of his life. This is clearly expressed in his deep desire to learn the languages: Arabic, Persian, Urdu, and Turkish.

It should be said at this stage of this chapter that if Houben sparked in his intellectual desire for Islamic Studies; Troll's discernment on his desire, the Gospel values and the teachings of the Vatican II and especially the teachings of the Pope Paul VI in *Ecclesiam Suam* turned these sparks into a glow of fire. The fire blazed along as Troll deepened his desire to serve the Church in the field of dialogue with Muslims. Moreover, it is important to note that Troll creatively brought to fruition the spiritual and intellectual dimensions of mission right at the beginning of his mission among Muslims.

Learning in the Presence of the Other

Troll's Engagement with Muslims, His Understanding and Practice of Dialogue with Muslims as a Catholic Theologian.

The first section presented the gradual development of the religious thinking of Troll from a biographical perspective. It was shown that Troll blossomed as a Christian scholar of Islam and an advocate and promoter of Christian-Muslim relations as he seriously sought knowledge of Islam and Muslims in the company of many Muslims. It was noted that ***discernment*** and ***witness to faith*** nourished this growth. It is not an exaggeration to say that his Catholic faith underpins his engagement with Muslim religious thinking.

This second section presents an analysis of Troll's scholarly work that is marked by the same elements: *discernment* and *witness to faith*. This analysis is done by reading the written texts of Troll. In his extensive writings, Troll covers a vast range of subjects in his writings that includes: Islam in general and Indian Islam in particular, Indian Muslim thinkers, Indian Islamic mission movements, Islam and religious pluralism, religious freedom, themes on Christian-Muslim relations (dialogue), and witness to Christ in a Muslim milieu. His writings can be divided largely into the following two sections: Troll's engagement with Muslims; and his understanding and practice of dialogue with Muslims as a Catholic theologian.

The first section deals with Troll's engagement with the religious thinking of a number of Muslims specifically in South Asia. This brings to the fore Troll's deep desire to know and understand the heart and mind of Muslims and calls for attention to the importance of deep knowledge of the other as an essential ingredient for any serious dialogue. His dialogical journey is directed by both his faith and credible lives of Muslims. It will show Troll's **desire for knowing the faith of Muslims** and

his discerning love for Muslims are integral to his witnessing mission among Muslims. These desire and love underpinned his engagement with them. The second section will present Troll's theological engagement with Muslims. It will be laid bare that Troll's commitment to freedom of conscience and religious freedom in the pluralistic world fortified his theology.

Engaging with Indian Islamic Religious Thinking

The Role of Scriptures in Religious Conversation between Christians and Muslims: Troll's Engagement with Sir Sayyid Ahmad Khan

Troll engaged with the writings of Sir Sayyid Ahmad Khan (here after Sir Sayyid) while studying this Indian Muslim intellectual's life and work for his doctoral thesis. His work on Sir Sayyid is considered to be one of the standard works on the subject in the academic world. In the process Troll discovered a refreshing line of the religious thought of Sir Sayyid. It appears to this writer that Sir Sayyid's attitude towards the Bible shaped Troll's understanding with regard to the importance of Scriptures in dialogue between Muslims and Christians.

Sir Sayyid's Commentary on the Bible

Tabyin al-Kalam is the fragmentary commentary of Sir Sayyid on the Bible.[47] G. de Tassy interpreted Sir Sayyid's Commentary as a testimony to his open-mindedness and broad vision, and commented that *Tabyin al-Kalam* as 'informative', 'interesting', and a 'synthesis of Eastern and Western learning and scholarship'.[48] After a careful study of this Commentary, Troll affirms that *Tabyin al-Kalam* is an extraordinary text that Sir Sayyid composed and published in 1862 at the age of 42 and republished it in 1885.[49] Troll observes the text was "... not an aberration of his younger year literary adventurism".[50] It is worth mentioning here without going into many details that *Tabyin al-Kalam* comprises three parts: (1) Prolegomena to the Study of the Bible; (2) Translation of, and commentary on, Genesis 1-11; (3) Translation and Commentary on Matthew 1-5.[51]

Muslims Cannot Reject the Bible Since the Bible Witnesses to the Oneness of God [*tawhid*]

Sir Sayyid emphasized that the Bible should be studied and commented upon by Muslims since the Bible witnessed to *tawhid*. This position is the key to his overall understanding of the Bible, radically in contrast to the general Muslim understanding that the Bible is a corrupted scripture.[52] One cannot miss this courageous approach of Sir Sayyid's approach towards the Bible in India. Troll makes note of this and writes: "The question of the corruption of the Scriptures (*tahrīf*) is an age-old issue among Muslims, Jews and Christians. It had deliberately been made the central point of the controversy [in India] by Pfander and the subject of special treatment by Kairānawi in his *I'jāz-i 'Īsawi*. [However] Sir Sayyid claims that the errors and contradictions that doubtlessly are found in the present biblical Scriptures can be solved without the postulate of a deliberate, general textual corruption of the Biblical texts".[53]

Troll confirms that Sir Sayyid believed in the relevance of the Gospel of Jesus. Troll writes: "… freed from the distortions and errors of dogmatic interpretation and in the light of the Qur'ân's uniquely clear message of God's Unity, [Sir Sayyid believed that] the gospel of Jesus continues to be relevant".[54] It is important to observe that though Sir Sayyid would recognize corruption in the text and distortion of dogma, however he would also hold that since the Bible in its totality witnesses to *tawhid*, it should be studied and commented upon by Muslims. In short, the position of Sir Sayyid was that Muslims cannot afford to reject the Bible.[55]

One should not lose sight of the implications of Sir Sayyid's stand that the Bible witnesses to *tawhid*. In other words, Sir Sayyid affirms that Muslims should recognize that Christians are thoroughgoing monotheists.[56] His affirmation is important since the Trinitarian Monotheism of Christians is often misunderstood by Muslims to be tri-theism!

The Bible Could Help Muslims to Grow in their Spiritual Life

Moreover, Sir Sayyid drew from the Bible, the Qur'ân and sound ḥadīth while interpreting biblical concepts like 'disciples', 'kingdom of God' and 'seeing God'. Troll affirms that for Sir Sayyid, Jesus uncovers the inner truth and the essence of the teachings of the Bible and thus helps Muslims to be attentive to the inner meanings of the teachings of the Qur'ân. Thus, the Bible could help Muslims to grow in their spiritual life. He insisted that a Muslim should deepen his/her faith in the light of the true moral teachings of the authentic pre-Qur'ânic scriptures. Troll stressed this significant element of the courageous endeavour of Sir Sayyid for the much-needed promotion of interreligious scholarship in India and beyond for the present times. Troll vibrated with the religious thinking of Sir Sayyid vis-à-vis his approach to the Bible.

Sir Sayyid basically makes two important assertions: Muslims cannot afford to reject the Bible since the Book witnesses to *tawhid,* and Bible could help Muslims to grow in their spiritual life. Sir Sayyid's attitude towards the Bible appears to have an impact on Troll's own thinking on the use of Scriptures in relations between Christians and Muslims. Troll has come to recognize that both Christians and Muslims need to read one another's scriptures if they want to deepen their understanding of one another and if they want to grow in mutual appreciation of one another.[57]

Reading One Another's Scriptures: Critical Theological Questions

Troll is aware of the critical theological questions that could come up in reading one another's scriptures. For example; while using the Bible and the Qur'ân in religious conversation between Christians and Muslims, he suggested that the following questions could not be avoided: "we cannot escape serious work on hermeneutics: first within our respective faith community, which passage do we privilege and which interpretation do we favour and for what reason? Secondly, how do we read each other's Scriptures cross-culturally and religiously, and what status we accord to them?"[58]

In the light of critical questions, Troll lays down an important ground rule for profitable interaction between Christians and Muslims while bringing together the Bible and the Qur'ân.[59] He writes that Christians and Muslims should "grasp the basic point that in the two faiths the Word of God addressed by God to the human race is understood in significantly different ways".[60] Christians and Muslims should not fail to grasp the profound differences in their convictions about the nature and message of their scriptures, otherwise conversations between them will not move beyond the irrelevant criticism and confusion.[61] Revelation of the Qur'ân as the Word of God is understood by Muslims as "the final, unique and fully authentic manifestation of the Word of God, addressed to humankind through the ministry of Muhammad".[62] For Christians the story of revelation comes to its fulfillment in Jesus of Nazareth, who is the Word made flesh (John 1:14), and public revelation ends with the death of the last Apostle.[63] So Muslims should recognise that for Christians the Word did not become a book but it became incarnate in the person of Jesus. Christians should recognize that the Muslims believe that God's word is preserved in the book, the Holy Qur'ân.[64] Muslims might ask: what about the Bible? Is it the Word of God? Muslims have the right to know about Christian thinking on this subject. Christians use the term Word of God in a different way to that in which Muslims use it in reference to the Qur'ân. For Christians, the Word speaks in and through the words of men and women, the authors who composed the various books in the Bible.[65] Limitations of the writers' cultures, languages and customs are part and parcel of the Bible. This human agency should not be seen as corruption of the Bible as argued by the medieval Muslim scholars.

Christians should recognize the spiritual significance of the Qur'ân in the lives of Muslims as the Book shapes the lives and spiritualities of more than a billion Muslims today. To enter the world of Muslims, Christians need to understand the status and agency of the Qur'ân and the way in which it is respected by Muslims.[66] Similarly, Muslims should recognize the place of the Bible in the lives of Christians for any meaningful interaction between them on the level of theology.

In the spirit of openness, Troll finds that there are Muslims and Christians who feel that it "is part of their vocation to get to know one another"[67] by studying one another's scriptures. Among Muslims, many are "increasingly aware of the need to learn something from Christians themselves about their own understanding of the Bible" and "take the Bible seriously and get to know it properly", as is the case with Christians who learn about the Muslim understandings of the Qur'ân.[68]

'Scriptural Reasoning': Muslims and Christians Studying the Bible and the Qur'ân Together

Troll affirms that the "intense reading of paired passages from the Qur'ân and the Bible" as an important initiative.[69] The project, called 'Scriptural Reasoning' attracts educated Muslims and Christians to study the Bible and the Qur'ân together.[70] M. Ipgrave finds that for any real progress in Christian-Muslim relations, Christians and Muslims should take both the Qur'ân and the Bible and study seriously their contents and teachings.[71]

In Scriptural Reasoning the onus is on the believer to explain his/her scriptures in the light of one's faith as well as awareness towards the presence of a believer, who believes differently. Thus the rules of exegesis are drawn in the light of one's faith with sensitivity towards the faith of the participant in religious conversation. Though Sir Sayyid did not expand his thinking to the level of the *Scriptural Reasoning*, it should be acknowledged that Sir Sayyid walked an uncharted path; acknowledging and emphasizing the theological place of the Bible for spiritual blossoming of a Muslim.

Troll further clarifies explicitly: "it is a non-negotiable basis for dialogue that each side should acknowledge that the Scripture on which the faith of the other community is founded forms the basis and the norm for the understanding and expression of that faith. This point, which was recognized at the Muslim-Christian Congress held in Tripoli, Libya, in February 1976, also implies the importance of Christians studying the Qur'ân and Muslims studying the Bible if the dialogue between them is to be meaningful".[72] While Troll constantly discerned a sympathetic approach towards the Qur'ân, he maintained without any vagueness that a Muslim who read the Bible should recognize unambiguously that the Bible on which the faith of the Christian community is founded forms the norm for understanding and expression of Christian faith and is not based on the Qur'ânic vision. Thus Troll keeps openness towards Muslims and witness to his faith in a healthy dialogical tension. Discernment plays a vital role in this process. Thus it could be affirmed that Sir Sayyid's new approach towards the Bible has certain theological impact on Troll's thinking on Scriptures in dialogue between Christians and Muslims.

While Troll's work on Sir Sayyid's theological thinking enriched his theological reflection on the place of the sacred scriptures in dialogue, his engagement with a number of other scholars have shaped his idea of dialogue between religions in the pluralistic world of today where different religions intermingle with one another everywhere. Troll recognizes that a shared intellectual and spiritual striving in response to the Word will enable Christians and Muslims to address difficult issues.

The next important issue that Troll gives specific attention to while dialoging with Muslim scholars is this: "how does a particular scholar deal with the question with regard to the establishment of a political state or *shari'a* state?"

The Islamic Social and Political Order

Some Muslim thinkers emphasise that the establishment of an Islamic State is essential to an Islamic thinking and way of life. It is important to discuss Troll's engagement with a scholar who promoted the Islamic social political order.[73]

Maulana Maudūdī (d.1979): Capture the Political Leadership, Establish an Islamic State[74]

Troll analyses the work of Maulana Maudūdī (hereafter Maudūdī) in a number of his articles.[75] Maudūdī is an important Muslim thinker from the subcontinent who fired the imagination of Muslims arguing a case for political expression of Islam as the essence of Islam initially in South Asia and eventually around the Muslim world. Before one comments on Troll's approach to Islamist, it is useful to present Maudūdī's key ideas.

Faith in Allāh is a Contract, not a Metaphysical Relationship

Maudūdī understood the concept of human life in the light of a human person's relationship with Allāh. What does this relationship entail? Man should repose his faith in Allāh. This act of reposing one's faith in Allāh is called a 'bargain' (Cf. Q 9:111). Faith in Allāh is not a metaphysical relationship between Man and God, but it is a contract. This contract necessitates that man barters his life and properties with Allāh in exchange for paradise in the life hereafter.[76] In other words, Allāh is Creator, Master and Sovereign. Allāh created humanity. Human persons should therefore live according to the decrees and guidance of God.[77]

Man has to Submit to Allāh Alone

Maudūdī recognised that the true meaning of *din* demands that one gives up all forms of servitude to man and submit to Allāh alone. Allāh alone is sovereign, the supreme ruler. Man has neither autonomy for deciding for himself nor power to rule over another. Pursuing an independent path is open rebellion against God.[78] 'God's will' is the primary source of law. All persons who surrender themselves to the will of God are welded together into a Muslim community; 'Ummah'. 'God's will' is enshrined in 'Shari'ah'. 'Ummah' should adopt 'Shari'ah' to remain Islamic.[79] If 'Ummah' adopts a law other than 'Shari'ah' that contract gets broken and 'Ummah' turns to be un-Islamic. Maudūdī envisaged a political system based on three principles. These principles are as follows: *Tawhid* (unity of God), *Risalah* (prophethood), and *Khilafah* (Caliphate). God is the creator and judge. Man is the representative of God and *Risalah* (prophethood) is the medium through which man receives the Law of God.[80] The main objective of Islam is to make people commit themselves to God and to worship Him alone. This objective cannot be met if the power lies with unbelievers and those who corrupted faith. In this context Muslims confine themselves to worship and prayer.[81]

Maudūdī's Response to Religiously Pluralistic India

Following Shah Waliullah (d. 1763) Maudūdī believed that Islam declined because the Ummah strayed from following the Qur'ân and Sunna and shifted from the God-fearing rule of Caliphs to wayward kingship.[82] Maudūdī thought that Muslims living in a culturally diverse and religiously pluralistic India without the benefit of an Islamic State would inevitably lead Muslims towards assimilation into the dominant ethos of Hinduism and thus lead them astray and Islam will decline further.

Maudūdī, while criticising the conservative Ulamâ for adding new regulations, took the modernists to task for allowing themselves to be seduced by an alien (non- Islamic) system. Thus both conservative Ulamâ and modernists drew a lot of flak from Maudūdī. Maudūdī wanted that a small dedicated and disciplined group should capture the political leadership and thus establish an Islamic state. He wanted shari'a to reign not only within Muslim families, but also that public life be organised according to the injunctions of Shari'a. It must be said that Maudūdī obviously focused on an Islamic state and certainly failed to recognise the composite culture where different religions have taken roots in the subcontinent. One can also say that the attempt of Maudūdī was a futile attempt to change the composite texture of Indian society where Islam had taken deep roots.

Islamists Ideology a Threat to the Pluralistic World

Picking up Maudūdī's inability to understand the plural texture of Indian society, Troll recognizes that understanding Islam *merely* in political terms is fraught with several serious issues. First and foremost, in a global village where people of different religions and people who reject any religion live together, Islamist ideology is a threat both to the peaceful coexistence of all people and a disservice to Islam itself; since such political expression ignores and conceals the spiritual dimension of Islam. Will Troll engage them in spiritual dialogue? It is pertinent to hear his words:

> It seems to me that there is no point in religious-spiritual dialogue with Muslims and Muslim groups who are attached to such a view of Islam, because the indispensable basic presuppositions for it to succeed are lacking. Genuine religious and spiritual dialogue in the context of our modern societies seems to me meaningful only with Muslims and Christians who share our fundamental secular, democratic values and logically, therefore ultimately recognise the separation of politics and religion, and are not working towards an Islamic, or for that matter, a Christian state. An alleged religious and spiritual dialogue with proven Islamists does not serve the truth. It represents a deception and bafflement of genuine servants of God, whether of the Christian or Islamic faith.[83]

Moreover, he advises Christians to discern and choose their Muslim dialogue partners carefully. He writes: "[Christians] should carefully consider what kind of Islam their [Muslim] dialogue partners advocate ... this prudence, which calls for a discerning knowledge is indispensible ...".[84] As a Christian scholar of Islam, Troll enters into a deep study of the work of other Muslim scholars and highlights their claim that is in contrast to the idea of Maudūdī, Islam does not demand a comprehensive Islamic social and political order. In this intellectual labour Troll continues to exercise the key elements of his mission; *discernment* and *witness to his faith* as a Jesuit priest *sent* among Muslims.

Confident Partnership with All: Maulana Azad (d. 1958)

To his delight Troll finds that several other equally important scholars do not subscribe to the views of Maudūdī. Maulana Abul Kalam Azad (hereafter Azad) is one among them. Like any religious and cultural tradition in India, diversity is at the heart of the Islamic intellectual tradition, affirms Azad. Azad reflects in the context of partition of the sub-continent in 1947.

First, on the political level, Muslims lost their prominence and leadership within India, since a large number from among the Muslim elite left India for Pakistan. The Islamic religious leadership that emerged at this juncture was largely inward looking and was unable to give clear directions to deal with issues in hand. Moreover, Muslims had to share political power with people of other religious traditions and live as equal citizens in an independent India.

At such critical juncture, Azad recognised the importance and centrality of citizenship in a multi-religious and multi-cultural secular country. He envisioned that Muslims should strive together with every other Indian to promote national values common to all Indians.[85]

Second, on religious level they were called to reconcile their faith with modernity in a multi-religious and multi-cultural India.[86] The deepest issue at stake is about how they were to correlate the new challenges with the revelation in the Qur'ân, and their future relationship with people of other religions in India.[87] Troll summarizes this situation in the following words: "In the final analysis, the problems of Indian Islam do not differ essentially from those facing the whole *Ummah* – and, in an analogous way, all major religions – namely, how to live as an important religious minority within the one pluralistic world of today – in harmony and in shared political responsibility with people of other faiths and ideologies."[88] This is the question that occupies the mind of Troll while engaging with fellow Islamic scholars.

Is a Comprehensive Islamic Order Essential?

Troll further writes:

> Azad assumed that Muslims would not be able to establish their own political order on the Indian soil. Azad held that once political independence was obtained, the Indian Muslims would have to live in equal citizenship with a majority of non-Muslims. In other words, they would not be able to enjoy complete autonomy nor the possibility of implementing a comprehensive Islamic order political, social, cultural, and religious ... [he] came to the conviction, on the basis of his reading of the Qur'ân, that Islam did in fact not necessarily demand such a comprehensive, autonomous realization.[89]

Qur'ân Urges a Wise Participation in the Human Condition[90]

Troll suggests with K. Cragg that the greatest contribution of Azad is "his courageous decision to attempt in justifying rationally, in terms of the Qur'ân and Islamic thought, Muslim participation with others in forming a common statehood".[91] Troll further writes: "Azad and like-minded Muslims rejected the explicit or implicit claim of the advocates of territorial separatism that, as Muhammad's mission, then in Medina, included essentially the exercise of political and military power in the name of Islam, so now an Islam worthy of its name and fit for survival today could not hope to be viable or genuine and complete without striving for the realization of that power".[92] Troll points out that Azad courageously evoked a number of aspects of the Qur'ân which urge a wise and sincere participation in the human condition. Thus, *hijra* for Azad is not political exclusivism but a call for a spiritual and moral commitment within humanity.[93]

Confident Partnership in a Diverse Nation

Further, Troll writes, Azad "invoked those aspects of the Qur'ân ... [and] envisaged an Islam not of sectarian belligerence but of confident partnership in a cultural and spiritual diversity where a strident divisiveness would be its betrayal. He shared in the effort to align Islam in India with Hinduism and Buddhism as far as loyalty allowed, because he was not of the opinion that living without the benefit of Islamic statehood would inevitably entail a slow assimilation of Muslims into the dominant ethos of Hinduism."[94]

Thus Azad's theological opinion rooted in the Qur'ân challenges the attitude that Maudūdī held towards cultural and religious diversity.[95] Troll thus highlights this openness of the spirit of Azad. Azad's political commitment drew from the deep springs of genuine Qur'ânic spirituality that he nurtured. In the efforts of Azad, Troll recognises a wholesome initiative to understand his [Azad's] inherited faith in the context of culturally and religiously pluralistic societies. Troll positively affirms the effort of Azad. In such positive affirmation that comes after careful reading of a Muslim scholar, Troll lives up to his vocation to be a Christian scholar of Islam.

Syed Vahiduddin: Adapt Creatively

It has been noted earlier that Troll acknowledged Vahiduddin as one who made him [Troll] understand and appreciate essential aspects of the Qur'ânic idea of God and of the meanings of Islamic prayer. Troll affirms that Vahiduddin Khan tried to re-awaken in all especially Muslims, the awareness of the hidden and yet ever-present Mystery. According to Vahiduddin Khan the serious challenge, to religious consciousness of the human person, comes not from science and technology but from a secular culture guided by autonomous morality.

Summarising Vahiduddin Khan on this point Troll writes: "This shift towards a secular outlook in aesthetic, moral and metaphysical consciousness affects, on the rational plane, theological consciousness, and hence dogmatic positions and involves a formulated creed".[96] More seriously, due to this shift, the transcendental vision is affected. As a result personal religious commitment is in danger of losing its relevance. What should one do to remain authentic in the contemporary situation? Vahiduddin argues that in order to demonstrate convincingly the existential import and inner dynamics of religion, a religious believer should make room for creative adaptation to ever emerging new situations.[97]

Qur'ân Continues to Engage with New Situations

Troll shows that Vahiduddin carries forward this discussion and argues that Islam should not be identified with its historical manifestation at any particular point of time.[98] The message of the Qur'ân continues to engage with new situations and opens up new possibilities for Islam in diverse situations. Consequently, Vahiduddin rejects all efforts of fundamentalist organizations who want to seize political power and to establish a shari'a state.[99]

Moral and Spiritual Aspects have Universal Validity. Those which are Contingent are Relative and Time-bound.

For Vahiduddin the Qur'ân is the living voice, and he wanted Muslims to approach the holy book with deep humility and to listen to its voice in all predicaments of life.

He considered the only adequate way of approaching the Qur'ân is appreciating the mystery that lies behind the Qur'ânic revelation in both hidden aspect (*batin*), which is at the level of the transcendental, and in its manifest aspect (*zahir*) at the metaphysical level. In the hidden aspect God is infinitely remote beyond all analogies. In the manifest aspect, God reveals man's origin and destiny. At the historical level, the Qur'ân addresses both the spiritual and moral dimension of the human person. The spiritual aspect guides the believer towards God through 'inner purification', and the moral aspect provides a moral code of conduct in the way of the seeker's quest for God.

Vahiduddin asserts that there are other instructions that are contingent and conditioned by concrete and shifting situations of history. While moral and spiritual aspects have universal validity and demand compliance without any compromise, the contingent ones are relative and time bound. This argument precisely goes against the arguments of the Islamist quest for establishing an Islamic political state. Troll meticulously notes of this commitment of an Islamic scholar who distinguishes between categorical and contingent aspects of the Qur'ân. Troll recognises the originality of the thinking of Vahiduddin Khan and his efforts to interpret the Qur'ân for his fellow believers in a pluralistic world. It should be noted that Troll in his engagement with the texts of Vahiduddin and in his personal friendship with him undoubtedly practised his vocation of a Jesuit scholar among Muslims by highlighting the new thinking that emerges in the thinking of Vahiduddin.

Maulana Wahiduddin Khan (b.1925)[100]

Troll has a long standing academic friendship with Maulana Wahiduddin Khan and has known him personally for years. Wahiduddin Khan is one of the important Islamic scholars in India.[101] His writings attract a vast readership and influence religious thinking among Muslims in India and elsewhere. His al-Risala Movement, a movement to propagate the ideals of Islam in a peaceful way, and the publications of the movement attract the attention of not only Muslims but also of non-Muslims.

Islam has Come to Convey the Proper Understanding of the Link between God and Humanity

Troll recommended that the present writer give special attention to Wahiduddin Khan's understanding of religion -'*din*'- which is central to his religious thinking. Wahiduddin Khan explains that Islam has come to convey the proper understanding of the link between God and humanity. Man and woman are servants of God and consequently fear and love should mark their relationship with God. Islam prepares them for the last day, the Day of Judgment. According to Wahiduddin Khan, this understanding is the essence of Islam. He points out that the political discourse about the establishment of the Islamic state based on Qur'ânic injunctions does not form the central message of Islam.[102]

Muslims Should Use 'Reason' and Practice 'Ijtihad' to Remain Adapted to Changing Times.

Moreover, Wahiduddin Khan emphasises that Islam must be explained *anew* in the modern world. For him explaining *anew* does not mean reform or revision of Islam but re-application (*ijtihad*).[103] He argues that the doors of *ijtihad* have never been closed, as they are thought to be so, and this principle of *ijtihad* should be applied in Islamic Law and Islamic thought in order to keep up with the times.

First, he asserts that, since Islamic scholars have never stopped applying this principle in their writings, one cannot claim that the doors of *ijtihad* were ever closed.

Second, times keep changing and bringing up ever new questions, so how should one deal with the new questions that are thrown up? Wahiduddin Khan argues that since the human person is endowed with reason, he/she has to use it and find ways to deal with new questions within the framework of Islam. Qur'ân states the principle that Islam is to remain always practicable (Q 22:78) ... It means that a Muslim should use 'reason' and practice 'ijtihad' to remain adapted to changing times.[104]

As mentioned above, Wahiduddin Khan is convinced that the effort to set up Islamic regimes is not an essential part of Islam and certainly not a condition for its growth and spirituality. For him, *Hudaybiyya* is a foundational model for living together will all people of different religious and cultural persuasions.[105] This "prophetic manner of acting as al-Hudaybiyya is a foundation model for imitation by the Muslims till the day of Judgement. It is especially important for Muslims today to follow this model, working out superior solutions by adopting a 'higher strategy' as it were."[106]

Wahiduddin Khan emphasizes "in the living process of the *ijma* of the ummah under the guidance of God." He believes that Islam should be cleansed of all the additions that Muslims have made out of their ignorance or viciousness. For an example some ulema have taught that Islam is incompatible with democracy. It is an ignorant addition to the thinking of Muslims by the ulema. In his understanding, Muslims are not asked to impose the Islamic System upon people of other religions. Muslims are asked to communicate the message in a peaceful way. Muslims have the duty to practice *da'wa,* the Islamic mission.[107] It is *islamically* illicit to employ any violent means to establish the rule of Islam on others. Hence any violence in the name of Islam has to be avoided and condemned.[108]

Wahiduddin Khan formulates: "Islam as a political system is lawfully established only by the free choice of the people, not by forceful imposition upon the populations".[109] For Wahiduddin Khan, only true and licit Islamic activism is one that operates on the lines of witness and invitation.[110] Islam must be studied in the spirit of *ijtihad.* Troll appreciates Wahiduddin Khan for strict separation of matters religious and political and the dire consequences of blending the two provide much food for thought.[111]

Maulana Abul Hasan 'Ali Nadwi[112]

Nadwi emphasized that the relationship between God and human beings is one of creator and creature or Lord and slave. This form of relationship entails that human beings give primary importance to acts of worship (*'ibadat*), various forms of *dhikr* and bidding prayers. He further argues that acts of worship along with the other four pillars of Islam hold within the overall organization of religion a fundamental and central position.

Troll highlights the importance that Nadwi gives for ritual worship and devotional practice. Nadwi argued that the leading ulema of the past emphasized the importance of developing a deep spiritual life in the nearness of God, intimacy, love and wonder. It could be said that Nadwi represented a *bhakti* (devotional) movement within Islam. Deep devotion alone can remove every form of associationism (tendency to associate God with created realities) from the hearts and minds of Muslims. Associationism is considered to be the greatest sin in Islam. Troll recognises that a number of Muslim scholars are quite concerned about the narrow vision of Maulana Maudūdī that reduced Islam to a socio-political organisation that pressed for the establishment of a theocratic state. As a Christian scholar of Islam, Troll brings to the knowledge of Christian readers and creates in them an interest to gain a deep knowledge of contemporary Muslim thinking that argues for peaceful coexistence on the Qur'ânic foundation.

Troll's Assessment: Re-interpreting Islam Could Hold the Key to the Future[113]

Through Troll's interaction with scholars and their written texts, he brings his intellectual seriousness bear upon his relations with Muslims. Troll recognizes the conflict in the minds of many Muslims between authenticity (in matters of life and doctrine as presented in the Qur'ân) and modernity that argues for progressive nature of truth. In the era of modernity, the human mind plays a vital role in interpreting and analysing the foundational texts for modern man and woman.[114]

In his efforts, Troll recognizes three types of Islam: *cultural Islam*, *Islamist Islam* (which has inherent tendency to be radical) and the *Islam of reinterpretation* that is based on the spirit of the letter.[115] Cultural Islam is "understood to be Islam as it is believed, experienced and practised in a given society."[116] This form of Islam takes a number of local elements into its legacy, and but it is perhaps not critical enough to scrutinize the demands of blind imitation that could destroy the vitality of the religious faith. An Islamist interprets the commandments of Allāh in a literal way, unconditioned by the historical circumstances. Such literalist reading of the Qur'ān inspires an Islamist to impose the commandments of Allāh even if it is through political militancy or even through terrorism. The proponents of *Islam of reinterpretation* try to identify the spirit behind the letter of the Qur'ān. As a result of his careful reading of Islamic scholars, Troll came to recognize that the *Islam of reinterpretation* could hold the key to the future because it responds flexibly to the challenges of modernity without denying continuity with at least some of the historical understanding of Islam.

Troll recognises that the proponents of *Islam of reinterpretation*, unlike the reformers of the 19th and 20th centuries, see reason not simply as universal reason or self-evident criterion, but as a socially constructed ability which exists with a variety of practices and different discourses on theory. They emphasise the following: freedom of thought and individual consciousness of freedom. They understand modernity as the critical light that modern knowledge has generated. They are convinced: "it is not sufficient to modernize Muslim societies in the fields of science and technology without at the same time probing the corpus of tradition religious interpretations."[117] Thus, Troll recognises that intellectual reconstruction and spiritual regeneration are key issues for progressive thinkers.

According to Troll, the true religious significance of the religious text emerges when academic scholarship enriches the devout religious approach to the text. In the process the devout approach acquires an intellectually reliable basis.

The approach of progressive thinkers liberates the Muslim mind from seeing in the Qur'ân only its utilitarian and superficial aspects. It happens when an exegetic method subordinates the text of the Qur'ân only to *hadīth* and to the doctrinal and legal codes. As a result, the believer who uses this exegetic method would be confined to what is strictly useful. This narrows down the belief of the believer and brings to a halt the dynamism of his/her faith. What is beyond the basic meaning would be considered by such a believer as temptation and it should be repressed. It leads the believer to appreciate only what is certain, what brings calmness as prescribed by the past. In the event of a crisis, it leads either to indifference or violence.[118]

In contrast to the narrow utilitarian approach, the progressive thinkers' method, "proceeds critically and historically and can thus restore to the revealed Word the vitality of its language, its symbols and, by extension, its spiritual and intellectual power. This probably creates space for a different style of belief on which is founded on a sense of assuredness allowing the belief to remain open-minded to questions and contestations: one which is proud of the breadth of the mission of the Qur'ân; and one which is confident that this breadth can inspire in the believer an enhanced sense of humility and openness to others, whoever they may be, and however they may define themselves."[119] In short, Troll recognizes a contextual method in the approach of these progressive scholars, whose reflection is sensitive to the context and history.

The Qur'ânic View of Religions: Grounds for Living Together

Having interacted in depth with Indian Muslim intellectuals, Troll comes to recognise the Qur'ânic grounds for people of different religions living together. Troll sets up three steps to recognise these grounds for living together. First, he takes the context into account: as far as Islam is concerned, the developments of the last centuries culminating in the abolition of the caliphate have led to an erosion of the ummah. The traditional division of the world into *dar-al-islam* and *dar-al-harb* has lost much of its meaning. The frontiers of the ummah are no longer definable in terms of geography and political boundaries. While 'Islam as culture' and 'Islam as politics' remain strong and retain a wide and perhaps, even widening allegiance, 'Islam as conviction', a living faith, a commitment, including the dimension of metaphysical certitude as well as cultic observance, is in deep crisis.[120]

Moral Teachings and Metaphysical Vision

Troll argues that while the spiritual lives of Muslims illustrate their inner experience as believers in one God, the moral prescriptions of the Qur'ân pave the way for the quest of God in the heart and mind of a seeker. Thus, the moral teachings and metaphysical vision have universal validity. The social practices are relative and time bound. People who propose this vision will argue that Muslim and non-Muslim relations should not be tied down to a narrow Meccan and Medinan context but should be framed in the overall moral and ethical teachings of the Qur'ân.

Dawa (invitation)

The challenging invitation (*dawa*) of the Muslim ummah presupposes the freedom of individuals to accept or reject it. Because if God had wanted, he could have made all one; but God allowed the difference. Plurality is God's design for the world. Qur'ân teaches that all should vie with one another in doing good. After intense interaction with Islamic scholars, Troll comes to recognise that there are grounds for mutual interaction between Christians and Muslims, which he terms as Qur'ânic humanism.

Qur'ânic Humanism

Troll says that the concept of Qur'ânic humanism draws its authenticity from the concept of man as *caliph*. '*Caliph*' is the vicegerent who must carry out the will of God and yet is given freedom to deviate from his injunctions. God could have prevented any free decision of an individual or a group to deviate from the original unity. Yet He sanctioned a pattern for humankind that allows for differences in belief and behaviour.

In this context, a person's ability to promote what the Quran term *maruf* and oppose what it terms *munkar* is important.[121]

This forms the basis of the Qur'ânic humanism. The Qur'ânic imperative is that Muslims give witness to their faith in solidarity and in critical dialogue with all believers and defend their right to be different. Troll affirms that in order to make an impact on the ever-shifting world of social legislation and politics, Muslims must strive together with others to contribute to the construction of not only of their own sectional world but also of the common universe with the aim of achieving maximum universal justice. This universe necessarily is pluralistic, an open Muslim ummah whilst being globally indivisible, accepts and respects diversity, as may be seen in the Constitution of Medina of AD 623 promulgated by the Prophet of Islam himself. This Constitution brought into association, in a spirit of harmony, both Jews and Muslims and provided a foundation in theory and practice, for the right of the other to be different.[122]

Troll writes: "the spiritual attitude demanded of the Muslim believer as witness of God in a pluralistic and questioning world is one of listening to God who is near to each person. It is an attitude of respect for each person's loyalties and of harmony with all who are striving for what is true, good and beautiful".[123] In Troll's building the case for Qur'ânic humanism, one can easily find the impact of Vahiduddin Khan.

This section discussed the salient features of Troll's interaction with Muslims. When the Church assigned him the task of intense Christian-Muslim dialogue, he recognised that reading Islamic texts and meeting Muslims and discussing with them their theological thinking, was an essential expression of his priestly ministry. Therefore, in all his academic and personal interactions with Muslims Troll applied his critical mind and discerning heart. This helped him to recognize that though the political dimension of Islam, which is one of the historically dominant models, cannot reduce Islam merely to political expression. The spiritual dimension of Islam shapes the lives of millions of Muslims.

Thus, he affirms the deeper dimensions of Islam, especially its spiritual dimension, without any ambiguity.

Moreover, his interactions with varied Islamic theological sources helped him also to recognise and appreciate the grounds within the Qur'ânic thinking for the harmonious grounds for living together of people of different religious traditions. One recognises that deeper understanding of religious traditions opens channels of communication and dialogue.

Furthermore, Troll emphasises that spiritual and intellectual efforts to read one another's scriptures, adapting creatively to ever emerging situations and confident partnership with Muslims (indeed with people of all religions) in a culturally and spiritually diverse world is the way ahead. It should be confidently emphasized that Troll is involved in this intellectual and spiritual labour *consciously* as one sent among Muslims by the Church. His striving to understand the other, the labour of love itself is the powerful manifestation of his faith among Muslims. It should be said that through his mindful entering into Muslim life and their spiritual and intellectual systems, Troll transforms his intellectual labour into mission, the **witness to his faith**.

Engaging with Theological Issues in Christian-Muslim Relations
The last section presented an overall picture of the efforts Troll made to develop his approach towards Islam and Muslims through intense interaction with Muslim thinkers, either through their texts or in personal conversation with them. His approach is marked by commitment to his faith and by an ongoing discernment of the Spirit in his dialogical contact with Muslims. It will be shown that for Troll, dialogue with Muslims is conversation in which words proceed from the inner freedom of the person. In this religious conversation Troll as a Christian and his Muslim interlocutor express the inner truth they are committed to. The inner truth expressed in deep dialogue transforms both. Thus, both participants discover the dialogical character of truth. In such deep religious conversations, the inner meaning of truth reveals itself

as love. Love makes this endeavour fruitful.[124] It is obvious from the previous sections that love for Muslims underpins Troll's intellectual and spiritual journey among them.

Magisterium: A guiding Force in Dialogical Journey

In the last chapter it was noted that the philosophical trends of Existentialism and Personalism had an impact on the thinking of Courtois. These philosophical trends impacted the 20th century Catholic theology.[125] This new theological current was termed as *'nouvelle théologie'* (new theology). Catholic theologians who followed *'nouvelle théologie'* based themselves on the Catholic concept of the Church, in which theology is more supervised by the magisterium and more rooted in the community. Another trend of the Catholic theology in the 20th century can be called 'kerygmatic theology'. This genre of theology emphasized that the contents of faith are primarily not speculative doctrine, but rather an object for solemn proclamation. Both these trends have profoundly affected the theology of the Second Vatican Council. As a Catholic theologian, Troll draws nourishment from the Vatican documents for his dialogical journey. One can affirm that these theological trends have impacted Troll's thinking and shaped his theology. He is deeply rooted in the teachings of the Catholic Church's magisterium and its approach in relationship with Muslims. Troll himself states that "the development of Catholic theological views of Islam is the fruit of the continuous interaction, between apostolic-missionary actions, on the one hand and, on the other, vision of faith and theological reflection".[126] The Catholic views on Islam and any efforts to build relationship with Muslims cannot afford to neglect the magisterium of the Catholic Church.[127] Troll operates creatively on the basis of magisterium.[128]

The Centrality of Mission in Dialogue

Both Christianity and Islam are committed to universal mission. In fact, mission is at the heart of both religions. Troll writes:

> To be a Christian means to share in the mission of Christ through active membership of God's pilgrim people, the Church. The Church is sent to make Christ and his message known and its identity can only be truly established in fulfilling this commission. The Christian Church, both as a whole and as its individual members, lives in, by and for mission. Mission consists of very diverse elements, ultimately incorporating all of life where it is lived out, in a Christian Spirit. Especially important expressions of mission include: prayer, worship and the celebration of the sacraments; serving the poor, sick, oppressed and exploited; contact, exchange, dialogue, and co-operation with adherents of other religions or world-views; proclaiming the Good News and inviting men and women to become members of the 'people of God' and to participate effectively as possible in the all-embracing witness of the Church to the truth, which is ultimately witness to the reality of the 'Triune God' revealed in the crucified and risen Lord Jesus Christ in the power of the Holy Spirit.[129]

He writes further:

> To be a Muslim means to belong to the Islamic community, the 'community of the prophet' (*ummaht al-nabi)*, which is constituted by Shari'ah derived by the divine revelation and which is commissioned by the Final Prophet sent by God to invite men and women to obey God's revealed will; with constant reference to the 'excellent model' (*uswatun hasanah*, Q 33:21) given in Muhammad himself. In other words, as a member of the Islamic community, a Muslim is commissioned to invite others to Islam, i.e. to obedient submission to the Will of the One God – as this has been formulated in the Shari'ah – and so to be a follower of the final, utterly uncorrupted and therefore supreme religion: Islam. 'True religion, in God's eyes, is Islam' (Q 3:19-20); so it is to Islam that Muslims are to invite others: 'Call people to the way of your Lord with wisdom and beautiful teaching ... Argue with them in the most courteous way' (Q 16: 125 also 12: 108).[130]

Thus Troll affirms: "Any attempt to improve relations between the two religions must take into account the missionary task of each of them, as well as the content of their faith."[131] This missionary task is rooted in the freedom of human person and it is lived out respecting and defending the right of every person. As a missionary he is fully committed to the freedom of his Muslim interlocutors in dialogue. Having noted the basic commitment to his faith and to the faith of his Muslim dialogue partners, Troll proceeds to deal with some of the substantial and weighty theological issues involved in such dialogues. While discussing these theological issues, he gives precise attention to the Muslim objections to them. As mentioned earlier, Troll is keenly aware that he was *sent* by the Church to give **witness** to his faith, and thus has to present the central beliefs of his faith in the presence of believing and theologically reflecting Muslim interlocutors. Thus, for him, the questions that Muslims ask are important questions. They need Catholic answers. He formulates those answers not just by repeating the Catechism. His answers respond to Muslim questions by drawing on Muslim faith convictions. Thus, in this ongoing conversation, Troll gives witness to his faith. He develops his responses precisely responding to those difficulties. This approach is contextual as well as dialogical.

Witnessing to Christian Faith among Muslims

Creation and Incarnation Flow from God's Nature as Bestower

Muslims consider that God has revealed His will for humanity; that the human person must obey the commandments of God and worship God alone. In Christian revelation, God's nature is revealed as Triune. In other words, One God unfolds in Trinity of Persons: Father, Son and Holy Spirit. Muslims find it unintelligible to ascribe words like 'Father' and 'Son' that primarily indicate fleshly realities to a transcendent God.[132] The words used to explain the Triune God in terms of 'nature' (*tabīa*) and 'person' (*shakhs*) do not help either, because *tabīa* technically alludes to created nature and *shakhs* hints at visible forms. Moreover, the Qur'ân does not refer to the third person of the Trinity anywhere. Troll discusses the Christian understanding of Triune God in the context of Muslim questions such as (1) Are you (Christians) really monotheists (*muwahhidūn*)? (2) Do you believe in three gods? (3) Who are these gods? (4): How can God be called Father or Son?[133]

Troll's starting point is a deep reflection on the 'Divine design for humanity'. Drawing from the works of Arab-Christian theologians, he states that God is by nature generous and thus God is the Giver of good. God out of His goodness created the universe and created the human being as God's representative on earth (*Khalīfa*). Man/woman is responsible for the universe as God's *Khalīfa*. God continuously seeks out human beings even before they search for God. If at all a human person searches for God, it is only a response to God's search. If God is essentially a Bestower, the Giver of good, God will never cease to bestow. God seeks human persons because He desires to give Himself to humanity. Troll writes: "[God] desires to share Himself and to unite Himself with the human person, the apex of His creation ... if then God is God – that is, the Bestower par excellence, then he will give nothing less than Himself".[134] Troll writes further:

> It is then one and the same movement which links the two actions or manifestations of God. If one admits the creation of the world by God, then one must also admit the incarnation. By Creation God bestows something whereas in the Incarnation God bestows Himself. To say that God incarnates Himself means to say that God is so much in search of man that He wants to unite Himself to him, and that He does so intensely that, finally, He realizes this union in the Incarnate Word.[135]

Troll has a deep respect for both the doctors of Islam and Sufi saints who respond to this Christian position. He presents an example from each category. F. Rahman is one of the renowned modern scholars of Islam. He cannot but conclude this Christian position as nothing less than the sin of associationism (*shirk*). For Rahman, God's mercy reaches its logical zenith in God's guidance for humanity through books and prophets.[136] Though intellectually challenged by the depth and commitment of scholars like Rahman, Troll did not find pointers for mutually deep conversation in this approach.

However, he was fascinated by the remarkable phenomenon of Sufism and the undeniable spiritual depth of Sufis like al-Hallaj.[137] Troll writes:

> I have always become convinced that although Sufis do not add anything essential to what Christians have in their religious culture ... the Christian believer can and should draw (spiritual) profit from it ... by 'reflecting' the light of Sufism in the mirror of a Christian thinking ... in order to see its image, to understand it, recognize and appreciate its values ... along with advancing my Christian spiritual formation I discovered values in Sufism – in all its variety – highlighting the central truths of my own spiritual tradition.[138]

A Sufi intends to discover himself in the hands of God. A Sufi is conscious of God creating him and in the act of creation wanting him to come to him in total freedom. The created nature (*nāsūt*) in so far as it is creature is infinitely apart from the divine nature of the creator. In so far as it is *creative* (*lāhūt*), the *creative being* (the creator) encloses in itself the effect of its act of creation. Thus, humanity manifests its creative sublimeness. There exists in effect a pre-eternal relation between (*nāsūt*) and (*lāhūt*). *Nāsūt* as manifestation of *lāhūt* in place of truthful witness unites itself to the unique word of God, which proclaims the divine Unicity and Lordship and which at the same time, creates the being which it [humanity] is, in its authentic purity.

Troll engages this in-depth experience of Sufism with the spirituality of the Gospel. He writes:

> The Christian doctrine responds to the same problem by a mediation of the mysteries of Trinity and Incarnation. Put very shortly: The Word of God is His Word, the second person of the Trinity, made flesh in Christ Jesus. Jesus is 'the faithful witness' (Rev 1,6) who declares in front of Pilate, 'I came into the world for this, to bear witness to the truth, and all who are on the side of truth listen to my voice' (Jn 18, 37). And: 'these who were born not from human stock or human desire or human will but from God himself' (Jn 1, 13). Thus, for the believer in God, the Truth through Christ, with him and in him, can render the same authentic testimony as Jesus. Born from God he [human person] will be son of God by adoption. It is man in the authenticity of his humanity that has been created in the Christ, by and in him. The truthfulness of Christ's witness is based on the reciprocity of the two testimonies, that of the Father and

of the Son, and man can, though, in and with Christ, give an equally authentic and truthful testimony. But to make sure of the authenticity of this testimony Christ has sent His Spirit (John 15, 26-27).[139]

Troll has shown how the two traditions authentic to their spiritual and theological foundations open and enrich each other. In such engagement Troll witnesses to his faith. As was noted, Troll draws on from Muslim sources to build a spiritual togetherness that remains faithful to each tradition.

Bestower (*ad extra*) is Bestower (*ad intra*) in the Trinity[140]

Troll carries his logical and philosophical reflection on creation-incarnation connection forward into a theological depth. He states clearly that God the Bestower in relation to the human person (*ad extra*) is also Bestower within Himself (*ad intra*) in the Trinity. He writes:

> This continual, inner-divine Gift which manifests the mystery of the Trinity of Persons in the absolute Unity of the Substance is prolonged outside, as it were, in Creation and it perfects itself in a unique way in the Incarnation. We are thus led to the Trinitarian nature of God, rising from his actions (creation and incarnation) to His being (Love=Trinity). Because God is Gift not only outside Himself but also and above all inside Himself. The *processio ad intra* simply signifies the internal dynamics of God.[141]

Troll says that the unity of God as a common element between Christians and Muslims needs to be approached carefully; for when Christians talk about God, they talk about one who "is known and worshipped as Father, Son and Spirit". Muslims do not accept the Trinitarian understanding of God and would think that Christians have compromised their faith, and the Qur'ân would even accuse them of being polytheists (associators) (Q 5: 33, 72 and in some other places by implication).[142] There are fundamental differences in the understanding of God between these two religious traditions. However, the Christian understanding of Trinity is not a watering down of monotheism, but its radicalization.[143] So, he says, "it is important for Muslims approaching dialogue with Christians to understand that this Trinitarian monotheism is central to Christian belief and worship and is not an aspect of Christianity that can be negotiated away".[144] He cautions that future conversations need to take an approach "which takes utterly seriously the points at which Christians and Muslims differ, and does not encourage a diplomatic evasion of these points for the sake of a dialogue which would suffer as a result".[145]

Furthering his reflections, Troll correlates his Christian faith in the context of Islam and its spirituality and highlights three important elements for deeper reflection and mutual enrichment. First, Troll states that for a Christian, union of God with each human being is real and possible in Christ. Every Christian who lives his/her faith authentically is a Sufi, a mystic united with God. Troll stresses that thanks to the mystery of Incarnation, what is characteristic of a small group of Sufis is the basic norm for Christian life.[146] Secondly, through Incarnation God has made the human person a participant in His nature and, consequently the wholesome way to promote the rights of God is to promote the rights of men and women. Islam emphasizes 'the rights of God'. Troll notes that emphasizing human rights is the way to stress the rights of God. This is another area where Christians and Muslims could profitably work in defence of human rights. Thirdly, in the Christian vision, Incarnation completes itself in the Eucharist. In the Eucharist a Christian believer is transformed and made a participant in the life and goodness of God. The incarnation of God and divinisation of the human person meet each other. The Eucharist expresses the dynamic of divine kenosis in all its fullness.

God's Self-emptying Love – The Heart of Christian Faith

Troll notes that God's self-emptying love (divine *kenosis*) is at the heart of the Christian faith. He affirms that the presentation and explanation of this key concept of the Christian faith might assist Muslims to recognize the core of that faith.[147] God's mercy is manifested in Christ who is God's own son (Luke 20,13). However, this mercy was rejected in the ignominious and humiliating crucifixion. While all seems to be lost, God turned the rejection into the ultimate redemption for humanity. Jesus emptying himself is inconceivable without Him being offered by the Father. Consequently, God's act of *handing over* and Jesus' act of *self-emptying* are one and the same act of God. It is the foundation of Christian revelation.[148] Troll writes: "I should think that this kind of theological approach could be of significant 'use' in our meeting in faith with Muslims and our task 'to give account of our faith' (1 Peter 3, 15), when they request that we do so".[149]

Allāhu Akbar and *Allāhu Mahabba*

Moreover, Troll also correlates this self-emptying love of God with an important expression for God that is close to the Muslim heart: *Allāhu Akbar*, which literally means 'Allah is greater'. This expression articulates 'proclamation of praise' of Allah and a 'cry of hope' on the lips and in the hearts of Muslims. This expression is whispered in the ears at birth and death of every Muslim; and five times a day, the muezzin cries it out from the minarets of mosques across the world. Troll asks if another exclamation carrying similar weight of importance should be found, it should be *Allāhu Mahabba*. It is the greatness of the love of God as manifested in the total self-giving and self-abasement (the *kenosis*) of Christ, which lies at the heart of Christian faith.[150] God's greatness is qualified in God's self-emptying love. One cannot easily dismiss the mutual enrichment that could be drawn from fraternal conversation between Muslims and Christians on these two correlated themes.

Vocation to Service in Christian-Muslim Contexts

Further, this self-emptying love (*divine kenosis*) of God is understood in the historical Christ-event.[151] The Christian faith underscores that Jesus Christ – not withstanding his divine condition – chose to empty Himself of His Godhead out of love of us even as the least of humans, a slave. As a slave Jesus submitted to the will of the Father. Thus, Christ enables and invites every Christian to follow Him and live the same. This way of life is of fundamental importance to every Christian, which urges them to refuse power and understand authority as service. In this context, as a Christian scholar on Islam, Troll makes an observation on Islam vis-à-vis power.[152] He writes: "I perceive Islam as a religion of power, a religion which seeks, in the name of God with all legitimate means, to take power and having once attained it, in the name of God to hold on to it. There exists in Islam the tactics of power and a great ability to arrive at the final goal, in the name of God".[153] How do Christians respond to this? Troll urges that Christians are fully conscious of their call to give witness of self-less service to all in the pattern of Christ. He further writes: "Christians as individuals, as groups and as Church will have to discern ever anew what are the proper ways of living their vocation to service in given Christian-Muslim circumstances".[154]

Appreciating the Faith of the Other in the Mirror of One's Faith

A couple of comments are in place, before proceeding further. Troll sees clearly in the mirror of his faith the beauty of the faith of Muslims. He appreciates and recognizes deep spiritual values that are found in Islam and the life of Muslims. By doing this, he implicitly invites Muslims to see in the mirror of their faith the beauty of the Christian faith. At the same time Troll also invites his fellow believers to listen to the piety, culture and the wisdom of Islam.[155] Troll is clear that the critical areas should be spelt in a transparent manner since fruitful conversations cannot be built on ambiguous foundations. Troll points out the profound differences between Islam and Christianity in the following words:

> ... in Islam, the extended and transcendent God of creation and prophetic guidance; in Christianity, the triune God of free self-giving in creation, redemption, and reconciliation. In Islam the law as the normative system potentially regulating every area of life; in Christianity the normative example of the radical love shown in the self-sacrifice of Jesus, consisting in the basic commandment to serve one's neighbour unconditionally and, as the law of Christ, claiming to represent the radical fulfilment of the old law. In Islamic perspective, the human person as the servant and vicegerent of God, called to responsibility and obedience to the Will of God, as this is finally and definitively revealed in the Qur'ân; in Christian perspective, the adoption of the human person as a child of God, renewed in the image of Christ through the power of the Holy Spirit.[156]

Troll affirms that the differences are "not simply a matter of variations in the practice of religion determined by economic and social conditions, but differences at the normative, doctrinal level".[157] In order to ensure enduring progress, Troll stresses that differences should be taken seriously.[158] Troll emphasises that both Christian and Muslims should recognize the weight and importance of differences between Christians and Muslims.[159] Recognition of differences is an expression of mutual respect. In other words, differences do not mean that there cannot be talking points, but they can be a source for learning, mutual appreciation, and enrichment. One can notice that Troll is consistently drawing from what is close to Muslim understanding and theology to build a Catholic response or a way of witnessing to his faith. In this whole process, it is important to note that Muslims could recognise the intelligibility of Troll's response as it takes Muslim faith seriously.

Human Sinfulness and Redemption

After questions concerning the nature of God, the second most important set of questions Muslims ask are focussed upon the question of 'redemption'. Muslims ask: How can God suffer and die on the Cross? How do you believe an innocent person's suffering can wipe away the sins of humanity? Since God can wipe away the sins of human persons even as they repent, where is the need for sacrifice?[160] Why is Christianity so pessimistic in portraying human nature as radically evil? These questions have set the stage for Troll's ongoing religious conversation with them.

Do Christians Overstate the Gravity of Sins?

Troll affirms the Muslims' right to ask for responses from Christians on these questions. He knows the theological positions of Muslims that give rise to these questions. Muslims understand that sin is chiefly breaking moral and social conventions, and everyone is responsible for their own deeds and will be rewarded or punished accordingly. Human sin is disobedience to the laws of God. They affirm that God is abundantly forgiving. The human person can take the initiative and ask for forgiveness. God forgives. God's forgiveness even goes before human repentance as its cause. God forgives all sins except idolatry and apostasy. With these theological passions, Muslims complain that

Christians overstate the gravity of sin by saying that human sin offends God.[161] Troll knows that these perspectives are intimately connected with the distinctive monotheism of the Qur'ân.

The Corruption at the Heart of Humanity: The Tendency to Sin

In the face of the question Muslims ask and their underlying theological convictions, Troll presents the Christian case as witnessing to his faith. First, he tries to spell out the human orientation towards sin. Referring to St Paul, Troll states that every human person experiences a struggle between the good that they want to do, and the evil that attracts them (Romans 7: 21-25). No one can deny the attractive power of evil present at the heart of our human nature. Thus there is a tendency to sin in every person. Troll writes:

> From birth onwards, it is present in every child. The instinctive experience of the human race is not only of being in harmony and friendship with God, but also of 'inheriting' a 'nature' moulded by a long history of good and evil, and especially by a network of personal guilt. This undermines the possibility of understanding and unity, both among human beings and between them and God.[162]

A metaphor will help one to understand human sinfulness, the way the Christian tradition understands it. One could liken the tendency to sin with falling into quicksand. One who has fallen into quicksand can never liberate himself by his own efforts. The more one struggles to come out, the deeper one plunges into it. Someone has to come from outside to save the one sinking into the morass. One who is on sure ground alone can save the one who has fallen. Similarly, only one who is not sinful, can save sinful humanity. Jesus, the sinless One, is the one who in his obedience to the will of God, gave himself as a total gift to God, and his death and resurrection brought mankind a new hope from the abyss of sin. With St Paul, every Christian recognises that human beings are dependent on the forgiving grace of God given to humanity in Christ. Troll writes:

The death of Jesus on the cross is a historical fact which there are no good reasons for denying. I believe, however, that I can understand the reasons which cause the Qur'ân to deny it. The Qur'ân denies the death of Jesus on the cross in order to make clear God's gracious providence for those who are his own. It is therefore important to explain that according to the Christian faith, God did not abandon Jesus on the cross but raised him from the dead, and transformed his death into glory...[163]

The Distinctive Monotheism of the Qur'ân

However, the Qur'ân denies that the Jews killed Jesus. God sent prophets to different nations. Prophets preached the oneness of God and the need to obey God. Some obeyed the prophetic teachings, but many more disobeyed. Some wanted to kill the prophets, but God saved them from their hands. God is all powerful. This is the pattern that is laid out in the Qur'ân. Jesus is no exception. Troll writes: "It is ... [this] distinctive monotheism of the Qur'ân itself which leads to the conclusion that Jesus did not die on the cross".[164]

Troll makes it clear while writing about redemption, that redemption is not connected to an idea of an appeasement of a vengeful God by spilling blood. He writes:

Redemption is not the appeasement of a vengeful God who, in order to restore his lost honour, demands the sacrifice of an innocent person to bring about atonement on behalf of those who are guilty. Redemption is about the powerful revelation of the forgiving and compassionate love of God, in the life, death and resurrection of Jesus, who, by laying down his life for those whom he loves, gives to human beings the gift of fellowship with God and enables them to live lives empowered by love.[165]

Christians do not overstate the power of sin but rather recognise that the human orientation to sin and the helplessness of the human person in his struggle against the corruption of sin. Consequently, sin is not merely breaking the commandments of God, but it is an offence against the Bestower and touches upon the mystery of God's unconditional love for every human person shown by Christ. Responding to these questions Troll engages with Muslims; understanding and respecting their positions, he presents to them his faith convictions.

Can a Muslim and a Christian Pray Together?

This is an important question Troll deals within his mission of Christian-Muslim relations.[166] In our pluralistic world one cannot completely avoid participation in the worship of the other. The immediate danger that Catholic theologians apprehend in such participation is the danger of syncretism. The question becomes theologically nuanced when it has to deal with Christians and Muslims *praying together*. They address their prayer to One God in whom both place their faith, and commit themselves to bend their own wills to the will of the One God. However, their understanding of this One God is not the same.[167]

Christians and Muslim Believe in One God

Troll says that Christians and Muslims should recognize first of all that they worship none but One God, without forgetting the considerable difference between the Christian and Muslim confession of God's unity.[168] Recognition of differences is an expression of mutual respect.

If one relativizes differences then the significance of difference will be undervalued.[169] However, differences do not remove the meaning one can experience in depth in encountering another.[170] Christians should be aware that Muslim prayer is directed towards the living God; and the Islamic faith over the centuries has raised true worshippers of the one God. Christians also must know that the God of Muslims in not an idol, not a creature, not a lofty idea but the One in whom Christians also believe.[171]

We Stand Before One God

Secondly, the Christians' and Muslims' faith in one God, and their prayer to that God allows them an encounter with God in faith, standing before God in a real way. Standing together helps Christians and Muslims understand that it is God who binds them together, and that the encounter between them is God's gift. This encounter helps Christians and Muslims to live their profound differences in genuine respect. When Christians and Muslims seek to live their relationship with God in a conscientious way, they are together in spite of their differences and thus they are brothers and sisters.[172] Pope John Paul II stressed this aspect in his address to Muslims in the Philippines. He told them: "I deliberately *address you as brothers*: for that is certainly what we are, because we are members of the same family, whose efforts, whether people realize it or not, tend toward God and the truth that comes from him. But we are especially *brothers in God*, who created us and whom we are trying to reach, in our own ways, through faith, prayer and worship, through the keeping of his law and through submission to his designs".[173]

Every Authentic Prayer Guides them Towards Living in Peace

The spiritual efforts of Muslim brothers and sisters do not leave the hearts of their Christian brothers and sisters unmoved since they stand together before God and every authentic prayer is under the influence of the Spirit of God who intercedes insistently for us (Romans 8:26-27). When Christians and Muslims stand together and pray 'authentically' according to their traditions, they are moving towards living together in peace. Troll argues that one should not stop a Christian who is exploring with Muslims this 'togetherness' in prayer.[174]

Truth Claims

The previous sections presented Troll's engagement with theological issues that concern Christian-Muslim relations such as the nature of God, God's relation with humanity, and the responsibility of Muslims and Christians before the one God whom they worship.

It was shown that Troll emphasises that recognition of similarities and differences will assist both Christians and Muslims to esteem one another, draw inspiration from one another and give witness to each other's faith. Troll further declares that, though appreciation of both common elements and differences in the faith traditions are important steps in Christian-Muslim religious conversations, the conversation will remain inadequate if the question of mutual truth claims remains unattended.

At this juncture Troll brings in the aspect of interpreting scripture and tradition to new contexts in ways that are compatible with both faith and context.

A Fundamental Question: From Christian Position

The Church's claim for truth arises from its consciousness of being sent in the fullness and power of Jesus Christ. Troll raises a fundamental question: "Can the Church, which believes that it has been sent to be a sign and instrument of the truth given to it through revelation, seriously claim that within pluralistic societies it is able to tolerate the competing truth-claims of non-Christian individuals and groups which, at least in the case of Islam, make a similar claim to be witnesses to a universal and final truth?"[175]

The Church's Position and the Challenge of the Modern State: From the Pprimacy of Truth Over Error to Freedom of Religion

The issue of religious freedom has had a long and chequered history in the Catholic Church.[176] In the past the Church held the principle of the primacy of truth over error. The Catholic Church affirmed that only it possessed the truth. Since the Church was in possession of the truth; it had only religious freedom. Consequently, Catholic Church stressed that it had the sole right to exist as a state religion.

Moreover, the Church taught that error had no privilege over truth.[177] In other words, error had no rights.[178] This principle had a harsh implication on the human person. While truth remained abstract, the human person was reduced to an object of truth. Troll writes:

> Justice was not afforded the human person per se, that is to say, as an outflow of a person as being, or for the protection of a person's human freedom, but rather *only in the capacity and in so far as the human person was situated within the religious and moral truth*. So it was that in concrete life, where truth does not exist as an essence by itself, but rather as the conviction of real people, everything just lay in the hands of the one authority that determined what truth was. In practice only the Church and those who belonged to her were in possession of justice. In order to

secure religious freedom for all citizens, the modern state had no other alternative but to oppose this theory of the Church and to prevent her from putting it into practice. In this way modern state paved the way for religious freedom against the incipient resistance of the Church.[179]

Further, the Universal Declaration of Human Rights by the United Nations General Assembly (10 December 1948), and the declaration of the freedom of religion by the World Council of Churches in 1948 and 1961, furthered the concept of religious freedom.

'Dignitatis Humanae'

During the Vatican Council II some of the Council Fathers continued to hold that error has no right over truth. However, there was another group of Council Fathers who affirmed religious freedom as a civil and human right. They argued for religious witness and practice, and immunity against constraint to act against conscience. The latter position was accepted in the Vatican II.[180] The Council fathers linked human dignity with human freedom. True religious freedom rooted in human dignity is finally emphasized in the Vatican document 'Dignitatis Humanae'.

Religious Freedom Rooted on Human Dignity

Troll builds his case for true religious freedom on the sure foundations of decrees and declarations of Vatican II. It is important here to lay bare, albeit briefly, the Christian foundations for true religious liberty, so that it will be helpful to understand the Muslim side as analogous to the Christian side.

The Vatican II "Declaration on Human Freedom" (*Dignitatis Humanae*) teaches that religious freedom of every person is firmly rooted in the dignity of the human person.[181] The right to religious freedom is based on human nature itself. This Declaration affirms that this is known from both the revealed word of God and human reason itself and pleads that religious freedom should become a civil right.[182]

Every Person is a Dignified Person, Equipped with Reason and Free Will

The Declaration further advances this argument and establishes that every person is a dignified person and is equipped with reason and free will and thus is bound by a moral obligation to seek truth, religious truth. While seeking the truth, with God's guidance, many may be able to arrive at a deeper knowledge of unchangeable truth. The Catholic Church teaches further that all religious communities, not only individuals, have the freedom to believe and practise a particular religion of their choice without pressure from any quarters.[183]

Thus, the Catholic Church in the Vatican II document '*Dignitatis Humanae*' shifted its claim from the 'Rights of Truth' to the 'Rights of the Human Person'. The Church began to emphasise that the right to religious freedom is an unconditional right of the human person, and the human person has the right to practice a faith or no faith, as one's conscience demands. Here the intrinsic link between human dignity and human freedom is spelt out clearly. In other words, coercion will destroy dignity of the person. Living according to one's true conscience is the way to live a human life with dignity. This intrinsic link emerged as the Church emphasized the centrality of the human person in its reflection.

This *position* does not mean that the Church has renounced her *truth-claims,* or that the Catholic Church has chosen to live with indifference. Would not an indifferent life amount to a betrayal of mission? Troll affirms that the Catholic Church makes a distinction between **moral right** or the obligation of each person to seek and acknowledge, uphold and embrace truth; and the **legal right** of freedom of religion. However, this legal right to religious freedom, as '*Dignitatis Humanae*' emphasises, should be practised without interference with the moral obligations of others. All religious believers, who follow different religious paths as their conscience demands, will be able to work for common good of the pluralistic societies if they distinguish between their moral right to seek truth and their legal right to religious freedom. Such efforts, Troll writes; "Never overlook the need of different communities to be able to engage in dialogue of this kind in ways that do not involve compromise, but rather cohere with the core religious convictions to which they bear witness, and by which they are nourished".[184]

Dialogue is Possible as the Truth Possesses All

Christians consider that the Church which has received the fullness of revelation in Christ does not release it from the responsibility to listen and to learn.[185] Troll emphasises that Christians should be humble enough to recognise that they do not possess a monopoly of the truth, but that the truth possesses all. This implies that dialogue is not only possible but essential with the people of other religions, who do not accept the self-revelation of God in Christ, since the Spirit enlightens the hearts of all people with the rays of Truth (NA 2), thus they are deeply grasped by the truth. And therefore in dialogue, "Christians meet the followers of other religious traditions in order to walk together toward truth and to work together in projects of common concern".[186]

A Fundamental Question: From the Muslim Position

Having established the centrality of human dignity in Catholic thinking on dealing with faith-claims in a pluralistic society, Troll explores the position of Islam. In an earlier section it was shown that Troll highlighted the work of many progressive thinkers in Islam who have attempted intellectual reconstruction and spiritual regeneration in Muslim scholarship and life when they connected academic scholarship with a devotional reading of the Qur'ân. Those Muslim scholars demonstrate the Qur'ânic ground for people of different religious persuasions living together. Progressive Muslim thinkers recognise the freedom of the human person to accept or reject a particular way of life. In other words, freedom of religion should be fundamental for regeneration.

Religious Liberty Crucial for Fruitful Relations between Christians and Muslims

After ascertaining sure foundations for religious freedom in the Catholic teachings, Troll explores how Muslims deal with this question. For Troll the question of religious liberty is very crucial for any fruitful relations between Christians and Muslims, since as shown in the previous paragraphs, religious freedom is integral to human dignity, and is part and parcel of human nature. Troll points out that in traditional Islamic thought the 'truth of faith' and 'correctness of acting' bind believers, individually and corporately. The Qur'ân calls attention to these two emphases since humanity has consistently *corrupted* truth and thus *rebelled* against God and spread *unbelief.* The Qur'ân teaches that the religion of God is Islam and thus it is the sole valid religion, and human beings have the basic duty to accept Islam. Moreover apostasy was not taken kindly by both the Qur'ân and Islamic traditions. At this context it looks as if it is a *cul-de-sac* situation for any discussion on religious freedom within Islamic traditions.[187]

The Singular Importance of the Human Person

Troll carefully *discerns* how Muslim thinkers respond to increasingly plural societies. He affirms that a number of Muslim organizations open themselves to the realities of life and display courage in revising their thinking on religious liberty and other related issues.[188] In these changing circumstances, many Muslim scholars explore certain themes that were not given prominence in pre-modern Islam. Troll writes:

> More and more Muslims participated in a way of life and outlook, at the center of which stands the human person, and which is characterized by a consciousness of subjectivity and individuality alien to pre-modern Islamic Culture.[189]

In other words, one could say that the singular importance of the human person is gaining currency among Muslim scholars. Troll warns his Christian readers that this should not make one think that in Islam anthropocentrism has replaced theocentrism. Troll explains:

" ... we certainly observe, however, that in comparison with medieval times, interest in exploring what can be said about God has waned in contemporary Islamic thinking, whereas interest in what God signifies to the human person has increased".[190]

Troll states that though the anthropological reflections ignited in the minds of many Muslim scholars for freedom and the dignity of human persons, so far these new beginnings have not sufficiently transformed any of the great institutes of Islamic learning or initiated any new movements in Islam.[191] He affirms that one cannot deny the influence of western thought patterns in these new beginnings. Troll does not deny the fact that Muslim thinking was aware of the concept of 'freedom'. He only states that this concept of freedom was not thought of either as an ethic of personal responsibility or a political category. A number of scholars, who are not professional theologians but prominent scholars and researchers in different academic disciplines, have contributed immensely to Islamic teaching on human dignity.[192]

The Universal Right to Religious Freedom

Religious pluralism and the interconnectedness of many in the public space is formally recognised by the UN Charter of Human Rights (1948) and by the Indian Constitution: No. 25 (1950). The right to religious freedom is the right to self-determination. It is the right to follow a particular faith and change it according to the dictates of one's conscience. In this light of modern development, the status of 'dhimmi' and laws regarding 'apostasy' stand in need of thorough revision. The growing insight into the sociological and psychological conditioning of religious faiths too leads to a greater tolerance or even respect for systems of meaning and meaningful acting other than one's own.

The integralist, monolithic reading of the Qur'ān emphasizes that the infrastructure that evolved in seventh century Mecca and Medina are to be followed everywhere and at all times. If this is not possible, at least one *should aspire* to that state. This denies any positive value to historical development. Such Muslims want to establish Medina everywhere... they do not distinguish the ethico-metaphysical teachings of the Qur'ân from the legislative textual interpretation.

The New Status of Human Dignity

The concept of the dignity of the human person and human freedom has had an impact on Muslim thinking. Troll points out to three categories of theologians that respond to the new questions that rise along with human freedom and human dignity. Troll states that new ideas do not come from the scholars who study and teach at Islamic faculties, or from Islamists who are graduates in the natural sciences. However, notable ideas come from the scholars who teach in European and American universities. They have had intensive training in Islamic philosophy, history, and Islamic theology, and they teach normally outside theological faculties and they claim to adhere to high standards of critical scholarship.[193]

Many contemporary Muslim scholars base their argument for human dignity based on the following Qur'ânic verses.

(1): The Qur'ân says: "We have **honoured** the children of Abraham" (Q 17:70). Muslim scholars say that this verse emphasises that God has bestowed inalienable honour on human beings.

(2): The Qur'ân says: "and when your Lord told the angels: 'I am putting a **successor/representative** on earth'" (Q 2:30). In this verse many Muslim scholars recognise that the human dignity rests on the representative role which is akin to what is held in the Bible... created in the image of God.

(3): The Qur'ân says: "We offered the **trust** to the heavens, the earth and the mountains, yet they refused to undertake it and were afraid of it; mankind undertook it – they have always been inept and foolish (Q 33:72) Troll states that this is the most important and frequently used verse in justification for human dignity. Here **'trust'** refers to human freedom and moral responsibility.

(4): The Qur'ân says: "When your Lord took out the offspring from the loins of the children of Adam and made them bear witness about themselves, He said, 'Am I not your Lord?' and they replied, 'Yes, we bear witness.' So you cannot say on the Day of Resurrection, 'We were not aware of this'" (Q 7:172). M.A. Lahbabi (d. 1993) notes that human dignity is illustrated in this verse as all people are called to witness to one God... this human calling is fundamental and a defining aspect of what it is to be human. Human dignity does not have to be earned; neither can it be lost.

The Link between Human Dignity and Human Freedom

Many conservative Muslim scholars do not link human dignity and human freedom. They consider human freedom as an additional or secondary gift given by God to humanity. A number of Muslim scholars find the link between human freedom and human dignity while giving closer attention to 'khalīfa' and 'amāna'. These scholars argued that if amāna is freedom then it implies that the dignity of man/woman consists in his/her freedom. If human person is the khalīfa, the representative of God on earth, then the human person should be free since God is eminently free. God is eminently creative, the one who represents God should be creative and creativity is impossible if there is no freedom. Human beings should be free to give witness to God. The freedom to give witness to God also presupposes the freedom of the person to refuse to do so.[194]

Troll concludes that the new ideas that emerge among Muslim scholars would influence the wider Muslim world if Islam was less focused on ideologies in Muslim majority countries. It is not the inner logic of Islam that stands in the way of understanding human dignity and freedom. The attempts to develop these concepts on the basis of Islamic tradition itself stand as a proof to ways of harmonizing these concepts with Islam. Moreover, these attempts stand as witness that Islam could contribute further to human freedom and human dignity.[195]

Troll avers unhesitatingly that modern Muslim thought accentuates freedom of will.[196] This freedom is the precondition for man and woman to have responsibility for their actions.[197] An important question arises in this context. How does human freedom correlate with the unconditional human obligation to obey the will of God? The conservatives would assert that the right to freedom against the enactment of Shari'a does not exist. The right to freedom is the fruit of an unconditional obedience to God. In other words, the right to freedom flows from the human person's obedience and not from the context in which human person gives his obedience to God. Those who uphold the modern ethos would pine for freedom and affirm that God desires free obedience. They would argue that the revealed norms would be put into practice by free and personal commitment, not by external pressure. Obedience to revealed norms is always a free and moral act. Troll concludes that when Islam is less exploited by ideologies of unification and harmonization, the new ideas that emphasise human dignity and human freedom will influence the Muslim masses. Troll states that it is not the inner logic of Islam that stands in the way of human dignity and human freedom. There are efforts to identify the resources in the Islamic texts and traditions that undergird and elaborate human dignity and human freedom. The resources not only tolerate human dignity and human freedom but also contribute to their future development.[198]

Democratic Society, a Prerequisite for Dialogue

Muslims and Christians live in a complex world. If Christians want to establish relationships with Muslims, Troll recommends that Christians should listen to Muslims and carefully read the type of material they publish. He writes:

> it is important to establish to what extent the fundamental outlook of any particular mosque is compatible with a harmonious and respectful co-existence with the laws and values of the country in which it exists. Only on such basis is it possible genuinely to accept each other and to develop a range of forms of respectful co-existence by building on what is held in common… In other words, clarifying whether there is the will on both sides to live together on the basis of the conditions and underlying

assumptions of a secular, democratic society is an essential prerequisite for an honest and fruitful interreligious encounter. Within that framework Christians and Muslims meet as witnesses to the understanding of God and of humanity as derived from their respective faiths in order to contribute to the wider good.[199]

Need for Renewal: Establish True Personal Relationships

Studying a religious system from an intellectual perspective is much easier than establishing relationship with people who follow a religion other than one's own. Relationships demand accepting the other as other with all that is important for them. In context of Christian Muslim relations, Troll writes:

> therefore, we are called upon, [both Christians and Muslims] first of all, to help to establish **true personal relations**. This implies an acceptance of the Muslim as the persons they are, and aspire to be, and a concentration on the problems of today rather than on the problems of the past.[200]

Deep personal relationships strike roots in the ambience of true hospitality. Troll asks:

> does hospitality, in a wider and deeper sense, not ask us to accept persons as truly as they are, with their own historical background, their own feelings and their own patterns of thought; in short, to make room for the other?[201]

Deep personal relationships will further create "awareness of and respect for the tenets of another's faith ... [and] true coexistence in a mutual acceptance of differences".[202] At this level of sincere and deep relationships one would eventually recognise that God is using different religions to draw people to Himself. Christians recognize that human history is tending towards the kingdom of God. Christian witness should be part of this dialogical tension that proceeds towards God's kingdom on earth.[203]

Summary Remarks

The chapter identified the noteworthy features of Troll's contribution that make his voice significant to Christian-Muslim relations in India. A few preliminary remarks are in place before proceeding further.

The discussion in this chapter shows: first, that **discernment** is at the heart of Troll's approach towards Muslims. He discerned assiduously the ways of God in the life of the Church and in the lives of Muslims, their cultures, and their faith. Discernment is an important tool for any serious engagement with people of other religions. Troll uses this tool very conscientiously in his erudite academic pursuits as well as in personal interactions with Muslim believers. It should be pointed out with certainty that proper discernment lays the foundation for ongoing dialogical relations with Muslims. Troll's life-long work confirms that any religious conversation with Muslims without adequate discernment would build resistant walls instead of connecting bridges.

Secondly, he developed longstanding friendships with many Muslims. Transparency and cordiality marks his personal and academic relationship with Muslims. It is evident that objectivity, scientific approach and sympathy marked his approach in the study of the Muslim religious thought. These three characteristics are important for anyone who wants to appreciate the spiritual, cultural and intellectual treasures of others. As a result there is mutual trust between him and his Muslim friends.

Thirdly, he held differences at the normative/doctrinal level should be carefully recognized and affirmed. He stressed that failure to recognize differences may end up in some form of eclecticism or syncretism. That is not true dialogue. Fourthly, he is always aware of being missioned by the Church for the ministry of dialogue with Muslims. This mission awareness makes him a bridge builder between two great religious traditions: Christianity and Islam. Fifthly, he was able to transform his labour of love that is studying in depth Islamic faith and practice into mission that is witnessing to his faith. The fruit of this mission is better understanding and mutual cooperation.

Solid Foundations: Anthropology and Theology

It should be said that Troll builds his dialogical efforts firmly on the anthropological and theological foundations that Catholic theology, especially the Vatican II and post-Conciliar documents which provide for religious conversation with people of other religious persuasions and especially with Muslims.

Anthropological Foundation: Human Dignity and Human Freedom Central to the Dialogical Thinking of Troll

Human dignity and freedom are unshakable elements of Christian anthropology. Human beings are religious and their dignity is inviolable. Troll holds that the value of the human person as a moral self with freedom, dignity and responsibility are central in his efforts towards dialogical relationship with Muslims. Drawing from *Dignitatis Humanae*, he affirms that the human person in his/her conscience has the right to follow a religion of his/her choice. The quest for truth is embedded in the nature of the human person. He asserts that any allurement or coercion in matters of religion and faith would destroy the dignity of the person. Any such violence to human conscience amounts to the violation of human rights. The discussion on 'Truth Claims' makes the theological position of Troll clear: he unambiguously affirms that human dignity and human freedom are central to his dialogical thinking.

Theological Foundation: The Triune God Relates with Humanity in Many Different Ways

The Catholic Church's commitment to dialogue is not just anthropological but primarily theological. The theological foundation for dialogue is the holy Trinity itself. The evangelical counsels; faith, hope and charity, dispose every Christian to live in relationship with the Trinity. The human relationship with God is built by knowing God in faith, placing one's hope in God, and loving God for God's sake. Further God wants each human person to participate in his triune being. In the Father the whole humanity forms one family. Jesus Christ is the Word of God and the seeds of the Word are scattered everywhere. The Spirit who accompanies the Church helps to discern the signs of the Spirit everywhere, and inspires it to reject nothing that is good. Thus the triune God relates with humanity in many different ways.

Bearing Witness to One's Faith Excludes Relativism and Syncretism

In response to this God of life, in his intellectual and spiritual journey with Muslims, Troll always remains true to his faith and gives witness to his faith. This 'giving reasonable account to his faith' is integral to his life and commitment as a Catholic priest. In other words, Troll never gave up his moral obligation to present the Gospel to Muslims. This approach becomes clear in the web page he maintains in several languages that answers Muslim questions about Christian faith. Troll further insists that both Christians and Muslims should give witness to their faith in relating with one another. Mission and *d'awa* have to be actively lived out in their mutual interaction. Christians have a moral obligation to give witness to their faith among Muslims and Muslims, have a moral obligation to extend d'awa to Christians since *mission* and *d'awa* are at the heart of their faith. Christians and Muslims should be deeply aware of the witnessing dimension of their faith: duty to bear witness and proclaim. This attitude excludes relativism and syncretism.[204]

Thus Troll affirms that any effort for mutual relationship between Muslims and Christians that does not give sufficient attention to the *'witness dimension'* of their faiths is bound to be either superficial or ephemeral. As noted in the chapter that would be a like castle built on sand having a short-lived durability. Also any effort to force one's religious conviction on the other is an insult and an affront to the dignity of the other. In short, it is an abuse of freedom.

'Labor of Love' in the Islamic Milieu is a Way of Giving Reasonable Account of One's Faith

What is very significant is that Troll gave witness to his faith not by preaching the Gospel to Muslims as many evangelists and missionaries did in the past. Rather he entered into the world of Islam. This 'incarnational' approach respects the other and their religious convictions and recognizes the presence of God in the other. It is like entering into a holy ground where God is present. He studied in depth Islamic philosophy, theology, culture, history, languages, and law. This led him to meet Muslims at the heart of their faith. This deeper study and analysis of Muslim positions is certainly due to his love for Muslims expressed in his intellectual labor. Such 'labor of love' in the Islamic milieu itself is a form of witness to his faith since he enters into this Islamic locale not as a secular researcher but as a committed Christian missioned by the Church to reach out to Muslims.

Knowledge of Islam and Witnessing to Christian Faith among Muslims: Two Sides of the Same Coin

In India a number of Jesuit scholars like Roberto de Nobili (d. 1656) and Constantine Beschi (d. 1747) wrote eloquently about Hinduism with an eye towards similarities and differences from Christianity. They believed that the Catholic response to other religions should be well grounded in detailed knowledge of the religions and cultures. Like those illustrious predecessors, Troll worked with great intensity to acquire a deep knowledge of Islam and of Muslims in India. His work shows his profound engagement with Muslim society. Therefore, it is not an overstatement to say that his missionary life and scholarly interests coalesce to enhance the overall intensity of his work. His desire is not to highlight the flaws in Islam and prepare a way to **convert** them to Christian faith. He has an unwavering commitment to the teachings of *Dignitatis Humanae*. This commitment makes his dialogical efforts genuine. There is no tension inherent in his scholarship and his mission as both seek to acquire a profound knowledge and give witness to his faith. His deep commitment and work bring to the fore the intricate but real and authentic connection between gaining knowledge of Islam and Muslims and witnessing to one's faith. Looking at the work of Troll, one cannot but say at this juncture that any future dialogical relations with Muslims that disregards an effort to gain accurate and truthful knowledge of Islam would not be fruitful.

However, it is very important to register how Troll differed from many of those distinguished predecessors. In the Pre-Vatican II era studying Islam and its culture was considered important essentially as strategic part of the missionary vocation for a number of missionaries. It is like 'know-Islam-well-so-that-you-can-guide-Muslims-to-Christian faith'. In contrast, a few pioneers like Massignon and Courtois opined that a Catholic can learn and get inspired as well from the Islamic sources. The implication is that Islam contains deep moral and spiritual values. Troll recognises the transforming spiritual values of Islam.

Political Expression Neglects and Conceals the Spiritual Dimension

It has been noted that the 'labor of love' also includes making a discerned interpretation of Islamic intellectual traditions. Troll carefully reads south Asian trends in scholarly Qur'ânic interpretation that is faithful both to the text and context. The political expression of Islam is one of the crisis points of Islam in its relationship with people of other religions and the world. If Muslim theologians could interpret Islam in pluralistic societies the crisis could be faced. Does Islam support a merely political expression of it? Troll has shown in his work that political expression neglects and conceals the spiritual dimension. If Islam has to contribute to the changing world … it has to work with people of other religions… Azad, Vahiduddin Khan, Wahiduddin Khan and Ali Nadwi affirm the centrality of citizenship in a multi-religious and multi-cultural country like India and sincere participation in the human, moral and spiritual conditions of that country. Troll underlines their call for creative adaptation of Islam to ever changing situations. Moral and spiritual aspects have universal validity.

Throughout such engagement Troll's approach to Islam and Muslims is always marked by a spirit of friendship and sympathy. A positive scholarly tradition can counter negative and prejudicial images of one another. The only future for the pluralistic, globally networked societies of the world is a shared future. If we wish to avoid the 'clash of civilizations', there is no alternative, whether in the Western world or elsewhere, to sustain a dialogue between religions and cultures that is honest, critical, and open. If the goal is coexistence in diversity, then all religious communities need to ask themselves how their inherited faith, moral principles, and religious laws should be understood and applied in the context of culturally and religiously pluralistic societies.

Mutual Enrichment is a Mark of a Deeper Form of Dialogue

Moreover, with a number of Muslim scholars he entered into deep and prolonged conversations on faith elements that unite Christians and Muslims as well as their differences between them. In these conversations he was able to contribute elements that could enrich some of the Muslim positions, and learnt elements that could challenge and enrich his own spiritual life, as well as Christian journey of dialogue with Muslims. One could cite the reflections on *Allahu akbar* and *Allahu muhabba* as one example for this level of conversation. Troll shows that Christian understanding of God can deepen and enrich the Muslim understanding of God. The greatness of God is the love of God. Many Muslims would not agree to this point.

In every stage of his conversation Troll very carefully discerns and remains faithful to his faith commitment as well as to the faith and dignity of his Muslim interlocutor. Finally, it should be stressed that Troll's work helps one to realize that interreligious encounter helps one to better know the truth, to understand truth and live by it. In this religious conversation, Christian and Muslim can purify and deepen one's own faith. They can share with and listen to one another for mutual enrichment. Experience will teach them that simply knowing another's faith will in fact deepen one's own faith.

Troll's work suggests that Christians working on the area of Christian Muslim relations should not attempt to prove the Christian mysteries to Muslims. Muslims do not have a common ground with Christians with regard to the Christian mysteries of Faith. These mysteries though are not against reason but above it. Discussion on a rational level only clarifies objections. Faith is a gift, not a truth to be proved. One should bear witness or teach, not prove or argue.

His work further shows that in his dialogical engagement with Muslims, Troll envisaged an open, honest and critical dialogue with Muslims so that both Christians and Muslims understand one another better and together could work for peace and justice drawing from their sources and inspiring one another in this venture. Mission is impossible if one does not listen to the Spirit of God in a conversation of the heart and mind. Listening to the other is giving witness to one's faith among others. In this process both Christians and Muslims allow Truth to overwhelm them.

Christianity and Islam Need One Another to be More Creative, and thus More Effective

That the pre-Vatican II scholars largely do not accept Islam as a 'genuine religion' is obvious. They felt that calling Islam a 'genuine religion' would amount to the betrayal of Catholic faith.[205] However, in the post Vatican II era, scholars like J. Jomier viewed Islam as a distinct and original religion that has a purifying and reforming function vis-à-vis Christianity. R. Caspar wanted to meet the Muslim believer as profoundly as possible for mutual edification in order to search together, in the light of the Spirit, the will of God as Christians and Muslims.[206] Troll is convinced that **Christianity and Islam need one another in order to be more creative and thus more effective**. Otherwise they may run out of inspiration without mutual input, and even hurt one another if they continue to consider themselves as rivals, as it happened in the past history.

Endnotes

[1] C.W. Troll, *Dialogue and Difference: Clarity in Christian-Muslim Relations* [Maryknoll, New York: Orbis Books, 2009], 1.

[2] 'Discerning love' functions critically when a Christian responds to the influence of God directing his/her life. See M.E. Thibodeaux SJ, *Ignatian Discernment of Spirits in Spiritual Direction and Pastoral Care* [Chicago: Loyola Press, 2020].

[3] L. Swidler, "Deeper Meaning of Dialogue Today," *Journal of Ecumenical Studies* 48, no. 2 [Spring 2013]: 143-144.

[4] H. Roborgh, "Transformation through Interfaith Dialogue," *Salaam* 34, no. 4 [October 2013]: 160-162.

[5] V. Courtois, "Editorial," *Notes on Islam* 10, no.1 [1957]: 51.

[6] The Declaration was signed on 10 December 1948 by 44 nations. Many other countries signed later. A total of 171 nations participated in the World Conference of Human Rights held in Vienna in June 1993.

7 Documents of the II Vatican Council, "Dignitatis Humanae," www.vatican.va/archive/hist_councils/ii_vatican_council/documents/vat-ii_decl_19651207_digntatis-humanae_en.html [accessed January 1, 2014].

8 The works of A. Shourie clearly shows the dilemma and misunderstanding. See A. Shourie, *Harvesting Our Souls: Missionaries, Their Design, Their Claims* [New Delhi: Rupa & Co, 2001]; A. Shourie, *Missionaries in India* [New Delhi: ASA Publications, 1994].

9 The word *calling* is used to indicate an inner voice that called Troll to serve God as a priest.

10 C. W. Troll, "Foundations of Dialogue: Obedience to Truth and Respect for Others," in *Seeking Communion: A Collection of Conversations*, ed. J.V. Edwin SJ [ISPCK: Delhi, 2018], 47-64.

11 Ibid.

12 Ibid.

13 C.W. Troll, "On Being Servant of Reconcilation," https://www.sankt-georgen.de/fileadmin/user_upload/personen/Troll/troll52.pdf [accessed January 1, 2014].

14 C. W. Troll, "On Being a Servant of Reconciliation," in *Christian Lives Given to the Study of Islam*, ed. C. W. Troll and C. T. R. Hewer [New York: Fordham University Press, 2012], 115-27.

15 C. W. Troll, "Foundations of Dialogue: Obedience to Truth and Respect for Others," in *Seeking Communion: A Collection of Conversations*, 47-64.

16 Ibid.

17 Ibid.

18 Ibid.

19 Ibid.

20 Ibid.

21 Ibid.

22 C.W. Troll, *Dialogue and Difference: Clarity in Christian Muslim Relations*, 154.

23 Documents of the II Vatican Council, "Lumen Gentium," www.vatican.va/archive/hist_councils/ii_vatican_council/documents/vat-ii_Const_19641121_lumen-gentium_en.html [accessed January 1, 2014].

24 C.W. Troll, "Changing Catholic Views of Islam," in *Islam and Christianity: Mutual Perceptions since the mid-20th century*, ed. J. Waardenburg [Leuven: Peeters, 1998], 19-77; C.W. Troll, "Catholic teachings on interreligious dialogue: analysis of some recent official documents, with special reference to Muslim–Christian relations," in *Muslim–Christian Perspectives of Dialogue Today: Experiences and Expectations*, ed. J. Waardenburg [Leuven: Peeters, 2000]: 233–275.

[25] Prof. Troll made this remark in a telephonic conversation with the author on October 12, 2010.

[26] Documents of the II Vatican Council, "Nostra Aetate," www.vatican.va/archive/hist_councils/ii_vatican_council/documents/vat-ii_decl_19641028_nostra-aetate_en.html [accessed January 1, 2014].

[27] C.W. Troll, *Dialogue and Difference: Clarity in Christian Muslim Relations*, 154. One must note that the synod urged Christians and Muslims 'to forget the past'. How do we understand this phrase? "I am rather intrigued by the exhortation 'to forget the past'. George Santayana, literary philosopher, had stated insightfully that 'those who do cannot remember the past are condemned to repeat it'. I am sure that it was known to the learned authors that those who do "forget" their history can only replicate it, and am inclined to think that what they were advocating was not the "forgetting" of the past, but the "letting go" of the rancor and bitterness that has been a legacy of the past especially for Muslims". Prof. Riffat Hassan (University of Louisville, Kentucky), e-mail message to author, September 12, 2020.

[28] C.W. Troll, "Changing Catholic Views of Islam," in *Islam and Christianity: Mutual Perceptions since the mid-20th century*, 24.

[29] C.W. Troll, *Dialogue and Difference: Clarity in Christian Muslim Relations*, 154.

[30] C.W. Troll, e-mail message to author, September 29, 2010.

On the 6th of August 1964 Pope Paul VI, during the work sessions of the Second Vatican Council, presented to the public the Encyclical letter *Ecclesiam Suam* where he officially opened the path of dialogue (the term dialogue appears here for the first time in an ecclesial document) in the new perspective of renewal of the Church, including the one with all the believers in God (non-Christian religions).

[31] A number of papal documents and popes' speeches in different places emphasize this point. See Pope Paul VI - Ecclesiam Suam 107 "Then to adorers of God according to the conception of monotheism, the Muslim religion especially, deserving of our admiration for all that is true and good in their worship of God". http://www.vatican.va/content/paul-vi/en/encyclicals/documents/hf_p-vi_enc_06081964_ecclesiam.html [accessed January 1, 2014].

Pope Paul VI – To *the New Ambassador of Pakistan* (*Rome, 9 September, 1972*), "We would also like you to know that the Church recognizes the riches of the Islamic faith – a faith that binds us to the one God" http://www.vatican.va/content/paul-vi/en/speeches/1972/september/documents/hf_p-vi_spe_19720909_ambasciatore-pakistan.html [accessed January 1, 2014].

Pope John Paul II – To Representatives of the Muslim Community in France (L' Osservatore Romano, Weekly Edition in English, 23 June 1980) – "It is with great joy that I address my greetings to you Muslims, our brothers in faith in the one God," https://insidethevatican.com/news/archbishop-fitzgerald-popes-friendly-outreach-muslims/ [accessed November 11, 2020].

Pope John Paul II – To the people of Pakistan – Karachi, 16 February 1981 (L' Osservatore Romano, Weekly Edition in English, 2 March 1981) – "It is especially gratifying to witness *how the bonds which unite all those who believe in God have been strengthened in recent years*. I am thinking in a particular way of the bonds of dialogue and trust which have been forged between the Catholic Church and Islam. By means of dialogue we have come to see more clearly the many values, practices and teachings which both our religious traditions embrace: for example, our belief in the one almighty and merciful God, the Creator of heaven and earth, and the importance which we give to prayer, almsgiving and fasting. I pray that this mutual understanding and respect between Christians and Muslims, and indeed between all religions, will continue to grow deeper and that we will find still better ways of cooperation and collaboration for the good of all". See B. L. Sherwin and H. Kasimow, eds. *John Paul II and Interreligious Dialogue* [Eugene, Oregon: Wipf and Stock Publishers: 1999], 59.

Pope John Paul II – To the Communities of the State of Kaduna (Nigeria), and in Particular to the Muslim Populations – Kaduna 14 February 1982 (John Paul II, Insegnamenti, 1982, V/1 pp. 434-436) – "We both believe in one God who is the Creator of man. We acclaim God's sovereignty and we defend man's dignity as God's servant. We adore God and profess total submission to him. Thus, in a true sense, we can call one another brothers and sisters in faith in the one God. We are grateful for this faith ...", http://www.vatican.va/content/john-paul-ii/en/ speeches/1982/february/documents/hf_jp-ii_spe_19820214_musulmani-nigeria.html [accessed January 1, 2020].

[32] For further discussion, see L. Provost, "From tolerance to spiritual emulation: an analysis of official texts in Muslim–Christian dialogue," in R. Rousseau, ed., *Christianity and Islam* [Scranton, PA Ridge Row Press,1985]; F. Gioia, ed., *Interreligious Dialogue: the Official Teachings of the Catholic Church. 1963–1965* [Boston, MA: Pauline Books and Media,1997]; PCID, *Recognize the Spiritual Bonds which Unite Us: 16 Years of Christian–Muslim Dialogue* [Vatican City: PCID, 1994]; M. L. Fitzgerald, "Twenty five years of dialogue: the Pontifical Council for Inter religious Dialogue," *Islamochristiana* 15 [1989]: 109–120; F. Arinze, "The engagement of the Catholic Church in interreligious dialogue since Assisi 1986," *Pro Dialogo* 95 [1997]: 211.

[33] C.W. Troll, e-mail message to author, October 12, 2010.

[34] C. W. Troll, "Foundations of Dialogue: Obedience to Truth and Respect for Others," in *Seeking Communion: A Collection of Conversations*, 47-64.

[35] Ibid.

[36] Ibid.

[37] Ibid.

[38] Ibid.

[39] Ibid.

[40] One should not forget in the first half of 20th century C.F. Andrews came to India to preach the Gospel and not to engage in proselytization. See S. Chandra, *Continuing Dilemmas: Understanding Social Consciousness* [Delhi: Tulika, 2002], 284-287.

[41] C. W. Troll, "Foundations of Dialogue: Obedience to Truth and Respect for Others," in *Seeking Communion: A Collection of Conversations*, 47-64

[42] Ibid.

[43] Ibid.

[44] Ibid.

[45] Ibid.

[46] Ibid.

[47] See C. W. Troll, C. Ramsey and M. B. Mughal, *The Gospel According to Sayyid Ahmad Khan (1817-1898): An Annotated Translation of Tabyīn Al-Kalām (Part 3)*, vol. 38, History of Christian-Muslim Relations [Brill: 2020].

[48] M. Hasan, "Religions of the Edge: Perspectives on Faiths and the Faithful," in *A Moral Reckoning: Muslim Intellectuals in Nineteenth-century Delhi, The Mushirul Hasan* Omnibus [Delhi: OUP, 2010], 102.

[49] C.W. Troll, "Sayyid Ahmed Khan (1817-98)'s Commentary on Mathew, Chapters 1-5, with special reference to his comments about the Beatitudes (Mt 5, 3-12)," [lecture, Aligarh Muslim University, Aligarh, March 22, 2013].

[50] C.W. Troll, "Some remarks on Sayyid Ahmad Khan's Commentary on Mathew 5" [Paper presented at the Jesuits Among Muslims Meeting, New Delhi, April 4, 2013].

[51] Ibid.

[52] See C. Adang, *Muslim Writers on Judaism & the Hebrew Bible: From Ibn Rabban to Ibn Hazm* [Leiden: E.J.Brill, 1996]; T. Pulcini, *Exegesis as Polemical Discourse* [Atlanta: Scholars Press, 1998]; H. Lazarus-Yafeh, *Intertwined Worlds: Medieval Islam and Bible Criticism* [New Jersey: Princeton University Press, 1992]; N. A. Newman, ed., *The Early Christian-Muslim Dialogue: A Collection of Documents from the First Three Islamic Centuries (632-900) Translations with Commentary* [Hatfield, Pennsylvania: Interdisciplinary Biblical Research Institute, 1993]; *The Oxford Encyclopedia of the Modern Islamic World*, II, 412-413; C.W. Troll, *Muslims Ask, Christians Answer* [Multimedia Affairs: Lahore, 2012], 18.

[53] C.W. Troll, "Some remarks on Sayyid Ahmad Khan's Commentary on Mathew 5," [Paper presented at the Jesuits Among Muslims Meeting, New Delhi, April 4, 2013].

[54] CW Troll, discussion paper series III – 3 "Modern Trends in Indian Islamic Thought – The Recent past," [lecture, Sophia University, Tokyo, Japan].

[55] C.W. Troll "Christian-Muslim Relations in India: A Critical Survey," *Islamochristiana*, no. 5 [1979]: 126.

[56] C.F. Andrews, *The Renaissance in India: Its Missionary Aspect* [Edinburgh: Foreign Mission Committee of the Church, 1972], 86.

[57] C.W. Troll, "Recent Studies in Nascent Islam," *Vidyajyoti* 44, no.5 [May 1980]: 227.

[58] J. Basset, "Has Christian-Muslim Dialogue already begun?" in *Muslim-Christian Perceptions of Dialogue Today* [Leuven: Peeters, 2000], 287. See GRIC, *The Challenge of Scriptures* [Maryknoll: Orbis Books, 1991]. In this volume the contribution by M.A. Mensia (chapter 6) discusses a way in which people of different religious traditions could look at each other's scripture in fruitful ways.

[59] C. W. Troll, "Bible and Qur'ân in Dialogue," *Bulletin Dei Verbum* 79/80, http://www.sankt-georgen.de/leseraum/troll37.pdf [accessed December 10, 2010].

There are a number of studies on some of the exemplary approaches to studying the Qur'ân and the Bible in a comparative way. The following are some of them: L. Lefebure, *True and Holy: Christian Scripture and other Religions*, [Maryknoll: Orbis Books, 2013]; L. Kugel, *In Potiphar's House: The Interpretive Life of Biblical Texts* [San Francisco: Harper Collins, 1990], 28-65; M.R. Waldman, "New Approaches to 'Biblical' Materials in the Qur'ân," *The Muslim World* 75, no. 1 (1985): 1-16.

[60] C.W. Troll, *Dialogue and Difference*, 132.

[61] M. Borrmans, *Guidelines for Dialogue between Christians and Muslims* [New York: Paulist Press, 1990], 104-105.

[62] Ibid.

[63] K. Rahner, "Revelation," in *Sacramentum Mundi: An Encyclopedia of Theology*, ed. K. Rahner, C. Ernest, Kevin Smyth, vol. 5 [London: Burn & Oates], 358. It is important to note that within Catholic theology there are two different ways in which revelation is understood. Most Catholic theologians before K. Rahner recognized revelation as truths revealed by God. These revealed truths were gathered in a deposit of faith. These revealed truths should be acknowledged as true on the authority of God as mediated by the Church for one's salvation. This could be called the static understanding of revelation. In this stream of thought the revelations possessed by non-Christian religions were considered to be preparation for the gospel. In this stream there would be no place for the Qur'ânic revelation as it came after Jesus Christ. In contrast to this first school, K. Rahner argued that revelation is not static but dynamic. It is God's self communication to which human person respond. Since revelation occurs within historical situations there could be Jewish, Islamic, Indic revelations. See R.P. McBrien, *Catholicism* [New York: HaperCollins, 1994], 252. See also Rene Latourelle, *Theology of Revelation* [Staten Island: Alba House, 1987]; G. Moran, *Theology of Revelation* [New York: Herder and Herder, 1966]; A. Shorter, *Revelation and its Interpretation* [London: Geoffrey Chapman, 1983]; A. Dulles, *Models of Revelation* [Garden City, NY: Doubleday, 1983].

[64] See especially, Chapter 2 [The Qur'ân as Sign of God] in G. Dardess, *Do we Worship the same God: Comparing the Bible and the Qur'ân* [Cincinnati, Ohio: St Anthony Messenger Press, 2006], 27-39.

[65] It is quite pertinent to quote C. Chapman. He writes: "While Christians see all the books of the Bible as inspired Scripture, they do not believe that the process of inspiration was such that every single word was dictated to the writers. They believe that these writers were thinking about what they wrote, each with their own style of writing, but that the Holy Spirit of God was at work in their minds.

The letter of 2 Timothy, traditionally attributed to the Apostle Paul, describes the Old Testament in these words: '... the holy Scriptures ... are able to make you wise for salvation through faith in Christ Jesus. All Scripture is God-breathed (*theopneustos*) and is useful for teaching, rebuking, correcting, and training in righteousness...' (2 Timothy 3. 15-16). The Second letter of Peter describes the process of inspiration in the books of the prophets in these words: '...prophecy never had its origin in the will of man, but men spoke from God as they were carried along (*pheromenoi*) by the Holy Spirit' (2 Peter 1.21; 'men they were, but, impelled by the Holy Spirit, they spoke the words of God.' NEB).

Christians therefore think of Scripture as *both* the Word of God *and* the words of human beings at the same time. They believe that the minds of the writers were fully active as they received the message that God communicated to them. God was at work in their minds as they wrote. The Word of God has come to us *in* and *through* the words of the human writer. Although the human element in the process of revelation means that people wrote within their normal limitations, it does not mean that what they wrote is not true and reliable". See C. Chapman. *The Bible Through Muslim Eyes and a Christian Response*, Grove Biblical Series [Cambridge: Grove Books Limited, 2008], 5.

[66] Christian medieval scholars considered the Qur'ân as a human document compiled by Muhammad. See N. Daniel, *Islam and the West: The Making of an Image*, 55-59.

[67] C.W. Troll, *Dialogue and Difference: Clarity in Christian Muslim Relations* 136.

[68] Ibid.,137.

[69] Ibid., 139.

[70] D. Ford and C.C. Pecknold eds. *The Promise of Scriptural Reasoning* [Oxford: Blackwell, 2007]. There are five important considerations that are operative in the Scriptural Reasoning Project. *First*, the scriptures are central to identity, beliefs, ethics, worship and ways of living for both Muslims and Christians; *second*, both believers should continually study and interpret the scriptures in order to be faithful to God in new circumstances; *third*, they can learn from each other and engage in dialogue around the scriptures together; *fourth*, a shared intellectual and spiritual striving in response to the Word will facilitate Christians and Muslims to address

difficult issues; and *fifth*, serious discussion around scriptures would help them to identify a common ground. See M. Ipgrave ed. *Scriptures in Dialogue: Christians and Muslims Studying the Bible and the* Qur'ân *together* [London: Church House Publishing, 2004], 144-145.

[71] Ibid.

[72] C.W. Troll, trans. D. Marshall, *Muslims ask, Christians Answer* [Lahore: Multimedia affairs, 2012], 21

[73] Said Qutb (d. 1966) is one of the foremost Muslim ideologues who called for the establishment of the sharia first in Muslim countries and then all over the world. Said Qutb, an Egyptian Islamic thinker argues on the basis of the overarching unity of human experience that it is improper to separate religion and society (*Social Justice in Islam*, trans. J.B. Hardie [Oneonta, N.Y.: Islamic Publications International, 2000], 32) to build a human system that split sacred and secular would violate the principle of *Tawhid*, the oneness of God. He further argued that separating religion and society will remove ethical values from the public space. As a result, one cannot avoid the creation of unjust societies. Islamic society which is rooted in the Qur'ân and Sunnah does not separate sacred and secular. Thus, Islam is a comprehensive and perfect system and its final realisation will lead to justice-filled world. In other words, Islam is a blueprint for social justice.

Qutb wanted to establish a vanguard to lead to the final realization of a fully Islamised society. Jihad, for Qutb is the way to achieve this vision. He stressed that Jihad is not merely defensive as interpreted by many other Muslim scholars. Islam, as a movement, has the right to take initiatives to advance its conviction. This movement will not go unchallenged. Entrenched interests will oppose it. How to deal with this reality? Qutb advised the vanguard to wage jihad and respond in kind against all that oppose the Islamic movement. What about the people of different religious persuasions? Would they be forced to accept Islam? Qutb suggested that they should be helped to reach the Islamic vision through preaching and persuasion. What about the secular institutions? Qutb was candid: the secular institutions have enslaved human masses and they (secular institutions) should be demolished so that people would be free to respond voluntarily to the call of Islam (S. Qutb, *Milestones*, trans. A.Z. Hammad [Indianapolis: American Trust Publications, 1990)]. Qutb's writings are popular among many Muslims. Some marginal groups, being inspired by thinkers like him, do not hesitate to unleash wanton violence upon innocent people (There is an interesting work that connects Qutb's thoughts to al Qaeda's actions. See B. Lincoln, *Holy Terrors: Thinking about Religion after September 11* [Chicago: Chicago University Press, 2006]).

While the concept of the Islamic State puzzles many non-Muslim populations; this is an existential question for people of different religious traditions. Troll engages with an influential Islamist who argues his case for the establishment of the Islamic State, and with a number of other prominent Islamic thinkers who argue that the Islamic State is not the essence of the Muslim faith, and the Qur'ân should be interpreted in harmony with the pluralistic nature of the world and its peoples. Troll interacts with them fruitfully and recognises and highlights in their Qur'ânic ground for peaceful coexistence.

[74] For more information on Maudūdī 's life and his religious and political thought, see K. Ahmed and Z.I. Ansari, eds., *Islamic Perspectives: Studies in Honour of Mawlānā Sayyid Abul A'lā Mawdūdī* [Leicester: Islamic Foundation, 1979]; S.V. R. Nasr, *Mawdudi and the Making of Islamic Revivalism* [Oxford: Oxford University Press, 1996]; R. Jackson, *Mawlana Mawdudi and Political Islam: Authority and the Islamic State* [Abingdon, UK: Routledge, 2011]; and A.R. Moten, "Islamic Thought in Contemporary Pakistan: The Legacy of 'Allāma Mawdūdī', in *The Blackwell Companion to Contemporary Islamic Thought*, ed. I.M. Abu-Rabi' [Oxford: Blackwell, 2006], 175-194. It is important to note that the name Maudūdī is spelt in different ways by different authors. This book considers the following way of spelling his name: Maudūdī.

[75] C.W. Troll, "Divine Rule and its Establishment on Earth: a contemporary South-Asian Debate", in *Faith, Power and Violence: Muslims and Christians in a Plural Society, Past and Present*, ed. John J. Donohue, S.J. and C. W. Troll, S.J. [Roma: Pont. Istituto Orientale, 1998], 223-239.

C.W. Troll, *Institute of Asian Cultures (Sophia University, Tokyo) Paper Series III*, 1-4. June-July 1986. No. 1 "Islam in the Indian Subcontinent - The Legacy of the Past." Pp. 27. No. 2 "Islam in the Indian Subcontinent - Muslims in Secular India." Pp. 19. No. 3 "Modern Trends in Indian Islamic thought - The Recent Past." Pp. 31.

[76] S.B. Ahmad "Maudūdīan Concept of Islamic State," *Islam and Modern Age* [November1983]: 243-44.

[77] A. Saeed, 'Maudūdī and the Challenges of Modernity', in *Tradition and Modernity: Christian and Muslim Perspectives*, ed. D. Marshall [Washington DC: Georgetown University Press, 2010], 125-132.

[78] Ibid.

[79] Puritan Muslims believe that God's will can be known by these divine laws (Sharia). A person should obey the Sharia in every aspect because the sole purpose of human life is to obey God's will by fully implementing the Sharia. Those who deny, dilute, or even argue about the Sharia are either infidels, hypocrites or iniquitous. Puritan Muslims insist that those who obey the Sharia are rightly guided whereas those who disobey are misguided. Moreover, puritan Muslims believe they can create a social order that reflects divine truth perfectly. Besides obeying the Sharia in their own lives, they actively and aggressively demand that all human beings should follow the Sharia. To achieve his goal, they are ready to destroy those who oppose them.

[80] S.B. Ahmad "Maudūdī an Concept of Islamic State," *Islam and Modern Age* [November1983]: 243-44.

[81] S.A. Maudūdī, *The Islamic movement: Dynamics of values, Power, and Change*, ed. Khurram Murad [Leicester: Islamic Foundation, 1984].

[82] C. Adams, "The Ideology of Maulana Maudūdī," in *South Asian Politics and Religion*, ed. D.E. Smith [Princeton: Princeton University Press, 1966], 384-385.

[83] C.W. Troll, "Can Christians and Muslims Pray Together?" *The Way*, [January 2011]: 63-64.

[84] Ibid.

[85] C.W. Troll, "Sharing Islamically in the Pluralistic Nation State of India: The Views of Some Contemporary Indian Muslim Leaders and Thinkers," in *christian Muslim Encounters*, eds. Y.Y. Haddad and W. Haddad [Miami: University of Florida Press, 1995].

[86] At this juncture Azad has to deal with the Shari'a. Azad envisioned the Shari'a as an aggregate of divine commandments for a comprehensive scheme of human welfare. This vision provides space for abrogation of some of the elaborate details of the Shari'a by appealing to the principles of the idea of the Shari'a.

[87] W.C. Smith, *Islam in Modern History* [New York: Mentor Books, 1959], 289.

[88] C.W. Troll, discussion paper series III – 4 "Modern Trends in Indian Islamic Thought – The Contemporary Scene" unpublished papers ... Sophia University, Tokyo, Japan, 3.

[89] C.W. Troll, discussion paper series III – 4 "Modern Trends in Indian Islamic Thought – The Contemporary Scene" unpublished papers ... Sophia University, Tokyo, Japan, 3-13.

[90] C.W. Troll "Islam Lived and Perceived from within a Pluralistic Nation and World: The Case of Maulana Abul Kalam Azad," *Salaam* 29, no. 1 [January 2008]: 8-23.

[91] C.W. Troll, discussion paper series III – 4 "Modern Trends in Indian Islamic Thought – The Contemporary Scene" unpublished papers ... Sophia University, Tokyo, Japan, 3-13.

[92] Ibid.

[93] Ibid.

[94] C. W. Troll, discussion paper series III – 2 "Islam in the Indian subcontinent – Muslims in Secular India" unpublished papers ... Sophia University, Tokyo, Japan, 6.

[95] Azad rejected *taqlid* (repetition) with regard to understanding the Qur'ân. He wanted the thick veils of Qur'ânic interpretations, which are alien to its genuine message, to be lifted up. These veils, he held confuse and disguise the deeper meaning of the Qur'ân. He argued that the Qur'ân should be allowed to speak for itself. He proposed a new path to contemplative study of the Qur'ân. He argued that the

Qur'ân directly appeals to the nature, senses, conscience of every reader. In other words, the Qur'ân communicates directly with the reader. His focus was not to take one back to language and reasoning of the Qur'ân but to help readers to recognize essential message of the Qur'ân.

[96] C.W. Troll, e-mail message to the author, 29 September 2011.

[97] CW Troll, discussion paper series III – 4 "Modern Trends in Indian Islamic Thought – The Contemporary Scene" unpublished papers ... Sophia University, Tokyo, Japan, 19.

[98] *'What is Islam? The Importance of Being Islamic'* by Shahab Ahmed is an important book in this context. Shahab Ahmed presents a view that Islam is a human-historical phenomenon and it cannot be labelled simply as such as 'religion', 'culture', 'civilization', or 'symbol-system' nor can it be identified with some 'essence' or 'core'.

He argues that Islam has to be conceptualized in such a way that it accounts for, as Shahab Ahmed puts it, 'Balkan-Bengal-Complex' where from 1350 CE to 1850 CE Islam has settled across the geographical and cultural situations holding diversities and even contradictions. Such broader conceptualization will avoid reductive essentializing like 'Islam is the legal core of the religion' or pluralizing Islam by giving up the search for coherence and thus not taking Muslims seriously when they define themselves.

Further, the author in responding to the question, 'what is Islam?' notes that 'Islam is a hermeneutical engagement with its search for meaning in the Pre-Text, Text, and Con-Text'. The Pre-Text is Truth that lies beyond and behind the Text of revelation given to Muhammad.

This Pre-Text is ontologically prior to the Text. The Sufis and philosophers engage with the Pre-Text through mysticism and philosophy. The Sufis, for example the Chisti sufis, embraced the concept of *Wahdat al wujud*. This concept emphasizes that there is only one existence, one *wujud* that is God. True existence belongs to God alone. Though in the phenomenal world we perceive diversity, in reality everyone reflects the existence of the One. In other words, everyone is one in the One. The philosophers emphasize that through reason one has access to Truth, the mind of God. Here the premise is that the Universal Reality of God-in the-Unseen whose truth is knowable.

The simple believers engage with 'Text' which is revealed from the Unseen-God-beyond this-world to a human messenger-in-this world, i.e., Muhammad. At this level the premise is that God-in-the-Unseen whose truth is seen in the Text.

The Con-Text is the way Muslims historically lived through cultural, linguistic, expressions often expressed through art, poetry, and architecture. The problem with the contemporary conceptualization of Islam is, in Ahmed's view, that it defines Islam solely by the Text of Revelation. Revelation has, in effect, been downsized to Text alone, whereas historically Islam has been "nothing other than the hermeneutical engagement with Revelation in all its dimensions and loci" (p. 355-6). See S. Ahmed, *What is Islam? The Importance of Being Islamic* [Princeton and Oxford: Princeton University Press, 2016].

[99] CW Troll, discussion paper series III – 4 "Modern Trends in Indian Islamic Thought – The Contemporary Scene" unpublished papers ... Sophia University, Tokyo, Japan, Ibid., 18-19.

[100] C.W. Troll, "A Significant voice of Indian Islam: MualanaWahiduddin Khan," *Encounter* no. 254 [April 1999].

[101] C.W. Troll, "Plurality of religion and plurality in religion: Christianity and Islam" in *Religious Pluralism in South Asia and Europe*, eds. Jamal Malik and Helmut Reifeld [New Delhi: Oxford University Press, 2005], 77-106.

[102] Interview with Maulana Wahiduddin Khan, 10 February 2014.

[103] C.W. Troll, "Plurality of religion and plurality in religion: Christianity and Islam" in *Religious Pluralism in South Asia and Europe*, 93.

[104] Interview with Maulana Wahiduddin Khan, 10 February 2014.

[105] Muhammad made a treaty with the Quraysh at al-Hudaybiyya. It is said that Muhammad conceded to humiliating demands of the Quraysh. Wahiduddin Khan argues that Muhammad accepted this treaty for what he considered the overall benefit of Muslims.

[106] Interview with Maulana Wahiduddin Khan, 10 February 2014.

[107] C.W. Troll, "Plurality of religion and plurality in religion: Christianity and Islam" in *Religious Pluralism in South Asia and Europe*, 94.

[108] Ibid

[109] Interview with Maulana Wahiduddin Khan, 10 February 2014.

[110] Ibid.

[111] However, it is important to notice a certain sense of ambiguity in Wahiduddin Khan's statement on Islam as a political system: 'Islam could be lawfully established only by the free choice of the people'. The key word in Wahiduddin Khan's statement is 'the free choice of people'. A host of questions cannot be avoided: How free is the *free choice*? Does *free choice* include freedom to change one's religion including the freedom to leave Islam and embrace any other religion of one's choice? How this choice is created? Qutb suggested that this choice is created after demolishing the secular and non-Islamic religious foundations. Though Wahiduddin Khan's over all thinking does not allow Qutb's thinking, however, it cannot be denied that there remains certain ambiguity in the thought of Wahiduddin Khan. Troll pointed out whether Wahiduddin Khan in principle accepts religious diversity and separates politics from faith or takes religious diversity as an unavoidable situation and interprets the Scripture to put up with the given reality. The coherence of Wahiduddin Khan's thinking is yet to be established by a scholar from the academic world.

[112] C.W. Troll, "The Meaning of Din," in *The Akbar Mission and Miscellaneous Studies*, vol. 1 *Islam in India: Studies and Commentaries*, ed. C.W. Troll [New Delhi: Vikas Publishing House, 1982], 168-177.

[113] C.W. Troll, "Progressive Thinking in contemporary Islam," *Encounter* no. 317-318 [February 2007].

[114] Samir Khalil Samir SJ, argues that Islam is having great difficulty in facing modernity. He writes: "Modernity is a concept that is foreign to many Muslims. This is exacerbated due to the fact most Muslim countries suffer from widespread illiteracy and are governed by authoritarian political regimes or dictatorships. The concept of 'human rights' is foreign to a large segment of the population.

There is an additional psychological barrier to accepting modernity. Many Muslim countries have experienced diverse forms of European colonization over the past two centuries. As a result, their attitude toward the West, modernity's birth place, is ambiguous. This is a mixed attitude, one of simultaneous attraction and rejection. Moreover, because the West has become increasingly secularized in modern times, that is, rejecting many ethical principles and values that were common to both peoples, modernity appears to Muslims as a breeding ground for atheism and immorality.

Finally, the memory of the glorious period of the Middle Ages, especially between the ninth and twelfth centuries, when intellectual and scientific activities in the Muslim world had peaked and actually exceeded the achievements of the West, make the current scientific and intellectual decline even more difficult to accept". See S.K. Samir, *111 Questions on Islam* [Ignatius: San Francisco, 2002], 17.

[115] ICAP – **I**ntegralists (Islamists) approach, **C**onservative approach, **A**doptionist approach, and **P**ersonalist approach. J. Renard writes that Islamists insist on "a literalist reading of the Qur'ân, whose absolute validity remains pure, universal, and unconditioned by historical circumstances", Conservatives are "cautious and suspicious of all major change, this approach prefers to let stand the full record of Muslim history", Adoptionist favour "fresh interpretations of Qur'ân and Sunnah in terms of changing needs", and finally Personalist lean towards political activism. See J Renard, *Responses to 101 Questions on Islam*, [Mumbai: Better Yourself Books], 144-145.

[116] C.W. Troll, e-mail message to the author, 29 September 2011.

[117] C. W. Troll, "Progressive Thinking in Contemporary Islam," *Encounter* no. 317-318 [February 2007]: 10.

[118] Ibid.

[119] Ibid., 13.

[120] C.W. Troll, e-mail message to the author on 12 March 2013.

[121] Ibid.

[122] Ibid.

[123] Ibid.

[124] A.A.R. Crollius SJ, "Interreligious Dialogue: Can it be Sincere?" in P-H Kolvenbach SJ, E. Farahian SJ, C. van Nispen SJ, and A.A.R. Crollius SJ, ed. *Understanding and Discussion: Approaches to Muslim-Christian Dialogue* (Inculturation and Interreligious Studies XX) [Roma: Editrice Pontificia Universita Gregoriana, 1998], 64-65.

[125] R. Jukko, *Trinity in Unity in Christian – Muslim Relations: The Work of the Pontifical Council for Interreligious Dialogue* [Leiden, Boston: Brill, 2007], 49.

[126] C.W. Troll, "Changing Catholic Views of Islam", in *Islam and Christianity: Mutual Perceptions since the mid-20th century*, ed. J. Waardenburg [Leuven: Peeters, 1998], 68.

[127] Ibid.

[128] C.W. Troll, "Witness Meets Witness: The Church's Mission in the context of the encounter of Christian and Muslim believers today," *Vidyajyoti Theological Reflections* 62, no. 3 [1998]: 152-171.

[129] C.W. Troll, "Dialogue as Encounter in Faith: problems and prospects," [A Public lecture delivered on 26 November 2008, at IAIS Malaysia, IAIS Occasional Papers Series 3], 8.

[130] Ibid., 9.

[131] Ibid., 10.

[132] D. Madigan, "The Trinity in Christian Muslim Dialogue", *Salaam* 6, no.1 [January 1985]: 4-12.

[133] C.W. Troll, *Muslims Ask, Christians Answer* edited by David Marshall, [Lahore: Multi Media Affairs, 2012], 59-60.

[134] C.W. Troll, "Who is Jesus Christ in a world of many faiths?", *Report of the Swanwick Christology Conference- September 1999* [London: CCIFR/CTBI, 1999], 19.

[135] Ibid., 22.

[136] F. Rahman, *Major Themes in the Qur'ân* [Minneapolis/Chicago, 1980], 9.

[137] Commenting upon Roger Arnaldez's book *Hallaj ou la religion de la croix* (Paris : Librairie Plon, 1964), Troll mentioned to the present author, that R. Arnaldez offers a deep, fascinating interpretation of the spirituality of al-Hallaj.

[138] C.W. Troll, "Who is Jesus Christ in a world of many faiths?" *Report of the Swanwick Christology Conference- September 1999*, 23.

[139] C.W. Troll, "Who is Jesus Christ in a world of many faiths?", 24.

[140] The Qur'ân makes several observations about different aspects of the Christian faith. Some of these observations, Muslim exegetes claim, deny the Christian teaching on the Trinity. The Qur'ân seems to challenge Christians on three important aspects of their faith with regard to the triune nature of God. 1. Is Jesus God? 2. Is God, the third of three? 3. Does God have a son? A closer look at different passages elucidates this. Students of Muslim writings on Trinity are hugely indebted to the long-term

work of Prof. D. Thomas who has prepared critical English translations with foot notes and introductory essays on the key writers. See D. Thomas, *Christian Doctrines in Islamic Theology* [Leiden: Brill, 2008].

For the Christian understanding of Trinitarian Monotheism among many works one can consult the following for reference: K. Rahner, *The Trinity* [London: Burns & Oates, Herder & Herder, 1970]; K. Rahner, *Foundations of Christian Faith* [London: Darton, Longman & Todd, 1978], 133-137; K. Rahner, "God's Oneness and Trinity," in *Vidyajyoti Theological Reflections* 46, no. 8 [September 1982]: 366-379. Rahner stresses that if the Transcendent God has come close to us, then 'medium' through which he has done is none other than Himself.

Also see Y. Congar, *The Revelation of God* [London, N.Y.: Darton, Longman & Todd, Herder & Herder, 1968]; C. Geffre, "The One God of Islam and Trinitarian Monotheism," in *Concilium* 1-3, no.1 [2001]: 85-93; N. Ormerod, "Augustine and the Trinity: Whose crisis?" in *Pacifica* 16, no.1 [February 2003]: 17-32.

[141] C.W. Troll, "Who is Jesus Christ in a world of many faiths?" *Report of the Swanwick Christology Conference- September 1999,* 24. A comment on Trinity is in order here. St Augustine defended the Christian understanding of the Trinity by steering a careful course between Tritheism – a doctrine that holds Father, Son and Spirit are three gods – and Modalism – Which holds Father, Son and Spirit are mere names. He situated Father, Son and Spirit as Subsisting Relations. That means within the Godhead Father, Son and Spirit are relations. Relations within the Godhead distinguish and unite. Within the one Godhead, Father is relation to Son and Holy Spirit; the Son is relation to Father and Spirit; and Spirit is relation to Father and Son.

[142] D. Madigan writes: "The Qur'ân is a little unsure just how to categorize us. We are most often considered monotheists (2: 62, 3: 10-115; 4: 55; 5: 69,82) although sometimes classified as unbelievers (5: 11, 72-73; 9: 30) or as polytheists ...", See D. Madigan, "The Trinity in Muslim/Christian Dialogue," in *Salaam* 6, no.1 [September 1985]: 4.

[143] D. Madigan, "The Trinity in Muslim/Christian Dialogue," in *Salaam* 6, no.2 [September 1985]: 53.

[144] C.W. Troll, e-mail message to the author on 12 March 2013.

[145] Ibid.

[146] C.W. Troll, "Who is Jesus Christ in a world of many faiths?" *Report of the Swanwick Christology Conference- September 1999,* 26.

[147] "In the face of the Islamic vision of the human creature before God, and of divine guidance conveyed by the prophets which – from the view of Christian faith – does not perceive and even obscures in some respect, the true depth of God's self-giving love, the Church has the duty to show forth and to witness to the full truth revealed in the person and career of Christ, in integral obedience to God and His

word and in delicate, serving love towards the Muslims". See C.W. Troll, "Witness Meets Witness: The Church's Mission in the context of the encounter of Christian and Muslim believers today," *Vidyajyoti Theological Reflections* 62, no. 3 [1998]: 166.

[148] C.W. Troll, "Who is Jesus Christ in a world of many faiths?" *Report of the Swanwick Christology Conference- September 1999*, 28.

[149] Ibid.

[150] C.W. Troll, "Allāhu Akbar: as a Central Theme of Religious Conversation with Muslim Believers," *Encounter* no. 272 [February 2002]: 1-11.

[151] Emeritus Pope Benedict XVI while addressing the participants gathered for the seminar organized by the Catholic-Muslim Forum on November 6, 2008 at Clementine Hall said: "The Christian tradition proclaims that God is Love (cf. *1 Jn* 4:16). It was out of love that he created the whole universe, and by his love he becomes present in human history. The love of God became visible, manifested fully and definitively in Jesus Christ. He thus came down to meet man and, while remaining God, took on our nature. He gave himself in order to restore full dignity to each person and to bring us salvation. How could we ever explain the mystery of the incarnation and the redemption except by Love? This infinite and eternal love enables us to respond by giving all our love in return: love for God and love for neighbor. This truth, which we consider foundational, was what I wished to emphasize in my first Encyclical, *Deus Caritas Est*, since this is a central teaching of the Christian faith. Our calling and mission is to share freely with others the love which God lavishes upon us without any merit of our own." Pope Benedict XVI, http://www.vatican.va/holy_father/benedict_xvi/speeches/2008/november/documents/hf_ben-xvi_spe_20081106_cath-islamic-leaders_en.html [accessed November 10, 2013].

[152] C.W. Troll, "Who is Jesus Christ in a world of many faiths?" *Report of the Swanwick Christology Conference- September 1999*, 30-31.

[153] Ibid. 31.

[154] Ibid.

[155] C.W. Troll, *Dialogue and Difference: Clarity in Christian Muslim Relations*, 95.

[156] C.W. Troll, "Dialogue as Encounter in Faith: problems and prospects," [A Public lecture delivered on 26 November 2008, at IAIS Malaysia ... IAIS Occasional Papers Series 3], 14.

[157] Ibid., 10.

[158] Ibid.

[159] C.W. Troll, "Can Christians and Muslims Pray Together?" *The Way* 50, no.1 [January 2011]: 53-70.

[160] C.W. Troll, *Muslims Ask, Christians Answer* ed. David Marshall, [Lahore: Multi Media Affairs, 2012], 33.

[161] Ibid., 34-35.

[162] Ibid., 38.

[163] Ibid., 44.

[164] Ibid., 37.

[165] Ibid., 45.

[166] C.W. Troll, "Common prayer of Christians and Muslims," *Theology Digest* 53, no. 4 [Winter 2006]: 321-330.

[167] G. D'Costa, "Interreligious prayer between Christians and Muslims," *Islam and Christian-Muslim Relations* 24, no. 1 [2013]: 1-14.

[168] C.W. Troll, "Can Christians and Muslims Pray Together?" *The Way* , 56; A. Teipen and A. Pumphery, "Muslims and Christians praying together, or not: some observations on German Protestand attitudes toward common prayer," *Journal of Ecumenical Studies* 50, no. 1 [2015]: 143-152.

[169] C.W. Troll, "Can Christians and Muslims Pray Together?" *The Way*, 56.

[170] Ibid., 57.

[171] Ibid., 56.

[172] Ibid., 59.

[173] John Paul II, *Interreligious Dialogue: The Official teaching of the Catholic Church from the Second Vatican Council to (1963-1995)*, ed. F. Gioia [Boston: Pauline Books and Media, 1997], no. 363.

[174] C.W. Troll, "Can Christians and Muslims Pray Together?" *The Way*, 70.

[175] C.W. Troll, e-mail message to the author on 12 March 2013.

[176] J. Lecler, *Toleration and Reformation* [New York: Association Press, 1960].

[177] It is interesting to note in the third century of the Common Era, Tertullian (C.E. 212) argued for freedom of worship and religion before the Roman Proconsul Scapula. In the fourth century of the Common Era 313, the Edict of Milan ensured freedom for Christians and all others to practice the religion they followed. See A. Dries, "Religious Freedom" in *The Modern Catholic Encyclopedia*, ed. M. Glazier and M.K. Hellwig [Collegeville, Minnesota: The Liturgical Press, 1994], 734.

[178] A. Dries, 'Religious Freedom' in *The Modern Catholic Encyclopedia*, 734-36.

[179] C.W. Troll, e-mail message to the author on 22 April 2013.

[180] A. Stacpoole, *Vatican II Revisted, By Those who Were There* [Minneapolis: Winston Press, 1986].

[181] The dignity of the human person flows from the fact that every human being is created in the image and likeness of God (Genesis 1: 26-27). See Vatican II, "Pastoral Constitution of the Church in the Modern World, Gaudium et Spes," (1965): nos. 12-22.

Every human person is capable of self-knowledge, self-possession, and ability to give oneself freely to others and gifted to enter into communion with others. See

Pontifical Council for Peace and Justice, Compendium of the Social Doctrine of the Church, no. 108.

[182] Cf. Pius XII, Radio Message (December 24, 1942), John XXIII, Pacem in Terris (April 11, 1963); C W Troll, "Religious Freedom in Modern Islamic Thought: A Catholic Perspective" in *Religious Liberty: A Theme for Christian-Muslim Dialogue*, ed. The Pontifical Council for Interreligious Dialogue, the Commission for Religious Relations with Muslims, [Vatican City, 2006], 56-57.

[183] Ibid.

[184] C.W. Troll, *Dialogue and Difference, Clarity in Christian Muslim Relations*, 51.

[185] Ibid.

[186] Secretariat for Non-Christians, *The Attitude of the Church toward Followers of Other Religions: Reflections and Orientations on Dialogue and Mission* [Vatican City, 1984], Section 13.

[187] C. W. Troll, "Religious Freedom in Modern Islamic Thought: A Catholic Perspective" in *Religious Liberty: A Theme for Christian-Muslim Dialogue*, 57-59.

[188] See E. H. Douglas, "The Theological position of Islam concerning Religious Liberty," in *The Eccumenical Review* 13, vol. 4 [1961]: 450-462.

[189] C. W. Troll, "Religious Freedom in Modern Islamic Thought: A Catholic Perspective," *Religious Liberty: A Theme for Christian-Muslim Dialogue*, 60.

[190] Ibid., 61.

[191] Ibid.

[192] Ibid., 62.

[193] C.W. Troll, *Dialogue and Difference: Clarity in Christian-Muslim Relations*, 57-62.

[194] C. W. Troll, "Religious Freedom in Modern Islamic Thought: A Catholic Perspective," 66.

[195] Ibid., 77.

[196] Ibid., 66.

[197] Ibid., 65

[198] Ibid., 67-75.

[199] C.W. Troll, "Dialogue as Encounter in Faith: problems and prospects," [A Public lecture delivered on 26 November 2008, at IAIS Malaysia ... IAIS Occasional Papers Series 3], 19-20.

[200] C.W. Troll, "A New Spirit in Muslim Christian Relations" *The Month* [September 1973]: 297.

[201] Ibid.

[202] Ibid.

[203] Ibid.

[204] Address of His Holiness Pope John Paul II, Peace: a Single Goal and a Shared intention 2002, 89-92 and Exhortation apostolique post-synodale, "Ecclesia in Europa," *Pro Dialogo* 118: 9-10.

[205] C.W. Troll, "Changing Catholic Views of Islam," in *Islam and Christianity: Mutual Perceptions since the mid-20th century*, 69.

[206] Ibid., 72.

Chapter 5

Paul Jackson:
Standing with the Other

It is abundantly clear that this whole process of initiating dialogue requires a deep Christian faith, for it is more directly focused on receiving than on giving. It seems to be the very antithesis of the why and wherefore of the life of a Christian missionary – to share one's faith experience of Jesus Christ with other. This is not so. In actual fact, it is an incredibly liberative experience. **It liberates us from the delusion of thinking that ultimately words, of themselves, can produce faith in another person.** Even more startling is the realization that this also applies to our deeds, no matter how noble they may be in themselves, for words and deeds can, in the ultimate analysis, be instruments by which we try to control another person. **In dialogue our focus is on the other person and we strive to be as fully open and present to that person as possible. This conscious effort to be enriched by God as experienced by this other person means that we are looking up to the [that] person as Christ looked up to His Father.** What greater tribute can we pay a person than this? Surely it is the Holy Spirit who produces and sustains such an attitude of heart and mind and fully incorporates it into God's loving, providential plan for the welfare of all?[1]

Introduction

Paul Jackson entered the Indian Muslim religio-cultural milieu through his painstaking work of translating *The Hundred Letters* of Sheik Sharafuddin Maneri (d. 1381) (hereafter, Maneri), a Sufi saint from

Bihar (India), from Persian into English. Muslim scholars appreciate and greatly value his scholarly work. S. Vahiduddin Khan writes:

> It is to the credit of Dr Paul Jackson to have introduced us to a remarkable seeker of God. His excellent translation of *The Hundred Letters* of Sheik Sharafuddin Maneri has found a very appreciative response from students of mysticism. It was readily recognized as a valuable contribution to the understanding of Sufism in general and of its flowering in the Indian subcontinent in particular. That a Christian scholar found in the Sufi saint of Bihar a kindred soul is no coincidence: however Christianity and Islam may differ in their dogmatic formulation, there is a close affinity in those spheres of experience which words cannot convey.[2]

His mentor and guide Prof. Syed Hasan Askari writes:

> Fr. Jackson undertook the ... translation [of the hundred letters of Maneri] in order to comprehend the teaching of Sharafuddin, a teaching that flowed from the wellsprings of the saint's profound inner experience of God. [...] Fr Jackson has succeeded in conveying the Muslim saint's experience to a largely non-Muslim audience. It is for me a work of inspiration comparable in breadth and subtlety to the original Persian text.[3]

Another Indian Muslim scholar Dr Asghar Ali Engineer writes: "Jesuit scholar Paul Jackson's contribution to Islamica is very precious. His competence in reading, understanding, and translating the texts of the Sufi saint Maneri is praiseworthy".[4]

The Patna University awarded the degree of Doctor of Philosophy for Jackson's thesis "*The Life and Teaching of a Fourteenth-Century Sufi Saint: Sharafuddin Maneri*". His thesis was examined by Annemarie Schimmel, a world-famous scholar of Sufism from Harvard University; K.A. Nizami, the leading Indian scholar of Sufism, from Aligarh Muslim University; and Syed Hasan Askari, the acknowledged expert of Sufism in Bihar. Their formal approval of his thesis made him confident that he had produced a coherent work based mainly on contemporary Persian manuscripts.[5]

In his thesis Jackson established "an indisputable causal relationship between the personal experience of Sharafuddin Maneri and his spiritual teaching. In other words.... his [Sharafuddin Maneri's] teaching is ultimately, the fruit of experience".[6] Jackson established this connection by examining the primary sources: especially the translation of the spiritual letters and related texts of *Makdhum Sahib* (the revered teacher) Maneri.

Jackson's work facilitated the wider world to come to recognise and appreciate the depth of spirituality that is found in the teachings of Maneri, a saint from Bihar. He writes:

> When I arrived in Bombay in 1961, I heard the first disparaging remarks about Bihar and its people. My personal encounter with the anti-Muslim riots of January 1964 in Calcutta made me realize the precarious situation of Muslims in India. My work among the Bihari Muslim refugees from Bangladesh in June 1971 vividly exemplified the plight of the Bihari Muslims. They were universally looked down upon. I wanted to make known, not only to the people of India, but also to a wider public, something they could be rightly proud of – their great Sufi saint, Sharafuddin Maneri! I wanted this to be a disinterested yet meaningful service that I, a Christian priest, was offering them. This was such a simple, perhaps even simplistic, goal, that I suspected that few Muslims would believe me, so I did not speak of it. My hope was that my efforts would bear testimony to it.[7]

Indeed, his work is being recognized as his service to Muslim world. The aforementioned scholars bear testimony to this service.

The translation of Manerian texts into English is a highly technical and nuanced job of an academician. Jackson did not simply remain an academic. He, however, added a 'heart-dimension' to this skilled work of translation. An anecdote will substantiate the 'heart-dimension' of his work. Thomas V. Kunnunkal SJ (the present President of Islamic Studies Association) organized a meeting between Christians and Muslims at *Nadwat ul Ulema* in Lucknow in the autumn of 2001. Jackson was present at the meeting. He was asked to make a comment on his 'translation work'. He said: "I read the text. **I listen to the voice of Maneri in my heart**. I render Maneri's teaching in English".

Jackson's remark indicates, (1) an intensive engagement with the text and the voice of Maneri that helped him to render in English the spiritual wisdom of Maneri that was locked in the age-old manuscripts,

(2) the importance of 'feeling one with the other' as an integral part of his work. In passing, it might be mentioned that in general hermeneutic theory (Paul Ricoeur) the text stands by itself and speaks for itself. The author has no control over the text. In his comments Jackson, emphasizing an element of devotion to the author, adds lustre to his translation. Jackson appears to develop a 'hermeneutic of experience' which is very close to Friedrich Schleiermacher.[8] It appears that his 'listening' to Maneri taught him that 'listening' is the essential ingredient in one's effort to understand the other and thus at the heart of dialogue between two individuals.

His 'translation work' connected him with the Muslims of Bihar and elsewhere. He interacted with them at the Sufi shrines of Bihar, in the number of *madaris* (the plural form of *madrasa* – Muslim religious seminary) that dot the landscape of Bihar, mosques, bazaars, public places and in their homes. In all his interactions, Jackson is firmly rooted in his identity as a Christian and respects his Muslim friends' identity as Muslims. He never compromises the fundamental aspects of these two great faith traditions in his interaction with Muslims the 'religious other'.

This engagement with the text and people won him a place in the hearts of many Muslims in Bihar and elsewhere. This ongoing interface with the spirituality of Muslims helped Jackson to see God through the eyes of his Muslim friends without ever losing his Christian vocation but only deepening it. It is no exaggeration to say that he considers Muslims as essential components of his own spirituality and life. He lives out his fundamental Christian vocation in a uniquely new and deeply Christian way. His love and concern for Muslims is recognized by the Muslims of Bihar. A Muslim friend of Jackson told him: "Since you [Jackson] came to Patna, the Muslims know that the Christians are concerned about them".[9] Another Muslim confirmed it in the following words: " ... in 1976, Paul [Jackson] came to Patna, and a new phase of Christian-Muslim dialogue began".[10]

Jackson's deep dialogical experience and reflection on experience liberated him from a false assumption that words can produce faith in the other. In contrast to this attitude of Jackson, one finds the Jesuits at Akbar's court believed that their logical arguments on behalf of the 'truth' of Christianity would lead the emperor to the Catholic faith. Alas! They won many battles, but lost the war! Polemics between Christians and Muslims results only to bitter conflicts and suspicion but never to mutual understanding and respect. Jackson himself initially felt frustrated when he was not able to speak about Jesus to the boys whom he served in a Jesuit school hostel in the early years of his arrival in India. Jackson's dialogical transformation is an indication he continues the new approach of Courtois. Jackson's Jesuit predecessors focused on 'giving', namely, convincing Muslims about the truth of the Christian faith, Jackson in contrast focused on 'receiving'. One cannot forget the context: his Jesuit predecessors simply reflected the anti-Muslim mindset of the 16th century, whereas Jackson reflects the light of his listening to Maneri and the Muslims, and the teachings of the Vatican II.

This chapter proposes to demonstrate that the spirituality of Maneri made a huge impact on Jackson's efforts for fruitful dialogue with Muslims. In other words, Jackson's experience of engaging with the text, voice of Maneri and credible lives of many contemporary Muslims, poor and rich, shaped his understanding of Islam, Muslims and dialogue with them.

Jackson is convinced that one *knows Islam* only by *knowing Muslims*. He essentially discovered that an openness to 'receive' and not to be obsessed with 'giving' is at the heart of dialogue. Experience and reflection on experience is the key to 'receive' and 'share' the spiritual riches. This discovery led him to the conviction of 'standing with the other as the quintessential aspect of dialogue'. Jackson's model calls for a paradigm shift in mission by emphasizing 'receiving' rather than 'giving'. This paradigm shift is the significance of his reflection based on experience. This is the significant contribution of Jackson to Christian Muslim relations in India.

Being Totally Present to the Other is the Quintessential Aspect of Dialogue

Jackson recognizes that a committed Christian, who is fully open and present to a committed Muslim in dialogue, opens up to God. In this process, both are enriched by God. Jackson makes sense of this dialogical experience in the following way: for a Christian it is like "looking up to the [that] person [Muslim] as Christ looked up to His Father". Jackson has learnt to be totally present to his Muslim friends in such dialogue. Jackson recognizes that being *totally present to the other* is the quintessential aspect of dialogue. Jackson carries forward what Courtois affirmed: "in mutual witnessing, we see the features of our heavenly father in the other".[11] In his dialogical openness, Jackson brings forth a new level in being Christian among Muslims. They also could learn to be fully present to the other as disciples of Jesus. Jackson's life is a lived-out invitation to his fellow Christians to reach out to their Muslim neighbors. The 'experience of receiving' reaches its peak in 'standing with the other'.

Jackson further affirms that the Holy Spirit sustains and sanctifies this solidarity between a Muslim and a Christian. These words of Jackson simply emphasize oneness of humanity. The implication is that we come from God and we return to God. His words also allude to the Catholic anthropology that every person is created to be oriented into Christ. This thought is based on the Pauline foundation that all are to be gathered in Christ. Jackson seems to suggest that by being totally present to the other, the practitioner of dialogue respects both the other and the inscrutable ways of God. It is easy to make all these assertions but, it is important to establish them coherently. This is what this chapter is all about.

This chapter has three sections. The first section will consider how God has prepared Jackson for the special ministry of service among Muslims. One can recognize how the call to 'reach out' to Muslims fell into Jackson's heart as gently as the spring rain falls on the bosom of the earth. Often the call to a mission is a gentle whisper that needs a sensitive heart. This section will present some biographical details of his life journey before he 'met' Maneri.

The second section is the heart of this chapter. This section will highlight how the teaching of Maneri fine-tunes Jackson's attitude for the deeper form of dialogue with Muslims. This section will have two subsections. In the first subsection the basic teachings of Maneri will be presented. This is a crucial prerequisite for the second subsection that will present how Maneri's teaching and his interaction with Muslims impacted and formed the heart and mind of Jackson for dialogue.

The third section of the chapter proceeds to show that Jackson shares the fruits he gathered over the years with his fellow believers through two equally important major interventions: the Islamic Studies Association (New Delhi) and his 'Islam Exposure' to theology students at the Regional Theology Centre (Danapur, Patna).

Biographical Notes

'I would Like to Write Something Helpful for Others'

Jackson is from Brisbane, Australia. As a young boy he was inspired to write something meaningful for others. This is an early indication of what was going to be his lifelong work: it is to write something meaningful for others. It could be safely assumed that he would not have known that he would bring to light in English the spiritual treasures of a Muslim saint who lived in the 14th century! Jackson writes:

> In our final year we went to a Carmelite monastery to make our retreat. Apart from talks by the priest conducting the retreat, a generous supply of pamphlets on various religious topics was made available to read. The writings of an American Jesuit priest, Daniel A. Lord, struck a chord within me. He was writing for teenagers. What he wrote came across to me as being 'deep and meaningful.' A desire to write something deep and meaningful' was enkindled within me and eventually led to a desire to become a Jesuit, like Fr. Lord, and write something that was helpful for others.[12]

He writes elsewhere:

> I should also mention how attractive I had found the writings of Fr.
> Daniel A. Lord, an American Jesuit, whose pamphlets I enjoyed reading
> during retreats organized for us during our last years at school. He
> 'spoke' to me in a very meaningful way, and I thought that I would like
> to write something deep and meaningful for people but had no idea
> what it might be.[13]

Jackson's words ... "he spoke to me" has a special significance. In the
introduction to this chapter, it was noted that while translating, 'he
listened to the voice of Maneri'. In passing it should be noted that
reading spiritual literature becomes very fruitful when the reader allows
the writer to play an important role!

Jackson wanted to write something so that others could benefit.
In other words, he wanted to give something to others. God brings to
fulfilment the initial gift of inspiration to a brilliant end in an astonishing
way by making Paul the recipient of precious wisdom of a Muslim saint,
Maneri! Inscrutable are the ways of God!

An Attraction to Live in Union with Jesus

An attraction to live in union with Jesus is the soul of Jackson's work.
This attraction emerged as he kept exploring the future. Initially, Jackson
wanted to be an army officer like his father. Not having a robust health
for a career in army, he considered the profession of a physician. It is
pertinent to listen to him.

> While thinking about my future I had first thought of becoming an army
> officer like my father, until I realized I did not have the health for that. My
> next option was to become a doctor, a physician, definitely not a surgeon!
> Slowly, however, another thought came to me, the idea of becoming a
> Jesuit. I felt Jesus was attracting me to live in union with Him as a Jesuit.[14]

Jackson joined the Society of Jesus in Melbourne in 1956. This desire
for intimate union with Christ will fructify in dialogue. For Jackson,
being present to Christ leads him to be fully present to the other. Being
present to the other is looking up to that person as Jesus looks up to
the Father.

On Being Chosen for the Mission in Hazaribag!

At the end of 1960, without his volunteering, he was missioned to Hazaribag Region in the state of Bihar, India. He was happy to come to India, as he interpreted this mission as God's will for him.

He writes:

> In the late 1960 the Australian Provincial selected me to go with Peter Jones to the mission of the Australian Jesuits in Hazaribag, India. This came as a surprise, as thoughts about going to our Hazaribag mission had never been occurred to me. Now, obviously, it was what God wanted.[15]

He arrived in Bombay by boat on 18 January 1961. He was sent to work in St Xavier's English-medium School in Hazaribag. The work was varied, as he had to teach and also supervise 450 boys in various hostels. Although he threw himself wholeheartedly into the work, he experienced a growing discontent as he was not supposed to talk to the boys about Jesus. He felt that the whole purpose of coming to India was to tell people about Jesus.[16] It was a spiritual crisis.

Jackson writes:

> Jesus Christ gave meaning to my life at the deepest level of my being. When I came to India I wanted to share the joy of that sense of meaning with others. That summed up my mission as far as I was concerned. The focus of my life was crystal clear.
>
> Three years later, having been unable to speak about Jesus to the boys, for there was no question of trying to convert them to Christianity, I was disturbed. The one thing I wanted to do was the very thing I was told not to do. I could speak about God, but not about Jesus. What was I doing in India? At least in Australia I would be able to speak about Jesus to the boys in our schools.[17]

He was not left in that crisis for long. Soon the tide was about to change. Vatican II was about to happen. The renewed understanding of mission was about to change the horizon of the missionary work in ways that no one had imagined at that time. The sixties were momentous times for the world-wide Church. It was the decade of Vatican Council II.

Church Should Reach Out to All Groups of People!

On 25 January 1959 Pope John XXIII announced the opening of the Second Vatican Council while speaking to a group of Cardinals at St Paul–outside–the–Walls, Rome. His announcement surprised most Catholics. There was both surprise and excitement in the air. The Council met in four sessions: 11 October to 8 December 1962; 29 September to 4 December 1963; 14 September to 21 November 1964; and 14 September to 8 December 1965.

During the fourth session of Vatican II, on 28 October 1965, the Church's relationship with non-Christian religions was discussed and approved. The Declaration discussed the bonds of Christians with Islam and other world religions, besides the common religious patrimony of the Jews. This new approach of 'reaching out' to the 'religious other' in contrast to the former 'inward-looking attitude' encouraged the members of the Church to initiate a new way of relating with people of other religions. In India, Courtois anticipated this new approach. He was, however, a solitary missioner reaching out to Muslims! Referring to the spring time of Vatican II and the inspiration he got from one of the Jesuit theologians who attended the Council, Jackson writes:

> Fr J. Putz, the famous Jesuit theologian and expert at the Second Vatican Council (1962-65), had just returned from the 1963 session. He gave a talk to the members of the community. He spoke about the vision of Pope John XXIII: "After the Council of Trent, the Church was like a fortress on a hilltop defending itself. That is not my idea of the Church. We must open all our doors and windows and reach out to all groups of people.[18]

Let Me Try to Do Something for Muslims!

'We must open all our doors and windows and reach out to all groups of people' kept echoing in the heart of Jackson. Jackson writes:

> Walking on the college terrace, I surveyed Calcutta by night, which lay spread out below me. I began to reflect on the Pope's desire that the Church should reach out to all groups of people. It was clear that, in our Hazaribag mission, we were reaching out to the tribal people, the Adivasis, the "original inhabitants" of our region. The next group was that of upper caste Hindus. Most of the boys at St Xavier's School belonged

to this group. Then there were the low caste Hindus, known as Harijans in those days, but now referred to as Dalits, a word denoting oppressed people ... Was there any other group? The answer to this was simple – the Muslims! Was anyone trying to do anything for the Muslims? The simple answer was "no". Was anyone likely to do anything? Well, you would have to learn Urdu to do so, and no one was studying Urdu or was likely to do so ... I made a resolution: "Let me try to do something!" I had no idea of what this "something" might be, except that it would involve learning Urdu after I had studied Hindi.[19]

From that night onwards his life had a specific direction – doing something for the Muslims of Hazaribag – without having any clear idea what this ultimately would be.

I realized that working with Muslims probably mean that I would spend my life as a missionary without the prospect of any 'conversions' to my credit. I accepted that. My focus changed. Instead of focusing on my personal faith in Jesus I wanted to be of assistance to Muslims at the deepest level of meaning in their lives. I felt a concern for them. This was strengthened within a couple of weeks when a terrible wave of killing and destruction swept over the Muslims in Calcutta. I had gone to bring the boys back to Hazaribagh in early January, 1964, and was caught up in this killing spree. I felt that, no matter what the position of Muslims might be elsewhere in India, they live in fear of attack at any time. They were vulnerable. I would do what I could do. My focus shifted from myself and what I wanted to do and was now directed toward other and what they needed. A conversion occurred...[20]

When he returned to Hazaribag he took up reading about Islam whenever time permitted. He read carefully every issue of *Notes on Islam* edited by Courtois. He interacted with Muslim lads in the hostel.

He writes that he discovered deep within another conversion had taken place! He writes:

I had discovered that there was not a single priest in whole of India whose apostolate was directed towards Muslims. Instead of being discouraged I found my resolve was strengthened even as the realization became clearer that I could not expect conversions among Muslims. Between remaining apart from Muslims and reaching out to them was clear what the Christ-like option was: reaching out to them. After all Christ reached out to us. The conviction grew that this was what God wanted. Another shift of focus occurred: this reaching out was a divine work. It held no prospect of personal aggrandizement.[21]

He realized that reading about Islam and reaching out to Muslims is a fine combination of mind and heart at work. He writes:

> Without any conscious action plan on my part, this original way of acting actually became the pattern of my life. It would be devoted to serious study, combined with meeting and befriending Muslims. This symbiotic pattern of study leading to friendships, and of friendships encouraging and sustaining me over long years of study, has proved most enriching.[22]

His illustrious predecessor Courtois lived out such a symbiotic pattern: serious studies that led to several publications and heartening relationships with many Muslims both rich and poor; studies and relationships mutually enhance and deepen one another. Like Courtois, Jackson, relentlessly pursued the knowledge of Islam and Muslims, by taking up a serious study of the Sufi dimensions of Indian Islam. Like Courtois he would never hide his love for Muslims. It could be said that Jackson naturally assimilated some of the inspiring qualities of his predecessor Courtois.

A couple of things should be noted here, before moving further. One is that he experienced a conversion from 'what he wanted' to 'what others needed'. The second, 'do something for others', got enriched, transformed and matured when Jackson was made a recipient. His journey appears to indicate that his pilgrimage moved him from the attitude of giving to humble receiving.

Study and Personal Contact – A Pattern Natural to Jackson

Jackson was sent to St Mary's College, Kurseong to study theology as an immediate preparation towards his priestly ordination. In Kurseong, he volunteered to teach English during his spare time. He taught English to the children of a small school attached to a nearby mosque.

He writes:

... [the] keenest student was the children's teacher. When the class was over, he would give me a lesson in Urdu and I then went to another teacher for a second lesson in Urdu. This was the routine for two afternoons each week for quite some time. Again the 'study and personal contact' pattern naturally fell into place.[23]

After his sacerdotal ordination he worked for a few years in the Hazaribag mission in schools. After that he was freed for the 'Muslim apostolate'. He went to Delhi, after an unsuccessful stopover at Aligarh. He started to study for an MA degree in medieval history. He also earned a diploma in Urdu from the Delhi University.

He made conscious efforts to recognise and appreciate the brilliant and exceptional qualities of individual Muslims. It is worth listening to him as he explains one such event.

... I met Prof. Mujeeb, the vice chancellor. When I explained that I was interested in studying Urdu, he realized the practical difficulties involved and suggested I study Medieval Indian History ... Unfortunately Mujeeb Sahib had a stroke and never formally taught me. I used to visit him regularly, however, and was amazed at how he retaught himself English and Urdu. His patient and yet persistent application was a far more valuable lesson than anything taught in a lecture hall. He was graciousness personified.[24]

"I Want to Work on a Sufi"

Doing something for Muslims took a concrete shape while he was a student at Jamia Millia Islamia. He decided to study the life of a Sufi. The reason: Sufis bring people together! He writes:

While I was doing preparatory studies in Indian History and Urdu, I was invited to attend an International Seminar in Delhi on Baba Farid, a famous early Chisti Sufi. As I expected, there were Muslim scholars as participants. I also met two Catholics, George Anawati, a Dominican priest from Egypt, and Louis Gardet, a famous scholar of Sufism from France. I was surprised to find some Hindu scholars there. What surprised me most, however, was the fact that there were also some Sikh scholars participating. This was because some *slokas* in the *Guru Granth Sahib* were supposedly composed by Baba Farid. I made a simple observation, "The Sufis bring people together." I felt inspired to say, "I want to work on a Sufi![25]

Attending this seminar had a profound impression on him. He writes:

The impact of the Baba Farid celebration was the realization of the importance of bringing people of various faiths together for a good cause. This was a far, better thing than simply focusing on one's own religion and not worrying about, or being at all interested in, the faith-life that sustained and gave meaning and substance to the lives of other people. Jesus prayed for unity, not for uniformity. Helping people of different faiths grow in mutual understanding is even one step further towards the divine activity symbolised by the sun's shining on one and all alike.[26]

A large number of Sufi writings in India are in Persian. Any serious study on the life and teachings of a Sufi demands a thorough knowledge of medieval Persian. Jackson was assigned to learn Persian either in Afghanistan or Iran. He went to Afghanistan and found the political situation was not conducive for his language learning. He proceeded to Iran. He began attending classes on written, classical Persian in the University. At that time he was still to decide on a Sufi whose life and teachings he was supposed to study.

This was the time he contacted Simon Digby at Oxford University through the kind intervention of his friend and colleague Christian W. Troll who was preparing a thesis in London. It is pertinent to hear him explaining how he discovered his Sufi. Jackson writes:

He [Digby] suggested two names. The first was Gesu Daraz of Gulbarga. 'That is South India,' I thought, 'but I want to work on a Sufi from North India!' Then I read the second name: Sharafuddin Maneri of Bihar Sharif! My astonished reaction to this was to marvel that Bihar had a famous Sufi. I had never even heard his name mentioned. I checked out some information about him, such as the large number of works written either by him or about him, and the fact that these writings were all in Persian. Here was my Sufi right on my door step, so to speak.[27]

The Mandate of the Society of Jesus After a Deep Spiritual Struggle

The mandate of the Society of Jesus to study the life and teachings of Sharafuddin Maneri did not come easily. It is significant to listen to Jackson how he was consoled after a long-drawn struggle to be given this mandate.

> I returned to India ... and went to Hazaribagh before beginning Tertianship, the final spiritual program of my Jesuit training. ... Unofficially some Jesuits said that I would be staying at St Xavier's School, teaching history at St Columba's College, and doing my doctorate. In realistic terms, the choice was simple. I could either stay in Hazaribagh and teach or go to Patna to make use of my Persian and study the life and teachings of Sharafuddin Maneri ... I would be able to meet my new superior only after the completion of the Tertianship.

> The whole point of the thirty-day retreat was to be able to turn to God in total, loving submission to his will and thus be enabled "to find him in all things." Even before the retreat began, I fell sick. It was a combination of an allergic reaction to something in the air ... with a real dilemma as to what God wanted me to do: teaching history in Hazaribagh or go to Patna and do a doctoral study of Sharafuddin Maneri's life and teaching. I wanted to run away before the retreat began. I could use my sickness as an excuse. The real reason, however, was my apprehension that I might be asked to give up all ideas of a doctoral study of Maneri and devote my life to teaching history at the local college. The struggle was that I knew I would do what my superior told me to do, as this would be clearly God's will for me, but it might go totally against all that I aspire to do.[28]

Finally after the retreat he met the concerned authorities in the Society of Jesus and discussed all issues at stake in a detailed way. "At the end, however, everyone agreed that this was clearly the course I should take, namely to go for a doctoral study of Maneri and then follow wherever this led me. This was my mandate from the Society of Jesus in March 1976 and it still holds good until today".[29]

To sum up: Jackson emerges fundamentally as a Pilgrim. He wanted to do something meaningful for others while he desired to live in union with Jesus. A Christian disciple is called to be with Christ and to be sent among people for doing good among people. Jackson's desire to live in union with Jesus fostered his inner journey. Several Christian spiritual writers like John of the Cross and Teresa of Ávila pointed towards such inner journey (ascents and descents) seeking to find and live in union with Jesus.

It is important to recognize a special spiritual gift in the life of Jackson. It is his ability to listen to the voice of the spiritual writers while reading their texts. Jackson himself has acknowledged that he 'listened to the voice' of Daniel Lord, the Jesuit spiritual writer, and to Maneri while he read their respective texts. Jackson *engaged* with Maneri for about four decades. There is a spiritual confluence of the text of Maneri, the voice of Maneri in the heart of Jackson, and Jackson's own spirituality. Such confluence becomes powerful in terms of bringing about transformation in the lives of people, in this case, in the life of Jackson and possibly many readers of his 'translations' and other learned articles. In Indian sacred space, people recognize the confluence of rivers as a holy place. The Allahabad Confluence 'sangam' where three rivers: two real rivers and one mythical river commingle and make the space sacred. The mythical river rises in people's faith and in their experience. The voice of Maneri could be likened to the mythical river. It rises in the heart of Jackson when he read the text.

The aspect of discernment in the life of Jackson needs to be highlighted. He discerned in the light of his faith and commitment to the Society of Jesus in which he was a member. His discernment is underpinned by his determination to bend his will to the will of God. This act of discernment continually called him to trust God and allow God to work in his life.

The spirit of Vatican II provided Jackson an impetus to reach out to others. He recognized that the experience of living in union with Christ took him to others and his quality time with others brought him closer to Christ. He wanted to reach out to a group of people who are generally considered to be out-of-boundaries for the Catholic Church. They were (are) Muslims. Jackson reached out to them. After Courtois, the 'Muslim apostolate' unfortunately had fallen into oblivion. Jackson, however, arrived in the scene as one who would revive the ministry and take it further. Troll joined Jackson and gave a fillip to the ministry. Jackson's work is being done essentially in and through the channels of the Society of Jesus and of the Church. Jackson who is trained in the way of Spiritual Exercises (a Catholic spiritual discipline) meets the religiously other, Maneri. The next section will introduce first Maneri and his teaching; secondly, the impact of Maneri's teaching on Jackson and his work in the field of Christian Muslim relations.

Introduction to Maneri and His Teachings

Maneri: The Man

Sharafuddin Maneri was born, about the year 1290,[30] to Yahya Maneri and Bibi Razia. Both Yahya Maneri and Bibi Razia were fully committed to the Sufi path to God.[31] They were a pious couple.[32] Jackson writes: "hence it was that, from his infancy, the fact that God reigned in the lives of his parents made an indelible impact on him. He spontaneously accepted God's reign in his own young life".[33] Maneri began his education 'In the name of God, the Merciful, the Compassionate' when he was 'four years – four months – four days' old. The first lesson was traditionally learning and writing a few alphabets. Maneri continued his education learning Persian and Arabic. Later, he went to Sonargaon in Bengal (1310 – 1323) for his further studies. There he attended lectures given by many Muslim scholars. While still there in Sonargaon, he fell ill and a physician prescribed intercourse. Accordingly Maneri took a slave girl and had a son born of that union.[34] This form of arrangement was quite lawful in his times and in his society.[35] However, Maneri preferred celibacy and lived as a celibate from the moment he left Sonargaon in 1323 until his death in 1381.

Guidance Along the Path to God

Maneri returned to his hometown with his son in 1323. His father died before he returned. Maneri did not stay home for long. Jackson writes: "the yearning of his heart was too great for him to settle down quietly in Maner. His need for guidance to find the path to God became so compelling for him that, entrusting young [his son] Zakiuddin to his mother's care, and urging her to consider him as her son in place of himself, he set out for Delhi with his elder brother, Khaliluddin".[36]

In Delhi, he met Nizamuddin Auliya, the famous Sufi of the times. Though Maneri was impressed by the holiness of Nizamuddin, yet, he did not feel called to become his disciple. Maneri called upon Bu Qalandar of Panipat and found the Panipat Sufi was lost in ecstasy most of the time. Maneri was not keen on taking him as his guide. Maneri was disappointed and almost decided to return home. His brother, however, encouraged him and took him to Sheikh Najibuddin Firdausi. Out of consideration for his brother, however, he agreed to visit him as a last attempt to find a spiritual guide for himself in Delhi. He was quite unexpectedly overcome emotionally at this meeting and was deeply affected by it. Without the slightest hesitation he asked to become his disciple. Maneri stayed in Delhi about eight years. He remained with Sheikh Najibuddin Firdausi till the death of the latter.[37]

In Pursuit of Union with God

Maneri left Delhi shortly after the death of his guide. On his way back home instead of entering his hometown, he veered off into the jungle of Bihia.[38] He wanted to give himself wholly to the pursuit of union with God. After living a brief period of complete isolation, he moved to a cave in Rajgir beside a spring. This spring is known even to this day as 'Makhdam kund'. He began to go to the nearby Bihar (now Bihar Sharif) for Friday congregational prayer that enabled people to meet him easily. At times he felt irksome to receive many visitors requesting his intercession with the local administrator. A visiting sheikh, however, advised him not to hesitate to take up the 'burden of people'. Maneri eventually moved to Bihar town and helped people in terms of writing recommendation letters on behalf of them to administrators and guided many seekers in the ways of God.

Spiritual Guidance: In the Hundred Letters

Maneri compiled a number of letters on various spiritual topics, on the request of Qazi Shamsuddin, the governor of Chausa in western Bihar throughout the year 1346-1347 CE. These letters were copied and compiled by Zain Badr Arabi. *The Hundred Letters* gained fame within Sufi circles of Bihar and elsewhere. The royals too paid attention to the teachings of this spiritual genius. Sultan Muhammad bin Tughluq (d. 1351) asked for further advice on some points that were raised in *The Hundred Letters*. The Indo-Persian Mughal elite read *The Hundred Letters* that had been copied for their reading and thus were undoubtedly influenced by it. Undoubtedly Sufi literature has a great spiritual and historical value.[39]

It will be helpful to know that Maneri was not the only Sufi master who compiled his teachings as letters. Sheikh Ahmad Sirhindi (d. 1621) left behind an enormous corpus of 542 letters called Maktubat-i Imam Rabbani. Sheikh Ali Hujwiri compiled Kashf al-jahjub. *The Hundred Letters* of Maneri is a special collection in the gallery of such spiritual literature. Why are *The Hundred Letters* considered to be special?

Bruce B. Lawrence writes:

What distinguishes *The Hundred Letters* from Kashf al-Mahjub is its artful balance – between reflection and conduct, between explanation and advocacy, between detachment to the Law and pursuit of the Way, between sobriety and ecstasy, bondage and freedom, death and life. *The Hundred Letters* ... may be less personal than the correspondence of Sheikh Ahmad Sirhindi, less comprehensive than the Kashf al-Mahjub of Sheikh Ali Hujwiri ... but they are unrivalled – and cannot be surpassed – as an invitation to experience the Sufi Way as a Sufi master experienced and described it, to join him in the endless struggle, which has been ordained for man alone in the whole order, to seek perfection while clinging to the pain of love.[40]

It is imperative here to turn one's attention to the basic teachings of Maneri.

Teachings of Maneri

Be a Pilgrim ... Be Aware of Obstacles

God sows the seeds of divine attraction in the hearts of pilgrims.[41] Pilgrims are on the path that leads towards God. A pilgrim is not a tourist. A tourist stops and often gets lost in the beauty of what he sees on the way. A pilgrim, however, is focused on the destination. The end is of prime importance for a pilgrim. Pilgrims have to traverse the spiritual wilderness towards their destination. Maneri warns seekers to be aware of many obstacles on the way. He compares obstacles to a band of robbers who lie in wait to plunder the travelers. He cautions them to keep a sharp eye on the pitfalls. He instructs them not to be lost on what they see on the way. He advocates the need of a spiritual guide for pilgrims.[42]

Why does a pilgrim take a perilous journey in the first place? Why should a pilgrim burn his boats behind and take a journey to uncertainty? The pilgrim sets out since he thirsts for more in life.[43] What gives one the assurance to take such a risk, a journey to uncertainty? 'Faith', answers Maneri poignantly.

Faith Inspires One to be a Pilgrim

Maneri teaches that it is faith that inspires one to become a pilgrim. Faith shows the way to God. The grace of God stirs the heart of persons to don the pilgrim's garb. God alone calls persons for this journey. The initiative lies with God. Only those who yearn for more solitude can respond to the invitation and set out for the pilgrim journey. Once on the pilgrim journey, one never knows for sure when the grace of God will come and draw the person towards Himself. Anyone who sets upon this journey on his own, succumbs to the temptations of austerities which may result in pride, or even a loss of faith. God's invitation never comes to an ignorant person. Maneri tells us that all baseness can be traced back to ignorance![44]

The Pilgrim Should Trust God

Maneri teaches that pilgrims should trust God absolutely. He gives the following graphic illustration to drive home his point. Imagine a person who is fully aware of his sinfulness and hears a heavenly voice that says that only one person will enter heaven. The sinful person believes that he is that person! That is 'trust in God'. It is relying upon God fully without any reserve.

Maneri explains that the more a pilgrim relies on God and not on his efforts, the more he recognizes that he is united with God and shares already to some degree, in the absoluteness of God's power. In other words, God provides for those whom he calls for this pilgrimage. God cares for the pilgrim like a mother cares for her children. God makes the way easy for the pilgrims. Finally, God leads the pilgrim towards total union with Himself.

God's Call and Human Responsibility

Maneri teaches that any form of the mystical knowledge of God or an experience of God, is a gift from God. Pilgrims should recognize that their experience of God is not the fruit of their searching. It is not a payment for labour undertaken on behalf of God. It is simply God's gift. Maneri, further, teaches his listeners that a person 'sees' God not because he sought God relentlessly, but because God chose to show Himself to the pilgrim. Thus, Maneri urges pilgrims to focus on God and not on oneself.

Maneri also reminds his disciples of the human dimension in response to God's call. He singles out the courage of the pilgrim in the face of challenges that keep him in good stead in his resolve to reach the goal.[45] Commenting on human responsibility in answering God's call, Jackson writes:

> 'Is everything so utterly dependent on God's will alone that man has nothing at all to do?' The answer must be a clear negative. While in no way wishing to limit the sovereign power of God, Sharafuddin asserts clearly that man has a very real role to play. He presupposes qualities of

mind and heart without which no substantial progress can be expected on the part of a disciple. In a broader perspective, his entire teaching effort, together with each quotation he makes from the Qur'ân, Tradition or the fund of Sufi sources he is acquainted with, presupposes that he has to say to man who must, in turn, be able to understand what he is saying. Otherwise it would be pointless either for him to write, or for people to study his writings. It was mainly the many long years of earnest effort which, under the guidance of Sheikh Najibuddin Firdausi and crowned by divine grace, enabled him to give meaningful advice and encouragement to his disciples. Finally, it should be noted that the four decades or more devoted to teaching, some of which was in written form, constitute an irrefutable assertion that man has a role to play, otherwise all this effort directed to explaining the Way to others and encouraging them along it would be utter nonsense.[46]

Importance of a Spiritual Guide

Maneri insists on the necessity of the assistance of an experienced guide for a pilgrim. How would a pilgrim recognize someone as his guide? Maneri suggests that God through a special grace of inspiration will help the pilgrim to identify his guide. Maneri makes it clear that the pilgrim when he finds his spiritual guide will feel a great attraction towards that particular guide and a confidence to entrust himself to him. An experienced guide will be able to guide the pilgrim in the ways of God since he himself has gone through an orderly progress.[47]

Jackson writes:

Even a sheikh's own mistakes can be helpful in guiding others, for he himself can learn valuable lessons by wandering off the Way for a time. The sureness of touch with which Sharafuddin describes some of the dangers along the Way, particularly the most subtle imaginable, indicates he had learnt his lesson the hard way.[48]

It is important to give attention to how Maneri explains discipleship. Jackson writes:

[...] discipleship is a matter of wanting something from heart. As we become aware of beautiful objects, a stirring occurs within our hearts. The more noble the object, the more noble the stirring. A person who desires

Reality itself will be helped by God, for such a desire is pure, stripped of anything base, or even of motives, and is free from inconstancy.[49]

Pilgrim's Progress: Repentance

Repentance is the first step in the way to God. Repentance for Maneri, is 'turning back' to God. Ordinary folks repent out of fear that God may punish them. They turn away from their sins and observe God's commandments. Pilgrims are more aware of God than the ordinary folk. Pilgrims observe commandments not out of fear but for God's sake. Pilgrims wish to be faithful to the commandments out of love of God. The pilgrims, in the words of Jackson, observe the commandments "because of a stirring love and reverence for Him that has arisen within us".[50] Maneri recognizes the touch of divine grace when he highlights 'reverence'.

Maneri encourages his disciples not to lose heart if they repeatedly fall into sin. He counsels them not to succumb to the satanic deception that repentance is futile. He was able to perceive even a modicum of good will and generosity in his disciples to fight evil within oneself. He highlighted that generosity and encouraged them to repent continually. There is no place for complacency; the disciples should press on and remain always a struggling penitent. God alone can effect a radical transformation of a person's heart. He alerts pilgrims that the human person always will have something 'other than God' and they should keep repenting, even if that otherness is their own very self![51] Beginners should show an earnest resolution to abandon sin. This earnestness to abandon sin is achieved not merely by crying for God's forgiveness but also by rectifying the damage that was brought about by one's sin.[52] Repentance also means transforming one's nature with the grace of God. Finally, Jackson points out that Maneri's teaching is born of deep personal insight on repentance. Jackson writes:

> He [Maneri] informs us that ... people should not forget the sins of the past but keep them continually in mind. The reason is to prevent them from growing proud. This seems sensible enough, but he adds that ... others think that repentance means forgetting entirely about sins of

the past. This is because the whole endeavour of a Sufi is to become a lover. This opinion also has much merit to it. On the other hand, a lover should keep his past infidelities in mind, according to Sharafuddin, who then goes on to say that the seemingly contradictory nature of the two positions vanishes if people take 'forgetting' to mean that the attraction of sin must be expunged from one's heart. This implies an ever-increasing love of God in comparison to which sins lose their attraction.

The reason for making this assertion is quite simple. Although it is within man's power to say 'No' when he is tempted, it is not within his power to expunge the attraction exercised by sin. What can and does take place is that it is subsumed by a far more powerful attraction – that of God Himself. Sharafuddin's solution is found on this attraction, and is an implicit avowal that he himself has felt it.[53]

Maneri envisions that a pilgrim needs training in *serving the other, devotion to God* and *discernment.*

Service to the Needy

Maneri makes an insightful comment when he says that a man attains freedom in the service of others. A servant is a free person. A free person can experience the joy of union with God. As long as one considers oneself as somebody, he is nobody in the eyes of God. Maneri's idea of service is intimately joined with self-negation. A person's service for the other is tried and found sound only when he considers himself rejected and valued useless. Maneri stresses that one can belittle oneself in one's own estimation by denying oneself and serving the other.[54]

Maneri affirms that genuine service trains the pilgrim to be humble. It makes the person radiant both internally and externally. A pilgrim in authentic service to the other would learn that such service is impossible unless he entirely abandons his own wishes, desires and control over others. If a pilgrim progresses in authentic service in the way Maneri indicates he will be able to deal with inordinate self-love effectively.

Devotion to God Through Prayer

Maneri emphasized that 'prayer without ceasing' is at the heart of a pilgrim's devotion to God. Prayer should be embellished by other forms of spiritual exercises like restraining one's speech, praying for others, spiritual conversation, and instructing someone who is in need of religious knowledge. Maneri also recognized that 'the unexamined life is not worth living' and stressed that pilgrims should carefully examine their life: thoughts and actions.[55]

Watching Over One's Heart

The motivation for God experience is often tinged with lesser motivations. A spiritual guide will be able to identify and help the pilgrim. Man's worth is measured according to his purity. It takes time, patience and guidance to purify one's intention. Purity of heart is the prerequisite of the mystical experience of God. Actions born of pure intentions will bring one closer to union with God. Actions bereft of purity of heart are utterly useless. The whole purpose of purifying one's heart is to seek God.[56]

Provisions for the Journey

After the initial preparation, a pilgrim has a long way to go. Maneri emphasizes that pilgrims have some provisions for the journey. First, Maneri recommends a '40 days retreat' to pilgrims. He emphasizes that a '40 days retreat' will bring about an overwhelming change in the very nature of the person who undertakes it. After the retreat, the retreatant will emerge completely a new person.

The retreat helps him to live a humble, self-disciplined, and God-oriented life. At this stage the pilgrim will experience an attraction to God and experience mystical illumination.[57] Jackson writes: "This attraction to God and abundance of mystical illumination indicate conclusively that the divine activity has, to some degree, 'taken over' his life ... the implication is that a person's life is no longer self-centered, but flows outward towards God and his fellow human beings".[58] Second, Maneri recommends listening to or singing spiritual hymns that bring out the spirituality of a pilgrim that is hidden in heart, like hammering on an iron rod brings out fire that is hidden in the rod. Singing is of no spiritual consequence if the heart is empty.[59] Thirdly, Maneri recommends begging to foster a pilgrim's trust in God. Begging is a good form of asceticism and helps to acquire freedom of heart. Begging also helps one to become aware that we all belong to God. When the pilgrim begs he is begging from God. God provides the pilgrim through another.[60] Jackson adds a comment: "It seems as though Sharafuddin actually has the spiritual guide in mind rather than some beneficent rich man".[61] Fourthly, Maneri warns pilgrims not to become proud. All mystical experiences are due to God's grace.[62] Fifthly, Maneri reminds us that the sincere pilgrim is content with whatever comes from the grace of God including disappointments. A sincere pilgrim is fully aware even the most disappointing moment could be the most graceful moment of his life.[63] Sixthly, Maneri encourages pilgrims to deal with fear along with hope. Jackson writes: "Sharafuddin tells us that hope and fear are like the sun and shade. Both are needed if any fruit is to ripen. It is by experiencing both that a person grows to full maturity of spirit".[64] Finally Maneri encourages pilgrims by emphasizing "time and again ... the eternal covenant which exists between God and the entire human race. 'Am I not your Lord?' ... This Qur'ânic verse is at the heart of Sharafuddin's conception of the Way to God".[65] The brief exposition of his teaching does say a lot about the person of Maneri and his spiritual disposition. The following paragraphs will highlight two important qualities of Maneri's life as a spiritual guide which Jackson finds inspiring, and of Maneri's sanctity, as Jackson has experienced.

Maneri, a Man of Encouragement

Maneri was a wonderful spiritual director. He encouraged his listeners that God himself would be their guide if they sincerely try to live the will of God in their lives. Bending one's will to the will of God is not oppressive but in fact liberating, since God Himself becomes his guide and walks his beloved through. Jackson resonates with this spirituality of Maneri. Jackson himself has gone through this though at that time he had not yet begun to study Maneri. It has been noted that while he was in his final year of formation in Hazaribagh, his whole being cried out to study Maneri. He was aware of another possibility that could deny him the opportunity to study Maneri. Finally, he was determined to do the will of God that would be given to him as mission by his higher authorities. That was a liberating experience for him. Jackson himself experienced being guided by the Spirit in those moments that later resonated with a similar experience and teaching, which came from Maneri.

Maneri did not Draw Attention to Himself

The teachings of Maneri were recorded carefully by his secretary Zain Badr Arabi. These accounts are known as *malfuzat*. Maneri used a lot of stories in his teachings. These stories were about Muhammad, his companions and the early Sufis. "In his didactory role, he occasionally related an incident from his own life. While doing so his whole attention was focused on making his teaching as clear as possible for his listeners, not to talk about himself".[66]

Jackson writers further:

Sharafuddin, unlike Ibn Battuta and others, was not dictating his memoirs. The occasional personal references in the various collections of discourses have to be hunted down with great patience. They occur while he is preoccupied in explaining some point or other. They slip out, almost unnoticed, in the form of illustrations of what he is saying. This fact greatly enhances their value, for they are quite definitely not 'tailored' in any way.[67]

Sanctity of Maneri

Jackson is deeply convinced of the sanctity of Maneri and Maneri's power of intercession. He writes the following after his visit to the shrine of Maneri.

It was a satisfying, enlightening. and enriching religious experience. It afforded me valuable insights into the religious mentality of the ordinary people. I perceived it was far closer to my own mentality than I had thought. The comparable situation that comes to my mind is Lourdes. I felt that anyone in the *dargah* would feel completely at home at Lourdes, for the type of faith involved in both places is basically the same – a deep faith in the power of the intercession of one of God's 'holy ones'. Both places have the tradition of God's having answered some of the prayers of the devotees in a miraculous manner. Both places have an atmosphere of living faith about them.[68]

Summarizing remarks: Maneri's life is marked with hunger – a keen desire for the knowledge of God, and a hunger for a deep experience of God. He travelled towards the east (Sonargaon) and then to north-west (Delhi) in search of knowledge and experience. Throughout his search his gaze was fixed on God and he longed for union with God. He felt a call to guide others in the ways of God. He taught his listeners that faith is God's gift which inspires one to be a pilgrim in search of God-experience. A pilgrim should trust God. He emphasized that every pilgrim should have a guide who would train him in the art of service to others, devotion to God and to remain vigilant throughout his pilgrimage. Jackson put it in a nutshell in the following words: "God sows the seed of divine attraction in a person's heart. After undergoing a period of sincere repentance, a person goes in quest of a spiritual guide who can lead him through the difficulties that anyone who sets out on the path to union with God can expect to encounter. The three main areas to concentrate on are those of divine worship, service of others and discernment ... Union with God in this life will blossom into 'the vision of God himself' ...".[69] The ultimate aim of the pilgrimage is "to attain, by divine grace, union with God in this life and, in the next, the eternal, joy-filled vision of God Himself."[70]

Maneri wielded enormous influence on people. It is a paradox that a man who sought nothing but union of God, could exercise authority on people. What was the reason? The reason was simply people considered that Maneri was close to God. In the times of Maneri, the Sultans wielded power. People considered that the Sultan's authority came from God and a Sultan was responsible to God alone. As noted, people recognized Maneri's proximity with God and affirmed his authority. His authority is bringing consolation to people. Maneri guided people to liberate themselves from self-seeking chains and helped them to taste the sweetness of God.[71]

People still revere him as Makhdum Sahib (the master, one who is served). God alone is one who is served. Why should people call Maneri 'one who is served', who was devoted to prayer and service to people? A Muslim is one who bends his will to the will of God and does everything according to the commands of God. One cannot do any particular service to God directly. The disciples of Maneri believe service to Maneri who is so close to God is tantamount to service to God. That is the reason people revere him as Makhdum sahib. Such is the spiritual influence of Maneri on large sections of people.[72]

Having briefly outlined the teachings of Maneri and his influence on people; the attention now will be focused on two essential points: How Maneri and his teaching impacted Jackson and how Jackson's interaction with Muslims formed his heart for a deep understanding of dialogue.

Impact of Maneri and His Teaching on Jackson

Maneri's Spirituality 'Astonished' Jackson

Maneri's faith and spirituality that is found in his Letters amazed Jackson. Jackson writes: "It is faith like this which calls for the profoundest Christian response".[73] Maneri teaches that a pilgrim is astonished at the grace upon grace in the beginning of one's pilgrim journey. This first astonishment leads to the final astonishment when the pilgrim realizes that however poor the pilgrim is, nothing can affect his union with God. It is important to quote Maneri and then Jackson's words to show the impact of Maneri's spirituality on Jackson. The following are the words of Maneri as rendered in translation by Jackson:

> Hence it is that they say that the first stage of a Sufi is astonishment and also his final stage is that of astonishment. The first is experienced on the occasion of blessings conferred, just as when a man is extolled and raised up by some great person, he lowers his head, abashed. The second occasion for astonishment is when a person realizes this fact: 'no matter how poor and needy I may be, this can never affect my union with God'. So, the whole story begins with astonishment and ends on the same note.[74]

Responding to these words of Maneri, Jackson writes:

> How beautifully these words capture the experience I myself have tried
> to understand and share with you. The astonishment of being called by
> God and entrusted with a lofty mission which gradually matures into
> the quiet contentment experienced by anyone who has become rooted
> and grounded in God. This quality shines out clearly in Maneri's life, as
> beautifully expressed in the above quotation. It also has meaning for me.
> It is like the ripeness of fruit that is ready to be plucked.[75]

Jackson insists on the importance of listening to the other. Otherwise,
however noble it may be, the relation still remains a monologue. This
Jackson makes explicit, while commenting upon the mission of Jerome
Xavier (d. 1617). Jackson writes:

> ...we appreciate Xavier's prolonged effort to learn Persian, as well as his
> awareness of the need for an elegant as well as an accurate style of writing,
> but it was all geared to an exposition of Christian writings. It was all in
> the line of a religious monologue rather than a dialogue. Xavier does
> not seem to have made any effort to acquaint himself with the spiritual
> legacy of Islam, Sufism, including its rich Indian dimension. For example,
> Abul Fazl mentions the works of Sharafuddin Maneri among the books
> in Akbar's library that are continually read out to His Majesty. Abul Fazl
> also quotes Maneri. While it would not be fair – the point still needs
> to be made, he [Xavier] would have enhanced his grasp of Persian as
> a vehicle for sharing his own spirituality, as well as opened himself up
> to the treasures of Maneri's Sufism, by reading such books. The result
> would have been at the level of spirituality, rather than that of polemics
> about specific Christian doctrines and the person of Muhammad. This
> point also serves to underscore the importance of listening in the whole
> realm of interreligious dialogue, a listening that strives to sense the spirit
> animating the religious outlook of the other person.[76]

One could say according to Jackson, that the spirituality of dialogue
is born when one opens oneself to the spirit. Jackson has consistently
emphasized the importance of listening to the other. When the Islamic
Studies Association convened its 13th National Convention in Jhansi he
stressed that the focus of the convention is to help "the local Christians
to come to know and experience the faith of Muslim neighbors. It is
also to see how faith empowers them in their life".[77]

Looking Towards God Through the Heart and Mind of Maneri

Jackson explicitly makes clear that he feels comfortable to look towards God through the heart and mind of Maneri. He writes:

> As I look towards God I do so as a Christian; a Catholic priest; and a Jesuit. When I look towards Him through the heart and mind of Maneri, I feel very comfortable. I do not experience any discordant note within my being. I feel I am in the presence of a man who was as sincerely dedicated to God and His service as was Ignatius Loyola, the founder of the Jesuit order to which I belong and which gives the most distinctive and all-embracing tone to my life. I instinctively feel that Maneri and Ignatius had an unutterable devotion to God and a profound, experiential grasp of the essential features of what such devotion entails. While Ignatius had great organizational skills, Maneri was more linguistically endowed. Maneri is, for me, like a second, confirmatory spotlight which highlights features which, while present and visible in the Christian spotlight, are further illuminated by light coming from a completely different direction.[78]

Jackson's words indicate how a deeply committed Christian and an equally committed Muslim can look towards God in and through the eyes of one another. In that spiritual disposition there is neither syncretism nor spiritual shallowness. In the deeper realms of spirituality an insight from a Muslim can illuminate and console a Christian in his journey towards God and similarly an insight from a Christian can illuminate a Muslim in his commitment and his onward journey toward God. In other words, the insights born of profound personal experience ultimately point towards a common ground. In this common ground a pilgrim sojourns beyond words and symbols but rooted in one's religious commitment.

While emphasizing their common ground, Jackson reveals that the common ground is a time of grace for him. He writes:

> [Maneri's] grasp of the spiritual life is in perfect accord with what I find in the Gospels and in the Spiritual Exercises of St Ignatius, and the teaching of St John of the Cross. It is, of course, presented in an Islamic setting, but its authenticity has stood the test of time. It is as valid today as it was for people living in the fourteenth century Bihar. Many conversations

about him and his teaching have been occasions of grace for me and all taking part.[79]

Jackson Resonates with Maneri

While translating *The Hundred Letters* Jackson experienced a resonance with the spirituality of Maneri especially with regard to the desire for union with God. As a youngster he desired to live in union with Jesus. That desire led him to the Society of Jesus. As a Jesuit (member of the Society of Jesus) he was moulded in the *Spiritual Exercises* that formed him to live a life of union with Jesus. What he found in the spirituality of Maneri resonated with the spirituality of the Society of Jesus that he makes effort to put in practice. He writes:

> As I was reading Maneri's letters in the original Persian, I grew increasingly astounded at how his spirituality dovetailed into what I myself had experienced through my exposure to the Gospels, the *Spiritual Exercises,* and my actual life as a Jesuit. This in effect meant that I would be conveying, through my translations, a spirituality that I myself resonated to, yet in a form wholly acceptable to Muslims. These translations would also give Christian readers the opportunity to form their own opinion on the intrinsic merit of Maneri's spiritual teaching.[80]

It is fair enough to say that Jackson experienced coherence in the realm of spirituality. A Christian and a Muslim can recognize God's inscrutable ways and God's presence in one another's life. Moreover, it is possible for a Christian to delve deep into the spirituality of a Muslim that is born of God experience without losing the Christian identity and help fellow Christians to recognize the spiritual depth of Muslim spirituality.

Jackson Lives a Synchronized Spirituality

Jackson emphasizes that a principle that has guided him over the years is that of transparency. He is keen to see his words and actions follow from what is in his heart. This involves the "cultivation" of the heart, so to speak, so that wholesome thoughts and actions can spring up like flowers.

Jackson is deeply aware that he not only brought some knowledge of Persian to the task of translation but also a lived-in experience of what Maneri was attempting to inculcate in his readers. "Time and again I was confronted with a real challenge to understand something Maneri was saying until an insight, based on my own experience, shed instant light on what he wanted to convey. Nowadays, we have synchronized events in the Olympic Games and elsewhere. It seemed to me that Maneri and I had what might be termed 'synchronized spiritualities.'"[81]

Further he confirms his Christian spirituality helps him to understand Maneri. He writes:

> [While translating Maneri's work] sometimes an allusion escapes me but, drawing on his own Islamic background, he [Prof Askari, Jackson's guide and mentor] has no difficulty in elucidating the point for me. Similarly, I sometimes draw on my own Christian experience in order to grasp a profound point being made by the author, Maneri, to the joy of Askari sahib.[82]

This teaching has a profound impact on Jackson. It was indicated in the beginning of this chapter that he wanted *to write something useful for others*. As a Jesuit in Hazaribagh he wanted to *reach out to Muslims and do something for them*. These are initial desires to serve others. As a Jesuit Jackson knew these desires needed to be purified. These desires were purified in the crucible of discernment. The discerned decision guided him to study medieval history, Urdu and later Persian. There was, however, a struggle in his heart. He was troubled in his heart over what would happen if he was missioned to something which was not his desire. His desires had exercised a great influence on him. However, the Jesuit formation had fine-tuned it and brought to a spiritual stage where he was ready and willing to obey his higher superiors whatever they found appropriate for him in the area where he could do something for Muslims. He remained committed to do something for Muslims. The deep interaction with Maneri in and through his *The Hundred Letters* helped Jackson to recognise the deeper coherence between the spirituality of Maneri that is found in *The Hundred Letters* and his own

Christian spirituality. He recognized the deeper one goes the more one can find common ground between spiritualities. In other words, universal wisdom emerges as a fruit if one strives to listen and learn from the other. Jackson experiences this as 'synchronized spirituality'.

From what Jackson writes one can draw a simple conclusion saying without doubt the spirituality of Maneri made an impact on him. He has learnt to listen to Maneri and his spirituality. This attitude of listening alone would bring desired fruit in dialogue. This synchronised spirituality eminently prepared Jackson for dialogue with Muslims.

Interaction with Muslims

Jackson Reaches Out to the Other at the Religious Level

His fundamental interaction with Muslims took place in the Khuda Bakhsh Library. It is pertinent to listen to him. He writes:

> For thirty-three years, five days a week, initially for about eight hours a day, and subsequently for about two hours a day, any of the mainly Muslim readers in the reading room of the library would see me seated with a Persian manuscript – or several manuscripts – on a stand, with a copy of the Persian-English dictionary of Steingass propped up beside it, and a notebook on the table in front of me on which to write my translation. They could not miss me, as I was normally the only foreigner sitting in the reading room. For a dozen years or so they would have seen Askari Sahib seated beside me, and would have noticed that we occasionally spoke to each other. Curiosity made them want to find out who I was and what I was doing, but politeness dictated that they inquire from someone else and not disturb me ... As long as Askari Sahib was still alive we had an almost daily interaction. I treasured these moments. A deep bond of respect and affection grew up between us. Because he was held in such high esteem, some of it rubbed off onto me. Many knew that he was my guide and friend, and were happy to see this relationship. These twin factors also came into play whenever I visited a number of madrasas and Sufi shrines over a period of twenty-five years in a dozen different towns in Bihar. My objective in visiting these places was to arrange for two students of theology to come in order to learn at firsthand about Muslims. This meant I walked into many madrasas and shrines alone. Apart from a few occasions when I was recognized, the normal reaction was one of polite suspicion. Soon, however, my talk about Maneri, the

> Khuda Bakhsh Library and Askari Sahib melted all resistance, and I was
> warmly welcomed. Maneri provided me with a key to open hearts of
> many Muslim brothers and sisters.[83]

Jackson's reflection on interfaith dialogue is born of his own long and fruitful interfaith journey. It is important to make a quick observation here. Jackson prefers 'inter-religious' dialogue to 'interfaith' dialogue since the former is more inclusive. In many an inter-religious dialogue meetings, he observes that the religious leaders who are invited to speak generally follow a particular trend: first, they state their faith and practice and then affirm how "their religion inspires them to help those in need".[84] Jackson finds that this approach, though it brings consolation, is inadequate and thus will not flourish. He argues that if inter-religious dialogue has to prosper one has to *reach out to the other at the religious level*. This could be done through learning about another's religious tradition. This learning brings new knowledge about others and thus wipes away ignorance. Knowing the other from close quarters intellectually and experientially will also challenge prejudices born of an obstinate and fixed mind-set. Thus men and women enlightened by such a journey can help their fellow religionists to learn to appreciate the good and beautiful in the other religious traditions. Jackson writes: "It would be of immense benefit ... if the religious leaders could mandate some promising young scholar to study another tradition".[85] He refers to the attitude of the Catholic Church at this context. He writes: "We see such efforts in the Catholic Church in India after Vatican II. Although numerically few in number, such people have proved to be of great assistance to the Church in reaching out with understanding to people of other religious traditions and, in varying degrees, in promoting and encouraging inter-religious dialogue".[86] This is based on his own personal journey as well.

Importance of Mutual Respect and Esteem

Prof Askari Sahib was a veritable second father to Jackson. For more than a dozen years Askari Sahib collaborated with Jackson in translation work. In the context of this collaboration a profound friendship developed.[87]

Reflecting on his own collaboration and dialogue with his guide and mentor, Jackson writes that mutual esteem and love drive away prejudices.

> When two people collaborate in a venture which both esteem and consider eminently worthwhile, they have the most favorable milieu for sustained in-depth dialogue. This results in a fruitful symbiosis in which the collaboration sustains the dialogue, and the dialogue sustains the collaboration. This in turn leads to a mutual widening of interests and one's circle of friends. Each partner, out of love and respect for the other, tends to project a very favorable image of his partner to his own circle of friends, thus providing them with personal knowledge – albeit second-hand – and esteem as the basis for judgments. People in this situation are not easily influenced by stereotypes, for they have a norm derived from experience which they can utilize as the basis for their judgments.[88]

Friendships born of mutual collaboration and dialogue teach each partner the importance of listening to one another, and the need to interpret the other in the light of personal experience. Jackson's comments indicate the best possible way to contribute to the well-being of all is to enter into sincere collaboration with people who are open and interested in such alliances. The art of listening to one another is the key to such liberating relationships.

Jackson Appreciates the Spiritual Dimension of Islam

The fruit of his reaching out to the other at the religious level animates him to recognize the beauty of what is at the heart of Islam and Muslim life: deep love for Muhammad. Jackson is able to recognize and appreciate the place of Muhammad in the lives of Muslims and comment on Muhammad's encounter with God positively.

Jackson writes:

> As had become his custom, Muhammad was praying in the cave when he had an experience which is commonly held to be recorded in these words: 'Recite in the name of your Lord who created man from clots of blood' (Q 96:1) [...] Muhammad is called upon to recite what is revealed to him by God. This revelation is contained in the Qur'ân. It is important to note that it originated in a spiritual experience [...] this experiential dimension of his encounter with God lies at the very heart of Islam.[89]

This experiential dimension of encounter with God is the solid foundation on which many Muslims build their lives. Jackson highlights this in his writings. The following would be a beautiful illustration of Jackson's approach.

> Four years ago, about 40 miners went underground [...] to commence their shift. Unbeknownst to them, disaster was to strike. Adjacent to the coal mine where they were working lay an abandoned mine which was full of water [...] suddenly the narrow wall separating the two mines caved in and an enormous torrent of water gushed into the mine. The miners were all swept off their feet and carried along by rushing torrent. After a while one of them, Salim Ansari, a poor Muslim miner, felt a ledge and climbed onto it. Feeling around in the dark he touched an empty jam tin. The rush subsided and he became enveloped in silence and an all-encompassing darkness. He shouted out, but received no reply. After a while a thirst forced him to scoop up some water with his tin and drink it. He remained in the watery silence and darkness for 138 hours. Just imagine what it must have been like! The silence and the darkness! Suddenly he heard human voices. He cried out and was rescued. Afterwards people asked him, the sole survivor of the disaster, how he had coped with the silken, the darkness and the uncertainty. His simple answer was: 'I put my trust in Allah!' It is obvious that Allah for him was the Reality which permeated his whole life, not simply a word or a concept. This statement applies to untold number of Muslims, like the old lady of ninety years of age who still fasted, and when asked what she did, replied that she simply spent her time praying to Allah.[90]

As mentioned earlier, Jackson's interaction did not begin and end on the desks of a library. Undoubtedly, the texts of Maneri sparked a fire in his heart. This fire continues to glow in contact with many Muslims, both poor and rich. Thus, Jackson emphasizes the importance of personal contacts with Muslims.

Jackson, commenting on the work of his colleague Troll, writes: "it should serve as a stimulus to do something very simple, namely, reaching out in friendship to Muslims, as acknowledged ... by Troll himself ... Personal contact is the most efficacious way to grow in mutual understanding ... [nothing can ever] replace the understanding gained as the fruit of personal experience."[91] He further advocates the efficacy of the efforts of ordinary Christians reaching out to Muslims. Such 'reaching out', Jackson stresses should presuppose the overriding dignity of the individual persons as the basis for interpersonal relations.[92] Jackson also stresses that Christians reaching out to Muslims should recognize and respect Muhammad and his position in the hearts of countless Muslim men and women.[93]

He encourages his fellow believers to thirst for Reality, and appreciate all that is good and beautiful everywhere. He writes: "We need dogmas to help guide us along the path to God, but not to serve as blinkers. We also need courage to look at our Muslim brothers and sisters and strive to understand how God is at work in them."[94]

The Spirituality of Interfaith Relations

Jackson has learnt that dialogue not only opens oneself to the other and to God but eventually transforms one and deepens his faith and deepens one's commitment for learning from the other. Jackson writes:

> [...] each partner is challenged to perceive and understand the other as he or she really is. The role of a person's deepest commitments slowly becomes clear to each, leading not merely to increased mutual respect, but also to an on-going self-analysis by means of which one begins to discern faith reality as distinct from verbal expression. One realizes that, in so far as one's faith is merely nominal – i.e. at the level of verbal expression – it has little transforming impact on our lives, but once we begin to acquire a sense of the reality referred to, we are changed, not suddenly and dramatically, but slowly yet perceptibly. Our gradual transformation bears eloquent testimony to the deepening reality of our faith.

He further writes:

> Thus, in the context of ongoing collaboration a dialogue involving religiously committed people [...] should lead to a mutual transformation which will, in turn help promote such a transformation in others.[95]

> [...] there has been much enriching sharing of personal beliefs and practices. Explicit discussions of the Bible and specific Christian beliefs, such as the mystery of the Blessed Trinity, have been rare and discouraging.

The mechanism operative seems to be that of living organism dealing with a foreign body. It is rejected. This occurs at the level of theological information, and is in sharp contrast to the interest generated by what may be termed 'evocative exchanges', i.e. discussions based on sharing personal experience.[96]

Jackson makes it explicit that 'evocative exchanges' lead the dialogue partners towards transformation. Jackson over the years has made efforts to share what the fruits of his dialogical journey with Maneri and present day Muslims with fellow Christians through the Islamic Studies Association and exposure programs he held at the Regional Theology Centre (Patna).

Experience at the Heart of Christian Muslim Relations

Islamic Studies Association

Jackson has contributed immensely through the various activities of Islamic Studies Association. The Association for Islamic Studies was founded at a consultation called in Agra by the Dialogue Commission of the Catholic Bishops' Conference of India (CBCI) in March 1979. In 1983 this association changed its name to Islamic Studies Association (ISA), using the Arabic form of the name of Jesus, to encourage dialogue between Christians and Muslims.[97] The mandate of ISA is to carry out the directive of Vatican II to work for mutual understanding and collaboration between Christians and Muslims.[98] It is a Catholic organization and it functions in consultation with this commission. The archbishop of Delhi continues to be its patron.[99]

The memorandum states the following aims and objects:

In the name of God and His ever greater service, to promote national integration of all Indian cultural, social, and religious groups and support Government programs for this purpose.

To work towards harmonious relations among Muslim, Christian, Hindu and other religious and social communities in India.

To promote, study, research, and teaching regarding the history, religion, culture, socio-economic conditions and other aspects of Islam.[100]

Any effort to bring about mutual understanding and collaboration is a worthy endeavour in the present situation of our country. Moreover, the initiatives to help people of different religious backgrounds to understand and appreciate one another need to be strengthened.[101] ISA has been at service for the last several years.

The regular public face of ISA has been the conventions it organizes every second year in different towns. Based on his learning that 'experience is transformative', Jackson as the President of the Association gave a basic structure to this convention. The convention focused on helping Catholic Christians, of a particular town where the convention is organized, to come and meet Muslims and listen to them what they say about Islam. This gives Christians an opportunity to interact with Muslims. Jackson writes:

> Experience has shown that the most practical way of doing this is to have one day during which Muslim speakers, from a variety of backgrounds, speak about their personal experience of what it means to be a Muslim in India today ... the following day, those who have a keener personal interest have the opportunity to visit Muslims in their own setting in places like madrasas, mosques, charitable hospitals, Sufi shrines and any prominent institutions in the city or town. On the first day, Christians play host. On the second day, the Muslims have an opportunity to extend hospitality to their Christian visitors.[102]

Several conventions have taken up the theme of "An Experience of Muslim Life". The Muslim speakers shared with the listeners, usually local Christians, their experience of what it means to be a Muslim today. "It is hoped that the cumulative effect of listening to their varied stories will prove to be a veritable experience of Muslim life".[103]

Jackson feels it is unfortunate that the relationship between Christians and Muslims is more often like ships passing one another in the night than interpersonal engagement.[104] Often many Christians, strange as it may seem, have no personal contact with Muslims. In the absence of such personal contacts and experiences, the shifting sands of largely negative and sensational media images play havoc and generate negative opinion and image of Muslims in the minds of Christians. These conventions provide opportunity for a more personalized experience.[105] In Christian-Muslim relations, Jackson cautions that Christians should be aware of the role of bias, prejudice, and ignorance in their attitude towards Muslims.[106]

The conventions organized by the ISA have an important role in view of the increasing polarization that is taking place. Jackson says:

> Events in the Middle East tend to make it more difficult for us to live harmoniously together. Viewed in this context [these conventions] ... may seem of negligible significance. This may be so, but initiatives which aim at helping people of different religious backgrounds understand and appreciate one another are urgently needed nowadays ... what has to be rejected is a mind-set which pounces on the deficiencies of a few members of another group, magnifies them and completely ignores the special beauty and goodness of the vast majority of its members.[107]

Jackson has contributed greatly to the quarterly journal of ISA, *Salaam*. As the editor of this journal for many years he encouraged young religious men and women to share their positive experience with Muslims, thus *Salaam* has become a veritable treasure of experience-based articles. *The Muslims of India: Beliefs and Practices* is the most important publication of ISA. This is the fruit of the labour of eight members of ISA in which Jackson played a key role as the editor of the volume.[108] This volume is put to greater use not only by students who prepare to become priests and nuns but also by students of different religious persuasions since this book has been recommended by IGNOU (Indira Gandhi National Open University, New Delhi) in their reading list.

It should be noted that undoubtedly Jackson emerges as a pilgrim who goes about doing good by removing resistant walls of prejudice and building bridges that lead to mutual understanding and appreciation between Christians and Muslims in India.

Patna: Islam Exposure Program

In 1983, when the Patna Jesuits established their Regional Theology Centre (RTC) at Danapur, the Dean asked him to give a course in Islam to the first-year theology students. He was given a mandate that the course should be based on an exposure program. The students were sent to different towns with important Muslim population and institutions. Over the years students have been sent to Bihar Sharif, Patna City, Darbhanga, Muzaffarpur, Sitamarhi, Siwan, Ara, Munger, Bhagalpur, Nawada, Masaurhi, Aurangabad, Gaya, and Phulwari Sharif. Before the students were sent Jackson would himself go to towns where students were due to be sent and secure accommodation for them either in the parish or in schools run by the Church personnel. He would go to the important madrasa in the town and introduce himself as a Christian priest and tell the madrasa officials about his long years of work on the manuscripts of Maneri Literature. He would enquire whether he could send two students who are studying to become Christian priests to learn about Islam. The Madrasa officials usually accept to meet Christian students. Then Jackson would move to a Sufi shrine. He always received a much warmer reception in a Sufi shrine than from the madrasas. Through the help of Catholic priests or nuns who work in those towns in Christian institutions, he would make contact with Muslims both middle class ones and poor ones. Jackson completes these preparations at least two weeks before the students go to those towns.[109] Maneri was Jackson's key to open Muslim doors in Bihar.

He would meet students and have a session with them for instructions with regard to the program. These instructions were: first, practical guidelines to reach the town where they are missioned, where do they stay, whom to meet [...]; secondly, general instructions about Muslim etiquette and meeting Muslims; and thirdly, possible questions that they could ask Muslims as they start their conversation. The students were instructed that after meeting people Jackson had arranged, they should meet a few more Muslims and have conversations with them. The students should write down every detail of their conversation with the Muslims they met. The students should ask questions, seek clarification, agree or disagree with what has been said; but no arguments.[110]

Students went off to the destined towns on Monday, and return on Wednesday of the following week. It gave them at least eight days of fruitful interaction with Muslims. On their return they were invited to share their experience, the knowledge gained as well as their reflections on their experience. After individual sharing the whole group reflect together on what they have learned from this program. Then Jackson deals with some issues and questions that have emerged during the sessions. The students write a short paper on their experience and reflections. Their reflections have been published in *Salaam* (the Journal of the Islamic Studies Association) over the years.[111]

Most students do feel certain trepidation while they set out to meet Muslims. Some students who have had good experiences with Muslims do not have any hang-ups to meet Muslims. When they return, their overriding emotion is one of achievement. The hospitality they received at Muslim homes and Muslim institutions lifts up their spirit in joy. They joyfully acknowledge the changed learning curve that the exposure brought in their life.

Over 250 students have been involved in these exposure programs over the years. Their information seeking sessions often turned into dialogue sessions. One student explains his transformative experience.

> It is a common belief that experiential knowledge leaves a more lasting impression on the human mind than knowledge gained through books or lectures. Experience, by influencing first the heart and only then the mind, changes one's attitude.

> At my home in Mangalore, until I was sixteen years of age, I had had no direct experience of a Muslim community. Brought up in an orthodox Mangalorian Catholic family I was indoctrinated by my parents, relatives and neighbors – practically all Christians – in the traditional approach to other religions. I was given the impression that Muslims were cruel – only Muslims slaughtered cows in Mangalore – and that they cheat in business and are therefore not to be trusted. The stories of Tipu Sultan's persecution of Christians and the cunning and cruelty of some of the Muslim rulers in India –at least the way we were taught - supported my belief imbibed from my elders at home.

> Whether I acquired a lot of knowledge of Islam was not the result that I was looking for, but I felt close to a community which earlier had hardly

any place in my life. This attitudinal change was possible only by this lived-in experience with Muslims. I can certainly say that today I can trust Muslims and relate to them as a friend. Even the arch conservative Maulanas are open to friendship and dialogue.[112]

First, he theoretically acknowledges the transformative power of experience. Secondly, he admits the predominant prejudices that he picked up from others in his early upbringing. Thirdly, he shares the fruit of his transformative experience. Experience is at the heart of learning and the door that opens up new vistas for much deep dialogue with Muslims.

It was not only the students acknowledged the change in their learning curve but also the higher authorities in the Society of Jesus recognized and appreciated Jackson's work.

> The credit goes to Fr Paul Jackson for introducing younger Jesuits into the process of interfaith dialogue. The lived-in experience among Muslims is a much-appreciated program for the RTC [Regional Theology Centre] students at Danapur. It helps us to open our eyes to a great reality of the lives of the ordinary Muslims of the state. I myself benefited from such experience.[113]

Jackson explains his methodology in the following ways.

> For some twenty-five years, I have conducted introductory courses on Islam in various seminaries and houses of formation for religious sisters. The most fruitful of these has been an "Exposure to Islam" program conducted for the first-year students of theology at our small regional theologate in Khaspur, near Patna. I would visit various towns in Bihar and meet people in *madrasas* and Sufi centers. I would rely on the assistance of one of our schools to make contact [with] middle-class Muslims, and evening schools, social centers, and dispensaries to make contact with poorer Muslims. I would get permission from the people I met to send two students of theology to learn about Islam directly from Muslims. After briefing the students and giving them written instructions, I would send them in pairs to the towns I myself had visited. Usually they stayed with the local Catholic priest but some managed to stay in madrasas and others with Muslim families. They would leave on a Monday morning and return on Wednesday of the following week. This would be followed by three days of sharing and reflection on their experience. If some points

> needed further elaboration, this task would fall to me. Each student then had to write a paper on his experience and his reflections on it [...] the program [...] gave them [students] experience-based knowledge of Muslims, which helped them become more objective in assessing reports of communal disturbances, for example.[114]

A number of things should be observed in this methodology. First, the title indicates that 'experience' has a decisive role in this course. A student is exposed to the reality of Islam through the followers of that faith. The ensuing experience is the teacher. This experience calls for transformation. As a result what would they say about Islam or Muslims would be from what they have experienced themselves. Experience is an anti-dote to prejudice. Prejudice and bias flourish when ignorance reigns. Learning based on personal experience will remain both authentic as well as deep rooted and convincing. This also opens us new vistas for faith based reflections with a critical bend of mind. Students learn new ways of relating with Muslims as priests and religious *sent* by the Church. Secondly, in this 'exposure' the local church has a vital role to play. The priests, sisters and lay people 'help' the students to meet Muslims in their localities by making initial contacts.

Summarizing Remarks

This chapter set out to analyze the work of Jackson and find out his significant contribution to Christian-Muslim relations in India. In conclusion it should be said that the three key attitudes that he discovered and practised and shared with his fellow believers stand out as significant to Christian-Muslim relations and dialogue in India. They are as follows: **'Listening'** is the key to enter into dialogue with others... **'Receiving'** not 'Giving' is at the heart of dialogue ... **'Standing with the other'** is the quintessential aspect of dialogue.

For Jackson, looking to God through the eyes of a Muslim is the deepest form of solidarity. In this form of solidarity Jackson is celebrating 'freedom' which is intrinsic to Christian faith. Did not St. Paul defend freedom in the following words: 'for freedom that Christ has set us free' (cf. Gal 5:1)? Scripture scholars clarify that St. Paul is referring primarily to the interior freedom enjoyed by Christians. This interior freedom attunes Jackson to take a stand in solidarity with Muslims who worship One God along with Christians. His focus is to pray that the will of God might be accomplished in them and through them. This is a very *Massignonian* attitude. Massignon with his monumental doctoral study of the Muslim mystic Mansour Al-Hallaj brought to western conscience the elements of love, mystical union, and sanctity found among Muslims. It is not an exaggeration to say by his serious study of Maneri, Jackson has brought to Christians everywhere the deep spirituality of a Bihari Muslim saint. Massignon after studying the life of al-Hallaj came to pray in the aforementioned way and Jackson's inner journey with Maneri has guided him to personalize such an attitude.

One can recognize the long journey the Jesuits had in this ministry. Jesuits in the court of Akbar condemned Islam totally. They did not find anything of worth in the faith of Muslims. They could see in Islam nothing but corruption and evil. If one recognizes that Jesuits at Akbar's court touched the rock bottom of Christian-Muslim relations it will not be an exaggeration to state that the new Jesuit journey that started at the Jesuit theologate in Kurseong especially by Courtois has scaled great heights in the life and ministry of Jackson.

Jackson in his mission among Muslims demonstrates the **discerning prudence** to choose the right way from among the many that present themselves to him, and the **complete trust** in the Lord who guides him into unknown horizons. He affirms the importance of mutual respect. He writes: Just as Muslims are invited to respect the Christian belief in Jesus as the Son of God, so too are Christians invited to respect the Muslim belief in the Qur'ân as the Word of God. There can be much fruitful discussion on a whole variety of questions that deal with historical matters and theological elaboration, but the fruitfulness of such interactions depends on this basic, sincere, mutual respect.[115]

One cannot but appreciate the lucid style of Jackson's writing. He uses words adeptly and constructs elegant portrait of events and personalities through his illustrative words. He wears on his sleeves a method of

writing that blends description with insights. He is a collector of gems...
consciously identifying, appreciating, highlighting and learning from
the outstanding human qualities of the individual Muslims he met.

It should be said that at this juncture of Jackson's spiritual journey
that Maneri further perfected Jackson's intention to serve others. Jackson
realized that he had to abandon his **wishes, desires and control over
others**. He realized that the **whole process of dialogue requires deep
Christian faith**, for **it is more directly focused on receiving than
on giving**. He also experienced an inner liberation that liberated him
from the delusion of thinking that ultimately words, of themselves, can
produce faith in another person. In dialogue the focus is on the other
person and one strives to be as fully open and present to that person
as possible.[116]

Jackson's dialogue is not limited to Muslims only. As a Jesuit and
a Catholic priest he reaches out to his fellow believers in dialogue. He
shows them a new path, in the light of the teachings of the Vatican II,
which they could consider in their relations with Muslims. Jackson's
writings and edited works on Indian Islam and Sufism and Christian-
Muslim dialogue continue to inspire a number of his readers and guide
them to find a new resonance with their Muslim neighbors. Through
his lectures, weighty theological articles in journals based on his work
on the manuscripts, talks to different groups, and popular essays on
Christian-Muslim relations in *Salaam*; he communicates the way to
understand Islam and Muslims better. His written words as well as spoken
words challenge the age-old prejudices against Muslims and encourage
Christians to meet Muslims with an open mind. The principle of his
approach is '*know Islam* by *knowing Muslims*'. The idea of '*knowing
Muslims*' is to meet them and establishing friendship with them. It is
to know what motivates them, what energizes them and what sustains
them. This intimate knowledge based on experience is the fruit of
commitment to such long standing relationships. This principle is an
antidote for those who seem to know Islam *a priori* from one's own
perspective or from the press which often advocate negative images of

Islam. One cannot deny the incarnational approach that Courtois began in India maturing in the dialogical activities of Jackson.

Spiritual consolation is an important indicator in all dialogical pilgrimages. Jackson's life journey is no stranger to this phenomenon. His dialogical journey could be mapped in the following way: as a young man, Jackson wanted to ***write something meaningful*** for the other. One could term this as his original inspiration. It is fascinating to find God fulfils this *original inspiration* of Jackson in ways that Jackson did not expect. God *called* him for a **mission** in the fold of the Society of Jesus. God *surprised* him with a **missionary** vocation, then *inspired* him to accept **a special call to enter into the world of Islam**, then *astonished* him with the **deep spirituality of Sufi saint Maneri**, then *guided* him to **make the hidden treasure of Muslim Sufi spirituality available to a wider world**, *endeared* him **to many Muslims in their homes and religious institutions**, *led* him to continue to contribute for the mutual understanding between Christians and Muslims. Put simply, God is at work! Jackson with his whole heart and mind participates in the mission of God. This mission, Jackson as a Jesuit understands in the light of the mission of Christ.

Jackson shows in and through his life and work that dialogue is not merely a cognitive but affective as well. Dialogue blossoms at the confluence of hearts. Dialogue is in the will, it is a volitional act. Dialogue can in turn generate convergence: convergence of values, understanding morals and ideals. In this convergence, in other words, in this **flowing together**, co-pilgrims deepen their roots and take wings! Knowledge is necessary but by itself it is inadequate. Jackson's approach is the approach of the heart and experience without neglecting the importance of knowledge. Experience transforms one to a new way of being a human. Experience transforms a Christian who has a specific mission to a new way of witnessing to one's faith.

In conclusion it must be said Jackson essentially discovered that an openness to 'receive' and not to be obsessed with 'giving' is at the heart of dialogue. This discovery led him to the conviction that 'standing with the other as quintessential aspect of dialogue'. Jackson's model calls for a paradigm shift in mission by emphasizing 'receiving' rather than 'giving'. This paradigm shift is the significance of experience-based reflection. This is the significant contribution of Jackson to Christian-Muslim relations in India.

Endnotes

[1] P. Jackson, "Christian-Muslim Dialogue in Patna: Past and Present," *Salaam* 17, no. 3 [1996]: 107.

[2] S. Vahiduddin Khan (in the foreword), P. Jackson, *The Way of a Sufi: Sharafuddin Maneri* [Delhi: Idarah-I Adabiyat-I Delli, 1987].

[3] S.H. Askari, in the preface of *Sharafudin Maneri: The Hundred Letters* (Translation, Introduction and Notes by P. Jackson), The Classics of Western Spirituality [New York: Paulist Press, 1980], xiii.

[4] A. Engineer, "What I believe," in *Journeying together in Faith: A Collection of Inner Pilgrimages in Honor of Jesuit Father Paul Jackson*, ed. V. Edwin and E. Daly [Anand: Gujarat Sahitya Prakash, 2008], 39.

[5] P. Jackson, "The Dialogue of Religious Experience," [Paper presented at the Jesuits Among Muslims' Meeting, New Delhi, 4 April 2013].

[6] P. Jackson, "The Life and Teaching of a Fourteenth-Century Sufi Saint of Bihar (Sharfuddin Ahmad Maneri)," [PhD thesis, Patna University, 1979], iii.

[7] P. Jackson, "The Dialogue of Religious Experience," [Paper presented at the Jesuits Among Muslims' Meeting, New Delhi, 4 April 2013].

[8] See F. Schleiermacher, *On Religion: Speeches to its Cultured Despisers* (Cambridge Texts in the History of Philosophy) [Cambridge: Cambridge University Press, 1996].

[9] C. W. Troll, "Paul Jackson's Approach to Muslims and Islam," in *Journeying together in Faith: A Collection of Inner Pilgrimages in Honor of Jesuit Father Paul Jackson*, 27.

[10] Ibid., 27.

[11] V. Courtois, "Editorial," *Notes on Islam* 7, no. 2 [1954]: 45.

[12] P. Jackson, "Synchronized Spiritualities," in *Christian Lives Given to the Study of Islam*, ed. C. W. Troll and C. T. R. Hewer [New York: Fordham University Press, 2012], 103.

[13] P. Jackson, "The Dialogue of Religious Experience," [Paper presented at the Jesuits Among Muslims' Meeting, New Delhi, 4 April 2013].

[14] P. Jackson, interview by author, February 15, 2012.

[15] P. Jackson, "Synchronized Spiritualities," in *Christian Lives Given to the Study of Islam*, 103.

[16] P. Jackson, "The Dialogue of Religious Experience," [Paper presented at the Jesuits Among Muslims' Meeting, New Delhi, 4 April 2013].

[17] P. Jackson, "A Jesuit journey into Islam," *Salaam* 21, no. 1 [2000]: 33-34.

[18] P. Jackson, "Synchronized Spiritualities," in *Christian Lives Given to the Study of Islam*, 104.

[19] Ibid.

[20] P. Jackson, "A Jesuit journey into Islam," *Salaam* 21, no. 1 [2000]: 34.

[21] Ibid., 35.

[22] P. Jackson, "Synchronized Spiritualities," in *Christian Lives Given to the Study of Islam*, 105.

[23] Ibid.

[24] P. Jackson, "Synchronized Spiritualities," in *Christian Lives Given to the Study of Islam*, 106.

[25] P. Jackson, "The Dialogue of Religious Experience," [Paper presented at the Jesuits Among Muslims' Meeting, New Delhi, 4 April 2013].

[26] P. Jackson, "A Jesuit Journey into Islam," *Salaam* 21, no. 1 [2000]: 35.

[27] P. Jackson, "Synchronized Spiritualities," in *Christian Lives Given to the Study of Islam*, 107-108.

[28] Ibid., 108.

[29] Ibid., 109.

[30] A beautifully narrated story of Maneri is found in P. Jackson, "Maneri's Story," *Salaam* 31, no. 4 [2010]: 147-155.

[31] P. Jackson, "Maneri in Ignatian Perspective," *Ignis* 20, no.5 [1994]: 246.

[32] P. Jackson, "Maneri's inward journey and its impact," *Salaam* 25, no. 3 [2004]: 194.

[33] P. Jackson, *Bihar's Makhdum Sahib: Sharafuddin Maneri* [Patna: Navjyoti Prakashan, year not mentioned], 3.

[34] P. Jackson, "The Life and Teaching of a Fourteenth-Century Sufi Saint of Bihar (Sharafuddin Ahmad Maneri)" [PhD thesis, Patna University, 1979], 40.

[35] R. Levy, *The Social Structure of Islam* [Cambridge: Cambridge University Press, 1969], 234.

[36] P. Jackson, *Bihar's Makhdum Sahib: Sharafuddin Maneri*, 6.

[37] P. Jackson, "The Life and Teaching of a Fourteenth-Century Sufi Saint of Bihar (Sharfuddin Ahmad Maneri)" [PhD thesis, Patna University, 1979], 43-65.

[38] Jackson reports a tradition that a Hindu family nursed Maneri when he fell ill. On this tradition Jackson comments: "there is nothing improbable in the tradition". Ibid., 71.

[39] P. Jackson, "The Historical value of Sufi literature," *Salaam* 12, no. 2 [1991]: 68-77.

[40] B.B. Lawrence (in the Foreword), *Sharafudin Maneri: The Hundred Letters*

(Translation, Introduction and Notes by P. Jackson), The Classics of Western Spirituality [New York: Paulist Press, 1980], xix.

[41] P. Jackson, "Understanding a Sufi: Sharafuddin Maneri," *Omega* 10, no. 2 [December 2011]: 97.

[42] P. Jackson, "The Life and Teaching of a Fourteenth-Century Sufi Saint of Bihar (Sharfuddin Ahmad Maneri)" [PhD thesis, Patna University, 1979], 167.

[43] P. Jackson, *The Way of a Sufi: Sharafuddin Maneri* [Delhi: Idarah-iAdabiyat, 1987], 166.

[44] Ibid., 165-166.

[45] Ibid., 168-169.

[46] Ibid., 170.

[47] Ibid., 176.

[48] Ibid., 176-77.

[49] Ibid., 177

[50] Ibid., 171.

[51] Ibid., 172-173.

[52] Ibid., 172.

[53] Ibid., 174-175.

[54] Ibid., 178-180.

[55] Ibid., 184-85.

[56] Ibid., 185-88.

[57] Ibid., 190.

[58] Ibid.

[59] Ibid., 193-195.

[60] Ibid., 195-197.

[61] Ibid., 196.

[62] Ibid., 197-199.

[63] Ibid., 200.

[64] Ibid., 201.

[65] Ibid., 203.

[66] P. Jackson, *Bihar's Makhdum Sahib: Sharafuddin Maneri* [Patna: Navjyoti Prakashan, year not mentioned], 2.

[67] P. Jackson, "The Life and Teaching of a Fourteenth – Century Sufi Saint of Bihar (Sharfuddin Ahmad Maneri)" [PhD thesis, Patna University, 1979], 29.

[68] P. Jackson, interview by author, February 15, 2012.

[69] P. Jackson, "Understanding a Sufi: Sharafuddin Maneri," *Omega* 10, no. 2 [December 2011]: 97.

[70] P. Jackson, "Maneri in Ignatian Perspective: 2," *Ignis* 20, no. 9 [1991]: 290.

[71] P. Jackson, "Understanding a Sufi: Sharafuddin Maneri," *Omega* 10, no. 2 [December 2011]: 97.

[72] P. Jackson, "Understanding a Sufi: Sharafuddin Maneri," 96-97.

[73] P. Jackson, "Inside Islam," *Salaam* 10, no. 2 [1989]: 66.

[74] P. Jackson, "A Jesuit Journey into Islam," *Salaam* 21, no. 1 [2000]: 36-37.

[75] Ibid., 37.

[76] P. Jackson, "The Jesuit Muslim Encounter in India," *Salaam* 28, no. 1 [2007]: 9-10.

[77] J.V. Edwin, "Christian and Muslims discuss life and faith at Jhansi," *Salaam* 28, no. 2 [2007]: 45.

[78] P. Jackson, "A Jesuit Journey into Islam," *Salaam* 21, no. 1 [2000]: 38-39.

[79] P. Jackson, "Christian-Muslim Dialogue in Patna: Past and Present," *Salaam* 17, no. 3 [1996]: 106.

[80] P. Jackson, "The Dialogue of Religious Experience" [Paper presented at the Jesuits Among Muslims' Meeting, New Delhi, 4 April 2013].

[81] Ibid.

[82] P. Jackson, "Beyond Dialogue," *Salaam* 8, no. 2 [1987]: 92.

[83] P. Jackson, "The Dialogue of Religious Experience" [Paper presented at the Jesuits Among Muslims' Meeting, New Delhi, 4 April 2013].

[84] P. Jackson, "Inter-faith Dialogue: Approaches and Modalities," *Salaam* 29, no. 1 [2008]: 5.

[85] Ibid., 7.

[86] Ibid.

[87] P.Jackson, "Focus on Patna," *Salaam* 12, no. 3 [1991]: 110.

[88] P. Jackson, interview by author, February 15, 2012.

[89] P. Jackson, "The Spiritual dimension of Islam," *Salaam* 25: 4 [2004]: 220.

[90] Ibid., 220-21.

[91] P. Jackson, "Dialogue and Difference," *Salaam* 31, no. 2 [2010]: 55.

[92] P. Jackson, "A Common Word," *Salaam* 32, no. 3 [2011]: 106.

[93] P. Jackson, "Devotion to the Person of Muhammad," *Salaam* 10, no. 3 [1989]: 91.

[94] P. Jackson, "Colloquium on 'Holiness in Christianity and Islam," *Salaam* 6, no. 3 [1985]: 128.

[95] P. Jackson, "Beyond Dialogue," *Salaam* 8, no. 2 [1987]: 93.

[96] P. Jackson, "Christian-Muslim Dialogue in Patna: Past and Present," *Salaam* 17, no. 3 [1996]: 106-107.

[97] P. Jackson, "Twenty-five years of ISA," *Salaam* 25, no. 3 [2004]:106.

[98] P. Jackson, "Welcome Speech," *Salaam* 17, no. 1 [1996]:11.

⁹⁹ See P. Jackson, "Twenty-five years of ISA," *Salaam* 25, no. 3 [2004]:106.

¹⁰⁰ A brochure published by Islamic Studies Association.

¹⁰¹ P. Jackson, "Presidential Address at the 12th National Convention of the Islamic Studies Association Jammu, 13th February 2005," *Salaam* 26, no. 2 [2005]: 66.

¹⁰² P. Jackson, "Twenty-five years of ISA," *Salaam* 25, no. 3 [2004]:110-111.

¹⁰³ P. Jackson, "Presidential Address at the 14th National Convention of the Islamic Studies Association Jammu, 28th February 2009," *Salaam* 30, no. 2 [2009]: 36.

¹⁰⁴ P. Jackson, "Presidential Address at the 15th National Convention of the Islamic Studies Association Bhopal, 26th February 2011," *Salaam* 32, no. 2 [2011]: 61.

¹⁰⁵ P. Jackson, "Presidential Address at the 14th National Convention of the Islamic Studies Association Jammu, 28th February 2009," *Salaam* 30, no. 2 [2009]: 36

¹⁰⁶ P. Jackson, "Inside Islam," *Salaam* 10, no. 2 [1989]: 55.

¹⁰⁷ P. Jackson, interview by author, Delhi, March 14, 2013.

¹⁰⁸ P. Jackson, "A Handbook on Islam," *Salaam* 10, no.1 [1989]: 30-35.

¹⁰⁹ P. Jackson, "Patna' Exposure to Islam Program," *Salaam* 27, no. 3 [2006]: 137-138.

¹¹⁰ P. Jackson, "Patna' Exposure to Islam Program," 139.

¹¹¹ Ibid., 140.

¹¹² P. Jackson, e-mail message to author, February 11, 2012.

¹¹³ J. Karayampuram, "An Inspiration for Interfaith dialogue," in *Journeying together in Faith: A Collection of Inner Pilgrimages in Honor of Jesuit Father Paul Jackson*, 11.

¹¹⁴ P. Jackson, interview by author, Delhi, March 14, 2013.

¹¹⁵ P. Jackson, "Do Christians believe that Jesus is the Son of God?" *Salaam* 30, no. 3 [2009]: 97.

¹¹⁶ P. Jackson, "Christian-Muslim Dialogue in Patna: Past and Present," *Salaam* 17, no. 3 [1996]: 107.

Conclusion

Our book set out to consider the following question: "What makes the contribution of Victor Courtois, Paul Jackson and Christian W. Troll enduringly significant, and why does it continue to inspire students and scholars of Christian-Muslim relations in India?" Our book demonstrated the following three characteristics in these pioneers: their love for Muslims, their intellectual curiosity and honesty in engaging with the intellectual traditions of Indian Islam, and their ability to integrate, and bring about coherence in their lives as Jesuit missionaries and promoters of Christian-Muslim relations. This is why their contribution remains relevant, stimulating and important in the present-day context.

It has been shown throughout the text that these Jesuits passionately promoted interfaith relations between Christians and Muslims. They laid strong foundations for building bridges between the followers of these two faiths through their scholarly and committed work. Their lives manifest a high level of integration in both the cognitive as well as the affective dimensions in building relations between Muslims and Christians.

Courtois, though originally assigned to Belgian Congo, left instead for Indian shores due to some exigency. While he was preparing to leave for India, he developed a special interest in the history of Mughal India and thus found a way to the heart of the Indian Muslims. Jackson arrived in India with a deep conviction to 'do something meaningful for others'. His desire to 'reach out to Muslims' was born on one eventful evening while looking over the cityscape of Calcutta, and reflecting on the work of the Hazaribagh Jesuits, of which he was a member, after listening to a Jesuit who just returned from attending a session of Vatican Council II. Troll arrived in India as an accomplished scholar on Islam in South Asia. He had already attained a good working knowledge of Arabic, developed a number of fruitful academic contacts, and had forged personal friendships with many Muslims around the world. His twelve years in India propelled him to deepen his understanding of Islam and love for Muslims.

It should be said that, besides their commitment to their faith in Jesus and their loyalty to the Society of Jesus, the three cultivated a common, deep desire to 'reach out to Muslims' and contribute something worthwhile for Christian-Muslim relations in this country. Thus, their life and work mark a new spirit in Christian-Muslim relations in this country. They wanted to reach out to Muslims and love them, even when most other Christians, including their fellow Jesuits, either ignored or at times denigrated Muslims in India. Their whole approach is a historic point in time, where a new departure in Christian Muslim relations occurred in India.

To appreciate this new spirit, the spirit of understanding, love and mutual respect that they developed towards Muslims, it was necessary to have a sense of the earlier relationships.

The first two chapters of this book presented a large canvas, in broad strokes, portraying these earlier approaches. Globally, the earlier approaches were often, though not always, marked by hostility. First, both groups interpreted their scriptures with regard to the other in an unsympathetic way. Secondly, political and military conquests often resulted in increasing mutual suspicion and antagonism. Thirdly, the lack of objective information about one another's faith often led to erroneous conclusions about others. In such a dreary climate of unfriendliness, distrust and antipathy, there were few oases in which few individuals or groups could make efforts to reach out to Muslims in a spirit of reconciliation and friendship. Among these, some emphasized 'love for Muslims' and others, 'knowledge about Islam'.

In India, the Jesuits who came to Akbar's Court used 'reason' as their weapon in their approach to Islam and Muslims in India. According to them, Christianity was the superior religion. They argued for this presumed superiority by insisting on the authenticity of Jewish and Christian scriptures in contrast to the fallacies of the Qur'ân, and holiness of Christ against 'irregularities' in the life of Muhammad. They attacked the Qur'ân and Muhammad both of which form the 'heart-beat' of the Islamic faith. The Jesuits' attitude was confrontational and did not connect hearts and minds. Unfortunately, they were not bridge-builders.

Later, Protestant Christian missionaries who came to India generally judged Muslims a priori through their Christian lenses. According to them, Islam was an inadequate religion. They considered the Qur'ân and Muhammad as stumbling blocks in evangelizing Muslims. They appealed to the feelings of Muslims and invited them to believe in Christ as their savior.

It should also be mentioned that both the Jesuits and Protestants largely imported to Indian soil the cultural and religious prejudices against Islam and Muslims that were prevalent in Europe. They practically ignored the level of cultural, social, political and intellectual integration Islam had achieved in India. Thus, they either disregarded or dismissed the intellectual and spiritual dimensions of Islam. In short, they failed to take the changed and changing contexts while trying to proselytize Muslims in the first half of the twentieth century. It is in this context that the authors studied in our book -- Courtois, Troll and Jackson -- usher in a new spirit that triggered a point of departure in Christian-Muslim relations.

Courtois envisioned Christians and Muslims as brothers and sisters, and that both belong to the family of God. This is his theological vision for Christian-Muslim relations in India. He embodied this vision in his mission and lived out that mission all his life. His mission was to reach out to Muslims not as adversaries but as brothers and sisters, giving attention not to what divides but what unites. He established contacts with Muslims not through debates, but through free-flowing family conversations. Throughout his life, Courtois emphasized the need for a profound knowledge of Islam and a deep love for Muslims. Thus, he challenged and reversed the earlier attitudes, and even anticipated the new attitude and direction of Vatican II in his relations with Muslims. For Courtois, love for Muslims would also include giving witness to his faith by sharing and living the love of God for all humanity that is revealed in Christ.

The weakness in Courtois's approach strategy probably includes his failure to give significant attention to what is now called the 'political dimension of Islam'. This should not be missed out in the present-day conversation between Christians and Muslims. It is important to observe that one who articulates the position of Courtois to Muslim friends needs to carefully explain his language, especially his calling upon God as Father. First of all, this is a foundational faith element of the Christian community in the light of revelation. Secondly, Courtois never urges his Muslim friends to accept God as father. Thirdly, recognizing differences is an expression of mutual respect. In short, his theological vision and the embodied vision that he lived out as mission should be emphasized as the new spirit through which he ushered bridge-building in Christian Muslim relations in India.

For Troll, commitment to 'freedom of conscience', 'religious freedom' and the 'dignity of the human person' emerges as the basic framework for Christian-Muslim relations. This basic framework is fortified and underpinned by the theological foundation that emphasizes how God (the Triune God in Christian theology) relates to humanity in different ways. His starting point for Christian-Muslim relations is solidly based on the teachings of the Vatican II.

If the conversation between Christians and Muslims is to be meaningful, it should be transparent and cordial, informed and free.

Discernment and witness to their faith ensure the continuity and fruitfulness of this religious conversation. Deep knowledge of one another's faith and love for one another, brings about fulfillment. Every participant in this conversation discovers in one another the presence of God. Troll's efforts for establishing and strengthening relationship, in other words, building bridges between Christians and Muslims, are nourished by Christian and Muslim spiritual and intellectual sources.

This model appears to fit very well for Christians and Muslims who adore and worship one God, and through their Sacred Scriptures connected with the Patriarch Abraham who is a connecting figure for the three Abrahamic religions, Judaism, Christianity and Islam. India is a nation of diverse religions and cultures. It is important to recognize that in India relations between Christians and Muslims cannot be built up in isolation. Christian-Muslim relations can neither neglect the majority of people who follow other religious traditions, nor leave out people who do not follow any particular religious tradition. The base for religious relations in India should expand and include those wider Indic spiritual traditions.

Troll greatly emphasizes the element of reason throughout his writings. Undoubtedly, it is an important dimension in South Asia. But in India, however, along with reason, experience must find a pride of place. Christian-Muslim conversation, to be meaningful, should integrate the experiential dimension of Christians and Muslims living together amidst people of different religious traditions for centuries.

From the writings of Troll, one sees that he has written extensively on different dimensions of the Muslim intellectual tradition and spiritual tradition. But he could not give adequate attention to the situation of various disadvantaged groups, castes, communities and genders. Christian-Muslim relations in India cannot afford to neglect this dimension in the future to make bridge-building even more solid.

Regarding the third author, Jackson's long years in India shaped his heart and mind for personal relations with Muslims to a much deeper degree than the first two authors. Jackson prescribes the following three key characteristics for interfaith relations: Listening, Receiving, and Standing with the other. These three underline how he has creatively integrated his knowledge of Islam and love for Muslims under the inspiration of a Muslim saint Maneri. Jackson had continually heard the voice of Maneri as he dug deeper to reach the spiritual treasures that were laid out by Maneri for anyone who seeks God. Jackson's personal contacts with poor Muslims in different parts of Bihar and his insistence that his students should come to know Islam more deeply, love Muslims through a lived-in experience with different groups of Muslims, and thereby build bridges establishes the fact that he is alive to the realities of Indian Islam and its various social, cultural and spiritual dimensions. Jackson, like Courtois did not comment on the formal political dimension of Islam that drew some extensive analysis from Troll.

When these three committed Jesuits are examined together, the organic connections growing from their new spirit of building bridges, reveal the fundamental leap that make their lives such a distinctive starting point.

In conclusion, therefore it should be said that:

- Courtois broke new ground in Christian-Muslim relations by crossing the bridge to meet Muslims who were kept out and away. He initiated a cross-border community building process through his deep knowledge of Islam and profound love for Muslims.

- Troll expanded the scope and content of interaction between Christians and Muslims by touching several wider contexts in their lives, histories, cultures, literature, modern politico-religious movements and theologies through his acquiring a deep knowledge of Islam in South Asia, and through his committed love for the freedom and dignity of his Muslim brothers and sisters.

- Jackson sharpened his focus on making Christian-Muslim relations a flesh-and-blood reality, in other words, an experience to discover the true Muslim. His other contribution was to open the spiritual treasures of Islam, found in the life and teachings of Maneri, to Christians and others. He builds bridges between Christians and Muslims founded on love for Muslims and their spirituality.

These authors have become beautiful models for interfaith relations, especially Christian-Muslim relations in India. Their lives highlight different dimensions of relations between Christians and Muslims. The significance lies not only in their writings but also the way their lives are lived in the context of Christian-Muslim relations. The creative integration of their lives and works rooted and founded on Christ make their voices significant in the field of Christian-Muslim relations. They have shown the way to build bridges between the followers of these two religions to live in harmony and peace.

Bibliography

'Abduh, M. *The Theology of Unity*. London, England: George Allen and Unwin, 1966.

Accad, M. "The Gospels in the Muslim Discourse of the Ninth to the Fourteenth Centuries: An Exegetical Inventorial Table." *Islam and Christian-Muslim Relations* 14 [2003]: 67-91, 205-220, 337-352, 459-479.

Adang, C. *Muslim Writers on Judaism & the Hebrew Bible: From Ibn Rabban to Ibn Hazm*. Leiden: E. J. Brill, 1996.

__________. "A Muslim Historian on Judaism: al-Mutahhar B. Tahir al-Maqdisi." In *Contacts between Cultures*, Vol. I. *West Asia and North Africa*, edited by A. Harrak, 286-290. Lewiston: The Edwin Mallen Press, 1992.

Addison, J.T. *The Christian Approach to the Moslem*. New York: Columbia University Press, 1942.

Anawati, G.C. "An Assessment of the Christian-Muslim Dialogue." In *The Vatican, Islam and the Middle East*, edited by K. Ellis, 51-68. New York: Syracuse University Press, 1987.

Andrae, Tor. *Mohammed: The Man and His Faith*. New York: Harper and Brothers, 1960.

Anees, M.A., S.Z. Abedin, and Z. Sardar. *Christian-Muslim relations: Yesterday, today, tomorrow*. London: Grey Seal, 1991.

Anees, M.A. "Christian-Muslim dialogue: myth or reality?" *Islam and the Modern Age* 23, no. 2-3 [1987]: 107-199.

__________. "Historical light on the present situation of Christian-Muslim relations." *Newsletter of the Office of Christian-Muslim Relations*, Hartford Seminary, no. 38 [1988]: 1-7.

Ansari, M. *Islam and Christianity in the Modern World*. 4th ed. Karachi: World Federation of Islamic Mission, 1965.

Ansari, Z.I. "Some reflections on Islamic bases for dialogue with Jews and Christians." *Journal of Ecumenical Studies* 14, no. 3 [1977]: 433-447.

Arberry, A.J. *Revelation and Reason in Islam*. London: Routledge Library Editions, 2008.

Armour, R., Sr. *Islam, Christianity and the West: A Troubled History*. Maryknoll, NY: Orbis Books, 2002.

Armstrong, K. *Holy War: The Crusades and Their Impact on Today's World*. New York: Anchor Books, Doubleday, 1991.

Arnold, T. W. *The Preaching of Islam: A History of the Propagation of the Muslim Faith*. Lahore, Pakistan: Sh. Muhammad Ashraf, 1961.

Atiya, A.S. *A History of Eastern Christianity*. Notre Dame, IN: University of Notre Dame Press, 1968.

Ayoub, M. "The Roots of Muslim-Christian Conflict." *Muslim World* 79, no.1 [1989]: 25-45.

Basetti-Sani, G. *The Koran in the Light of Christ: A Christian Interpretation of the Sacred Book of Islam*. Chicago: Franciscan Herald, 1977.

Basset, J. "Has Christian-Muslim Dialogue already begun?" In *Muslim-Christian Perceptions of Dialogue Today: Experiences and Expectations*, edited by J. Waardenburg, 277-291. Leuven: Peeters, 2000.

Bauschke, M. "Islam: Jesus and Muhammad as Brothers." In *Christian Approaches to Other Faiths*, edited by A. Race and P.M. Hedges, 191-211. London: SCM Press, 2008.

Beaumont, M. *Christology in Dialogue with Muslims: A Critical Analysis of Christian Presentation of Christ for Muslims from the Ninth and Twentieth Centuries*. Oxford: Regnum Books International, 2005.

Bell, R. *Bell's Introduction to the Qur'ân*. Revised by W. Montgomery Watt. Edinburgh, England: Edinburgh University Press, 1970.

————. *The Origin of Islam in Its Christian Environment*. London, England: Frank Cass and Co., 1968.

Bennett, C. *In Search of Muhammad*. London: Cassel, 1999.

Bethmann, E. W. *Bridge to Islam*. London: George Allen and Unwin, 1953.

Borelli, J. "The Goals and Fruit of Catholic-Muslim Dialogue." *The Living Light* 32, no.2 [1995]: 51-60.

————. "New Era and a New Model for Christian-Muslim Dialogue." In *A Common Word and the Future of Christian-Muslim Relations*, edited by J. Borelli, 93-110. Georgetown University: ACMCU Occasional Papers, June 2009.

Borrmans, M. *Guidelines for Dialogue Between Christians and Muslims*. Translated by R. Marston Speight. New York: Paulist Press, 1990.

Brown, S. W., trans. *The Challenge of the Scriptures: The Bible and the Qur'ân*. Maryknoll, NY: Orbis Books, 1989.

Buaben, J. *Image of the Prophet Muhammad in the West: A Study of Muir, Margoliouth and Watt.* Leicester: The Islamic Foundation, 1996.

Bulliet, R. W. *Islam: The View from the Edge.* New York: Columbia University Press, 1993.

Cash, W. W. *Christendom and Islam: Their Contacts and Cultures Down the Centuries.* London: SCM Press, 1937.

Chapman, C. *The Bible Through Muslim Eyes and a Christian Response.* Grove Biblical Series. Cambridge: Grove Books Limited, 2008.

Cooper, A., ed. *Ishmael, My Brother: A Christian Introduction to Islam.* Bromley, Kent: MARC, 1993.

Courtois, V. "Islam and Conversion." *The Clergy Monthly* 10, no.1 [July 1946]: 1-14.

__________, ed. *Al-Biruni Commemoration Volume (AH 362 – AH 1362).* Calcutta: Iran Society, 1951.

__________. "Christ and Muslims." *Indian Missionary Bulletin* 1, no.2 [1952]: 66-75.

__________. *Al-Biruni, a life sketch.* Calcutta: Iran Society, 1952.

__________. *Al-Biruni, a playlet.* Calcutta: Iran Society, 1952.

__________. *Intorduction to the study of Islamism.* Calcutta: Little Flower Press, 1952.

__________. *Mary in Islam.* Calcutta: Oriental Institute, Islamic Section, 1954.

__________. *The Christian Doctrine: An Exposition.* Calcutta: Oriental Institute, 1954.

__________. *The Christian Doctrine: An Exposition – Abridged Edition.* Calcutta: Oriental Institute, 1954.

__________, ed. *Avicenna Commemoration Volume (AH 370 – AH 1370).* Calcutta: Iran Society, 1959.

Cragg, K. *The Call of the Minaret.* 2d ed. Maryknoll, New York: Orbis Books, 1985.

__________. *The Event of the Qur'ân: Islam in Its Scripture.* London, England: George Allen and Unwin, 1971.

__________. *The House of Islam.* Belmont, California: Wadsworth Publishing Company, 1975.

__________. *The Mind of the Qur'ân: Chapters in Reflection.* London, England: George Allen and Unwin, 1973.

__________. *Muhammad and the Christian: A Question of Response.* Maryknoll, New York: Orbis Books, 1984.

__________. *The Pen and the Faith: Eight Modern Muslim Writers and the Qur'ân.* London, England: George Allen and Unwin, 1985.

__________. "The Riddle of Man and the Silence of God: A Christian Perception of Muslim Response." *International Bulletin of Missionary Research* 17 (October 1993): 160-163.

Daniel, N. *Islam and the West: The Making of an Image*. Oxford: Oneworld, 1993.

D'Costa, G. *The Meeting of Religions and the Trinity*, Edinburg: T & T Clark, 2000.

Denffer, A.v. *Some Reflections on Dialogue between Christians and Muslims*. Leicester: The Islamic Foundation, 1980.

Donner, F.M. "The Historical Context." In *The Cambridge Companion to The Qur'ān*, edited by J.D. McAuliffe, 23-40. Cambridge: Cambridge University Press, 2008.

Dulles, A. *Models of Revelation*. Garden City, NY: Doubleday, 1983.

__________. *The Christian Faith in the Doctrinal Documents of the Catholic Church*, New York: Alba House, 1998.

__________. *Christianity and the Religions: From Confrontation to Dialogue*. Maryknoll, NY: Orbis Books, 2002.

Dupuis, J. *The Christian Faith in the Doctrinal Documents of the Catholic Church*, New York: Alba House, 1998.

Esack, F. *The Qur'ān: A User's Guide*. Oxford: Oneworld, 2005.

Esposito, J.L. *Islam: The Straight Path*. New York: Oxford University Press, 1991.

__________. *Future of Islam*. Oxford: Oxford University Press, 2010.

__________. *The Islamic Threat: Myth or Reality*. New York: Oxford University Press, 1992.

__________, ed. *Voices of Resurgent Islam*. New York: Oxford University Press, 1983.

Al-Faruqui, I. "Islam and Christianity: Diatribe or Dialogue?" *Journal of Ecumenical Studies* 5, no. 1 [1968]: 45-77.

Fitzgerald, M.L. "Other Religions in the Catechism of the Catholic Church." *Islamochristiana* 19 [1993]: 29-41.

Ford D. and C.C. Pecknold, eds. *The Promise of Scriptural Reasoning*. Oxford: Blackwell, 2007.

Gaudeul, J.M. *Encounters & Clashes: Islam and Christianity in History*. 2 vols. Rome: Pontificio Instituto di Studi Arabi e d'Islamistica (P.I.S.A.I), 2000.

Ghazi bin Muhammad, "On 'A Common Word Between Us and You'." In *A Common Word: Muslims and Christians Loving God and Neighbour*, edited by M. Volf, G. Ibn Muhammad, and M. Yarrington, 3-17. Rapids, Michigan: William B. Eerdmans Publishing Company, 2010.

Gioia, F. *Interreligious Dialogue, The Official Teaching of the Catholic Church 1963-95*. Boston: Pauline Books and Media, 1997.

Goddard, H. *A History of Christian-Muslim Relations*. Chicago: New Amsterdam Books, 2000.

__________. *Christians and Muslims: From Double Standards to Mutual Understanding*. London and New York: Routledge Curzon, 2003.

__________. *Islam: Towards a Christian Assessment*. Oxford: Latimer House, 1992.

__________. *Muslim Perceptions of Christianity*. London: Grey Seal, 1995.

Goldsack, W. trans. *Selection from Muhammadan Traditions*. Madras: The Christian Literature Society for India, 1923.

GRIC (Muslim-Christian Research Group). *The Challenge of the Scriptures: The Bible and the Qur'ân*. Maryknoll, NY: Orbis Books, 1989.

Griffith, S.H. *The Church in the Shadow of the Mosque*. Princeton and Oxford: Princeton University Press, 2008.

__________. "Arab Christian Culture in the Early Abbasid Period." *Bulletin for the Royal Institute for Inter-Faith Studies* 1 [1999]: 25-44.

Griffiths, P.J., ed. *Christianity through non-Christian Eyes*. Maryknoll, NY: Orbis, 1990.

Gülen, M.F. *The Necessity of Interfaith Dialogue: A Muslim Perspective*. Somerset, NJ: The Light, Inc., Wisdom on to the faith series 10, 2004.

Haddad, Y.Y., and W.Z. Haddad, eds. *Christian-Muslim Encounters*. Gainsville, FL: University Press of Florida, 1995.

Haddad, Y. Y. *Contemporary Islam and the Challenge of History*. Albany, New York: State University of New York Press, 1982.

Hourani, A. Islam in European Thought. Cambridge: Cambridge University Press, 1992.

Haddad, Y. Y. , J. O. Voll, and J. L. Esposito. *The Contemporary Islamic Revival: A Critical Survey and Bibliography*. New York: Greenwood Press, 1991.

Heck, P.L. *Common Ground: Islam, Christianity and Religious Pluralism*. Georgetown University: Georgetown University Press, 2009.

Hewer, C.T.R. *Understanding Islam: The First Ten Steps*. London: SCM, 2006.

Hourani, A. *Islam in European Thought*. Cambridge: Cambridge University Press, 1991.

Huntington, S.P. *The Clash of Civilizations and the Remaking of World Order*. London: Simon & Schuster, 1996.

__________. "The Clash of Civilizations?" *Foreign Affairs* 72, no. 3 [Summer 1993]: 22-49.

Ipgrave, M., ed. *Scriptures in Dialogue: Christians and Muslims Studying the Bible and the Qur'ân Together*. London: Church House Publishing, 2004.

Jackson, R. *Fifty Key Figures in Islam*. London: Routledge, 2006.

Jackson, P. "Dialogue with a Muslim." *The Clergy Monthly* 37, [1973]: 430-435.

__________. "Dialogue in Patna." CMRI 1, no. 4 [1980]: 17-20.

__________. "Sufism." *CMRI* 2, no. 3 [1981]: 14-18.

__________. "A Comparative Study of Khair ul-Majalis and Khwan-i Pur Ni'mat." *Indo-Iranica* 35, no. 1-2 [1982]: 30-42.

__________. "Bihar Sharif Revisited," *Salaam* 4, no. 2 [January 1983]: 27-29.

————. "The Personal and Spiritual Perspective of a Jesuit in Islamic Studies." *Ignis* 13, no. 3 [May-June 1984]: 22-32.

————. "Colloquium on Holiness in Christianity and Islam." *Salaam* 6, no. 3 [1985]: 124- 128.

————. "Forth Convention of the Islamic Studies Association: Calcutta" *Salaam* 7, no. 1 [1986]: 24-26.

————. "The Alchemy of happiness." *Salaam* 7, no. 2 [1986]: 72-76.

————. "Ecumenism in Action." *Salaam* 7, no. 4 [1986]: 178-180.

————. "Beyond Dialogue." *Salaam* 8, no. 2 [1987]: 91-96.

————. "A Handbook on Islam." *Salaam* 10, no. 1 [1989]: 30-35.

————. "Inside Islam." *Salaam* 10, no. 2 [1989]: 53-67.

————. "Satanic Deception." *Salaam*, 10, no. 2 [April 1989]: 75-77.

————. "Devotion to the person of Muhammad" *Salaam* 10, no. 3 [July 1989]: 84-92.

————. "Islamic Studies Association's Sixth convention and General Body Meeting, Bombay, 15-18 November 1989." *Salaam* 11, no. 1 [January 1990]: 3-8.

————. "Dialogue in Brisbane." *Salaam* 11, no. 4 [1990]: 148-157

————. "Focus on Patna." *Salaam* 12, no. 3 [1991]: 102-110.

————. "Maneri in an Iganatian Perspective: Part I." *Ignis* 20, no. 5 [1991]: 245-252.

————. "Maneri in an Iganatian Perspective: Part II." *Ignis* 20, no. 6 [1991]: 285-292.

————. "Maneri in an Iganatian Perspective." *Encounter* no. 188 [1992].

————. "The Role of ISA." *Salaam* 14, no. 4 [1993]: 112.

————. "Ethics and Morality of Islam." *Salaam* 14, no. 2 [1993]: 29-40.

————. "The Neighbourly touch." *Salaam* 17, no. 1 [January 1996]: 3-8.

————. "Muslims of Darbhanga." *Salaam* 17, no. 1 [January 1996]: 30-33.

————. "Christian-Muslim Dialogue in Patna: Past and Present." *Salaam* 17, no. 3 [1996]: 83-107.

————. "Sufism and Jesuits in Bihar." *Ignis* 25, no. 4 [1996]: 53-61.

————. "A Journey into Islam." *Salaam* 21, no.1 [January 2000]: 31-39.

————. "Maneri's Inward Journey and its impact." *Salaam* 25, no. 3 [July 2004]: 184-201.

————. "Meeting Muslims in Calcutta." *Salaam* 26, no. 4 [October 2005]: 180-186.

————. "Dialogue in Blackwater." *Salaam* 27, no. 1 [January 2006]: 22-24.

————. "Patna Exposure to Islam Program." *Salaam* 27, no. 4 [October 2006]: 136-146.

————. "Pilgrimage to Deir Mar Musa." *Salaam* 27, no. 4 [October 2006]: 152-159.

__________. "Jesuit-Muslim Encounter in India." *Salaam* 28, no. 1 [January 2007]: 4-16.

__________. "Jesus and Muhammad." *Vagdevi* 2, no. 1 [January 2008]: 6-12.

__________. "Interfaith Dialogue – Approaches and Modalities." *Salaam* 29, no. 1 [April 2008]: 3-7.

__________. "Louis Massignon." *Salaam* 29, no. 2 [April 2008]: 70-73.

__________. "Letter of 138 – Historical Background." *Salaam* 29, no. 2 [April 2008]: 50-55.

__________. "Christian Muslim Dialogue in India at a Glance." *Jeevadhara* 38, no. 227 [September 2008]: 427-430.

__________. "An Inquiry." *Salaam* 30, no. 1 [January 2009]: 18-20.

__________. "National Convention ISA." *Salaam* 30, no. 2 [April 2009]: 35-37.

__________. "Jammu Convention." *Salaam* 30, no. 2 [April 2009]: 38-42.

__________. "Two Stories – Christian and Muslim." *Salaam* 30, no. 1 [January 2009]: 5-17.

__________. "Do Christians believe in one God?" *Salaam* 30, no. 2 [April 2009]: 43-50.

__________. "Al-Ghazali." *Salaam* 31, no. 2 [April 2010]: 76-82.

__________. "An Historical Text." *Salaam* 31, no. 1 [January 2010]: 4-14.

__________. "Maneri's story." *Salaam* 31, no. 4 [October 2010]: 147-155.

__________. "Maneri and poetry." *Salaam* 31, no. 4 [October 2010]: 174-180.

__________. "Dialogue and Difference." *Salaam* 31, no. 2 [April 2010]: 50-55.

__________. "Maneri on Islamic Law." *Salaam* 32, no. 1 [July 2011]: 6-12.

__________. "Understanding a Sufi: Sharafuddin Maneri." *Omega* 10, no. 2 [December 2011]: 85-100.

__________. "Suicide Bombers." *Salaam* 33, no. 2 [April 2012]: 69-77.

__________. "Rays of Light." *CMRI* 2, no. 1 [1980]: 23.

__________. "Rays of Light." *CMRI* 3, no. 1 [1981]: 45-46.

__________. "Rays of Light." *CMRI* 3, no. 1 [1982]: 34-35.

__________. "Rays of Light: Nizamuddin Auliya." *CMRI* 3, no. 2 [1982]: 35-37.

__________. "Rays of Light: Nazaruddin Chiragh Dehlavi." *CMRI* 3, no. 3 [1982]: 51-53.

__________. "Rays of Light: Abdulla Ansari." *CMRI* 3, no. 4 [1982]: 38-39.

__________. "Rays of Light: Abu Bakr Al Kalabadi." *Salaam* 4, no. 2 [1983]: 33-35.

__________. "Rays of Light: Living with a Sufi Master." *Salaam* 4, no. 4 [1983]: 28-32.

__________. "Rays of Light: Muzaffar Shams Balkhi." *Salaam* 5, no. 2 [1984]: 49-51.

__________. "Rays of Light: Attitudes of Heart and Mind." *Salaam* 5, no. 4 [1984]: 39-40.

__________. "Rays of Light." *Salaam* 6, no. 1 [1985]: 22-24.

__________. "Rays of Light: Two Letters." *Salaam* 6, no. 2 [1985]: 91-93.

__________. "Rays of Light: Abu Said of Mayhanah." *Salaam* 6, no. 3 [1985]: 121-123.

__________. "Rays of Light: The History of Sistan." *Salaam* 6, no. 4 [1985]: 180-182.

__________. "Rays of Light: Man's happiness consists in knowing God." *Salaam* 7, no. 1 [1986]: 27-29.

__________. "Rays of Light: The Alchemy of Happiness." *Salaam* 7, no. 2 [1986]: 72-76.

__________. "Rays of Light: Reynold A. Nicholson." *Salaam* 7, no. 3 [1986]: 121-123.

__________. "Rays of Light: The Greater Struggle." *Salaam* 8, no. 1 [1987]: 40-41.

__________. *Sharafuddin Maneri: The Hundred Letters*. New York: Paulist Press, 1980.

__________. *The Way of a Sufi: Sharafuddin Maneri*. Delhi: Idarah-i Adabiyat, 1987.

__________, ed. *The Muslims of India: Beliefs and Practices*. Bangalore: Theological Publications in India, 1988.

__________. *In Quest of God: Maneri's Second Collection of Hundred and Fifty Letters*. Anand: Gujarat Sahitya Prakash, 2004.

Jameelah, M. *Islam Versus Ahl al-Kitab: Past and Present*. Delhi: Taj Company, 1989.

John Paul II, Pope. "Message to Young Muslims in Casablanca." *Bulletin* 20, no. 3 [1985]: 249-257.

__________. *Recognize the Spiritual Bonds Which Unite Us: Sixteen Years of Christian-Muslim Dialogue*. Vatican City: Pontifical Council for Interreligious Dialogue, 1994.

Jomier, J. *How to Understand Islam*. London: SCM, 1989.

__________. *The Bible and the Koran*. Translated by Edward P. Arbez. Chicago, Illinois: Henry Regnery Company, 1967.

Joseph, S., and B.L.K. Pillsbury, eds. *Muslim-Christian Conflicts: Economic, Political and Social Origins*. Boulder CO: Westview, 1978.

Kalin, I. "Seeking Common Ground between Muslims and Christians." In *A Common Word and the Future of Christian-Muslim Relations*, edited by J. Borelli, 7-15. Georgetown University: ACMCU Occasional Papers, June 2009.

Kateregga, B. and D. Shenk, *Islam and Christianity*. Michigan: William B. Eerdmans Publishing Company, 1981.

Kerr, D. "Christian-Muslim Relations: lessons from history." In *The Road Ahead: a Christian-Muslim Dialogue*, edited by M. Ipgrave, 26-37. London: Church House Publishing, 2002.

Khalidi, T. "Learning from Muslim history." In *The Road Ahead: a Christian-Muslim Dialogue*, edited by M. Ipgrave, 39-44. London: Church House Publishing, 2002.

Kimbel, C. *Striving Together: A Way Forward in Christian-Muslim Relations*. Maryknoll, N.Y.: Orbis Books, 1991.

Kolvenbach, P-H., E. Farahian, C. Van Nispen, and A.R. Crollius. *Understanding and Discussion: Approaches to Muslim-Christian Dialogue*. Rome: Pontificia

Universitá Gregoriana, 1998.

Küng, H. *Islam: Past, Present & Future*. Oxford: Oneworld, 2007.

__________. "Christianity and World Religions: The Dialogue with Islam as One Model." *The Muslim World* 77, no. 2 [1984]: 80-95.

__________. "Christian Self-Criticism in the Light of Judaism." In *Christology in Dialogue*, edited by B. F. Berkey & S.A. Edwards, 229-247. Ohio: The Pilgrim Press, 1993.

__________. "The World Religions in God's Plan of Salvation." In *Christian Revelation and World Religions*, edited by J. Neuner, 25-66. London: Burns & Oates, 1967.

__________. "What is True Religion? Toward an Ecumenical Criteriology." In *Towards the Universal Theology of Religions*, edited by L Swidler, 231-250. Maryknoll: Orbis Books, 1986.

__________. "Towards an Ecumenical Theology of Religions; Some Theses for Clarification." In *Christianity among World Religions*, edited by H. Küng and J. Moltmann, 119-125. Edinburgh: T&T Clark, 1986.

Lazarus-Yafeh, H. *Intertwined Worlds: Medieval Islam and Bible Criticism*. New Jersey: Princeton University Press, 1992.

Lochhead, D. *The Dialogical Imperative: A Christian Reflection on Interfaith Encounter*. Maryknoll, NY: Orbis Books, 1988.

Malik, C. *God and Man in Contemporary Islamic Thought*. Beirut: American University of Beirut, 1972.

Marshall, D. *Learning from How Muslims See Christianity*. Cambridge: Grove Books, 2006.

Mawdudi, A. *Towards Understanding Islam*. Leicester: Islamic Foundation, 1996.

Michel, T. "Christian-Muslim Dialogue in a Changing World." *Theology Digest* 39, no. 4 [1992]: 303-320.

__________. "Islamo-Christian Dialogue: Reflection on the Recent Teachings of the Church." *Bulletin* 20, no. 2 [1985]: 172-193.

__________. "Islam and Terrorism: Are We Missing the Real Story." *East Asian Pastoral Review* 41, no. 3 [2004]: 240-247.

__________. "Muslim Approaches to Dialogue with Christians." *Islam and the Modern Age* 15 [February 1984]: 37-50.

__________. *A Christian View of Islam: Essays on Dialogue*. Edited by I.A. Omar. Maryknoll, NY: Orbis Books, 2010.

Meyendrof, J. "Byzantine Views of Islam." *Dumbarton Oaks Papers* 18 [1964]: 113-132.

Mingana, A. "The Apology of Timothy the Patriarch before the Caliph Madhi." *Bulletin of the John Rylands Library* 12 [1928]: 137-298.

Mohammed, O.N. *Muslim-Christian Relations: Past, Present, Future*. Maryknoll, NY: Orbis Books, 1993.

Monro, D.C. "The Speech of Urban II at Clermont, 1095." *American Historical Review* 11 [1905]: 231-42.

Moran, G. *Theology of Revelation*. New York: Herder and Herder, 1966.

Motzki, H. "Alternative accounts of the Qur'ān's formation." In *The Cambridge Companion to The Qur'ān*, edited by J.D. McAuliffe, 59-78. Cambridge: Cambridge University Press, 2008.

Nasr, S.H. *The Heart of Islam: Enduring Values for Humanity*. New York: HarperCollins, 2002.

__________. *Islam: Religion, History, and Civilization*. New York: HarperOne, 2003.

__________. "Islam and the Encounter of Religions." *Islamic Quarterly* 10 (July and December 1996): 47-66.

__________. "The Islamic View of Christianity." In *Christianity through Non-Christian Eyes*, edited by P.J.Griffiths, 126-134. Maryknoll, NY: Orbis Books, 1990.

Nazir-Ali, M. *Mission and Dialogue*. London: SPCK, 1995.

__________. *Frontiers in Muslim-Christian Encounter*. Oxford: Regnum Books, 1987.

__________. *Islam: A Christian Perspective*. Exeter: Paternoster Press, 1983.

Newman, N. A., ed. *The Early Christian-Muslim Dialogue: A Collection of Documents from the First Three Islamic Centuries (632-900 A. D.). Translations with Commentary*. Hatfield, Pennsylvania: Interdisciplinary Biblical Research Institute, 1993.

O'Mahony, A. "Christianity, Interreligious Dialogue and Muslim-Christian Relations." In *World Christianity: Politics, Theology, Dialogues*, edited by A. O'Mahoney and M. Kirwan, 62-92. London: Melisende, 2004.

Perry, M., and H.E. Negrin, eds. *The Theory and Practice of Islamic Terrorism: An Anthology*, New York: Palgrave Macmillan, 2008.

Phan, P.C. "Can We Read Religious Texts Interreligiously?" In *A Common Word and the Future of Christian-Muslim Relations*, edited by J. Borelli, 15-33. Georgetown University: ACMCU Occasional Papers, June 2009.

Pulcini, T. *Exegesis as Polemical Discourse*. Atlanta: Scholars Press, 1998.

Rahman, F. *Islam*. New York: Anchor Books, 1968.

__________. *Major Themes of the Qur'ān*. Chicago: Chicago University Press, 2009.

Rahner, K. "Christianity and the Non-Christian Religions." In *Theological Investigation*, 5: 115-34. London: Darton, Longman & Todd, 1966.

Ramadan, T. *The Western Muslims and the Future of Islam*, Oxford: Oxford University Press, 2004.

Riley-Smith, J. "The Crusading Movement and Historians." In *The Oxford Illustrated History of the Crusades*, edited by J. Riley-Smith, 1-12. Oxford: Oxford University Press, 1995.

Rissanen, S. *Theological Encounter of Oriental Christians with Islam during the Abbasid Rule.* Åbo: Åbo Adademis Förlag-Åbo Adademi University Press, 1993.

Robinson, N. "Massignon, Vatican II, and Islam as an Abrahamic Religion." *Islam and Christian-Muslim Relations* 2, no.2 [1991]: 182-205.

Rodinson, M. *Mohammad.* Harmondsworth: Penguin, 1976.

Rousseau, R.W., ed. *Christianity and Islam: Struggling Dialogue.* Montrose, Pa.: Ridge Row Press, 1985.

Sahas, D.J. *John of Damascus on Islam: 'The Heresy of the Ishmaelites'.* Leiden: Brill, 1972.

Khalil S. "Is Islam part of God's plan?" *Jivan*, February 2011.

__________, and J.S. Nielsen, eds. *Christian Arabic Apologetics during the Abbasid Period (750 -1278).* Leiden: Brill, 1994.

Saritoprak, Z. "How Commentators of the Qur'ân Define 'Common Word." In *A Common Word and the Future of Christian-Muslim Relations*, edited by J. Borelli, 34-45. Georgetown University: ACMCU Occasional Papers, June 2009.

Swanson, M.N. "Beyond Proof-Texting: Approaches to the Qur'ân in Some Early Arabic Christian Apologies." *The Muslim World* 88 [1998]: 297-319.

Siddiqui, A. "Fifty Years of Christian-Muslim Relations: Exploring and Engaging in a New Relationship." *Islamochristiana* 26 [2000]: 51-77.

__________. "Muslims' Concern in Dialogue: A Study of Christian-Muslim Relations since 1970." Ph. D. thesis, University of Birmingham, 1994.

__________. *Christian-Muslim Dialogue in the Twentieth Century.* London: Macmillan, 1977.

Siddiqui, M.H. "Muslims and Byzantine Christian Relations: Letter of Paul of Antioch and Ibn Taymiyah." *Greek Orthodox Theological Review* 31 [1986]: 33-45.

Sirry, M.A. "Early Muslim-Christian Dialogue: A Closer Look at Major Themes of the Theological Encounter." *Islam and Christian-Muslim Relations* 16 [2005]: 361-376.

Smith I. J. "Islam and Christendom: Historical, Cultural and Religious interaction from the Seventh to the Fifteenth Centuries." In *The Oxford History of Islam*, edited by J.L. Esposito, 305-346. Oxford: Oxford University Press, 1999.

Southern, R. W. *Western Views of Islam in the Middle Ages.* Cambridge, Mass.: Harvard University Press, 1962.

Speight, M. "Christians in the *Hadith* Literature." In *Islamic Interpretations of Christianity*, edited by L. Ridgeon, 30-54. Richmond, Surrey: Curzon Press, 2001.

Sweetman, J.W. *Islam and Christian Theology: A Study of the Interpretation of Theological Ideas in the Two Religions.* 4 vols. London: Lutterworth Press, 1945-1967.

Swidler, L., ed. *Muslims in Dialogue: The Evolution of Dialogue.* Lewiston/Queenston/Lampeter: Edwin Mellen Press, 1992.

Thomas, D. *Christian Doctrines in Islamic Theology*. London-Boston: Brill, 2008.

__________. "Early Muslim Relations with Christianity." *Anvil* 6, no.1 [1989]: 23-31.

__________. "Two Muslim-Christian debates from the early Shi'ite traditions." *Journal of Semitic Studies* 33 [1988]: 63-65.

__________. "The Doctrine of the Trinity in the Early Abbasid Era." In *Islamic Interpretations of Christianity*, edited by L. Ridgeon, 78-99. Richmond: Curzon, 2001.

Troll, C. *Sayyid Ahmad Khan: A Reinterpretation of Muslim Theology*. New Delhi: Vikas Publishing House, 1978.

__________, ed. *Islam in India: Studies and Commentaries. Vol. I: The Akbar Mission and Miscellaneous Studies*, New Delhi: Vikas Publishing House, 1982.

__________, ed. *Islam in India: Studies and Commentaries. Vol. II: Religion and Religious Education*. New Delhi: Vikas Publishing House, 1985.

__________, and Syed Vahiduddin eds. Islam in India: Studies and Commen*taries. Vol. III: Islamic Experience in Contemporary Thought:*. Delhi: Chanakya Publications, 1886. Pp. x+293.

__________, and Gail Minault, Ian Henderson Douglas, eds. *Abul Kalam Azad: An Intellectual and Religious Biography*. New Delhi: OUP, 1988.

__________, ed. *Muslim Shrines in India. Their Character, History and Significance. Vol. IV: Islam in India: Studies and Commentaries*. Delhi: Oxford University Press, 1989.

__________ and J. J. Donohue, S.J. *Faith, Power and Violence: Muslims and Christians in Plural Society, Past and present* [Orientalia Christiana Analecta 258], Roma: Pontificio Istituto Orientale, 1998.

__________, H. Reifeld and C.T.R. Hewer, eds. *We have Justice in Common. Christian and Muslim voices from Asia and Africa*. Sankt Augustin/Berlin: Konrad-Adenauer-Stiftung, 2010.

__________. *Muslims ask, Christians answer. African edition in English*. Nairobi: Pauline Publications Africa, 2010.

__________ and C. T. Hewer, eds. *Christian Lives Given to the Study of Islam*. New York: Fordham University Press, 2012.

__________, C. M. Ramsey, eds. *Sayyid Ahmad Khan's (1817-1898) Translation and Commentary of The Gospel according to Matthew, Chapters 1-5. Emendation of the original text, Presentation of the text in contemporary Urdu script, Translation, critical Annotations and Introduction*. Lahore: Maktabah-e Jadeed Press, 2017.

__________. "A Note on an Early Topographical Work of Sayyid Ahmad Khan: Asâr al-Sanâdîd." *Journal of the Royal Asiatic Society* [1972]: 135-46.

__________. "A New Spirit in Christian-Muslim Relations." *The Month* [September 1973]: 296-99.

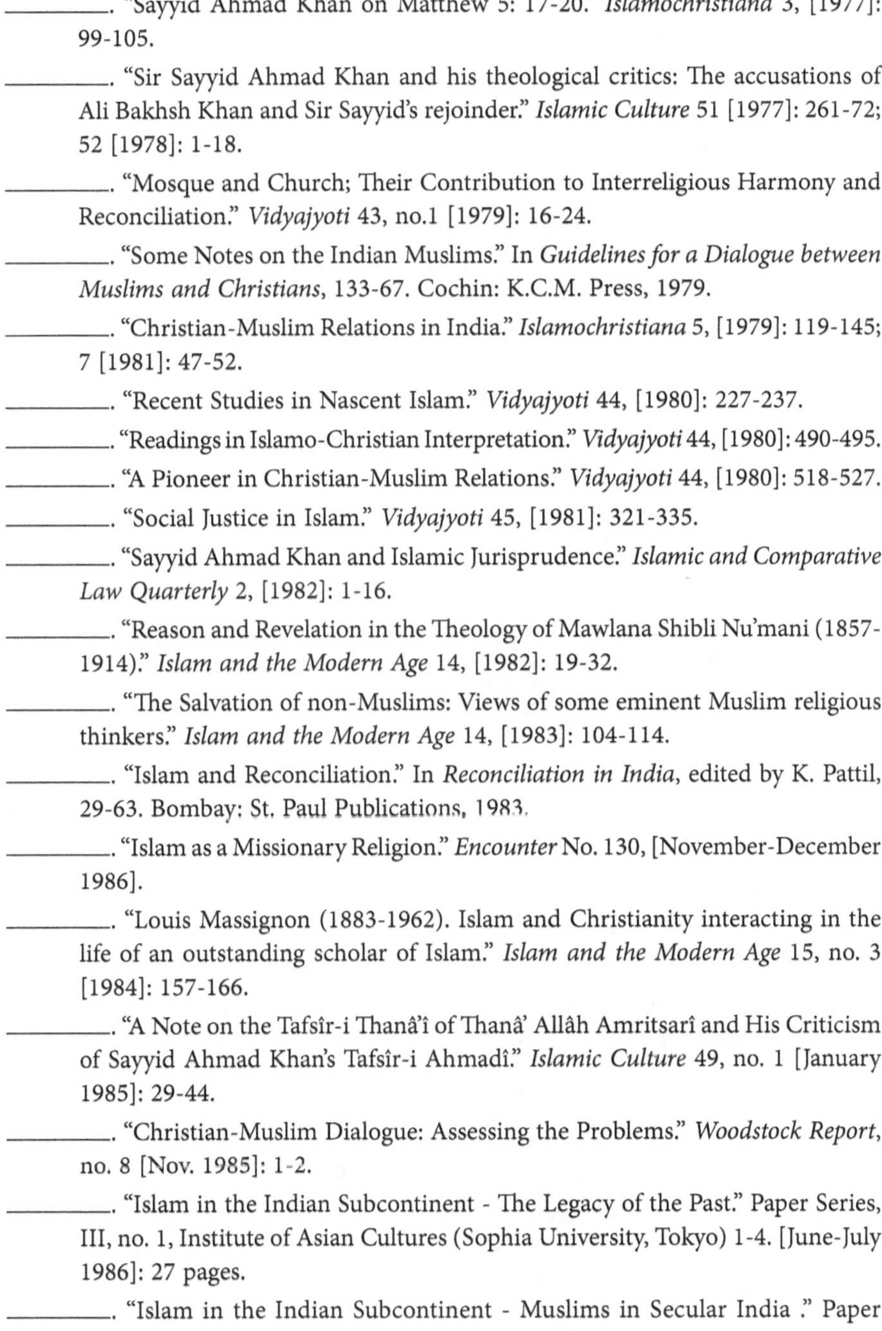

__________. "Sayyid Ahmad Khan on Matthew 5: 17-20." *Islamochristiana* 3, [1977]: 99-105.

__________. "Sir Sayyid Ahmad Khan and his theological critics: The accusations of Ali Bakhsh Khan and Sir Sayyid's rejoinder." *Islamic Culture* 51 [1977]: 261-72; 52 [1978]: 1-18.

__________. "Mosque and Church; Their Contribution to Interreligious Harmony and Reconciliation." *Vidyajyoti* 43, no.1 [1979]: 16-24.

__________. "Some Notes on the Indian Muslims." In *Guidelines for a Dialogue between Muslims and Christians*, 133-67. Cochin: K.C.M. Press, 1979.

__________. "Christian-Muslim Relations in India." *Islamochristiana* 5, [1979]: 119-145; 7 [1981]: 47-52.

__________. "Recent Studies in Nascent Islam." *Vidyajyoti* 44, [1980]: 227-237.

__________. "Readings in Islamo-Christian Interpretation." *Vidyajyoti* 44, [1980]: 490-495.

__________. "A Pioneer in Christian-Muslim Relations." *Vidyajyoti* 44, [1980]: 518-527.

__________. "Social Justice in Islam." *Vidyajyoti* 45, [1981]: 321-335.

__________. "Sayyid Ahmad Khan and Islamic Jurisprudence." *Islamic and Comparative Law Quarterly* 2, [1982]: 1-16.

__________. "Reason and Revelation in the Theology of Mawlana Shibli Nu'mani (1857-1914)." *Islam and the Modern Age* 14, [1982]: 19-32.

__________. "The Salvation of non-Muslims: Views of some eminent Muslim religious thinkers." *Islam and the Modern Age* 14, [1983]: 104-114.

__________. "Islam and Reconciliation." In *Reconciliation in India*, edited by K. Pattil, 29-63. Bombay: St. Paul Publications, 1983.

__________. "Islam as a Missionary Religion." *Encounter* No. 130, [November-December 1986].

__________. "Louis Massignon (1883-1962). Islam and Christianity interacting in the life of an outstanding scholar of Islam." *Islam and the Modern Age* 15, no. 3 [1984]: 157-166.

__________. "A Note on the Tafsîr-i Thanâ'î of Thanâ' Allâh Amritsarî and His Criticism of Sayyid Ahmad Khan's Tafsîr-i Ahmadî." *Islamic Culture* 49, no. 1 [January 1985]: 29-44.

__________. "Christian-Muslim Dialogue: Assessing the Problems." *Woodstock Report*, no. 8 [Nov. 1985]: 1-2.

__________. "Islam in the Indian Subcontinent - The Legacy of the Past." Paper Series, III, no. 1, Institute of Asian Cultures (Sophia University, Tokyo) 1-4. [June-July 1986]: 27 pages.

__________. "Islam in the Indian Subcontinent - Muslims in Secular India ." Paper

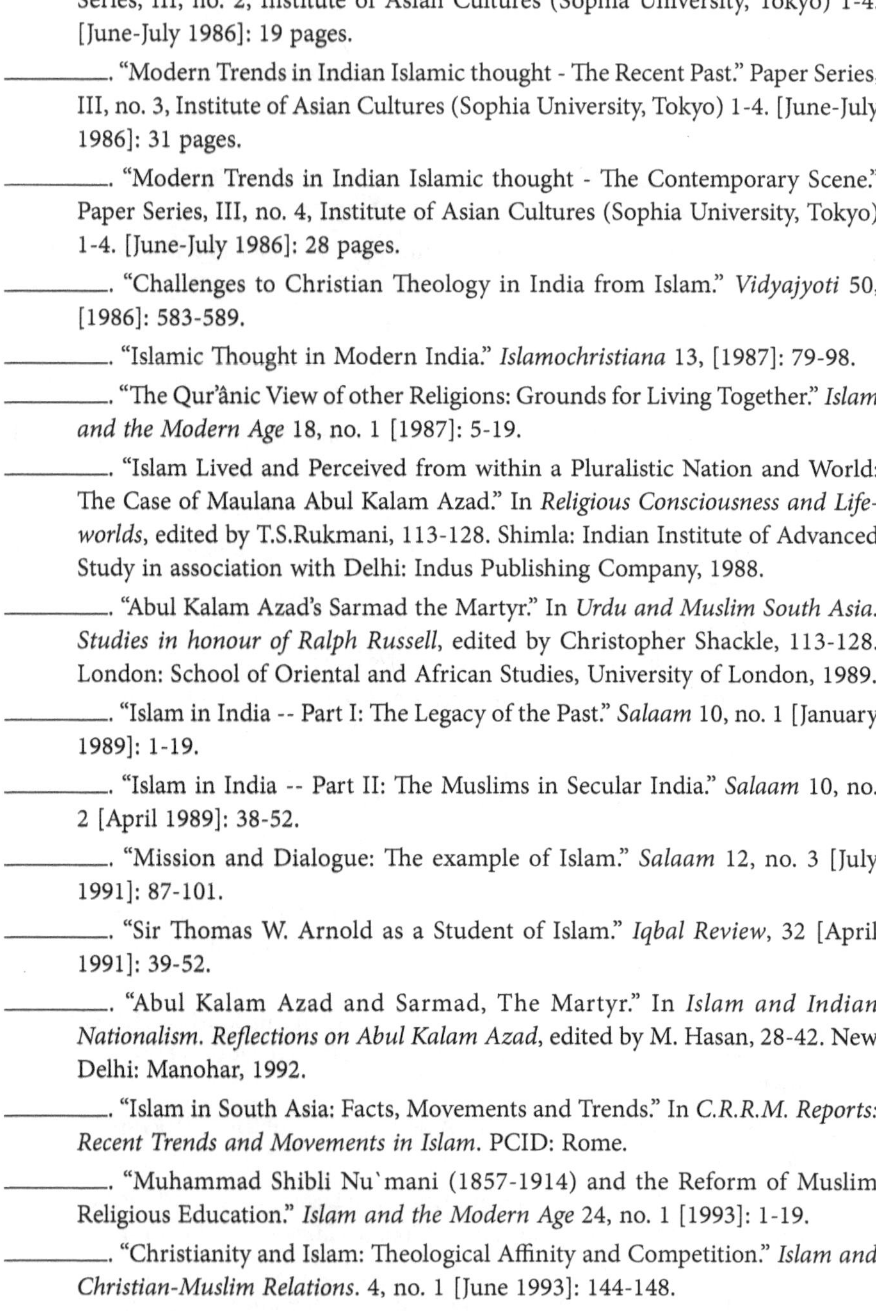

Series, III, no. 2, Institute of Asian Cultures (Sophia University, Tokyo) 1-4. [June-July 1986]: 19 pages.

__________. "Modern Trends in Indian Islamic thought - The Recent Past." Paper Series, III, no. 3, Institute of Asian Cultures (Sophia University, Tokyo) 1-4. [June-July 1986]: 31 pages.

__________. "Modern Trends in Indian Islamic thought - The Contemporary Scene." Paper Series, III, no. 4, Institute of Asian Cultures (Sophia University, Tokyo) 1-4. [June-July 1986]: 28 pages.

__________. "Challenges to Christian Theology in India from Islam." *Vidyajyoti* 50, [1986]: 583-589.

__________. "Islamic Thought in Modern India." *Islamochristiana* 13, [1987]: 79-98.

__________. "The Qur'ânic View of other Religions: Grounds for Living Together." *Islam and the Modern Age* 18, no. 1 [1987]: 5-19.

__________. "Islam Lived and Perceived from within a Pluralistic Nation and World: The Case of Maulana Abul Kalam Azad." In *Religious Consciousness and Life-worlds*, edited by T.S.Rukmani, 113-128. Shimla: Indian Institute of Advanced Study in association with Delhi: Indus Publishing Company, 1988.

__________. "Abul Kalam Azad's Sarmad the Martyr." In *Urdu and Muslim South Asia. Studies in honour of Ralph Russell*, edited by Christopher Shackle, 113-128. London: School of Oriental and African Studies, University of London, 1989.

__________. "Islam in India -- Part I: The Legacy of the Past." *Salaam* 10, no. 1 [January 1989]: 1-19.

__________. "Islam in India -- Part II: The Muslims in Secular India." *Salaam* 10, no. 2 [April 1989]: 38-52.

__________. "Mission and Dialogue: The example of Islam." *Salaam* 12, no. 3 [July 1991]: 87-101.

__________. "Sir Thomas W. Arnold as a Student of Islam." *Iqbal Review*, 32 [April 1991]: 39-52.

__________. "Abul Kalam Azad and Sarmad, The Martyr." In *Islam and Indian Nationalism. Reflections on Abul Kalam Azad*, edited by M. Hasan, 28-42. New Delhi: Manohar, 1992.

__________. "Islam in South Asia: Facts, Movements and Trends." In *C.R.R.M. Reports: Recent Trends and Movements in Islam*. PCID: Rome.

__________. "Muhammad Shibli Nu`mani (1857-1914) and the Reform of Muslim Religious Education." *Islam and the Modern Age* 24, no. 1 [1993]: 1-19.

__________. "Christianity and Islam: Theological Affinity and Competition." *Islam and Christian-Muslim Relations*. 4, no. 1 [June 1993]: 144-148.

__________. "New Light on the Christian-Muslim Controversy of the Nineteenth and Twentieth Century." *Die Welt des Islams* 34, no.1 [1994]: 85-88.

__________. "Two Conceptions of Da'wa in India: Jama'at-i Islami and Tablighi Jama'at." *Archives de sciences sociales des religions* 87, [July-September 1994]: 115-133.

__________. "Sharing Islamically in the Pluralistic Nation-State of India: The Views of Some Contemporary Indian Muslim Leaders and Thinkers." In *Christian-Muslim Encounters*, edited by Y.Y. Haddad and W. Haddad. Miami, 245-262. University of Florida Press, 1995.

__________. "Christianity and Islam: Mutual Challenges. Hans Zirker's recent work on Islam." *Orientalia Christiana Periodica* 61 [1995]: 571-580.

__________. "Islam and Islamic Thought in Modern Times." *Salaam* 18, no. 2 [July 1997]: 94-115.

__________. "Witness Meets Witness. The Church's Mission in the Context of the Encounter of Christian and Muslim Believers Today." *Vidyajyoti* 62, no.3 [1998]: 152-171.

__________. "The Islamic community and the Community of Mankind." *Encounter* no. 254 [May 1998].

__________. "Changing Catholic Views of Islam." In *Islam and Christianity: Mutual Perceptions since the mid-20th century*, edited by Jacques Waardenburg, 19-77. Leuven: Peeters, 1998.

__________. "Divine Rule and its Establishment on Earth: a contemporary South-Asian Debate." In *Faith, Power and Violence: Muslims and Christians in a Plural Society: Past and Present*, edited by John J. Donohue, S.J. and C. W. Troll, S.J., 223-239. Roma: Pont. Istituto Orientale, 1998.

__________. "A Significant Voice of Contemporary Islam in India: Maulana Wahiduddin Khan (b. 1925)." *Encounter*, no. 254 [April 1999].

__________. "Jesus Christ and Christianity in Abdullah Yusuf Ali's English Interpretation of the Qur'ân." *Islamochristiana* 24, [1998]: 77-101.

__________. "Who is Christ for me - in the context of encountering Muslims and studying Islam?" In *Who is Jesus Christ in a world of many faiths? Report of the Swanwick Christology Conference*, edited by Churches' Commission on Inter Faith Relations and Churches Together in Britain and Ireland, 16-36. [London, 1999]:.

__________. "Catholic Teachings on Interreligious Dialogue: Analysis of some recent official documents, with special reference to Christian-Muslim relations." In *Muslim-Christian Perceptions of Dialogue Today*, edited by J. Waardenburg, 233-275. Leuven: Peeters, 1998.

__________. "Allâhu Akbar as a Central Theme of Religious Conversation with Muslim Believers." *Encounter* no. 272 [2002]: 1-11.

__________. "The Word of God and Interreligious Dialogue." *Salaam* 27, no. 2 [2006]: 51-70.

__________. "Pope Benedict XVI at Regensburg University." *Salaam* 27, no. 4 [2006]: 160-164.

__________. "Progressive Thinking in Contemporary Islam." *Encounter* no. 317-318, [2007].

__________. "Is Muhammad a prophet for Christians also?" *Vidyajyoti* 72, no.1 [2008]: 38-52.

__________. "Paul Jackson's approach to Muslims and Islam." In *Journeying together in Faith. A collection of Inner Pilgrimages in Honour of Jesuit Father Paul Jackson*, edited by V. Edwin, SJ and E. Daly, SJ, 21-38. Anand: Gujarat Sahitya Prakash, 2008.

__________. "Reflections in the Light of A Common Word–An Introduction." In *We have Justice in Common. Christian and Muslim Voices from Asia and Africa*, edited by Christian W. Troll SJ, Helmut Reifeld, and C.T.R, Hewer, 19-22. Augustin/Berlin: Konrad-Adenauer-Stiftung, 2010.

__________. "Dialogue as Encounter in Faith: Problems and Prospects." IAIS Occasional Paper Series 3. Kuala Lumpur: Malaysia, 2009.

__________. "Dialogue and Religious Truth Claims in Christianity and Islam." In *World Christianity in Muslim Encounter. Essays in memory of David Ker*, edited by S. R. Goodwin, vol .2, 43-70. New York/London: Continuum International Publishing Group, 2009.

__________. "John Paul II and Islam." In *The Legacy of John Paul II*, edited by M. A. Hayes and G. Collins, S.J., 203-218. London: Burns & Oates, 2008.

__________. "Muhammad–Prophet for Christians also?" In *The Legacy of John Paul II*, edited by M. A. Hayes and G. Collins, S.J., 252-268. London: Burns & Oates, 2008. 252-268.

__________. "Can Christians and Muslims Pray Together?" *The Way* 50, no.1 [January 2011]: 53-70.

__________. "Catholicism and Islam." In *The Catholic Church and the World Religions: A Theological and Phenomenological Account*, edited by G. d'Costa, 71-105. London/New York: T & T Clark, International, 2011.

__________. "Christian Spirituality and Islam." In *The Bloomsbury Guide to Christian Spirituality*, edited by P. Tyler and R. Woods, 261-269. London/New Delhi/New York/Sydney: Blooomsbury, 2012.

__________. "The Ethical and Political Dimensions of Dialogue." Al-Maarif, [2012]: 21-41.

__________. "On Being a Servant of Reconciliation." In *Christian Lives Given to the*

Study of Islam, edited by C. W. Troll and C.T.R. Hewer, 115-127. New York: Fordham University Press, 2012.

__________. "The Christ Mysticism of Paul of Tarsus." In *Mysticism in East and West*, edited by H. Stamer, C. W. Troll , S.J. and T. Würtz, 122-143. Lahore: Multimedia Affairs, 2013.

__________. "Some Remarks on Sayyid Ahmad Khan's Commentary on Matthew 5." In *Muslim Renaissance Man of India*, edited by A.R. Kidwai, 322-228. New Delhi: Viva Books, 2017.

Vaporis, M.M., ed. *Orthodox Christians and Muslims*. Brookline: MA: Holy Cross Orthodox Press, 1986.

Voorhis, J.W. "John of Damascus on the Moslem Heresy." *The Muslim World* 24 [1934]: 391-398.

Waardenburg, J. "World Religions as Seen in the Light of Islam". In *Islam: Past Influence and Present Challenge*, edited by A.T. Welch and P. Cachia, 245-75. Edinburgh University Press, 1979.

__________, ed. *Muslim Perceptions of Other Religions throughout History*. Oxford: Oxford University Press, 1999.

__________, ed. *Scholarly Approaches to Religion, Interreligious Perceptions, and Islam*, Bern: Peter Lang, 1995.

Watt, W.M. *Mohammad at Mecca*. Oxford: Oxford University Press, 1953.

__________. "The Early Development of the Muslim Attitude to the Bible." *Transactions* 16 [1955 – 56]: 50-62.

__________. *Muslim-Christian Encounters – Perceptions and Misperceptions*. London: Routledge, 1991.

__________. *Islam and Christianity Today: A Contribution to Dialogue*. London: Routledge and Kegan Paul. 1983.

Woodberry, J.D., ed. *Muslims and Christians on the Emmaus Road*. California: MARC, 1989.

Young, W. G. *Patriarch, Shah and Caliph*. Rawalpindi: Christian Study Centre, 1974.

Zebiri, K. *Muslims and Christians Face to Face*. Oxford: Oneworld, 1997.

__________. "Relations Between Muslims and Non-Muslims in the Thought of Western Educated Muslim Intellectuals." *Islam and Christian-Muslim Relations* 6, no. 2 (1995): 255-277.

__________. "Muslim Perceptions of Christianity and the West." In *Islamic Interpretations of Christianity*, edited by L. Ridgeon, 179-200. Richmond: Curzon, 2001.